Therapeutic Interviewing

Essential Skills and Contexts of Counseling

Michael D. Reiter

Nova Southeastern University

PEARSON

Boston • New York • San Francisco
Mexico City • Montreal • Toronto • London • Madrid • Munich • Paris
Hong Kong • Singapore • Tokyo • Cape Town • Sydney

Senior Sponsoring Editor: *Virginia L. Blanford*
Series Editorial Assistant: *Matthew Buchholz*
Marketing Manager: *Erica DeLuca*
Production Editor: *Annette Joseph*
Editorial Production Service: *Publishers' Design and Production Services, Inc.*
Composition Buyer: *Linda Cox*
Manufacturing Buyer: *Linda Morris*
Electronic Composition: *Publishers' Design and Production Services, Inc.*
Cover Administrator: *Joel Gendron*

For related titles and support materials, visit our online catalog at www. ablongman.com.

Between the time website information is gathered and then published, it is not unusual for some sites to have closed. Also, the transcription of URLs can result in typographical errors. The publisher would appreciate notification where these errors occur so that they may be corrected in subsequent editions.

ISBN-10: 0-205-52951-8 (alk. paper)
ISBN-13: 978-0-205-52951-3 (alk. paper)

Library of Congress Cataloging-in-Publication Data
Reiter, Michael D.
  Therapeutic interviewing : essential skills and contexts of counseling / Michael D. Reiter.
    p.   cm.
  Includes bibliographical references and index.
  ISBN-13: 978-0-205-52951-3 (alk. paper)
  ISBN-10: 0-205-52951-8 (alk. paper)
  1. Interviewing. 2. Counseling. I. Title.

BF637.I5R45 2008
158'.35--dc22   2007026117

Printed in the United States of America

10 9 8 7 6 5 4 3 2 1   RRD-VA 11 10 09 08 07

This book is dedicated to my daughter, Maya Yumi.
May you listen to and be heard.

In memory of Mika

About the Author

Michael Reiter received a dual master's degree (Master of Education and Educational Specialist) in Counselor Education with subspecializations in Mental Health Counseling and Marriage and Family Therapy at the University of Florida and a doctorate in Family Therapy from Nova Southeastern University. He is currently Assistant Director/Associate Professor in the Division of Social and Behavioral Sciences of the Farquhar College of Arts and Sciences at Nova Southeastern University. He is a Certified Addictions Professional, a Licensed Marriage and Family Therapist, and an Approved Supervisor from the American Association of Marriage and Family Therapy. In terms of specific theories, he has tried to be open to the variety of theories available to counselors, and he finds it helpful to have taught counseling theories courses and family therapy theories courses at his university. His primary theoretical orientations are for some of the constructivist brief therapies, such as solution-focused and narrative therapies. However, he finds something intriguing about almost every theory.

Brief Contents

Contents

5 *Reflecting Skills: Exploring Content, Feelings, and Meanings of the Client's Story   93*

6   *Questions and Goal-Setting Skills: Asking Purposeful Questions and Developing Collaborative Therapeutic Goals   132*

PART FOUR • *The Contexts of Therapy*

Preface

One of the first courses I took as a master's student in Counselor Education was a counseling skills class. This was the first time I had taken a course on this material, and for our final exam, we had to conduct a mock therapy session with a classmate, videotape it, and then view the videotape with our instructor, to whom we would explain and justify what we did with the client. I remember that during that meeting with my instructor, he took me by surprise by saying that he was unexpectedly pleased by what he saw on the videotape. For some reason, he didn't think that I was going to do well. I'm not sure what led him to think that, and at the time, I didn't ask. But the exchange led me to think about what makes a good counselor: Is the ability to use counseling skills effectively something inherent in the personality of the therapist, or is it something a person can learn? I have come to realize that it is a combination of the two.

I believe that people become effective therapists by learning about and practicing the basic skills of therapy. However, those skills are enhanced by the therapist's personality; counselors need to be able to work well interpersonally with others. This book is my attempt to provide novice therapists with a basic understanding of therapeutic interviewing and how each of them can develop the skills needed to become a competent therapist.

I decided to write this book because, after having taught foundational therapeutic interviewing on undergraduate, master's, and doctoral levels, I have never found a textbook that provides my students with everything that I wanted them to know. I know that providing "everything" is an idealistic goal, and that this book cannot do that, but I think it can fill some of the holes that other textbooks have. I have not seen a textbook that both focuses on the microskills of therapy—so important for beginning therapists—and provides an introduction to the unique challenges an interviewer faces based on the context of the setting or the client. Because of this, I have always had to assign two textbooks. So I developed this textbook with my students in mind; I've written about the areas that I think are important for beginning therapists. In this book, I do not focus on specific skills that are located in specific theories, as this is the purview of more advanced theories classes. My intention is that students gain the foundational skills of therapeutic interviewing, along with an understanding of the formats and settings in which they might be providing these skills, so that they will then be able to tailor their skills to whatever theory they find resonates most with them.

I have been fortunate to engage in therapy in a variety of settings and with a range of clients. I have worked at a facility for individuals deemed incompetent to stand trial, a residential group home for developmentally delayed adults, community mental health centers, a hospital with patients with late-stage AIDS, an outpatient program for children and adolescents who have been sexually abused or have substance abuse issues, an in-home program for foster children, an in-home crisis program, a university outpatient program (with a one-way mirror and live supervision), and a private practice setting. My clients have ranged from very young adults to the elderly. I have worked with individuals, couples, families, and groups. I have been able to work with individuals from many cultural groups, given that much of my practice has been in the very diverse south Florida area.

When conceptualizing the book, I didn't want to make distinctions among the various types of professionals that conduct therapeutic interviews or the various therapies available. I do believe the foundational skills discussed in this book pertain to psychologists, psychiatrists, mental health counselors, marriage and family therapists, clinical social workers, professional counselors, pastoral counselors, and a range of other individuals who work with people in need. Although many people make distinctions between psychotherapy and counseling, for the purposes of this book, I will use the words *counseling* and *psychotherapy* interchangeably. I will leave it to the providers of those services to make any distinctions as to what is applicable in their own settings and what is not. I believe that most of what is presented in this book is relevant for any mental health professional.

How This Book Is Organized

The book is organized into four sections. Part One sets the stage for *understanding the relationship* that occurs during the therapeutic interview.

- Chapter 1 explores what interviewing and the therapeutic alliance are.
- Chapter 2 focuses on clients and the impact that coming to therapy might have on them.
- Chapter 3 addresses therapists and the impact that providing therapy has on them.

Part Two of this book focuses on the *microskills of interviewing*.

- Chapter 4 explains how therapists begin and maintain an interview.
- Chapter 5 provides concrete skills for developing empathy, including paraphrasing and reflecting skills.
- Chapter 6 explains the use of questions in the therapeutic interview and how they can be used to develop appropriate therapeutic goals.
- Chapter 7 highlights the various types of endings in therapy: specific issues, sessions, and termination as a whole.
- Chapter 8 focuses on the pitfalls of therapy, providing readers with guidelines for how they can avoid making these therapeutic mistakes.
- Chapter 9 explores how therapeutic interviewers can focus on client strengths and resources to enhance the interview.

Part Three of the book focuses on the various *contexts of clients.*

- Chapter 10 addresses the types of skills needed when conducting intake, assessment, and crisis sessions.
- Chapter 11 addresses the impact that culture has on the therapeutic interview.
- Chapter 12 tackles the issue of interviewing children.
- Chapter 13 focuses on interviewing couples and families.
- Chapter 14 deals with interviewing groups.

Part Four of the book highlights the various *settings* in which therapeutic interviewing occurs.

- Chapter 15 discusses office-based interviewing, including a discussion of private practice and how managed care impacts the therapy interview.
- Chapter 16 highlights the various issues involved in conducting therapeutic interviews in clients' homes.
- Chapter 17 addresses three main alternative contexts of therapy, including school-based, residential, and online counseling.

In addition to providing a wide range of what I hope is useful information, I wanted to write a book that would give students exposure to many of the issues that therapists face when conducting therapy and help them to develop the skills necessary to do this. Part of how I attempted to do this is through providing many practical exercises, personal reflections for the reader, case examples, and case scenarios. The case scenarios are primarily from my personal experience of working with clients. I do not present them as the best way to work with clients; in fact, in many I discuss what I think my mistakes were. They are provided for the reader to try to put a more personal spin on the material and demonstrate how some of the ideas really work in therapy.

A book like this is difficult to write on many levels, including determining the target audience, establishing the appropriate level for the material, and deciding how much to focus on ideas and theory versus skills. One decision I made as I wrote was to change the pronouns reflecting the client and the therapist from chapter to chapter, rather than to use the awkward he/she wording. Often I simply used the plural, but when the singular is used, I refer to the therapist as *he* and client as *she* in all odd-numbered chapters, and the reverse (the client as *he* and the therapist as *she*) in all even-numbered chapters. I also decided to use one chapter to discuss conducting therapeutic interviews with clients from different cultures. Although there is mention throughout the book of specific issues that arise when working cross-culturally, the reader should think about what is being presented and be aware that age, gender, culture, race, socioeconomic level, sexual orientation, and other such issues affect the therapy interview. Therapists should be conscious of how these might impact the client, self, or the therapy interchange.

Acknowledgments

This book has benefited from the assistance of many individuals. I want to thank Drew Wallace for his encouragement, support, and assistance. Drew went through this whole book with me and was a voice of honesty, letting me know which sections worked, which could be modified, and which should be omitted. He helped to shape this book into what you will be reading. I also appreciate the support and encouragement of my colleagues at Nova Southeastern University. I appreciate the suggestions of the following reviewers who let me know when I was being a bit too wordy, biased, and where I had left out some information: Casey A. Barrio, University of North Texas; Joshua Gold, University of Southern Carolina; Beulah M. Hirschlein, Oklahoma State University; Arthur Lyons, Moravian College; and Naijian Zhang, West Chester University of Pennsylvania. I want to thank Tracy Light, the best book representative out there, for always checking in and helping connect me to Allyn and Bacon. I also want to thank my editors at Allyn and Bacon who maintained faith in the project, especially Virginia Lanigan, who initially contracted the project, and Ginny Blanford, who has brought it to publication. I would also like to thank Holly Crawford for her meticulous copyediting to ensure a quality project.

I want to thank several musicians who were with me (at least musically) along the path of writing this book. The background ambience they gave me added to this project and my mind-set in writing it. These artists include Marillion, Spock's Beard, The Flower Kings, Transatlantic, and Pain of Salvation.

I have been mentored and guided by the various instructors who have given me feedback about my therapy skills and those who have provided me growth opportunities. This book was aided by my contact with all of my past clients and students. In classes, I was able to discuss many of the topics and issues that are presented in this book. Recently, many students read and gave me feedback on the first draft of this book. However, there were several students whose review of the book helped to ensure that it was of the utmost quality. I want to recognize those students: Janiqua Armbrister, Marilyn Berlanga, Cammie Cacace, and Denise Da Rosa.

Lastly, I want to thank my wife, Yukari Tomozawa, who from the very first thought of this book supported me more than any wife should. She provided me the room to work for hours on end in my office instead of being with her. She reviewed the work in progress, giving me suggestions and feedback, but always letting me know she was proud of me.

M.R.

1

Therapeutic Interviewing

Defining Therapy, Therapeutic Relationships, and the Interview

Sitting across from a client and knowing what to say, what not to say, how to sit, how to react, what strategies to use, and a host of other decisions in order to help the client with a problem is extremely challenging. Some people find that they have been helpful with friends or family members when those individuals have had problems, but having a real client (someone they do not know) sit across from them changes the rules of the game. The conversation between the two individuals becomes different based on the change of roles and rules inherent in such relationships. The interview in these two contexts will not be the same. The person who is a good interviewer in the friend-to-friend interview will have many more decisions to consider when talking with clients.

This book explores the dynamics, skills, and processes of one specific type of interview, the therapeutic interview. At its most basic, "an interview is a communication interaction between two (or more) parties, at least one of whom has a goal, that uses questions and answers to exchange information and influence one another" (Barone & Switzer, 1995, p. 8). Therapeutic interviewers operate in a multitude of ways. Some do very little talking, some predominantly use questions, some hardly use questions, while others use stories to help clients achieve their goals. There is no one right way to conduct a therapy session. This is both freedom and restriction. Therapists can operate in a variety of ways to achieve a positive outcome. Sometimes, however, especially for novice therapists, a blank canvas can be overwhelming. This book can provide a first step in helping novice therapists navigate the therapeutic landscape. The book highlights some of the core foundational skills that most therapeutic interviewers use, while also highlighting some potential pitfalls.

Dynamics of Interviews

A therapy session is an interview, yet it is distinct from other types of interviews such as employment, survey, recruitment, performance, research, and selection interviews. Berg (2004) explained that, at its simplest, interviewing is "a conversation with a purpose" (p. 75). The purpose of the interview is based on what type of interview it is, the context of that interview, and the goals of each person in that interaction. In any type of interview, two people (or more) mutually engage in a discourse in which each is contributing to the conversation. Although we might have the perception that one person (the interviewer) is the owner of the interview, this is not quite the case. Interviews are transactions, in which each person is both sender and receiver of communication. Each contributes to the overall output of the transaction.

Interviews are a unique form of human communication and are distinct in their structure, process, and guidelines. They are not the same as regular conversations. Conversations can range from extremely casual and meaningless (small talk to strangers) to extremely serious (conversations with significant others about important issues). Barnlund (1990) held that there were many similarities between therapeutic communication and ordinary conversation, yet therapeutic communication is more focused, structured, and is held for one distinct purpose, to help one person (client) get relief from some type of problem.

Most interviews, regardless of the context (for example, counseling, research, employment), are one-time occurrences. However, therapy, more than any other context of interviewing, has interconnected interviews. After an initial interview, the beginning of therapy interviews for second and subsequent sessions will follow up on the first interview. The interviews will be less about getting to know one another and more about integrating what occurred in previous interviews into the current one. The conclusion of therapeutic interviews is also different from that of most other interviews as it includes asking something of the interviewee. Perhaps the therapeutic interviewer asks the interviewee to do some type of homework or other such action that will take what was discussed during the interview and put it into practice to better the person's life. Thus, unlike most other interviews, the goal of the therapeutic interview is *change*.

All interviews are rule governed (Barone & Switzer, 1995). The more formal guidelines of therapy interviews are set by licensing and credentialing bodies. We call these guidelines "ethics." Therapists use these ethical codes to help them-

Reflection 1.1

Think about your perceptions of the differences between a normal conversation and an interview. What do you think are the main differences between the two? When would you engage in one rather than the other? What are your perceptions of the differences between the individuals involved? What roles might each of them play and how would that change their behavior during the transaction?

selves make decisions about their conduct with clients, colleagues, and the general public. Other rules of interviews are more covert and are based on the context of that interaction. Interviews have norms, for instance, that help determine what behaviors are and are not acceptable in the situation. One such norm is the norm of reciprocity. This is when each party of the interview engages in a back and forth manner of giving and receiving information.

People are not born good interviewers. As in all skill development, the old cliché holds that practice, practice, practice is what is important. (Do Exercise 1.1.) Therapeutic interviews are unique in skill development because an integration of *theory* and *practice* is necessary to become an effective therapeutic interviewer.

The Therapeutic Interview

The therapeutic interview occurs within a unique context of human interaction. It is perhaps one of the most sensitive of all types of interviews because it primarily deals with extremely personal issues of people's lives, such as their hopes, fears, feelings, and pain. At its simplest (a conversation between two people—a therapist and a client), the therapeutic interview attempts to lead to change for one member of the duo (the client). However, there is an imbalance in the amount of personal information disclosed; one person (the client) discloses the majority of the personal information, while the other person (the therapeutic interviewer) discloses a minimal amount of personal information. Although this is the same for many types of interviews (for example, an employment interview), the intensity of the material discussed is usually much deeper and more personal in the therapy interview. There is also an imbalance in the focus of the interview; the majority, if not almost all of the focus, is on the client. In most nontherapy relationships, there is equal reciprocity in the amount of time spent talking and the level of personal disclosure. This is known as the dyadic effect (Beebe, Beebe, & Redmond, 2005). The type of information one person discloses to another is expected to promote similar self-disclosure from the other. For instance, if one person tells someone where he or she went to college, the other person is expected to respond with the college he

Exercise 1.1   *Observing Rule-Based Interviews*

Watch an interview conducted between two people. This might be on the television or a videotape. Shows such as *20/20*, *Oprah*, or other talk shows usually have some type of interview during the show. Have a notepad and a pen. Pay attention to all of the overt and covert rules of conduct during the interview. Some of the things to pay attention to are who speaks first; who speaks last; who is the primary person to ask questions; who speaks longer; how much can people interrupt each other; what type of physical proximity is acceptable; how emotional can people get; and so forth. Then watch an interview that is occurring in a different context and conduct the same type of observation. What differences do you notice?

or she went to. In the therapeutic interview, there is usually an extreme imbalance of self-disclosure in the relationship context.

The therapeutic interviewer is highly trained in setting a context for conversations that helps open up possibilities for the client. Therapists, having gone to school and received training in various areas of helping, have expertise in developing conversations for change possibilities.

What is it that defines an interview as being therapeutic? Zeig and Munion (1990) explained that there are three areas that, in combination, determine an interchange as psychotherapeutic: relationship, change, and theory. Therapy is based on an encounter between two or more people where one of these individuals uses verbal and nonverbal skills, such as empathic understanding, to connect with the other person and help move the other person toward desired goals. This empathic understanding connects the two people in a relationship. Second, the therapeutic interview is a business relationship where the two parties contract with one another for the desired outcome of one person—the client—changing some aspect of her situation. Lastly, therapy is based on the therapist having some model of how problems form and how they are resolved. Although this explanation of what psychotherapy entails gives a very general overview of the field, many people have debates as to what therapists should, or shouldn't, be skilled at; how they should work with clients; what the therapeutic goals should be; and how therapists and their clients should get there. This book provides the reader with foundational knowledge of how to conduct a therapy interview, regardless of theory. However, the therapist's theoretical orientation impacts the way in which that therapist conducts sessions. Thus, therapists-in-training should take the material presented in this book and evaluate how it makes sense based on their own theoretical orientation, the clients they are working with, and the contexts they are working in. The next section of this chapter explores some of the ways in which psychotherapy has been understood.

Defining Therapy

The process in which the therapeutic interview is housed has been called many things over the past century, including psychotherapy, therapy, counseling, and helping. It is practiced by a variety of individuals including psychiatrists, psychologists, family therapists, mental health counselors, clinical social workers, pastoral

Reflection 1.2

How do you define *therapy*? What does therapy mean to you? What do you think the main ingredients of counseling are and what are they not? Where did your ideas of therapy come from? What assumptions do you have about what happens between therapist and client?

counselors, professional counselors, and other individuals involved in the mental health service industry. Regardless of the title of the person conducting the therapeutic interview, distinct skills are needed for working with other individuals. These skills are then used in a context defined by the theory of the therapist, how the client came to therapy, and where the therapy is taking place. The theory addresses what type of relationship to establish with the client; how much self-disclosure, confrontation, and support the therapist should give the client; and what the focus of therapy will be. The theory also informs with whom to meet, how often, and what goals will be addressed. Regardless of theory, a thorough understanding of psychotherapy is needed to place the skills of therapeutic interviewing into a framework of meaning.

One of the key components of the therapeutic interview is that its main purpose is *change*. Therapists use all of their skills and knowledge to assist clients in moving in a direction of change (be it behavioral, emotional, relational, or psychological). The intent of this change is for it to be lasting, so that the client does not have to keep coming back to therapy. Therapists attempt, over time, to get the client to eliminate or reduce a complaint situation. The time necessary to do this might be one session or hundreds of sessions over several years.

One thing that many novice therapists struggle with is the notion that the therapeutic interview is based within a contractual agreement between therapist and client in which the therapist has agreed to utilize his skills and resources to work *for* the client. The struggle is that the "work" in therapy cannot be one-sided in either direction. Both therapist and client must use the therapeutic interview to try to reach the treatment goals. If only the therapist is working, little to no change will happen for the client. If only the client is working, change may occur; however, it will probably not be as effective as if both parties are equally trying to complete the business transaction. Change that would probably have happened without the therapist's interventions wastes the client's time and money. Lambert (1992) discussed this type of change (where the client changes because of things occurring outside the therapy or because of personal traits) as extra-therapeutic factors. These account for approximately 40 percent of change for clients. Although this may make it seem as if the therapist has no influence in this area, during therapy sessions, therapeutic interviewers can build on extra-therapeutic factors to help increase this type of change.

Although it is a contractual agreement, the therapeutic relationship is different from most other business relationships. In a typical business relationship, one person is providing a service for another person and then gets paid for that service. The person paying usually does not have to do anything more than provide financial compensation. In a restaurant, besides eating, the customer does not have to do anything (that is, buy the food from food supply sources, prepare the food, plate it, bring it to the table, clear the table, wash the dishes, and so forth). This is one of the main reasons the customer is paying for this type of service. Psychotherapy is a unique business relationship because the customer has to pay and also is expected to do a majority of the work. Without the client's hard work, therapy is likely to be ineffective.

Reflection 1.3

What behaviors and personality traits do you look for in someone whom you feel comfortable opening up to? When meeting new people, what are the signs that you notice that let you know it is safe to self-disclose to that person? What are the signs that lead you to be hesitant to open up to someone? How do you define *safety* in an interpersonal transaction?

Therapeutic interviewing is the combination of a therapist's academic theory of how people function along with the therapist's own personality characteristics. These work together to help someone in distress. Therapeutic interviewers do not just "be" with clients. They have trained for years learning unique skills that most other professionals have not mastered, so that they can work with people for the goal of improvement. Being a therapist is a very difficult and rigorous endeavor. Clients come to therapists expecting them to solve the problems that are leading them to feel bad, miserable, anxious, or any of a thousand other emotions they do not want to have. Trained therapists use their knowledge, along with their personality, to connect with clients in a relationship whereby they conjointly develop a discourse that opens up room for change for the client. For the purposes of this book, there will not be a distinction between therapy and counseling, although it is acknowledged that people in the field do distinguish the two. Further, the two terms will be used interchangeably and defined as two or more people engaging in a professional interaction in which one person (the therapist), having learned certain unique skills of interviewing and change production, is providing services to assist another person (the client) in making some type of behavioral, emotional, relational, and/or psychological change.

The Helping Process

Many professionals discuss therapy as a process in which therapist and client come together, over time, and work toward reaching mutually agreed on goals (these goals being predicated on the client's wants and the therapist's theoretical orientation). Although the modal number of sessions that a client will attend with a particular therapist is one, the mean number of sessions a client meets with a therapist is between five and seven (Miller, Duncan, & Hubble, 1997). Even in a single session, there is a process that occurs. One therapeutic interview is all that might be needed to help a client get what is wanted out of therapy (Hoyt, 2000; Talmon, 1990). However long the process of helping, both therapist and client impact and are impacted by each other.

Therapy is primarily about setting the stage for change to happen. Cormier and Hackney (1999) provided four conditions in which the helping process occurs. The first is that someone is seeking help. Second, someone is willing to give help. Third, the person willing to give help is capable and trained to give that help.

Lastly, this interchange occurs in a context and setting that permits this type of interaction to occur. This may seem to be a simplistic explanation of the process, yet each condition is vital for the effective outcomes of therapy. If someone comes to therapy but is not seeking help (perhaps the person is court-ordered or forced to go to therapy by a family member), there is a more difficult connection and process in therapy along with a lower likelihood of positive outcome. If the therapist is not focused on the client or on helping (perhaps based on his own personal problems), the helping process is hampered. If the therapist was not trained properly or is not good at therapeutic interviewing (therapy is a skill based on personality characteristics of the therapist combined with knowledge of techniques and theories), a good helping process is not as likely. If the two people are not provided an arena in which they can explore the issues and goals for which the client is in therapy, the helping process can be difficult to work through. The arena can help, but can also hamper what happens in therapy. Case Scenario 1.1 demonstrates how the physical setting of the therapeutic interview might prevent a smooth process to occur.

As discussed, therapeutic interviews involve two people: therapist and client. Brammer and MacDonald (2003) provided a framework for the process of helping based on the combination of what occurs within and between therapist and client. The personality of the helper, along with whatever helping skills that person has, lead to growth-facilitating conditions for the client, which culminate in specific outcomes (goals) for the client. Therapy is thus based on who each person is and how those two people come together at that specific time and in that specific context. Consequently, therapy is never the same endeavor. Each client a therapist works with leads to a variation of therapy since the two will relate to one another differently from the way any other two people relate to one another. Further, no two therapeutic interview sessions with the same client and therapist will be the same. Both individuals come into each interview different from the way they were in the last interview they shared together. Since therapy is based on the connection between two people, it sometimes goes very well; other times, the outcomes are

CASE SCENARIO 1.1

I was supervising a master's degree intern who was working at an in-patient psychiatric hospital. Because some of the patients in the hospital could be violent at times, the hospital had a rule that therapists could not be alone in a room with a client with the door closed. Further, at this particular hospital, there were no therapy rooms. Therapists had to work with patients in a room that was used by the nurses and doctors to write their clinical notes. Also, there was a bathroom in this room, so that even if a therapist was working with a patient, a nurse might come in during the middle of the session, go into the bathroom, close the door, and use the facilities. Therapist and patient could hear the toilet flushing and to maintain confidentiality, would have to stop talking when the nurse first walked in the room and then again when the nurse walked out. Patients in this setting seemed to be hesitant to open up fully, and when they did, were faced with many interruptions to the flow of the therapy process. This situation served the interns as an example of how the context can impact (albeit negatively) the process of therapy.

not positive. Occasionally, people do not "click" and a strong therapeutic relationship does not develop. At other times, there is too much of a connection, which can also hamper therapy. Therapists need to understand themselves and their thoughts, try to understand the client's perceptions and situation, while also understanding what is occurring between the two of them within the context of the therapy agreement.

Since therapy requires both therapist and client to work actively in order to achieve the goals of the relationship, the process of therapy requires both people to apply themselves in the interview. This book focuses on those things a therapist can do during this relationship, part of which includes attempting to foster the motivation of the client to work and be productive in the therapy process.

Regardless of theoretical orientation, therapeutic relationships between therapists and clients have many similarities. Barone and Switzer (1995) suggested ten fundamental building blocks of all therapeutic relationships:

1. A helping relationship
2. Support for working through problems until resolved
3. A specific therapeutic setting
4. A plan of treatment
5. A method for accomplishing that plan
6. A positive expectation of help
7. Client self-awareness as the basis for change
8. A new way of viewing the problem
9. Support for trying out new behaviors
10. A therapist who is a model of self-acceptance and the courage to change. (p. 391)

Based on orientation, therapists will focus more intensively on one or the other of these components, which are all part of the therapeutic relationship. Unfortunately, for various reasons, some therapeutic relationships lead to client and therapist not being able to work together productively. Therapists have a tendency to attribute this lack of progress to client resistance, assuming the client is not following through with therapy and working in the process. This might be the case. However, there could also be many other reasons why the combination of that therapist, using that particular orientation, with that client was not successful. Therapists cannot force a positive relationship. What they can do is to create a context and ambiance for clients to enter into a dialogue that might be useful for them. Part of how they do this is by trying to establish a positive therapeutic alliance.

Reflection 1.4

What strategies do you use when initially meeting someone in order to forge a connection with them? How much of a natural leader are you? How much do you overwhelm a conversation? What type of interpersonal communicator are you?

Reflection 1.5

Think about some of your closest friends. What are the characteristics that each of you possesses that leads to a positive relationship? What do you bring to the relationship? What do you look for in someone when you want to engage in conversation? Think about how you are different with different people in your relational field. How are you different with your parents, friends, significant other, and acquaintances?

The Therapeutic Alliance

As we've seen, therapy is based on a relationship between two or more people in which one person is primarily assisting another person to reach certain goals. This relationship connects the two people as they are working together to solve a dilemma. It is not a relationship in which both people reciprocate in the same manner. Therapists focus their energy on helping the client. Clients focus their energy on helping themselves. Thus, there is an inherent disparity in the relationship. What connects the two people in the relationship is that they are there for a common cause: to help the client move closer to the client's goals. When these two people come together, a spark is triggered.

The interaction between therapeutic interviewer and client has been called many things including "therapeutic alliance," "therapeutic relationship," and "helping relationship." Regardless of what it is called, every theory of counseling and psychotherapy regards the working relationship between the parties in the therapy room as a very important one.

Many theories postulate that the therapeutic alliance is the main means of therapeutic change. Rogers and Stevens (1967) stated, "The quality of the personal encounter is probably, in the long run, the element which determines the extent to which this is an experience which releases or promotes development and growth" (p. 89). Theories such as psychoanalytic, person-centered, Gestalt, existential, and symbolic-experiential are all predicated on what occurs in the immediate connection between therapist and client. Teyber (2006) held that the working alliance is based on the client's perceptions of the therapist, stating, "A working alliance is established when clients perceive the therapist as a capable and trustworthy ally in their personal struggles—someone who is interested in, and capable of, helping them with their problems" (p. 44). Therapists can enhance this relationship when they are communicating an understanding of the client's situation, are empathic and supportive, and are perceived as allies, dedicated to helping the client with the problem.

Reflection 1.6

How much do you enjoy helping others in need? What is it about being able to be useful that is appealing to you? What are your thoughts on doing this as a full-time job?

By viewing the therapeutic process as based on a working alliance, the contractual relationship between the two parties shifts from a typical business relationship to a joint effort in which therapist and client need each other for a productive outcome. Without a positive relationship, the likelihood of positive change for the client is reduced. Just as in many other endeavors, the people working together need to be able to function well. Although in many other business relationships, the two people do not have to care about one another, therapy is about two people in close contact, discussing very intimate, personal, and serious issues. Thus, the ability to work together is heightened during the therapeutic interview.

The therapeutic alliance is also based on safety. Individuals must feel safe to express themselves as they are. Rogers (1989) described this situation, in which people are able externally to say and behave in ways that they are internally thinking and feeling, as congruence. People function more effectively when they feel as if they can be themselves in the transaction without negative consequences from the other person. This then provides more freedom to explore one's self, which can lead to better insight or connection to self and others. In this relationship, therapists use all of their skills, knowledge, and theory to connect with the client's motivations, knowledge, and resources to help the client progress.

Because the therapeutic alliance is based on the interactions between two unique people, the personality and attitudes of both people impact the quality of the alliance. The qualities of the client, qualities of the therapeutic interviewer, and the therapist's skills are the main components of the therapeutic alliance (Summers & Barber, 2003). This alliance is based on a mutual understanding of each other's role in the interview. Stine (2005) held that the therapeutic alliance focuses on the attitudes that client and therapist hold toward each other: cooperation, trust, mutual respect, and understanding. If therapist or client holds negative attitudes toward the other party, the quality of the therapeutic alliance could be hampered. One interesting caveat to this is that therapists do not need to like their clients. However, it tends to be more the actions and worldview the therapist might not like rather than the person. Most therapists would hold that if a therapist does not like a client, this dislike can come through in various ways and negatively impact the therapeutic process. If therapists find that they dislike a client, they are encouraged to (1) engage in self-exploration to figure out what it is about the client that is bothering them, (2) possibly discuss what they are experiencing in the therapeutic relationship with the client to see if some new perception can come to the surface, (3) talk with a colleague or supervisor to attempt to move past these feelings, and (4) refer the client to someone else if, after trying to work things out, the negative feelings continue to impact the therapy in detrimental ways.

The therapeutic alliance begins from the very first moment therapist and client interact with one another. This might be over the phone when the client is setting up the initial meeting or it might be in the waiting room when the therapist first greets the client. Therapeutic interviewers need to gain a sense of the client's experiences and set a collaborative relationship from the beginning of therapy. If they cannot, the connection may be hampered. The therapeutic alliance is enhanced when both individuals believe and experience that what they have to

Reflection 1.7

Think about someone you know whom you do not really like. Perhaps there is something about that person's personality that gets on your nerves. Or perhaps your dislike is based on how the person looks or acts. If you were to have to work together, how strong and positive would the bond be between the two of you? What could you do to improve the connection and ability to work together? What have you done in past situations to move beyond initially disliking someone to being able to work together?

say is important and heard. Therapists can set the tone of the therapy process by accepting and validating the client when the client discusses any and all issues during the very first encounter.

From the beginning, the therapist can attempt to gain a sense of the client's perspective and theory of change. Duncan, Miller, and Sparks (2004) viewed the therapeutic alliance as being predicated on three main issues: the agreement about goals, meaning, and purpose of the therapy; the client's view of the therapeutic relationship; and the means or methods used. When the therapist pays attention to each of these issues, along with having a desire to understand how the client perceives each of these, a stronger therapeutic alliance develops. Unfortunately, therapists can be blinded to what is occurring in therapy by focusing only on their own experiences and their own beliefs. Since therapeutic interviews occur based on a transaction between people, therapists should be conscious of their own and their client's positions, attitudes, and beliefs.

One key element of the therapeutic alliance is that the therapist has some sense of caring. This caring is a different type than therapeutic interviewers have for their parents, siblings, friends, or significant other. It is a caring about people in general. This nonromantic caring holds that the therapeutic interviewer cares about the way in which the client understands the world. One of the benefits of this type of caring relationship is that it binds both people in the interchange and helps to further the therapeutic alliance. Further, when therapists find that they are truly exhibiting this type of caring, they feel that they are really with the client, allowing their skills and personality to come out naturally (Halstead et al., 2002). The therapist cares about the client as a human being. It is not caring about what the person does, but that the person is a worthwhile person, who, if the situation allows, will move in a positive direction.

Characteristics of Effective Therapeutic Relationships

The relationships that develop during therapeutic encounters tend to be one of the primary factors that lead clients toward reaching effective outcomes. In outcome studies, approximately 30 percent of the variance of effective outcomes is due to the therapeutic relationship (Lambert, 1992). When clients are asked what was helpful for them in therapy, they tend to say that the therapist "was nice," "listened to me," and "was supportive" rather than discussing the techniques or theory the therapist used. Given that the use of a specific theory (and the associated techniques and interventions of that theory) accounts for only approximately 15 percent of the variance of outcome, it is imperative for training programs to spend more time focusing on helping therapists-in-training learn how to develop productive therapeutic *relationships* rather than on choosing a specific *theory* to operate from. Further, since it has been found that no one theory is more effective than any other theory (Miller, Duncan, & Hubble, 1997), therapists should pay attention to how they connect with clients; good connections can then enhance the effectiveness of any theory they choose to utilize. This is not to say that having a specific therapeutic model is not important; it is. Therapists need to have a framework and an understanding of what they are doing with clients. But what is more important, and this cuts across any theory the therapist might choose, is that the therapist knows how to connect with the client. When therapists perceive that the relationship they have with a client is not clicking, they should see what they can do to get the relationship back on track.

In perhaps one of the most seminal approaches to understanding the therapeutic relationship, Carl Rogers (1961) outlined his view of the characteristics of a helping relationship. Rogers asked himself several questions about the relationship:

1. Can I be in some way which will be perceived by the other person as trustworthy, as dependable or consistent in some deep sense? (p. 50)
2. Can I be expressive enough as a person that what I am will be communicated unambiguously? (p. 51)
3. Can I let myself experience positive attitudes toward this other person—attitudes of warmth, caring, liking, interest, respect? (p. 52)
4. Can I be strong enough as a person to be separate from the other? Can I be a sturdy respecter of my own feelings, my own needs, as well as his? (p. 52)
5. Am I secure enough within myself to permit him his separateness? (pp. 52–53)
6. Can I let myself enter fully into the world of his feelings and personal meanings and see these as he does? (p. 53)
7. Can I receive him as he is? Can I communicate this attitude? Or can I only receive him conditionally, acceptant of some aspects of his feelings and silently or openly disapproving of other aspects? (p. 54)
8. Can I act with sufficient sensitivity in the relationship that my behavior will not be perceived as a threat? (p. 54)
9. Can I free him from the threat of external evaluation? (p. 54)
10. Can I meet this other individual as a person who is in process of becoming, or will I be bound by his past and by my past? (p. 55)

A significant number of training programs have utilized Rogers's ideas as the foundation for what the therapeutic relationship should be based on. Some of the main ideas Rogers espoused were accurate empathic understanding, unconditional positive regard, and congruence (genuineness). Lambert, Shapiro, and Bergin (1986) stated that "virtually all schools of therapy accept the notion that these or related therapist relationship variables are important for significant progress in psychotherapy and, in fact, fundamental in the formation of a working alliance" (p. 171). Rogers's three core conditions of unconditional positive regard, congruence, and accurate empathy have become hallmarks of therapist training. This book focuses, especially in Part II in the discussion of the microskills of therapy, on how therapists can develop the skills necessary to provide accurate empathy. This book also holds that therapists should care about their clients as human beings as well as being "real" during the therapeutic interview.

Part of an effective therapeutic relationship is allowing the other person the full range of emotional expression. Usually, outside of the therapeutic relationship, people are not given the freedom to really explore themselves. If they begin to cry, the other person attempts to get them to stop by saying something such as, "Don't cry. C'mon. It will be all right." This action on the part of the listener attempts to deny the individual's feelings, or at least to stop them, usually because the listener is uncomfortable being in a connected position with someone who is having difficulties. This can be seen in the listener's quickly reaching for a tissue to give to the person crying, as this action is a message to stop crying and not to feel what it is the person is feeling.

In the last twenty years, therapy has shifted from being hierarchical, with the therapist the "all-knowing" expert and the client the "helpless" patient. It is now a much more collaborative process in which clients are experts on their lives while therapists are experts on engaging in conversation that helps move clients toward achieving their goals. Using his skills and personhood, the therapist provides certain conditions (empathy, warmth, validation, respect, congruence, unconditional positive regard, and so on) so that the client can add her perceptions to the therapeutic discourse and attempt to open up new avenues of thinking, feeling, and/or relating to others.

In summary, the therapeutic alliance/relationship is the cornerstone to effective therapy. Therapeutic interviewers should have this as a primary focus not only on first meeting the client, but also during the entire course of therapy. Fox (2001) summed up the therapeutic relationship through the acronym of AGAPE

Reflection 1.8

Think about your normal responses to friends and family members when they come to you with problems and dilemmas. How do you usually respond? When they begin crying or are upset or angry, what do you tend to say and do? How do you think a therapist's responses would differ from a friend's or a family member's?

(which is the highest form of love in Greek): *A* = *Acceptance*; *G* = *Genuineness*; *A* = *Actuality*; *P* = *Positive regard*; *E* = *Empathy*.

The Goal of Therapeutic Interviews

As previously established, therapeutic interviews occur in a contractual relationship in which one person is coming to another for help with some personal problem and is giving that person some type of compensation for this help. The client has certain ideas of why she is going to therapy, even if it is something as generic as feeling that she is "not happy." The client, based on her own personal belief system, has a certain understanding of what would constitute a positive outcome in therapy. The therapeutic interviewer, based on his theoretical orientation, has his own view of what should occur in therapy. Sometimes this coincides with the client's idea; sometimes it does not. For some therapists having the client gain insight is important. Others focus strictly on behavior change. Other therapists would like the client to think differently, while still other therapists want the client to experience differently. Regardless of orientation, the therapist has his own view of what "change" looks like. The therapeutic interview is predicated on the intersection of the therapist's and client's views of what can be different.

The therapeutic interview is purposeful in that it focuses on what the client has to say, particularly about what she wants for her life. Thus, the therapist attempts to understand what it is the client wants, based on the client's situation. Then, given the therapist's understanding of problem formation and problem resolution, he works with the client toward the client's goals. Each theoretical orientation has a somewhat different process of helping the client achieve these.

Whatever happens in the therapeutic interview, the ultimate outcome is what occurs when the client leaves the interview and lives life. Thus, there is a very distinct purpose for the therapeutic interview. It involves one person (interviewer) talking with a second person (interviewee) with the intention of helping the interviewee experience life in a more satisfactory manner. Although this sounds easy, therapists have been debating for over one hundred years on the best way(s) to make this happen.

Perhaps the primary goal of therapy is for the client to no longer need therapy. Some therapists frame this as getting the client to fire them. Yet, it is for them to be fired because the client does not need them anymore and not because they are ineffective and not useful. These therapists might start off the first session with a client by asking the following question: "What needs to be different in your life for you to know that it is okay to fire me?" By asking a question in this manner, the therapist shocks the client a little bit, but in a way that is playful while also framing the relationship as having a distinct purpose and a temporal aspect. This is another way in which the therapeutic interview is a very different business relationship from most others. In most business relationships, the goal for the service provider is to provide a positive service and have the customer keep coming back to utilize that service. In therapy, however, the goal is to get the client, as quickly as possible, to not need the service. Further, the goal is to have the client never come back! This goes counter to most business models.

The Therapeutic Contract

The therapeutic interview occurs based on a contract between two parties. This contract specifies the terms of the interaction. The therapist must abide by certain conditions, including confidentiality and an attempt to reduce possible dual relationship issues, among others; the therapist must follow certain ethical codes. The therapeutic contract contextualizes the therapeutic interview as a business and professional encounter; however, it is one that is quite charged with emotionality.

Either before or during the first session, the therapist informs the client about the parameters of the therapeutic relationship, along with explaining the process of therapy. This occurs via the informed consent. Clients have to consent to enter into this working relationship with the therapist. Instead of being secretive and coming from a "Buyer Beware" framework, the therapist uses informed consent and makes the guidelines of the therapy process overt so that the client freely enters into this arrangement. Clients should sign an informed consent agreement to demonstrate that they understand and agree to have this particular type of relationship with this particular individual.

There are three key aspects to the legal definition of informed consent: capacity, comprehension of information, and voluntariness (Corey, Corey, & Callanan, 2007). Capacity refers to the client's ability to make decisions on her own. Most underage individuals do not have the capacity to enter into the informed consent agreement and require consent through their legal guardian (note, however, that this is not always the case). Comprehension of information concerns how much the client understands her rights. Therapists need to word the informed consent document, along with their verbal explanation of it, in a way that the client can understand. In developing informed consent forms, therapists should ensure that the average person could make sense of them. Voluntariness means that the person freely chooses to enter into this relationship.

In other words, the therapy contract needs to be entered into willingly by the client where the client has the capacity to make the decision to do so based on the relevant information provided by the therapist. Children are not considered to have the capacity to make this agreement, so their parents or guardians must make the decision to do so for them. Therapists should check their state laws to learn who is considered capable of making their own choices about entering into therapy. When multiple people are involved in therapy (such as in couples or family therapy), every individual who is at the age of majority (usually eighteen) needs to sign the informed consent form. However, it is recommended that all parties who can write sign their name, as this helps everyone to feel included in the contract.

Most therapists develop their own consent form, which they ask clients to read before the therapy process begins. Agencies typically have a standard informed consent form, which can be used by therapists working at the agency.

These forms usually discuss the client's rights in therapy, goals of therapy, issues of confidentiality, expectations for the client, payment, consequences of missing sessions, qualifications of the therapist, risks and benefits of therapy, and a general explanation of the therapy process (Corey, Corey, & Callanan, 2007).

Therapists are encouraged to discuss with the client all aspects of the informed consent to ensure the client fully comprehends the issues surrounding the therapeutic process. One of the difficulties of informed consent is whether it truly is "informed." How much does the therapist have to tell the client about the purpose behind the interventions he is making? Does the therapist need to inform the client how he is conceptualizing the problem situation, and thus which techniques he is using? A rule of thumb is that the therapist should discuss with the client enough information for the client to make a reasonable decision about whether she wants to enter into this relationship. The specifics of theory are usually not considered to be integral to be disclosed, except if the therapist is going to be engaging in an unconventional method of treatment (for example, hypnotherapy, flooding/exposure therapy, or the like).

Therapy is not only a contract between therapist and client, but also between therapist and society. This contract is to provide services in the most ethical manner possible. To fulfill their responsibilities of this implicit contract, therapists must keep accurate case notes to document what occurs during the therapeutic process. Since the therapeutic system is connected to the legal system (court-ordered cases), the managed care system (insurance), and the medical profession, therapists need to ensure that they are providing services in the most professional manner.

Professionalism is a learning process. It takes time for someone in a field to learn the rules, laws, and ethics of that field, as well as the particulars of how to practice in that field. Therapeutic interviews are performed by people with various skills levels. This book is one step forward in helping therapeutic interviewers conduct effective therapeutic interviews that will help their clients move, as quickly as possible, toward the clients' goals. Regardless of the type of interview, interviewing is both a skill and an art. The therapist must know the technical aspects of interviewing. Yet, a really good therapist makes therapy an art form. Leon (1982) stated, "Interviewing is an art, a science, and a therapeutic tool all wrapped up in one complex package" (p. 4). Some people believe that being a good interviewer is an innate ability, that conducting good interviews is more of an art than a science. Others view it as a science that can be learned and perfected. Beginning therapists tend to view therapeutic interviewing as a skill set that can be learned. Novice therapists tend to spend so much time trying to figure out the skill part of interviewing (for example, what question to ask next, what the client's nonverbals mean, how much to talk or just listen) that they are not fully "there" in the therapy room. They do not create a drama in the therapy room that is exciting for both therapist and client.

Keeney (1990) imagined training a therapist to develop "communicational artistry" (p. 1). All persons in the interview would be engaged in a flowing process where each played off the other. This artistry of communication transcends the therapy room and also occurs when therapeutic interviewers work with their supervisors. Haley (1996) explained that like other art, therapy is learned and taught in an apprenticeship system.

One means of being a bit more artistic rather than scientific is to understand therapy as improvisation. Given that improvisation depends on two or more people working off one another—each not knowing what the other is going to say next—improvisation is lively and in the moment. The same is true for the therapeutic interview. If it were scripted with no deviation, the person of the therapist and the person of the client would lose importance. This book provides several guidelines and recommendations about how to conduct therapeutic interviews. However, it is not a cookbook. Therapists, based on their own personal characteristics and the theory or theories that make the most sense for them, will need to determine for themselves which of the skills in this book should be utilized at which times during the therapeutic interview. Further, these skills need to be incorporated into the therapist's personal style to be truly effective.

Are Therapeutic Interviews Effective?

Perhaps one of the first questions to ask when going into the field of therapy is how effective therapy is for clients. Does it work or are clients, and therapists, just wasting their time? What would be the point of going into a profession that doesn't produce positive outcomes for its consumers? Spiegel (1999) discussed how some people believe that psychotherapy is useless and potentially harmful. This can be seen in recent debates by celebrities such as Tom Cruise and other Scientologists who denounced the entire field of psychiatry. Although there is a distinction between psychiatrists who prescribe psychiatric medications and therapists who conduct therapeutic interviews, the distinction was ignored in the debates. Psychiatry has been associated with psychotropic medications, and those who denounced psychotherapy lumped it in with concern about overmedicating clients.

Epstein (1999) provided an interesting overview of the ineffectiveness of psychotherapy. He explained that the research base the field uses to explain its efficacy has not been sound. Epstein also held that there is self-deception in the therapy field when the therapist is attempting to ameliorate social problems by working with the individual agent instead of through a wider social context. This goes to the larger issue of what is leading to the difficulties that clients have. If some clients develop symptoms and problems because of the social context in which they live (for example, poverty, prejudice, and so forth), working with these individuals without addressing the larger context may not be a fully meaningful endeavor.

One of the difficulties of deciding whether therapy was helpful for a client is determining how to define effectiveness operationally. Who should be the person to judge whether therapy was useful or not? The therapist? The client? A third party? Is therapy effective when the client no longer has a DSM-IV-TR diagnosis? What happens if the client's initial concerns have been sufficiently addressed so that they are no longer concerns, yet there are other difficulties that were not present or mentioned in the beginning of therapy? This goes to a deeper issue of whose goals are honored during the therapy interview. For instance, whose goals are honored if a client is court-ordered to therapy because of alcohol issues yet the client and therapist do not think that alcohol is the problem, but rather that lack of self-esteem is? If the client improves her self-esteem to the point that both therapist and client are comfortable with it, yet the client is still drinking, has therapy been effective? Case Scenario 1.2 provides an example of how various goals can be involved in a therapy case.

It would seem to be common sense that "helpers" actually help the people they work with. This is assuming that all therapeutic interviewers are equally effective. This assumption isn't necessarily accurate. As in all professions, some practitioners are good at what they do while others are not. There appears to be a continuum of effectiveness from excellent to extremely bad. Where a therapist is on that continuum is dependent on how much training they have received, the quality of that training, their own personal experiences, their supervisor, the type of interpersonal relater they are, and other such qualities. However, it is not this simple. Effectiveness of a therapist is also related to clients. Thus, effectiveness depends on where a client is on the continuum of working on their problem and how that placement intersects with the therapist's place continuum of skill development and the therapist's personal characteristics.

So, is therapy effective? Therapists working in clinical practice know in their gut that what they are doing is working. However, given the climate of managed care's influence in therapy, individuals and companies want documented proof of effectiveness.

Saunders (1999), in exploring past research, concluded, "The evidence for the effectiveness of psychotherapy as a health intervention is overwhelming" (p. 82). Saunders (2002) later, based on scientific inquiry, explained that therapy is "an extremely efficacious treatment" (p. 251). Drisko (2004) reviewed meta-analyses of psychotherapy outcome research and noted two main points. First, having psychotherapy is more effective than not having psychotherapy. Those who had counseling did much better than those who didn't. The second finding is that there is little difference across psychotherapies, that they all seem to have the same amount of influence and effectiveness on outcome.

CASE SCENARIO 1.2

I was working with a family who had been referred to therapy because of allegations of neglect. The family consisted of a husband and wife, both in their midtwenties and their one-year-old daughter. The child protection services had deemed that there had been neglect and requested an in-home family therapy crisis program to work with this family. The couple disagreed that they had neglected their child. I then had three different goals operating when working with this family: the couple's, the child protective service's, and my own.

In conclusion, therapy has been shown to be more effective than no therapy. The type of theory the therapist uses has been shown not to make a difference in outcome (although operating from a theory does impact 15 percent of the variance of positive outcome). Thus, therapy is useful, regardless of theory. What many clinicians are now discussing is the connection between the person of the therapist and the person of the client as the major contributor to the therapy process followed by a connection between the types of techniques/approaches used based on the client's problem.

Summary

Therapy is a process wherein at least two individuals mutually agree to engage in a conversation that focuses on one person's current problematic situation(s) and to attempt to develop alternatives and possibilities for that person so that he or she will have more options to live life in the way that he or she desires. This conversation occurs based on a therapeutic relationship in which the therapist provides certain conditions that enable the client to feel safe enough to open up to the therapist and to explore his or her own experiences and feelings. Through the therapeutic alliance, therapist and client operate within the ethical rules of therapy to reach the client's goals.

Exercises

1. Interview several people about what they think therapy is all about. Interview people from different age levels, genders, educational levels, and occupations. Notice if any patterns emerge. Then examine how other people's definitions of psychotherapy are similar to or different from your own.

2. Watch several interviews conducted on television, or if you can, check out counseling videos from your local public or university library. What positive and negative skills do you notice the interviewer displaying? What impact do you notice the interviewer having on the interviewee?

3. With your classmates, debate the necessity of having to establish a positive therapeutic alliance. Half of the students should take the stance that a positive alliance is absolutely necessary for an effective outcome in therapy. Half of the students should take the stance that it is not the alliance that matters in therapy but what the client does differently.

2

The Therapy Client

Motivation and Understanding of Therapy

In Chapter 1, therapy was described as a relationship involving at least two people—one person with problems who is coming to another person for help. The therapeutic *relationship* is just that—a relationship *between* people. This chapter focuses on one of these people—the person coming to therapy. This person may be the most neglected focus of inquiry in trying to understand the therapeutic process, yet is the most important part of the therapy. Most training programs focus on who the therapist is and do not devote the attention they could to the characteristics of clients. Because of this, therapists may not have a good sense of who they are working with. This chapter focuses on why clients might come to therapy, who they are, and what they know about therapy prior to coming.

Definition of the Person Coming to Therapy

The person who comes to a therapist has been called many things throughout the history of psychotherapy. When therapy began, approximately a century ago, most therapists were psychiatrists with medical degrees who used the term "patient." Psychoanalysts, who were the primary conveyers of therapy for most of the last century, called the person the "analysand." When the Diagnostic and Statistical Manual (DSM), which is based on a medical model, became the common means of understanding what is occurring for people, "patient" continued to make sense. However, there has been a growing push in the field of therapy to be "consumer-driven"; thus, the term "client" has become in vogue. Other terms used include "helpee," "consumer," and "co-collaborator." For the purposes of this book, the term "client" will be used. It contains less pejorative meanings than "patient" as well as a less hierarchical distinction between the two parties.

Clients come to therapy with a variety of problems, experiences, personality characteristics, and ideas of what therapy is or is not. In terms of the problems that

Reflection 2.1

Think about the last time that you went to your medical doctor. How warm and friendly was your doctor? How much did you feel like a unique human being? When you saw the medical tech, nurse, or doctor walking around with your chart, what impact did that have on you? How "in control" did you feel of what was going on for you? How much of the time were you and the doctor discussing what was going on for you versus the doctor *telling* you what was going on for you? What sort of relationship do you want with your clients? Based on the position that you take, how do you think this will impact your work with your clients?

clients are dealing with, they range from what might be considered minor (for instance, wanting to stop a nail biting habit) to those that are life threatening (for example, homicidal or suicidal thoughts). For many clients, the decision to come to therapy is based on life not being as they want it. What they want different may be viewed by others as being important or not important. A client might be extremely wealthy, healthy, and have everything going for him, but if there is something, no matter how small, in that person's life that brings him discontent, then this is an important problem *for that particular client*. Therapists need to understand why this problem is significant *for the client*, rather than judging it from their own criteria of what constitutes a problem.

Other clients come to therapy because of issues that no one would ever want to deal with. These might be having been raped, losing a loved one in a car accident, having been kidnapped, or having experienced some other traumatic situation. Sometimes the problems clients are coming to therapy with border on the bizarre (Kottler & Carlson, 2003). Some clients come to therapy because they are having relationship difficulties. Others are exhibiting behaviors they don't like, such as compulsive hand-washing or masturbating. Other clients come because they are not happy with the way their lives are going. Still others come because they want to get a better sense of who they really are. How clients come to therapy, the issues they are dealing with, their expectations of therapy, along with their own personality and life experiences impact what occurs in therapy.

Who clients are and what they do have enormous impact on whether they reach their goals. Lambert (1992) found that approximately 40 percent of the improvement a client makes during the therapy process is due to client factors and extra-therapeutic influences. Extra-therapeutic factors consist of personal traits and attributes as well as chance events that happen outside the therapy and impact the person enough that the person changes. It would seem absolutely imperative to take these into consideration when working with a client. However, it is the client factors that will be discussed here, as these are the strengths, resources, and capacity for growth that the client comes into therapy with. Therapists can join and help clients toward goals by making a point of highlighting these client factors. Further, by focusing on client factors, therapists shift the dynamic of the relationship from expert–patient to co-collaboration. Clients then become primary change agents.

Motivation for Therapy

Clients arrive on the therapist's doorstep through their own initiative or through that of a parent, spouse, child, or third party. Clients who come on their own may have realized that there are things about themselves that they want to change or do not like. These things may have been pointed out to them by others or may be things they came to realize on their own. These changes may be that they want to stop using drugs, to feel less depressed, to overcome grief or a past trauma, or the like.

Haley (1996) suggested that a therapist can hold two views of who should go to therapy. The first is that therapy is for people who are experiencing some problem impacting their lives—problems that are in need of resolution. The second view is that therapy is useful for everyone because therapy helps people become better people. Depending on the therapeutic interviewer's perspective, she will accept certain people as clients and not others. A therapist does not have to work with every client who seeks help. Sometimes, telling a sad client that he is experiencing sadness appropriate to the situation (for example, grief after a loved one passes away) is to let them know that they are doing okay and do not need therapy. One of the most important things for therapists to be able to do is to quickly figure out who they can help and who they cannot.

Some clients come at the behest of another person very close to them. This tends to happen in couples or family therapy where one or more parties are coming because someone else in the family is upset with something. This also occurs with child therapy, where the parent brings a child to therapy because of behavior or emotional problems the child may be displaying. When working with clients who have come at the request of someone else, it is important to try to figure out quickly what it is that they themselves want out of the therapeutic experience. Case Scenario 2.1 describes an actual case where this helped to make a therapeutic connection.

At universities, some students are required to go to counseling if university personnel sense that the person is in need. Some therapy training programs require their students to attend therapy so that the students can work on their own issues before working with clients. A second benefit for these students is that they are able to experience what it is like to be the client in the therapeutic relationship. Most recently, in the United States, the legal system has been using the therapy system as a means of working with people who have committed crimes. For instance, individuals who have been involved in domestic violence may have to go to anger management courses, sometimes for as long as twenty-six weeks. Adolescents who commit crimes might have to go to therapy instead of juvenile detention. Case Scenario 2.2 highlights an actual case in which the goals of the legal

CASE SCENARIO 2.1

I met with a seventeen-year-old male who was brought to therapy by his mother because he was getting into trouble at school and his grades were dropping. While his motivation was driven (literally!) by his mother's demand he seek help, after meeting with him, I asked him why he thought his mother had brought him to therapy. He told me she was upset at how he was doing at school. I then asked him what it was that *he* wanted for himself from therapy. He revealed struggling with feelings of alienation and anxiety about his sexual identity, something he felt unable to reveal to anyone at home or school. I then focused on this as the primary issue in therapy in order to develop the most effective therapeutic alliance I could with him.

CASE SCENARIO 2.2

I met with a family of five where, after the thirteen-year-old son was caught shoplifting, the juvenile justice system gave the family a choice: The son could either go to the juvenile detention center for two months or the family could go to therapy until the therapist deemed that therapy was complete. The family opted to go to therapy. When asked what they wanted to work on, each member of the family stated that there were not any problems in the family and that the son had just committed a stupid act, which he had learned his lesson from. The son had shoplifted two bottles of hand lotion. I opened the conversation to what they might want changed for themselves as a family or as individuals. No one in the family took me up on this offer. I worked with the family for three sessions, and then reported back to the juvenile justice system about what occurred in therapy. In this case, I was unable to get the family members to be active in the therapy because their goals were not the same as the juvenile justice system's goals.

system and the therapy system did not quite mesh with a family's sense of what was happening.

Characteristics of Clients

What are the traits and characteristics of someone who enters into the therapeutic relationship as a client? In reviewing the literature, Clarkin and Levy (2004) found that people who exhibit emotional distress and psychological symptoms and who perceive their own mental health to be poor are most likely to be clients. This would seem to be common sense; however, there has been an increase in the number of therapy clients who do not show these symptoms. More people are utilizing

Exercise 2.1

On a piece of paper, write down ten characteristics of clients. What do you notice about this list? Are these attributes positive or negative? Where do you think you developed these perceptions?

the vast array of counseling services (from career counseling to therapy for relationship problems to requests for psychiatric medications). Who comes to therapy is also predicated on gender, culture, and age. Clarkin and Levy found that women tend to seek help more often than men, and younger individuals seek help more often than older individuals.

The National Institute of Mental Health (www. nimh. nih. gov) reported that about one in five adults in the United States is dealing with some type of mental disorder. Some people experience more than one mental disorder at the same time. Using 1998 U.S. Census figures, the estimated number of Americans who, in a given year, are dealing with mental disorders is 44.3 million people. This does not take into account the millions more who might not have a mental disorder but are impacted by those who do or who have serious issues in their lives that do not fit the criteria of mental disorders. NIMH also found that out of the ten leading causes of disability in the United States, four of them are mental disorders (major depression, bipolar disorder, schizophrenia, and obsessive-compulsive disorder). In a given year, about 10 percent of Americans eighteen and over have a depressive disorder (with a nearly two-to-one ratio of female-to-male). Approximately 13 percent of people eighteen to fifty-four deal with an anxiety disorder.

Clients range from infants to the elderly; from men to women; from homosexual to heterosexual to bisexual to transgender; and from a myriad of races, religions, ethnicities, and nationalities. Therapists-in-training are encouraged to work with as many different types of people as possible to gain the broadest perspective of client functioning as well as the best practices for working with each of them. Therapy is not exclusively used by those who have a diagnosable situation. People come to therapy to get over the loss of a loved one, for help with loneliness, to stop engaging in a harmful behavior (for example, smoking or alcohol addiction), to figure out how to be more successful in romantic relationships or how to focus better, and so on. However, only a small percentage of people who need mental health services actually go for therapy. This is due to a large number of reasons. The next section discusses help-seeking behavior and then explains how negative media portrayals have possibly led to clients and therapists being stigmatized so that people are not utilizing these services.

Help-Seeking Behavior

People's attitudes toward seeking help play a role in their willingness to seek help for themselves (Sheffield, Fiorenza, & Sofronoff, 2004). These attitudes are developed within a public discourse about who the people are that seek psychological services, who the people are that provide psychological services, and what transpires between the two.

The dominant discourse in the United States about psychotherapy is that those who seek therapy services are viewed negatively. Those who go to counseling are often thought of as weak and abnormal and as failures. Sparks (2002), in analyzing media representations of mental illness, found that many texts presented those defined as "mentally ill" as not being liked or wanted by members of the community, as being unpredictable, needing medication, requiring special treatment facilities, as being uneducated, dangerous, and unstable, and as chronicly ill. There are not many positive understandings and representations of the mentally ill in society or the media. This leads to real life consequences for what people think about them and how people respond to them. Just the term *mentally ill* presents a skewed sense of who these people are. Most individuals who seek therapeutic services do not have current severe problems or issues they are dealing with. This term would not seem to be relevant to them. However, just by going to see a therapist, societal perception of them might be that they are psychologically unstable.

The perception that people have of mental illness is closely related to their desire and willingness to seek therapeutic services. Leong and Zachar (1999) found that the more negative opinions people had about mental illness, the less likely they were to seek help from a mental health professional. Given that people are exposed to many negative mass media representations of mental illness, people are likely to adopt a corresponding perception about people who have been diagnosed with a psychological disorder. This is also problematic in that people will not seek therapeutic services early in the problem sequence. When a problem first occurs, people will attempt their normal problem-solving behaviors. If these solution attempts work, then the person will not seek services. However, if the solution attempts do not work, the person will continue to try to apply them to see if a solution only needs time and more effort. If this still does not work, they may change solution attempts or talk with friends and family members for a solution. If the problem persists or gets worse, they may then, depending on the problem and their concept of what therapy is and how (or if) it will help—plus the thought of how other people as well as themselves will view them if they go to therapy—seek out psychotherapeutic services.

Why would people not go to therapy because of what other people think? In the United States (and most other countries), there has been a stigma against people who seek psychotherapy services. This societal viewpoint has been present since the days when people who were seen by psychotherapists were placed in "insane asylums." Clients experience this negative stigma, which leads them to feel embarrassment, hurt, and anger (Wahl, 1999). Once a person (or group of people) is labeled as different and thus stigmatized, their range of opportunities in life are reduced (Goffman, 1965). Thus, those people who realize that they are in the stigmatized group will most likely come to view themselves as deficient. The stigmatization of being labeled as crazy is not a new phenomenon. People considered to be mentally ill have dealt with stigma throughout most of known history (Foucault, 1965; Mora, 1992; Simon, 1992).

The reasons why individuals seek out psychotherapeutic services have changed, especially in the last several decades. Whereas, in the past, individuals went to therapy when their condition was severe, today individuals are going to therapy for a multitude of reasons, many of which could be considered common and ordinary. Most individuals at some point in their lives have experienced some type of mental health problem in which the severity of the distress matches the symptoms and signs of mental disorder (Satcher, 1999). However, only a small portion of the population utilizes therapeutic services. This means that although a majority of the population experiences issues that would be appropriate for therapeutic services, only a small percentage actually seeks out those services.

Bram (1997) suggested that "the public may not have full confidence that psychotherapists are capable of or have the means to appropriately, therapeutically, and ethically handle the range of feelings evoked in them by their clients" (p. 175). He explained that the false perceptions of the public might lead some people to avoid seeking services for fear of being exploited or rejected by a therapist (erroneously thought to be self-serving and impulsive). People who are currently clients may hold back from full exploration in session based on false notions of who therapists are and what occurs in therapy. Therapists can understand these perceptions and can help to educate clients about the realities of therapy practice.

Psychotherapy is not utilized by every group of people in the same ways. Depending on culture, age, and gender, people may have different viewpoints and expectations for what therapy can do. Barry et al. (2000) explained that males and those under the age of forty, more so than women and those over forty, do not seek mental health services. This may be because of lower levels of awareness, lower confidence in mental health services, negative attitudes toward help-seeking, and the possibility of social stigma. Other groups that have lower than normal rates of psychotherapy usage are African Americans (Snowden, 2001), Asian Americans (Leong & Lau, 2001), and the elderly (Wetherell et al., 2004).

Media Presentations of Therapy

In the last several years, psychotherapy has become more prominently portrayed in the media. With television shows such as *Dr. Phil*, *Frazier*, and *The Sopranos* along with movies such as *28 days*, *Prince of Tides*, and *Good Will Hunting*, individuals who have never gone to counseling are receiving information about clients, therapists, and the therapy process. Yet, what seems to be portrayed is a rather negative view of therapists (for instance, therapists engaging in unethical behavior or being potentially psychologically disturbed themselves). Although the portrayals of clients, therapists, and the therapeutic process seem to be somewhat more positive since the 1980s (Wahl, 1995), overall they are still negative in that they do not shed a very positive light on anyone involved in therapy. Gabbard and Gabbard (1999) suggested that there was only one period in the history of cinema that portrayed therapists positively. They called this the Golden Age, which ran from the late 1950s to the early 1960s (only several years). Aside from this extremely brief period, most therapist and client portrayals in films have been negative. Although some people might not put too much weight on media depictions, this negativity can have an extremely powerful effect on how people develop an understanding of clients and therapists as well as on what happens between them during the therapeutic process.

The mass media's portrayal of clients has been more severe than that toward therapists. Clients are seen as people who are mentally ill, many of them as villainous and murderous (Wahl, 1995). In several studies in which researchers viewed samples of television presentations, the mentally ill were consistently presented in negative ways (Diefenbach, 1997; Signorielli, 1989; & Wahl & Roth, 1982).

Although these negative images can be harmful, preventing some people from seeking out therapeutic services or stigmatizing those who go to therapy, positive portrayals can also be problematic in that they may portray an idealized image that is not realistic (Gabbard & Gabbard, 1999). The public seems to have a split view of mental health professionals. On one side, they hold these individuals in high esteem because they have the knowledge to understand the workings of human behavior and what is going on in people's minds. On the other side, they hold contempt for them because they cannot solve all of society's problems and not necessarily even the problems of a single individual.

Television shows such as *Frazier* present therapists as neurotic. Movies such as *Analyze This, What About Bob, Color of Night*, and *Good Will Hunting* present therapists who might not be the most grounded people. When people watch *One Flew Over the Cuckoo's Nest* or *Girl, Interrupted*, they may fear entering into a treatment program (especially an inpatient program) or going to a therapist. This is partly due to the portrayal in many movies of the psychotherapist in a position of authority, usually in a manner that is overbearing and potentially harmful to the client (Walker, 2004). Brandell (2004a, 2004b) described several movies that have shown a more realistic portrayal of the therapy process, including *I Never Promised You a Rose Garden, Ordinary People*, and *The Sixth Sense*. Table 2.1 (page 28) lists a handful of movies in which clients, therapists, and the therapy process are depicted along with a brief description.

The importance of how client, therapist, and the therapy process are depicted in the media is not an insignificant matter. Charles (2004) explained, "When we buy our ticket to the movies, we're not just buying a few hours' entertainment. We are also, for that interim, buying a worldview and borrowing an identity—trying it on for size" (p. 67). Compounded on this is how and where psychotherapy is shown. Many movies have shown people being locked up in facilities such as mental hospitals and institutions. Walker (2004) suggested that this leads to an understanding of psychiatry (and counseling/psychotherapy gets lumped along with that) as being authoritarian and controlling. When people enter mental hospitals, they are usually not there by their own volition and they usually cannot leave until the mental health professional in charge says that they can. These movies provide the viewer with a perspective that the mental health field is repressive (Walker, 2004).

TABLE 2.1   *Movies Depicting Clients, Therapists, and Psychotherapy*

28 days: Sandra Bullock's character goes into an inpatient alcohol and drug rehabilitation clinic. Her therapist, Steve Buscemi, is an ex-user who does not seem to be fully healed.

Analyze This: Billy Crystal plays a therapist who at times is very bored with his clients and has fantasies of slapping them because the clients are being superficial. Further, Crystal's character gets caught up in the mafia goings-on of one of his patients.

Color of Night: Bruce Willis plays a psychologist who unintentionally pushes his client to suicide.

Girl, Interrupted: The inpatient hospital setting that Winona Ryder finds herself in is extremely restrictive and cold. Although Whoopi Goldberg's character has some sense of warmth, the head psychiatrist is cold.

Good Will Hunting: Matt Damon's character meets with several therapists before meeting his therapist, played by Robin Williams. The first therapist he accuses of being gay and wanting to "jump his bones." The second therapist attempts to hypnotize him, wherein Matt Damon makes fun of the therapist's attempts. Upon meeting Robin Williams's character, Matt Damon antagonizes him about his ex-wife so that Robin Williams grabs his neck and threatens to physically harm him, thus showing how he is somewhat unstable. However, the two develop a very close connection.

One Flew Over the Cuckoo's Nest: Nurse Ratched is portrayed as not caring for the self-hood of the patients in the psych ward. Patients are treated in a cold and harsh manner.

Prime: A therapist finds out that one of her patients is dating her son. She continues treating the client without discussing the situation with her.

The Prince of Tides: Barbara Streisand, playing a psychiatrist, falls in love with her newly deceased patient's brother.

What About Bob? Bill Murray's character is extremely phobic, but taken to the extreme of being farcical. Richard Dreyfuss's psychiatrist character is self-absorbed and uncaring toward his clients.

The popularity of Dr. Phil McGraw, along with his being named as "America's Therapist" (Ventura, 2005), presents a skewed view of what therapy is. Dr. Phil occasionally tells people that if they just listen to him and follow his directions exactly, that they will then get better. This presents a picture of the client as passive participant in need of the expert advice of the therapist. Although he is a clinical psychologist, on his television show, Dr. Phil doesn't quite do "therapy" as it is normally practiced.

When people who have no previous experience of what therapy is watch a television show such as *Dr. Phil*, or see therapy portrayed in a movie, they may develop a false perception of what occurs in the therapy room. This is potentially harmful since people's conceptions of mental illness are significantly developed through their exposure to the mass media (Wahl, 1995). People might be reinforced to view clients as being "crazy" and therapists as being "wacky" and unethical. Based on the predominance of media presenting therapists as incompetent, mentally challenged, overly sexual, or domineering, people may come to therapy with a negative perception. Further, clients might gain a sense that therapy calls for the therapist to tell the client exactly what is wrong with him and exactly what he needs to do to get better. This view detracts from understanding the therapeutic relationship as collaborative.

Given how clients, therapists, and the therapy process are portrayed in the media, therapists must work with clients to orient them to the reality of therapy instead of the false myth presented in society. It is very important for therapists to realize what clients think the therapeutic process is about. Therapists should talk with clients either before therapy begins or at the first session and give a brief overview of what the client can expect from the therapist and the therapeutic process. This will help ensure that therapist and client have similar expectations for the relationship.

Societal View of Those Who Seek Therapy

Going to see a therapist has not always been an accepted standard. In many countries outside of the United States (along with continuing segments within the United States), going to see a therapist is a sign of having a serious mental problem. It is an implicit admission that people cannot manage their lives on their own and thus need someone to help them. Many individuals, if asked to give a few adjectives of someone who goes to therapy, might say "crazy," "wacko," "insane," "psycho," or other such pejorative term.

During the early part of the twentieth century, if someone were to go see a therapist, that meeting probably occurred within a mental institution (sometimes called an "insane asylum"). It was so embarrassing to have a member of one's family sent to an insane asylum that families would construct stories about why that family member was not presently at home, similar to how they might if a daughter

Reflection 2.2

Imagine you were to be set up on a blind date (given that you were single). Your friend tells you that this person is nice, intelligent, attractive, and has a decent job, along with other positive attributes. They also tell you that the person is currently going to see a psychotherapist. How would that information impact your decision to go out on the date? What preconceived ideas might you have of the other person? How would you view the other person?

or sister became pregnant out of wedlock. Until the middle of the twentieth century, societies used institutions (that is, mental hospitals) to segregate those deemed different and insane. These feelings of embarrassment can be so severe that the family feels stigmatized (Dubin & Fink, 1992; Lefley, 1992).

It hasn't been until the last twenty to thirty years that a greater acceptance of therapy has shifted people's viewpoints. Although shows like *Dr. Phil* may generate a false perception of therapy, they have opened up the arena of therapy from being a private affair to becoming more public. Guests on *Dr. Phil* range in their struggles, from people exhibiting severe mental disorders to people who cannot keep their New Year's resolutions to couples who are fighting to parents who spank their children to overweight individuals trying to lose weight and the like. In the last several decades, people are realizing that going to counseling and therapy is not only for severe depression or suicidal thoughts, but also for career counseling, couples counseling, school problems, and a myriad of other normal life difficulties.

Today, most people know someone who is going or has gone to therapy. Managed-care insurance companies will most likely have some type of mental health coverage. Many people are talking more openly about going to see a therapist. Yet, there is still a sense that if someone has gone to therapy, there is something wrong with that person. Based on these perceptions, clients may come to therapy with a sense that something is truly wrong with them. They might be dealing with issues of embarrassment and isolation. Therapy might become a very private affair for them; they might not tell good friends or family members they are attending. These clients will probably feel somewhat uncomfortable during the first interview.

Opening Up in the First Session

The therapeutic interview might be one of the strangest contexts for two people to engage in a relationship. The normal expectations of human communication, such as reciprocity, do not exist in the therapy room. In agency settings, clients will be asked a host of extremely personal questions so that the therapeutic or intake interviewer can get enough information to complete a biopsychosocial assessment (an assessment to try to understand the biological, psychological, and social contexts of the person and how they relate to the person's complaints). This might occur even before the therapist and client make a simple, basic connection.

Therapists should allow clients room to become familiar with the situation so that they will be comfortable in disclosing the personal information that brought them to therapy in the first place. Unfortunately, some therapists might label this hesitance as "resistance" when in fact it would seem to be a normal interpersonal process. In most people's everyday lives, it takes a long time to develop sufficient interpersonal trust in another person so that people feel comfortable self-disclos-

Reflection 2.3

Think about the last time you went to a medical doctor for the first time and had to fill out the medical history form in the waiting room before you ever got to meet with the doctor. How comfortable were you writing down some of the past physical ailments that you've had? What was it like for you telling the doctor what was wrong with you or what concerns you had about your health? Now imagine what that must be like for a client going to a psychotherapist.

ing to that person and trusting that the person will keep the information confidential and won't think bad of them.

The Client's Experience in Therapy

As presented in Chapter 1, the personality and skills of the helper lead to growth-facilitation conditions for the client, which culminate in specific outcomes for the client. Clients have a unique way of understanding and being with different therapists. There is not always a correct "fit," even if the therapist is fully present with the client. Clients would have very different therapy experiences if they met with various therapeutic interviewers.

Clients want a safe place where they can open up and talk to someone who will not judge them. Therapists need to present an inviting arena for clients to be able to use the therapeutic interview to its full potential. To ensure this is happening, therapists can check in with clients during the course of therapy to assess whether what they are doing seems useful for the client. The following therapist response is one way of achieving that.

> *Therapist:* I just want to take a second to see if what we are doing here makes sense for you and is helping you at all. What are the things that we're doing that you are finding useful? What isn't quite useful to you?

The client's experience is also based on the right fit with the therapeutic interviewer. Some consumer guides for potential clients recommend that clients shop around for a therapist until they find one that they feel they are compatible with (Feltham, 1999). They can do this based on short telephone conversations with therapists or on an initial face-to-face interview. When a client initially calls a therapist for a first session, therapists might consider talking with the client about what the first session should be, albeit a therapy interview or a chance for the client to assess whether there is a good fit. Some therapists spend about ten to fifteen minutes on the phone with clients before a first session is ever scheduled so that clients can evaluate their initial impression of the therapist's way of working and personality.

Readiness for Change

Clients come to therapy at different points in their awareness of their problem(s) as well as with varying levels of desire to act on their problem(s) for change. Prochaska, DiClemente, and Norcross (1992) developed an understanding of client motivation for change, referred to as the "stages of change model." This model was originally developed to conceptualize clients dealing with addictions/smoking cessation (DiClemente & Prochaska, 1982), yet has been used with clients with all types of life difficulties. Prochaska and DiClemente (1992) explained, "As currently understood, the stages of change represent specific constellations of attitudes, intentions, and/or behaviors that are relevant to an individual's status in the process of change" (p. 185). The stages of change model is based on five basic stages of change: precontemplation, contemplation, preparation, action, and maintenance (Prochaska & DiClemente, 1992; Prochaska, DiClemente, & Norcross, 1992).

The use of the stages of change model is based on the client's relationship to one specific problem (Prochaska & DiClemente, 1992). Thus, a client might be at one stage of change in regards to one problem (for example, action stage with the problem of anxiety) yet might be at a very different stage of change in relation to a different problem (for example, precontemplation stage with the problem of drinking). Important with all clients, but possibly most important with substance abusers (DiClemente, 1999), an assessment of the client's motivation for help or change can set therapy on the right course. Miller, Duncan, and Hubble (1997) explained that one of the keys to developing a strong working relationship with clients is for the therapist to understand and work with the clients based on their level of readiness for change.

Petrocelli (2002) proposed that all people go through the stages of change, whether they do so with or without therapy. However, the stages of change model was not designed for those people who are not intentionally in the change process but are having change imposed upon them (Prochaska & DiClemente, 1992). Therapists can connect with the particular stage the client is currently in to enhance the therapeutic alliance and lead to a better chance of client change.

Precontemplation

The first stage a client goes through is the precontemplation stage. It is that point in which the client is "unaware, unwilling or discouraged when it comes to changing a particular problem behavior" (Prochaska & DiClemente, 1992, p. 186). The client is not planning to make any behavioral change attempts and tends to see the problem behavior as having more advantages than disadvantages (Connors, Donovan, & DiClemente, 2001). These clients are usually court-ordered clients or clients who are coming because someone in their family wants them to come to therapy. Connors, Donovan, and DiClemente (2001) delineated some common characteristics of individuals in the precontemplation stage: "defensive . . . resistant to suggestion of problems associated with their drug use [or problem behavior]

. . . uncommitted to or passive in treatment . . . consciously or unconsciously avoiding steps to change their behavior . . . lacking awareness of a problem . . . often pressured by others to seek treatment . . . feeling coerced and `put upon' by significant others" (p. 13).

Clients in the precontemplation stage tend to initiate few change attempts. If a therapist attempts to get the client to change, perhaps by giving him homework tasks, the client might become defensive (Prochaska & DiClemente, 1992). This would make sense in that the client is not really thinking about changing and is not ready for it. Just as you would not be motivated to change something about yourself if you didn't think there was a problem, clients might disagree with therapists (or most probably the referring person) about whether they have a problem. If the therapist tries to get an individual in the precontemplation stage to make active change efforts right away, the therapist is pushing too much, too fast.

Connors, Donovan, and DiClemente (2001) recommended that therapists working with a client in the precontemplation stage should do two things. First, they should not focus on behavioral change. Petrocelli (2002) also suggested that behavioral models of therapy do not work well with people in the precontemplation stage. Second, they should use motivational strategies so the client might perceive that the problem needs changing. These strategies are designed to get the client to focus inward. Prochaska and DiClemente (1992) stated, "In order to move ahead in the cycle of change, precontemplators need to acknowledge or take ownership of the problem, increase awareness of the negative aspects of the problem, and accurately evaluate self-regulation capacities" (p. 186). (See Case Example 2.1.)

Contemplation

Clients in the contemplation stage realize that they have some type of problem, but they have not yet committed to making a change attempt (Prochaska & DiClemente, 1992; Prochaska, DiClemente, & Norcross, 1992). They might start to look at themselves in relation to their problem and might even reevaluate their connection to the problem. These clients might also seek out information about the problem and evaluate the advantages and disadvantages of changing (Connors, Donovan, & DiClemente, 2001). Connors et. al. described some common charac-

CASE EXAMPLE 2.1

Penelope, a twenty-four-year-old graduate student, has been partying heavily for the last two months. She is staying out until four or five in the morning and is having difficulty concentrating in her classes. However, she hasn't received any grades this semester to let her know how her partying is impacting her. A classmate noticed that Penelope seems extra-tired in class and asked her about it. Penelope told the classmate she is doing fine and is having a great time going out.

teristics for individuals in the contemplation stage: seeking to evaluate and understand their behavior; distressed; desirous of exerting control or mastery; thinking
about making change; have not begun taking action and are not yet prepared to do
so; frequently have made attempts to change in the past; and evaluating pros and
cons of their behavior and of making changes in it (p. 19).

Connors, Donovan, and DiClemente (2001) recommended that therapeutic
intervention with a client in the contemplation stage deal with consciousness raising, self-reevaluation, and environmental reevaluation. Therapists can help these
clients understand what it is that they are doing in certain problem situations. In
order to move forward, these clients would need to make a firmer commitment to
change, and thus take the first step toward difference (Prochaska & DiClemente,
1992). (See Case Example 2.2.)

Preparation

The preparation stage occurs when the client has acknowledged that there is some
type of problem and has committed to actively taking steps to make things better,
but has not done so yet (Prochaska & DiClemente, 1992; Prochaska, DiClemente, &
Norcross, 1992). The client is preparing to change and might have taken the first
few small steps of change, but is not fully into the change process. The client has
decided to change and that the change will be in the near future. Prochaska,
DiClemente, and Norcross provided more rigorous criteria for this stage, "Individuals in this stage are intending to take action in the next month and have unsuccessfully taken action in the past year" (p. 1104). Connors, Donovan, and
DiClemente (2001) listed common characteristics of individuals in the preparation
stage:

> intending to change their behavior
> ready to change in terms of both attitude and behavior
> on the verge of taking action
> engaged in the change process
> prepared to make firm commitments to follow through on the action option
>   they choose
> making or having made the decision to change. (p. 22)

CASE EXAMPLE 2.2

Penelope is still enjoying going out four or five nights per week and staying out
quite late. She has noticed that she is not as engaged in class as she used to be and
that her papers have not been of the quality that she used to write. However, in her
undergraduate program, she spent so much time in the library that she felt she
missed out on having fun. She has decided to continue to party but to pay attention
to how much it is really impacting her school work.

For those clients in the preparation stage, therapists can utilize the same techniques they did in the contemplation stage (that is, consciousness raising, self-reevaluation, and environmental reevaluation) while also increasing the clients' commitment to change (Connors, Donovan, & DiClemente, 2001). To move to the next stage, clients need to be fully engaged in the change process. This comes through setting their goals and priorities to achieving the change. (See Case Example 2.3.)

Action

The action stage is that time when the client is actively doing things to change the problem behavior (Prochaska & DiClemente, 1992; Prochaska, DiClemente, & Norcross, 1992). The change at this stage is behavioral, with the client *doing* something differently. They work on effective strategies for changing the problem behavior and preventing possible pitfalls. They are also beginning to learn ways to prevent a reversal of the positive changes they are making. Connors, Donovan, and DiClemente (2001) provided common characteristics of individuals in the action stage: client has decided to make change; client has verbalized or otherwise demonstrated a firm commitment to making change; efforts to modify behavior and/or one's environment are being taken; client presents motivation and effort to achieve behavior change; client has committed to making change and is involved in the change process; and client is willing to follow suggested strategies and activities to change (p. 25).

Connors, Donovan, and DiClemente (2001) suggested that the therapist utilize interventions that are designed for overt behavior change. This is the stage that most therapists look for in clients, when both therapist and client are actively engaged in not only talking about change, but also making the actual change in behavior. Perhaps one of the main tasks for the therapeutic interviewer working with a client in the action stage is to help the client increase his level of self-efficacy. This would be achieved by working with the client to engage in certain positive behaviors and become better able to utilize these behaviors to help reduce the problem (for example, getting someone with anxiety problems to practice relaxation methods). (See Case Example 2.4.)

CASE EXAMPLE 2.3

Penelope has received several poor grades in school and has attributed them to her partying lifestyle. She believes that once she calms down and goes out less, she will be better able to focus on her school work. However, she is still going out several times per week. She has told herself that she will cut down on how much she is going out right after spring break, which is in two weeks, because she currently has some friends staying with her from out of town. They really like to party and she doesn't want to spoil the good time everyone is having.

CASE EXAMPLE 2.4

Penelope has decided that she does not want to let her partying lifestyle prevent her from performing well in her graduate program and jeopardize her career. She has decided that she will only go out on Friday and Saturday nights and that she will be home by 2 a.m. so that she is not exhausted the next day. Further, she has decided to cut back how much she drinks when she goes out so that she will have, at most, two drinks, instead of her normal four or five. She has begun implementing this new plan immediately.

Maintenance

The maintenance stage is the last stage of the change process. It occurs once the majority of change has happened (in the action stage) so that the client is engaging in behavior to ensure the positive change continues (Prochaska & DiClemente, 1992; Prochaska, DiClemente, & Norcross, 1992). Since relapse is the norm of most change attempts, clients need to be actively engaged in positive behavior to avoid falling back into previous problematic patterns. Connors, Donovan, and DiClemente (2001) provided common characteristics of individuals in the maintenance stage: client is working to sustain changes achieved to date; considerable attention is focused on avoiding slips or relapses; client may describe fear or anxiety regarding relapse and face a high risk for relapse; and client may face less frequent but often intense temptation to begin to use substances or to return to substance use (p. 30). (See Case Example 2.5.)

Spiral Pattern of Change

Clients tend to move through these stages of change, not in a linear fashion, but in a spiral fashion (Prochaska, DiClemente, & Norcross, 1992). They might cycle through these stages several times before the point of termination. Many therapists using this viewpoint will discuss it with their clients as part of the relapse prevention process of therapy. Some stages of change practitioners have devel-

CASE EXAMPLE 2.5

Penelope has cut back on how much she goes out and parties. She is only going out several times per month. And when she goes out, she is not drinking alcohol (perhaps one drink at the most). She is getting home by 2 a.m. Her concentration has improved in her classes and her grades have been getting better.

CASE EXAMPLE 2.6

Penelope's grades have improved back to the high level they were before she began going out and partying. She is enjoying herself when she goes out, but she is not drinking and is not staying out late. She has learned how to balance the rigors of her graduate program with personal enjoyment outside of school.

oped a sixth stage, termination. Prochaska and DiClemente (1992) described the termination stage, "This phase would represent some closure to the process of change, in that the behavior is either firmly established or extinguished and that further time and energy are not needed to sustain this behavior change" (p. 187). Thus, a client would have spent a considerable amount of time in the maintenance stage where a new pattern of behavior had taken hold. (See Case Example 2.6.)

Summary

Who clients are, why they are coming to therapy, what happens to them in their lives, what they know about therapy, and how they fit with the therapeutic interviewer all play a role in what happens during the therapy process. Clients have unique understandings of themselves, their problems, therapy, and therapists. Therapeutic interviewers can take time in the beginning of the first interview to talk with a client to gain a sense of the client's expectations for self, the therapist, and the therapy. They can then talk with the client to help educate the client if the client has any incorrect perceptions about the process. This understanding also happens within a context of the client's motivation for change. Therapists can assess what level of motivation the client has for change and work based on the client's position rather than expecting all clients to be similar in their interactions during the therapeutic interview.

Exercises

1. Interview several people who have never gone to therapy; perhaps they might be friends or family members. Ask them what their perceptions are of people who go see a therapist. Ask them what their perceptions are of therapists and therapists' characteristics. Ask them about what they think happens between client and therapist. Lastly, ask them where they developed their views. What have media representations taught them about therapy?

2. Write down ten reasons why you would go to a therapist. After you complete this, make a list of what you think the common issues are that lead clients to go into

therapy. How does your list for yourself differ from your list for clients? Next, go out into the community and ask people what they think are the main reasons why people go to a therapist. How much do their ideas correspond with yours?

3. Together with a classmate, develop a role-play that depicts a client at one of the various stages of change. Enact this role-play for the class and see if they can guess the client's stage of readiness.

3

The Therapeutic Interviewer

Motivation and Impact of Being a Therapist

Being a therapist can be one of the most rewarding professions out there. However, it can also be one of the most frustrating, challenging, and confusing professions. Therapists are usually not put on pedestals, do not make millions of dollars (or usually not in the hundreds of thousands range), and are intimately connected to people's pains and anguish. Therapists are human beings. They are not automatons that just ask questions or make responses. They are people who come into the therapeutic interview with a personality that makes them unique and that impacts the course of the interview while the interview in turn impacts the person of the therapist. This chapter discusses the person of the therapeutic interviewer, highlighting why people come into the field, characteristics of effective therapists, and issues of therapist self-care to help prevent burnout.

Motivations for Being a Therapist

Why would someone want to become a therapist? It is usually not a profession that most parents dream of for their child when the child is born. Deciding to become a therapist usually occurs late in people's schooling. Many individuals who come into the field come after having worked in another field, whereas most people going into medicine know from an early age, and usually from when they begin their undergraduate program, that they want to go into that field.

Many people come into the field of therapy because throughout their lives they have been a person to whom friends and relatives come when they are having issues and need someone to talk to. For some reason, others have found these people to be excellent listeners who make them feel better. Other people come into the therapy field because they had some type of trouble(s) early in life, went to a therapist, and found the experience to be life altering. Since they experienced the potential benefits of therapy, they want to help other people in the same way. Some people find immense pleasure in helping others. And then there are those who want to find out about themselves because certain things are not right in their own lives. These are people who tend to find living a happy life challenging and want to find out how they can make their own lives better. They believe that when they find this out they can also help other people. However, the more they search for their own answers, the less time and energy they have for helping clients find theirs.

Most individuals enter the counseling field because they care about other people. They care so much that they want to help other people past their struggles and pain. There seems to be something within them that has a hard time allowing another human being to suffer. Other people come into the field, not with a sense of caring, but wanting to be able to figure out what is "wrong" with people. They tend to be more detached and are more focused on being the person who can "cure" someone or on being "the helper" instead of truly having empathy for the other person's pain. Either points of this dichotomy are problematic. If clients do not believe the therapist actually cares about them, that they are just another patient there to make the therapist money, a positive therapeutic relationship will probably not be developed and movement toward change will probably be diminished. However, if therapists care too much, they might try harder than their clients to achieve the goals. When therapists are more motivated for change than their clients, they eventually become frustrated with the clients because the clients are not changing as fast as the therapist expects they should.

Some therapists go into the field because they want to be needed. This can be very problematic because the therapist is then partly focused on how to get his own needs met instead of trying to meet the client's needs and goals. Corey, Corey, and Callanan (2007) stated, "The goals of therapy can also suffer when therapists with a strong need for approval focus on trying to win the acceptance, admiration, and even awe of their clients" (p. 39). This is problematic because the focal point of therapy should be therapist-to-client and client-to-client, with both therapist and client operating for the client's growth. Case Scenario 3.1 describes how a therapist-in-training might come into the field for what seem to be the wrong reasons.

The therapist's motivation for going into the field is critical to how he will be as a therapist. This motivation leads to our orientation and framework of how therapists understand themselves via their clients (and other larger systems).

Reflection 3.1

Think about why you are going into this field. Is this the career that you wanted for yourself since you were an adolescent? When did you decide that you wanted to be a therapist? What were the other fields that you wanted to go into? Why did you chose this field over those? If you are making a change of careers, why did you decided to leave one career and enter this new one? What reactions have you gotten from friends and family members about this choice of career?

CASE SCENARIO 3.1

I supervised a master's practicum student who was having difficulties in some of her relationships with her clients. She became very upset if the clients did not change quickly and was overelated when the clients told her how useful she was to them. In my discussions with her, we talked about how it could be detrimental to therapy to look for the client to give her validation and that validation should come from within instead. She told me that all her life she had lived in the shadow of her sister and that she became a therapist to show everyone that she could achieve good things. Unfortunately, she had gone into the field for two main reasons. The first was that her life was not happy and she wanted to figure herself out. The second was that she was dealing with a sibling rivalry situation, in which all her life her sister was looked upon more favorably by her parents. Her sister was a successful therapist. My supervisee wanted to show her parents, her sister, and herself that she could be just as good. We then had several more conversations in which I attempted to get her to really think about the field and her place in it in a different manner.

Corey, Corey, and Callanan (2007) provided several questions therapists can ask themselves about their motivation for going into the field:

- How will I know when I'm working for the client's benefit or working for my own benefit?
- Even though I have personal experience with a problem a client is having, can I be objective enough to relate to this person professionally and ethically?
- How much do I depend on being appreciated by others in my own life? Am I able to appreciate myself, or do I depend primarily on sources outside myself to confirm my worth?
- Am I getting my needs for nurturance, recognition, and support met from those who are significant in my life?
- Do I feel inadequate when clients don't make progress? If so, how could my attitude and feelings of inadequacy adversely affect my work with these clients? (p. 40)

Therapists can ask themselves these questions along with taking a good inventory of why they decided to go into a field that can be so stressful, demanding, and confusing. If they find that their answers do not sit right for them in their stomach, they should talk this out with an instructor or a supervisor.

Characteristics of Effective Therapists

Just as clients come to therapy with varying personalities, styles, and worldviews, therapists also are unique and bring their own personhood to the interview. However, there are certain traits that most people in the mental health field would

Exercise 3.1

Either alone or with a group of classmates, brainstorm a list of perceived effective traits of therapeutic interviews. Then, develop a list of perceived ineffective traits. Examine the two lists and see what types of themes, similarities, and/or differences you notice between the two lists. After developing the list, discuss how some of the effective traits, might be ineffective in some situations. Conversely, discuss how some of the perceived ineffective traits might be effective in certain situations.

agree that effective therapists should have. Therapists are interviewers of people, and as such, should exhibit the following three features (Morrison, 1993). First, they need to obtain the largest amount of information possible that will help them work with the person to move that person toward her goal. Second, they should be doing this in the least amount of time necessary. Lastly, while getting all of the information they need in the shortest period of time, they should also be developing as good a relationship with the interviewee as possible.

Cormier and Cormier (1991) identified the following characteristics of effective therapists: intellectual competence; energy; flexibility; support; good will; and self-awareness. Each of these characteristics is important and the more therapists represent each of these, the more likely they will make a connection with clients. These are not the only traits of a good therapist. Neukrug and Schwitzer (2006) identified eight attitudes for the therapeutic interviewer to embrace: being empathic; being genuine; being accepting; being open-minded; being cognitively complex; being psychologically adjusted; being good at relationship building; and being competent. Case Scenario 3.2 highlights how a therapist-in-training might have difficulty utilizing her strengths and being confident as a person.

How supportive should the therapist be? The ability to confront a client can also be an important quality for the therapist (Young, 2005). Therapists can be more than solely a supportive source for clients; they can help confront clients about contradictions, realities, and possibilities the clients are not aware of. Therapists need to have enough confidence in themselves to be able to challenge other

CASE SCENARIO 3.2

I was supervising a doctoral level therapist who had a physical deformity. It was quite apparent that she had this disability because of its impact on her walk and partial lack of use of one of her arms. In the classroom she performed very well. She was very good at reading the book and paying attention in class so that she could do well on tests and papers. However, because of her disability, she was very self-conscious. This came through in her work with clients. She had difficulty engaging them in a strong alliance. Part of this was due to her lack of belief in herself as a person in transactions. In supervision, we talked about how she could translate her confidence in herself in the classroom to the therapy interview room.

people. Yet, this type of challenging needs to be housed within the other effective traits of therapists or else it will appear negative and disrespectful.

Part of being an effective therapist is to have a clear sense of one's goals. Long (1996) understood effective helper skills as being divided into three areas: attitudinal goals, behavioral goals, and affective experience. The attitudinal goals are the mind-set of the therapist, which then impacts the therapist's work with clients. These attitudes include respecting the client's capabilities and understanding that clients have the right to be themselves and the responsibility for making their own choices. The behavioral goals are those practices therapists use to put into place the attitudes they espouse. These include being genuine, having positive regard, and structuring the interview to help clients see the issues clearly. The affective experience of therapeutic interviewers, based on the attitudes and behaviors they have, leads to outcome goals for the helper. These outcomes can be seen in the impact the therapeutic interviewer has on the client including being a role model, a catalyst for change, and a facilitator of client growth.

Effective therapists are not only aware of what is going on for the client, but also what is going on within themselves and who they are as people. Corey (2005) provided a list of personal characteristics of effective therapists. It included having an identity, respecting themselves, being open to change, making their own choices, being life-oriented, being authentic, having a sense of humor, learning from their mistakes, living in the present, being culture-oriented, caring about others, deriving meaning from their work, and maintaining healthy boundaries. This list is not intended to be dogmatic. Therapists are human beings. They make mistakes, can become self-focused, and have their own lives to deal with. This is one of the challenges for therapists; people expect them to have no problems in their own lives. This is an unrealistic expectation. Life is difficult, and human beings are not perfect. Perfection is not a good goal for any person to strive toward because it is unrealistic. Therapists are fallible individuals who sometimes make sound decisions and sometimes do not. The goal is to make as many good decisions, both personally and professionally, as possible while learning from bad decisions. One way to attempt this is to strive to personify as many of these traits as possible. (Do Exercise 3.2.)

As previously mentioned, one of the main reasons people enter the counseling field is that they consider themselves to be caring people. Caring, in the therapy context, is extremely important, yet it can sometimes be detrimental if the therapist cares too much and does not know how to handle these feelings appropriately. One of the main issues for therapists is to have the capacity for caring. This capacity for caring is not something that some people are born with and others aren't. It develops based on a process of taking an other-orientation in which the individual tries to understand what is going on for another person. (Do Exercise 3.3.)

One of the main skills of a therapist is to help the client to become empowered. The more a therapist tries to take over for a client (perhaps because the therapist wants so much for the client to get better), the more likely the client will give up responsibility for her own actions and put that responsibility onto the therapist. Caring includes the notion of respect. Egan (2002) provided several norms for

Exercise 3.2   *Therapist Belief System*

Fill in the following statements about your views of yourself and people:

1. I think my best trait is _____.
2. I think my worst trait is _____.
3. People tend to be _____.
4. I believe that change occurs for people when _____.
5. Three characteristics of an emotionally healthy person are _____.
6. Three characteristics of an emotionally unhealthy person are _____.
7. When thinking about interacting with people I have never met, I _____.
8. My main strength is _____.
9. My main weakness is _____.

In looking at your answers, how do you think they will impact you during a therapeutic interview? When you get an opportunity, form small groups with your classmates and openly discuss how you think the personality and worldview of the therapist might impact the therapeutic interview.

---

therapeutic interviewers to follow to express their belief in the worth of the client: not doing harm; being competent and committed; expressing to the client that they are there for the client; assuming the client's goodwill; not rushing to judgment; and keeping the client's agenda in focus. Each of these norms suits the therapist well in connecting with the client and being effective. Case Scenario 3.3 provides an example of a therapist whose caring for her client impacted her emotionally.

Therapist Self-Care

Therapists are human beings. They behave, think, and feel. They have impact on their clients and are impacted by their clients along with what occurs in their own personal lives. Therapeutic interviewing is one of the primary work situations in which the service provider's personal life can have quite detrimental outcomes on the relationship and the client. When therapists are working with a client, they need to give their full attention to that person. Yet, therapists also have to bring something to the table, beyond their training and knowledge. They need to bring themselves.

In order to be able to help others, therapists must have something to give. This means that therapists should be aware of themselves and when they are moving on a positive or negative track. When they find that they are on that negative path, they need to do something to get themselves on a healthier path before they begin their next therapeutic interview. When on a positive path, they need to continue doing those things that are helping them function well.

One of the ways to get on a positive track is to take care of one's own self. This leads therapists to be able to consider not only their own wants and needs,

Exercise 3.3

How caring are you?

Strongly Disagree (1) Disagree (2) Neutral (3) Agree (4) Strongly Agree (5)

1. I cannot not help someone in need.	1	2	3	4	5
2. I feel guilty if I pass someone asking for help and I don't help them.	1	2	3	4	5
3. I think more about satisfying someone else's needs than my own.	1	2	3	4	5
4. I think that altruism is an important act.	1	2	3	4	5
5. I think that I can make a difference in people's lives.	1	2	3	4	5
6. I can accept the situation when I cannot help someone.	1	2	3	4	5
7. People have told me that I am a caring individual.	1	2	3	4	5
8. Sometimes I try to help others so much that they get upset with me.	1	2	3	4	5

Lower scores would indicate someone who can create boundaries between themselves and other people while higher scores indicate having a more difficult time distancing from someone in need.

CASE SCENARIO 3.3

I was supervising a master's Mental Health Counseling practicum student who was working in a child outpatient program. The student, a mother in her mid-thirties, began working with a five-year-old client who was experiencing a very turbulent home life. The student-therapist, a very caring individual, would cry after working with the client because of the client's bad situation. In supervision, she expressed her desire to want to adopt the child so that he could have a good life. She was having a very difficult time of caring for the client as a child who should not have to live in a bad situation while not being able to make the dramatic changes that might have been needed to alleviate his environmental problems. We worked in supervision of how she could care without letting it impact her to such a degree.

Reflection 3.2

How aware are you of when you become stressed? What signs do you pay attention to in yourself to let you know? When you are stressed out, what do you do to relax? What activities are done alone and which include other people? How do you take five minutes of your day to focus just on you?

but also the wants and needs of another person. Most people are aware that on airplanes, people are directed, in the case of an emergency, to put the oxygen mask on themselves first and then on the people who cannot do it for themselves. The person helping out needs to be in a stable position to function more effectively and to help the other person. This holds for the therapeutic interviewer who needs to be stable to function at his peak in the therapeutic interview.

In terms of self-care, there are things that therapists can do in their career and in their nontherapy life to enhance their performance. Brems (2000) provided some personal and professional strategies for maintaining well-functioning for therapists. On a professional basis, therapists can engage in continuing education, consultation and supervision, networking, and stress management strategies. Continuing education courses, conferences, workshops, classes, and reading materials provide therapists with updated information on the field so that their therapy does not become stagnant. Consultation and supervision allow the therapist to engage with another professional about providing more effective service. Networking connects the therapist with others who are experiencing similar issues. Stress management strategies include developing a diverse range of clients (to prevent stagnation), engaging in professional activities other than direct client contact, and ensuring that during the day there is free time to reenergize. On a personal basis, self-care skills comprise healthy personal habits, attention to relationships, recreational activities, relaxation and centeredness, and self-exploration and awareness. Part of personal self-care includes eating, sleeping, and exercising properly. Additionally, therapists should have a connection to other people who are not engaged in the therapy profession, as this helps to ensure a life away from therapy. One way of rounding out the therapist as a person instead of just a therapist is having hobbies and interests different from therapy. Therapists can also consider keeping a journal, meditating, or having personal therapy as ways to take care of themselves.

The Therapist and Mental Health

Therapy is a very remarkable interpersonal situation in that therapists work with people who may be having issues with mental health while therapists are expected to be well-adjusted so that they can work with those who aren't. Like other people, therapists have their own personal conflicts. What separates them from people in other professions is that they need to be more in tune with their own personal issues so they do not bring them into the therapy room.

Therapists are at risk for experiencing serious mental health and psychological problems based on their personal and professional life issues (Sayyedi & O'Byrne, 2003). Gilroy, Carroll, and Murra (2004) noted that therapists may be prone to depression due to the demands of therapeutic interviewing. In these researchers' study, 31 percent of the psychologists surveyed reported having taken antidepressant medications. Many of the therapists surveyed reported feeling isolated from their colleagues during times of depression. Therapy is an isolating experience. Although therapists are constantly interacting with others, their interactions are not the kind that most people experience during their average workday. During the therapeutic interview, therapists are so focused on the client that they tend to lose their own self to some degree. Because many therapists spend most of their working day with their clients, there is not much time at work for small talk. When they go home, many therapists tend to not talk about what occurred during their day because of issues of confidentiality and the nature of their work. At times, this can result in their feeling disconnected from people.

Because their jobs are stressful and their nonwork lives may also be stressful because they are normal people who have normal problems, therapists may seek therapeutic services from another therapist. Three of the main factors that lead health care professionals to go for their own therapy are marital problems, suicidal behaviors, and work stress (Katsavadkis, Gabbard, & Athey, 2004). On first thought, using the false perception that therapists should be mentally sound and their marriages perfect, this finding is surprising. However, many therapists have relationship problems, just like most people in relationships. Bamond-Hanson (2002) researched how being in a marital and family therapy training program impacted the spousal relationship of therapists-in-training. In reviewing the literature, she found that trainees, who are learning about family process, start to apply the knowledge they are learning in the classroom to their own lives. Since they are married, these therapists-in-training tend to personalize the material. One of the problems that occurs for them is that although they were probably at the same level emotionally and intellectually with their spouse when they first met and married, they are growing in these areas (especially in the area of self-enhancement) during the course of their training while their partner may not be. This then can lead to a chasm between the two.

Just as clients come to therapy with problems of various degrees of severity, therapists deal with their problems in many different ways. Some problems are easily handled and do not impact the therapist in the therapy room (for example, the therapist has high cholesterol), while others are more detrimental (for example, the therapist is going through an extremely contentious divorce). The type of problem and how it is impacting the therapist is extremely important, since therapists must be able to function competently. It is actually unethical for therapists to practice when their own personal problems are seriously impacting their therapeutic work. Therapeutic interviewers' livelihood is on the line when their personal problems begin to impact their business role. These issues may be best addressed when therapists go for their own therapy.

Therapy for the Therapist

As discussed, the therapist is a human being who is dealing with his own issues. He might be dealing quite effectively with them or he might need some assistance. Many therapists find themselves going to therapy to talk about their own problems. This makes sense, since they see value in their own work with others, that they would try to obtain this service when they see their personal need for it. Geller, Norcross, and Orlinsky (2005) explained, "Personal treatment for psychotherapists—receiving it, recommending and conducting it—is at the very core of the profession of psychotherapy" (p. 3).

What is interesting is that some therapists will not go because of the negative stigma that they think is associated with therapists (people helping others with mental health) seeking their own therapy. These individuals are not the norm. A majority of mental health professionals have had their own personal therapy (Norcross & Guy, 2005; Orlinsky, Ronnestad, Willutzki, Wiseman, & Botermans, 2005). Norcross and Guy reported that approximately 75 percent of therapists seek at least one session of personal therapy. And most of them go to therapy for a lengthy period of time. Orlinsky and others demonstrated that the phenomenon of therapists having personal therapy is worldwide. South Korea is the only country where a majority of the therapists did not have at least one session of personal therapy.

When psychotherapy was first practiced and psychoanalysis was the main mode of working with clients, therapy was required for all therapists. In order to become analysts, individuals had to go through analysis themselves. This analysis would last for several years, if not more. Other approaches, such as Bowen family systems theory and symbolic-experiential therapy, highly encourage therapists to explore their own situations so that they can be more effective in the therapy room. When other models became more prominent, especially the models of working with clients more briefly, this requirement changed. The question, then, is whether having therapy as a therapist is useful and effective. This needs to be answered on two levels, personal outcomes and professional development. In studies regarding the effectiveness of personal therapy for psychotherapists, outcomes consistently show that it was helpful (Orlinsky, Norcross, Ronnestad, & Wiseman, 2005). This was not the case for all psychotherapists in therapy, as some experienced no effects or even negative outcomes. The majority of therapists, however, find their own therapy to be personally useful. Therapists also rank their own personal therapy as one of the main sources of positive development in their training. Thus, personal therapy for the therapeutic interviewer seems to be beneficial on many levels.

Many graduate training programs either require or highly recommend that their students receive therapy. Corey, Corey, and Callanan (2007) provided several positive reasons for therapist trainees to engage in their own therapy. First, any issues the person has, such as low self-esteem or depression, can be addressed in a therapeutic manner instead of impacting the therapist's work with a client. Second, it gives the person an understanding of what it is like to be the client in the therapeutic relationship. Third, people have blind spots, and therapy might make them aware of these. Fourth, trainees can explore their own motivation for going into the counseling field. Macaskill (1999) listed several reasons for personal therapy for therapists:

a. Enhance the sensitivity and empathic awareness of the therapist by having the experience of being a client;
b. Improve the therapist's self-awareness by facilitating a better understanding of his or her own personality dynamics, which it is claimed will reduce personal blind spots;
c. Improve own psychological well-being;
d. Reduce levels of personal symptomatology;
e. Increase the trainee's awareness of his/her own problems and areas of conflict, which will then allow the recognition and appropriate handling of countertransference;
f. Lead to the resolution of personal conflicts;
g. Result in increased mastery of the techniques used via the close observation of an experienced therapist in action;
h. Lead to an increased conviction about the validity of the therapeutic model being used;
i. Lead to an increased conviction about the validity of the techniques being practiced, as the trainee will have had personal demonstrations about how the actual process works. (p. 143)

In looking at the reasons therapists report for going to therapy, one finds that they tend to go more for their own personal problems and personal growth than for professional or training purposes (Norcross & Connor, 2005; Orlinsky et al., 2005).

Based on these potential positive benefits, many of the theoretical approaches recommend that potential practitioners go for therapy. Many graduate training programs concur and suggest or require their students to go to therapy. Macaskill (1999), on the other hand, although discussing many potential positive benefits for personal therapy of the therapist, found that there was a lack of findings to support them and that therapists-in-training can receive many of these same benefits through class activities such as role-plays, diaries, and video-taping. One potential problem in graduate programs requiring students to enter therapy is that some students may not believe they need therapy and thus would not be ideal candidates for therapy. Students might be in the precontemplation or contemplation stage and would not utilize therapy because there was not something that they wanted changed for themselves or their lives.

In weighing the positive and negative potential of personal therapy for themselves, most therapists-in-training (or therapists) find it more beneficial to go to therapy. By going to counseling themselves, therapists can potentially reduce the possibility of their own issues impacting their work with clients. Further, as a

Reflection 3.3

For what reasons would you go to therapy for yourself? For what reasons would you not go for therapy? How do you think having been a client in therapy would impact your work as a therapeutic interviewer? What would be your thoughts about yourself as a person? Who do you think you would tell? Who wouldn't you tell? Why?

result of being clients (or past clients) themselves, therapists are less likely to view their clients in a negative manner.

Burnout

Engaging in therapeutic interviews for a living can take its toll on the therapist. Clients come to therapy not because things are going well in their lives, but because they are experiencing pain, anxiety, depression, confusion, anger, or a myriad of other emotions that could be deemed "negative." Listening to these types of situations and stories hour after hour, day after day, week after week, year after year can build up and severely impact the therapeutic interviewer. Kottler (2003) stated, "There are tremendous risks for the therapist in living with the anguish of others, in being so close to others' torments. Sometimes we become desensitized by human emotion and experience an acute overdose of feeling; we turn ourselves off" (p. 15).

This turning ourselves off is considered as burnout. According to Corey and Corey (2006), "burnout is a state of physical, emotional, and spiritual exhaustion characterized by feelings of helplessness and hopelessness" (p. 157). Therapists have been dealing with the potential of burnout since the beginning of the profession. It impacts people differently based on the conditions in which they provide services. Rupert and Morgan (2005) found that individuals in agency settings experienced higher levels of burnout than those in private practice. Practitioners in agency settings deal with more negative client behaviors than solo and group private practitioners. This might be because clients going to agencies have more severe problems.

Reflection 3.4

Imagine going to work five days a week, for eight hours each day, hearing about troubles, sorrows, pain, anger, hurt, guilt, anxiety, and a host of other intense feelings. Think about how open and receptive you would be at home to family members' upsets and gripes? How well do you think you could recharge yourself to be "present" for your own family? What strategies do you have for maintaining your emotional health while being surrounded by intense negative feelings?

People experience symptoms of burnout in a variety of ways. They might find job disillusionment, feelings of hopelessness, desire to be away from others, coping dilemmas, and loss of empathy (Burnard, 1994). A variety of situations might lead to therapist burnout, such as not having control over one's work, long work hours, heavy administration duties, fewer direct pay clients, and more negative clients (Rupert & Morgan, 2005). Therapists should stay alert to these risk factors and try to make changes in their therapy practice to prevent burnout from occurring.

Burnout in the field of psychotherapy is not a given. Therapists can prepare themselves to try to prevent burnout in a variety of ways. By being in tune with what is going on inside themselves, therapists can check in to see how they are feeling. When therapeutic interviewers end an interview and leave the context of the therapy, they should shift from life as a therapist to life as a person. Getting in touch with friends and family and participating in nontherapy-related activities, such as athletics, traveling, going to the movies, and hobbies, can help keep the therapist grounded.

All of these activities, which would seem not to be relevant to what a therapist does on a daily basis, actually help sustain therapists in their careers. Stevanovic and Rupert (2004) described several behaviors and activities they referred to as career-sustaining behaviors. These types of activities help prolong therapists' vitality in the field and prevent burnout: relationships with friends and family, self-awareness, a strong professional identity, keeping the various parts of life in perspective, especially their work role, and so on. Many of the clients who come to see therapists are there because they are not able to maintain balance in their own lives. Balance is difficult to achieve because of the many demands on people. Therapeutic interviewers need to understand that in order to be at the peak level of effectiveness, they will need to work at being better in the skills of therapy and in the management of their personal lives.

Therapists can also attempt to prevent burnout by meeting with other colleagues for informal or formal supervision. Dlugos and Friedlander (2001) provided a list of therapist behaviors that led to high levels of work commitment. These included sustaining boundaries between personal and professional roles, engaging in a variety of activities to provide freshness in life, maintaining a strong supervision, being spiritually grounded, taking on social responsibilities, and reframing stressors and obstacles as challenges.

Another thing that therapists can do to prevent burnout is to focus on the positive benefits of being a therapist. Therapists are not in this field because they are altruistic. Although most therapists truly want to help others, there is a joy and excitement they get when conducting therapeutic interviews. Therapists can pay attention to those times where they feel enthused by the job. Further, not everything discussed in a therapy interview is negative. Those therapists who can focus not only on their own strengths, but also on those of their clients, are helping themselves prevent burnout.

Burnout is possible at all stages of one's career; however, it tends to impact novice therapists differently from more experienced therapists. Williams et al.

(2003) found that novice therapists tended to be more conscious of their own anxieties and critical self-talk whereas experienced therapists had more issues with boredom and outside distractions. These researchers further found that while both the novice and experienced therapists experienced losing focus during sessions, the novice therapists told themselves more critical self-talk. How novice and experienced therapists handled these situations differed. The novice therapists used more self-disclosure to the clients, and experienced therapists practiced more thought-stopping techniques. In the beginning of their careers, novice therapists may feel more stress because they do not fully know what they are doing. Experienced therapists may feel more stress because of issues of boredom. Further, novice therapists might feel more stress because they are being evaluated more—by themselves, their clients, and their supervisors. Experienced therapists may have developed larger support systems and coping strategies over the course of their careers along with a sense of accomplishment that is not completely predicated on their role as therapists (Rosenberg & Pace, 2006).

Supervision

Therapists are continuously growing as both people and therapists. Having another professional to engage in conversations about therapeutic process and personal influence in the process is important to continue to update personal energy and therapeutic knowledge. Further, there are times during therapy when the therapist must make ethical decisions. Sometimes these decisions are not very clear and having another professional confirm or disconfirm the decisions can help protect the therapist legally and provides guidance and direction.

Supervision might be one of the most important components in helping to ensure that the therapist is competent (Corey, Corey, & Callanan, 2007). These authors hold that there are three main goals for supervision: improving the skills and knowledge of the trainee, protecting the client's welfare, and ensuring that the profession is taking in a qualified person. Supervision is a process that clients and society can rely on to help ensure that the people who are providing counseling services are able to do it effectively. Their effectiveness is predicated on knowledge, but also on certain orientations. Haley (1996) explained, "Supervising is the teaching not only of techniques of therapy but also of an appreciation and understanding of tragic human dilemmas" (p. 3). He stated that therapists need to be not only expert interviewers, but also sensitive human beings. The latter is much harder to teach, but can be developed in conjunction with a skilled supervisor.

Therapists-in-training receive a lot of supervision during their graduate years, sometimes having two or three supervisors at the same time. Even after graduation, novice therapists need to be supervised in order to become licensed in their particular area. Once licensed, however, the therapists' requirement for supervision diminishes. Therapists should take it upon themselves to seek out the necessary individuals who can guide them to expand their understanding of themselves, their clients, and the current state of the art in the field. They can do this in a formal manner where by they ask a more senior therapist to mentor and supervise them, or in a less formal manner, by simply talking with colleagues about cases, new approaches, and their feelings about being therapists.

One of the most difficult things for novice therapists is to be able to accept and utilize feedback from supervisors. Many therapist trainees come into their first practicum having been somewhat effective helping their friends and family over the course of their lives. Yet what worked with their friends usually does not work with actual clients, because of the huge difference in context. It is understandable that novice therapists might have some difficulty accepting constructive criticism (also known as feedback); they are feeling somewhat incompetent to begin with because this is a new field with hard-to-learn skills. Case Scenario 3.4 explains a situation with a novice therapist who had difficulty in accepting feedback.

Therapist Skill Growth

The process of becoming a therapist is a lifelong process. Therapists are continually growing as interviewers, clinicians, and people throughout the course of their lives. As in most processes, there are stages therapists go through during the course of their careers. Ronnestad and Skovholt (2003) elucidated a six-stage model for therapist growth as a therapeutic interviewer. The first phase is the lay helper stage in which therapists, before they are therapists, have friends, family members, and acquaintances come to them for help. In this phase, people use common sense, along with their gut, to inform themselves of how to help.

The second phase is the beginning student phase. In this stage, people realize there is a difference between the commonsense helping of friends and a more skilled approach. However, they have not learned these new skills sufficiently yet and are dealing with the anxiety of wanting to quickly learn what takes years to master. Becoming an effective therapeutic interviewer is a process that takes many years of study, hard work, and experience. It is an ongoing process of becoming and, along the way, the therapist never stops learning. Although some individuals

CASE SCENARIO 3.4

I was supervising a doctoral trainee who thought that she was already a good therapist, although she did not have that much clinical experience. In practicum class, she was quick to try to supervise her classmates and tell them what they should and should not be doing with their clients. Whenever I gave her feedback about something she was doing with clients, she would become very defensive. She would try to justify her actions and not be open to the possibility that there might be better alternative ways of working with her clients than the way she was using. Part of supervision then focused on working with her to accept feedback and learn how to be open to the possibility of growth and change.

come into the therapy profession because they have been good natural helpers to friends and family, the intricacies of therapeutic interviewing are much more complex and take active effort to master. Ivey and Ivey (2003) referred to people's spontaneous manner of being and working with others as their natural style. This natural style is usually somewhat effective for therapists in making others feel better, even before they have had their first course in counseling. However, this is not sufficient by itself. Personality without theory behind it is usually not that effective. Likewise, theory without personality usually is not effective. The combination of the two is what makes someone a good therapeutic interviewer.

The third phase is the advanced student phase. During this part of therapist development, the person has learned the basic skills of therapy and is trying to perform them as perfectly as possible, which usually leads to their being cautious and conservative. Through training, a person can become a better therapeutic interviewer. One of the benefits of a training program, whether it is at a university or in a clinic setting, is that the trainee gets feedback from a trained and qualified source. Barone et al. (2005) found that therapy trainees became better at accurate empathy when they were given feedback than those trainees who did not get feedback. This gives weight for therapists-in-training to try to get as much feedback as possible from fellow classmates, supervisors, themselves, and perhaps most importantly, their clients.

The fourth phase is the novice professional phase. This stage usually occurs when people finish graduate school and begin working on their own. The therapist begins to feel more freedom yet realizes that he or she has not been fully prepared for everything that practicing on one's own has in store. Novice professionals may read articles and books on topics and issues they are seeing but not fully knowing how to handle. They may also attend conferences and trainings to improve specific skills.

The fifth phase is the experienced professional phase. Here, the clinician has been practicing for many years with a variety of types of clients. These therapists find a way to be authentic as a person in the therapy room. Once licensed, the therapist is believed not to have all of the knowledge of the field, but to have a sufficient amount to be able to practice effectively. Licensing and certification boards require therapists to keep active continuously in trying to understand themselves, develop new skills, and become aware of current issues in the field by going to trainings, workshops, and conferences or by other means of acquiring continuing education units (CEUs). The field has grown and evolved so quickly that it would almost be hubris to think that any individual or approach understands everything needed to work with all clients in all contexts.

The last phase of therapist skill growth is the senior professional stage. The therapist in this phase has been practicing for over twenty years. He becomes a trainer for novice therapists and needs to figure out how not to become apathetic in the late stages of his career. Being a good therapist is a constant process of personal and theoretical growth. It requires effort, adaptation, and humility (Smith et al., 2004).

Through this model, a therapist can be viewed as constantly being in a state of learning. Even senior level professionals attend conferences, read up on the latest findings and theories through journals and books, and constantly evaluate their own work. This helps to prevent the stagnation that can potentially lead to burnout. While therapists are going through these stages, they also tend to find themselves changing in their personal lives.

Specialization Area

There is debate in the field about how much someone should be a generalist versus a specialist. Some individuals entering the therapy field know which client group they want to work with. Many want to work with children and/or adolescents (perhaps this is due to their love of children or the thought that if they can help these individuals early in life, they can then prevent later problems). Other students have no clue as to which client population or problem area(s) they want to work with. Regardless, it is recommended that therapists have as many options available to them as possible. Given that therapy is about increasing clients' response options, therapy training should be about increasing the therapists-in-training's response options. During practicum and internship experiences, therapists-in-training should explore areas that they might not have thought about working in, as they may not get these opportunities later in their careers once they have picked a specific type of clientele and setting to work in.

If trainees try to focus too quickly on one specific theory or client type, they will not gain the general exposure needed to work with the variety of clients and client issues that almost all therapeutic interviewers will encounter during their careers. However, if trainees do not learn anything in enough specificity and depth, they will probably flounder during the interview with whatever client might come in. Thus, trainees should gain enough knowledge in different theories and client issues so that they have a foundational knowledge that they can then build on during their careers. Case Scenario 3.5 (page 56) explains how a colleague focused, in my opinion, too quickly on one specific theoretical orientation. This led to her not being as flexible as possible.

Use of Self in Therapy

Therapeutic interviewers cannot be automatons. They must be able to use their knowledge of theory, proficiency of skills, and who they are as people to work at their optimum level. One of the most important aspects of being a therapist is being genuine. Clients can tell when a person is in "therapist mode" or is just being themselves and having their knowledge and skills come out through who they are.

CASE SCENARIO 3.5

During my doctoral program, one of my colleagues quickly veered toward one specific type of theoretical orientation. This was during the first semester of our four-year program. She was very committed to this approach and received extra training at the national training program for it. However, she was not open to other approaches, thinking that the approach she had adopted was the right one and the others were second best. This hampered her during practicum because there were times when the approach she was using (along with who she was in using the approach) was not working with some clients. Since this was the only approach that she really trained on, she was not able to switch her style to one that would work better with those clients.

One of Carl Rogers's main characteristics for effective therapists is that the person is being genuine while conducting the therapeutic interview. He explained:

> It has been found that personal change is facilitated when the psychotherapist is what he *is*, when in the relationship with his client he is genuine and without "front" or façade, openly being the feeling and attitudes which at that moment are flowing *in* him. (Rogers, 1961, p. 61)

One of the facilitative factors of therapy is that the client enters into a relationship with a real person. Otherwise, therapy could as easily (or perhaps even more easily) be done between the client and a computer program. Therapists should take the risk of being themselves in therapy, as most people can tell when others are playing a role and being "fake." This means they should be congruent rather than incongruent. Although no one is expected to fully attain this condition, the more the individual is able to hear himself, the more he can be himself without fear of who he is. This then is communicated in subtle ways to the client who can start to do the same.

This whole process is about taking an I-thou position where the "I" is the therapist, who is his own person, with thoughts, feelings, attitudes, a history, and beliefs. The "thou" is the other person who is her own person, with thoughts, feelings, attitudes, a history, and beliefs. Each person in an I-thou relationship understands this and allows the other person to be who they are instead of being a replica of themselves or an automaton. (See Case Scenario 3.6.)

Self-Growth

Besides growing as a therapist, the therapeutic interviewer should continually strive to grow as a human being. Being a good therapeutic interviewer is based on the combination of good utilization of skills, techniques, and theory along with one's own personality. Therapists should utilize their own self in the therapy inter-

CASE SCENARIO 3.6

It took me a while to really become a good therapist. During my master's program, I learned the techniques and theories and tried to apply them. I did all right with clients, but it wasn't until my second year in my doctoral program that I realized that I could work more effectively with clients if I let my personality come through. I like to joke around with people and do this often in my nontherapy life. But when I blurred the distinction between how I was in my therapist role and my nontherapist role, I found that not only did I enjoy doing therapy more, but also my clients seemed to engage in the therapeutic process with more gusto. Part of being genuine, for me, was self-disclosing with clients and being more playful with them. Although this is me being more genuine, it is not the same for other therapists who will find that when they really bring themselves into the therapy room, they will act very differently. I noticed this while I was supervising students in a live-supervision environment. A doctoral therapist-in-training was working with a couple. They were talking about an issue when, behind the one-way mirror, I thought of a joke that fit perfectly with their situation and that I thought might help the therapist build a better relationship with the couple but also would be helpful for the couple to think about as it could then work as a reframe. I called this in to the therapist, but since it wasn't her personality to really joke around like that with people, the joke (and the message) didn't come across as I intended. This is when I remembered that I needed to help the therapist bring out her own strengths and personality instead of having her try to imitate my strengths.

view. Thus, they should constantly explore who they are and try to grow intellectually, socially, emotionally, and culturally. One of the ways to do this is to go for one's own therapy. Another way is to do a lot of traveling. Through traveling, therapists are able to come into contact with a wide range of people and experiences. The more individuals are situated in only one way of doing things or only one culture, the less openness they will have for difference and potential change. Experiencing different people, different cultures, and different parts of oneself allows people to gain a deeper sense of who they are and a greater acceptance for others. Therapists-in-training might also expose themselves to various arts, literature, cinema, and cuisine to broaden their horizons.

There are many ways for therapists to grow, even for beginning therapists. Paris, Linville, and Rosen (2006) found that marriage and family therapy interns were influenced in their growth as people and clinicians through experiences that occurred in their clinical practicums as well as their lives outside the clinic. In terms of their growth as clinicians, outside practicum experiences that helped were personal therapy, related work experiences, personal relationships, spiritual beliefs, and generic learning. The clinical experiences that lead to growth as people included generic clinical experiences, supervision, personal reactions, and family system/family-of-origin theories.

Therapists are human beings who are influenced by what happens during the clinical interview, supportive clinical experiences (discussions with colleagues and supervisors), interactions with friends and family, and other areas of life that might not seem clinically related, but tend to have some impact. Bamond-Hanson (2002) recommended that training programs include some type of forum so that students could process the information and experiences that are occurring for them in the program. In this way they would be better able to handle, in their personal lives, the powerful ideas and events from the field.

Self-Disclosure

As discussed in Chapter 1, the therapeutic relationship is unique in that it shifts from the common mutual exchange of self-disclosure that most relationships exhibit. One of the general rules of the therapeutic interview is for one person (the client) to do most, if not all, of the self-disclosing while the other person (the therapist) self-discloses only a minimal amount of information. However, if the therapist does not self-disclose anything to the client, and is in essence a blank slate, he has the potential for shifting from being a real person to being only a role.

Therapist self-disclosure has the potential to aid the therapy, but can also hinder it in various ways (theories such as classical psychoanalysis do not encourage much therapist self-disclosure as this may hamper the appropriate amount of client transference). Once the therapist self-discloses to the client, he becomes a real person, which allows the client to feel closer to him in a two-person interaction. This connection helps facilitate the therapeutic alliance, leading to a more collaborative endeavor. Usually this a good thing; however, Egan (2002) held that some clients cannot handle this type of intimacy. Another negative possibility of self-disclosure is when the client takes the therapist's disclosure as a challenge that they should overcome this situation also, since the therapist did so in the past. Thus, when self-disclosing, the therapeutic interviewer walks a fine line of disclosing to help encourage clients to move forward versus discouraging them because their self-esteem is lowered.

How might the therapeutic interviewer know whether the disclosure is appropriate? A rule of thumb is to ask, "Who is this self-disclosure for, me or the client?" If it is more for the therapist to make himself feel better, it might be better to keep the self-disclosure private. If the revealing is for the client, then perhaps it might be useful.

Every communication that therapists make with clients is self-disclosing. As with most other techniques discussed in this book, self-disclosure has various levels. There is a formal self-disclosure during the heart of the session, in which the therapist might disclose that he experienced a situation similar to the one the client is currently struggling with. There is also an informal self-disclosure that usually happens at the very beginning or ending of a session, usually in the waiting room. For instance, a therapist might meet the client in the waiting room where the client makes a comment about the weather. The therapist's reply back gives the client information about the therapist, and also leads to the possibility of joining. If a therapist says, "I love this type of weather," this may seem like a very innocuous response. However, it is information that the client takes in, however she might.

Therapist self-disclosure can help the therapeutic process in many different ways. These might include giving clients permission to open up while also giving them permission to feel what they feel, providing a sense of universality for feelings or actions and effective role modeling (Welch, 2003). Self-disclosure can also allow the client to know why the therapist might have had to cancel an appointment or was not as present as usual in a session.

> **Therapist:** I wanted to apologize to you today. I was not as present as I could have been today. We found out yesterday that our dog has cancer.
>
> **Client:** I'm sorry to hear that.
>
> **Therapist:** Thank you. I'm sorry if I seemed a little distant. I just wanted to let you know that it was nothing about you.

Although there is not a hard-and-fast rule about self-disclosure, therapists can use a framework of appropriateness to determine whether they should or shouldn't self-disclose, and if so, what type would be useful. Egan (2002) presented several guidelines for using self-disclosure:

- Include helper self-disclosure in the contract.
- Make sure that your disclosures are appropriate.
- Be careful of your timing.
- Keep your disclosures selective and focused.
- Don't disclose too frequently.
- Do not burden already overburdened clients.
- Remain flexible. (pp. 208–209)

By being up front with clients, perhaps during the first therapeutic interview, that the therapeutic interviewer may discuss some aspects of his life that he thinks might be helpful for the client, without the need to be helpful for himself, therapists can prime clients to be aware that there might be a therapeutic benefit of these occurrences. Case Scenario 3.7 provides an example of how self-disclosure can be used to connect with a client as well as to help the client not be as anxious about the problem situation.

There are also many possible disadvantages to self-disclosing. These can include the client feeling overwhelmed or distracted by the disclosure, feeling perturbed because the self-disclosure is not similar or related to her own distress, thinking that the therapist is trying to outdo her, and feeling sympathy toward the therapist (Welch, 2003). Because there is the stereotype that therapists have their own problems that they need therapy for, some clients might perceive a therapist's self-disclosure as a desire to get his own therapy from the client.

In working with many students throughout my supervisory and professorial career, I have observed that novice therapists seem to prefer not to self-disclose. Many have learned a common counter to a client asking the therapist a personal

CASE SCENARIO 3.7

I was working with a twenty-five-year-old man who was coming in because of issues surrounding depression. During our second session, he was feeling quite low. He asked me if I ever felt depressed in my life. I told him that there were periods of my life when things weren't quite as I wanted them and that I felt down occasionally. I told him that it might not be at the level that he is feeling, but that I, he, and most people had periods of feeling down in their lives as well as periods of feeling up and happy. I then asked him about those times when he wasn't feeling down so that we could see the extent of his experience. After I did this self-disclosure, he seemed to be more comfortable with me and he didn't feel as overwhelmed about his problems.

question (even a fairly innocuous personal question): "How would it help you to know that about me?" Personally, I am not in favor of this counter as I think it sends a negative message to the client that the therapist cannot be a real person with the client. It would seem that therapists should develop the skills to be able to connect with clients (sometimes through self-disclosure), but be able to shift the conversation from themselves back to the clients. However, for clients who ask many personal questions of the therapist or seem to have some other agenda (perhaps avoiding focus on themselves or having an infatuation with the therapist), reduction of self-disclosure may be more appropriate.

The disadvantages of self-disclosure are enhanced when therapists make mistakes during the interview. Young (2005) described several mistakes therapists make in self-disclosure. The first is when the disclosure is too deep. When the therapist's self-disclosure (story) is too involved and intense, the client has to spend too much time processing the therapist's story instead of making a connection to their own story, which might help them move toward their own goals. A second mistake is when the disclosure is poorly timed. There are some times when shifting, even if only for a few seconds, the thrust of the conversation is not appropriate. This is especially so when the client has just stated something extremely significant, such as a trauma. The third type of mistake is when the therapist's self-disclosure is not in line with the experience of the client. (Do Exercise 3.4.)

With your classmates, discuss what you notice about which topics you would or would not self-disclose. Debate how various types of self-disclosure might or might not be useful during the therapeutic interview.

Reflection 3.5

Think about what you would be comfortable with a client knowing about you. What areas of your life and of who you are as a person would you be okay sharing with a client? Why would you not share other areas of yourself?

Exercise 3.4   Therapist Comfort with Self-Disclosure

For the following statements, state whether you would be comfortable self-disclosing this to a client or not and your reason for this.

1. I would self-disclose my name. _____
2. I would self-disclose where I earned my degree. _____
3. I would self-disclose how much experience as a therapist I have. _____
4. I would self-disclose what my primary theoretical orientation is. _____
5. I would self-disclose where I was born. _____
6. I would self-disclose whether I am married or not. _____
7. I would self-disclose whether I have children or not. _____
8. I would self-disclose whether I liked the client or not. _____
9. I would self-disclose what my religion is. _____
10. I would self-disclose my sexual orientation. _____

Summary

The person of the therapeutic interviewer is one key to a productive therapeutic process. Therapists are made up of skills, philosophy, strengths, faults, and continued struggle for growth. Therapists should constantly strive to connect with themselves in order to ensure that they are continuing to grow instead of stagnating or allowing their own issues to come through in the therapy room. This can be done through individual efforts at growth, supervision, and continued professional activity in the field. Therapists have the potential of burning out since they are sometimes isolated in their jobs and their work is based on the problems of others. Therapists should learn to foster pathways in their nontherapy lives as well as practices in their professional role to be able to work at their most effective level.

Exercises

1. Break up your class into two groups. One group should brainstorm traits they would attribute to effective therapists. The other group should brainstorm traits they would attribute to ineffective therapists. Come back together and compare the answers. Then have a discussion about whether there is anyone who does not, at some point, exhibit all of the traits.

2. Interview therapists in various specialty areas asking them how they got into the field, what they think the important characteristics of effective therapists are, strategies they use to prevent burnout, and ways that they maintain their own mental health.

4

Beginning Conversational Skills

Use of Language for Joining and Maintaining an Interview

At the outset of a first session, therapists are presented a choice of focusing immediately on the presenting problem or taking some time to get to know the client. Although either way can be effective, it is recommended that at least a portion of the first session be used to join and make a connection with the client. Especially during the first meeting, therapist and client need time to feel each other out and start to become comfortable with one another. The first interview is sometimes the most critical piece of the therapy process, and it usually sets the tone for the therapist–client relationship (Faust, 1998). If the modal number of sessions that a client comes to therapy is one, then the first session is many times the last session. Therapists should do all they can to make the most out of this session, either as a one-time event or as the beginning of future sessions. Although it is important to be as productive as possible about client concerns, the foundation of the therapeutic alliance needs to be established in the first meeting. Thus, a balancing act occurs wherein the therapist and client join with one another and get to know a little about who each other is, while also figuring out what the client's goals are and how the therapist can help move the client in the direction of those goals. This chapter covers various issues of beginning the therapeutic interview along with basic conversational skills therapists can use to keep the interview progressing.

Joining Skills

Joining is a process that occurs through the whole of therapy wherein the therapist attempts to make and maintain a connection to the client. Joining is perhaps one of the most invaluable skills a therapist can learn, since by connecting to the client, the therapeutic interviewer develops a therapeutic alliance with the client. Some therapists, such as Bender and Messner (2003), have as their primary goal(s) for the first meeting with the client to establish the therapeutic alliance.

Joining at the very beginning of therapy utilizes different skills from joining in the middle of therapy. When the therapist and client first meet, they do not know each other. Therapists can take the very beginning of the first session to get to know the *person* of the client instead of the *problems* that brought that client to therapy. The following brief transcript depicts how this might begin:

> *Therapist:* Before we get into the concerns that brought you to therapy, if you could tell me a bit about yourself.
>
> *Client:* Well, I'm thirty-three and a teacher.
>
> *Therapist:* What do you teach?
>
> *Client:* I teach third grade. Mainly English.
>
> *Therapist:* What's that like to teach third grade?
>
> *Client:* At times it can be stressful, with all those students in a class. But I love it. I wouldn't want to do anything else.
>
> *Therapist:* When did you realize that you wanted to be a teacher?
>
> *Client:* When I first started college, I was thinking about maybe accounting, but then I realized in my sophomore year that I loved kids so much that I needed to be a teacher.

Through this very brief interchange, the therapist has gotten to know something of the person of the client along with making the client feel comfortable and easing him into the therapy process. Further, the more information the therapist has about the client, the more she can contextualize the client's situation.

An initial part of the joining process is attending to, not only the client, but also the therapist herself. Sperry, Carlson, and Kjos (2003) provided three types of attending and joining skills: internal attending, physical attending, and verbal attending. Each of these skills helps to connect therapist and client while also laying the foundation of further conversation about future issues.

Internal attending is a mind-set that the therapist "needs to put aside personal concerns including any physical discomfort or immediate worries before beginning the counseling session and be present for the client" (Sperry et al., 2003, p. 38). Therapists cannot allow their own personal issues to negatively impact their effectiveness during the therapeutic interview. This can be achieved by the therapeutic interviewer's finding her *chi*. The term *chi* comes from the martial arts where the martial arts practitioner finds her center. By having this balance, the practitioner can more effectively use her mind and body to work the skills of the discipline. When first practicing this internal attending, the trainee might need to do thought stopping or other means of focusing.

The second type of attending and joining skill is physical attending. Physical movements of the client and therapist are important to keep in mind throughout

Exercise 4.1

Sit down in a chair, become internally aware of yourself, and find your center. Your center will be that part of your body where you find a balance. When you are sitting, this is usually between your stomach and your waist. Focus in on that center and allow that comfort to envelop your entire body. Once you can easily accomplish this, practice with a partner. Have your partner sit in front of you. Find your center and open yourself up to be ready to listen to whatever it is that the other person says to you. Don't say anything; just find the comfort in being willing and ready to listen to the other person.

the session. As the therapist, it is important that one's body conveys one's interest, connection, and desire to continue in the process of the therapeutic interview. Clients will tend not to engage as fully as they might in the therapeutic discourse when they think that the therapist is not there with them. To do this, the therapist should be facing the client, give proper eye contact, and have an open body position. Crossed hands and legs give off a closed stance, wherein clients might feel distance, no matter how slight, from the therapist. Distance is usually not beneficial during the therapeutic interview.

In understanding distance, the therapist and client might be physically close, yet there can be things between them that create distance. This goes to the notion that anything (both physical and emotional) that comes between the therapist and client can potentially bring distance between the two. Thus, therapists should not sit behind desks or as many practicum students in university settings tend to do, hold the client's chart during the session (as if it is a protective shield). Even notetaking can potentially distance therapist and client.

The third type of attending and joining skill is verbal attending. Sperry et al. (2003) explained, "Verbal attending is the words, phrases, and times of silence counselors use to indicate they are attending to the client" (p. 41). Therapists can use their words to, in very small ways, let clients know they are either paying attention or not paying attention to them. Beebe, Beebe, and Redmond (2005) talked about the differences between confirming and disconfirming responses, describing a disconfirming response as any response (or lack of) from one person that decreases the other person's self-worth. A confirming response is a response that increases the other person's self-worth. Directly acknowledging the other person's question or comment, answering someone, supportive responses, compliments, and clarifying what the other person said are all confirming responses. Therapists should attempt to use these types of confirming responses as much as possible and avoid any type of disconfirming response (for example, not responding, mumbling, being tangential in their response).

> *Client:* I'm feeling really bummed out today. I don't have the energy to do everything that needs to get done. What do you think I should do?
>
> *Therapist:* There are a lot of things you can do (*direct acknowledgement*). But I do want to note that although you felt bummed out, you still came here to

this session (*compliment*). It sounds like today has been tough on you, and I hope you feel better (*supportive response*).

Greeting the Client

Therapy is a business relationship. Business relationships tend to begin by a handshake between the two sides. Most therapists, when first meeting a client, will shake hands with the client. Handshakes are a form of behavior that leads to information about the other person while also sending a communication about ourselves. Too hard a handshake and the other person may shy away, feeling that the person is too dominant. Too limp a handshake might send the message that the person is weak or doesn't care. The male-to-female handshake can also be problematic, with one party or the other not knowing how firm to make it. It is recommended that therapists-in-training practice with their colleagues how to shake hands and get proper feedback to determine whether they are providing too hard or too soft a handshake.

Some therapists think that any form of physical contact with a client is inappropriate if it is therapist initiated. Thus, they might introduce themselves to the client and only shake hands if the client initiated the handshake. In U.S. culture, the handshake is the predominant means of introductions. In other cultures, other forms of initial greetings might be more important, such as a kiss on the cheek in some South American or European countries or a bow in some Asian countries.

When introducing themselves, therapists must decide how they want to present themselves. For those individuals with doctorates, the honorific "Dr." might be used. There are positives and negatives to its use. By saying, "Hello, I am Dr. Franks," the therapeutic interviewer might be perceived as placing herself in a higher position than the client, one that implies she is more the expert. This may gain her status and respect from the client. However, it could also put distance between her and her client. If the therapist introduced herself by saying, "Hello, I am Natalie," she may not gain as much status in the beginning of the encounter, which could hamper client movement. Yet, this might also place her on a more even playing ground where therapist and client become co-collaborators in the therapeutic endeavor. Therapists will need to make a determination of what they want clients to call them based on the context in which they are providing services as well as who the client is.

The greeting with the client is important because it is the first impression the therapist is making on the client. Many people form their impressions of another person within the first five minutes of an interaction. Therapists should come across as friendly, but not overly friendly; caring, but not overly caring; and reserved (so as not to dominate the other person), but not overly reserved.

Therapist dress is another factor that impacts the client's initial impression. Depending on the geographic area and the type of client (adult, adolescent, or child), a therapist's clothing can impact how the client views and engages with that person. For higher socioeconomic areas, business attire is more appropriate. In home-based sessions with clients of lower socioeconomic status, more informal clothing is appropriate. With children, clothing that can get ruined and stained should be worn since some type of play therapy is usually involved.

Framing the Purpose of Therapy

As discussed in Chapter 2, clients come to therapy with a wide range of perceptions and misperceptions as to what therapy is or is not. Some clients come having never been in therapy before and are extremely nervous and apprehensive as to what will occur. Other clients have been to therapy previously and might expect the current therapeutic interviewer to operate in ways similar to those of a past therapist. Therapists can use the beginning of the first interview to help orient clients to how they operate and the process of therapy. It is essential to set the ground rules of therapy from the very first interview so that clients understand what therapy and the therapeutic relationship are about (Kenny, 1998).

For clients, the beginning of a therapeutic relationship can provoke some type of anxiety. Clients are anxious to have the problem bringing them to therapy resolved, but they are also anxious about whether there will be a connection with the therapist so that therapy will be useful. Meier and Davis (2001) explained how potentially to relieve clients of some anxiety at the very beginning of therapy:

> Clients may find it helpful, however, to know that (a) they will do most of the talking, (b) they may experience painful feelings before they begin to feel better, (c) exceptions exist regarding the confidentiality of counseling, (d) persons in counseling are not inherently weak, and (e) most individuals in counseling are quite sane. (p. 4)

The more information that clients have up front about what will occur, the more comfortable and relaxed they will probably feel. (Do Exercise 4.2.)

Informed Consent

Informed consent is a process by which the client consents to treatment based on being informed about the parameters of the relationship and what will occur in therapy, in a general sense. Corey, Corey, and Callanan (2007) explained that it "involves the right of clients to be informed about their therapy and to make autonomous decisions pertaining to it" (p. 156). It consists of stating the therapist's credentials, confidentiality policy, payment issues (fees, billing procedures, and

Exercise 4.2

Develop an explanation of what therapy is and read it to a classmate. Have the classmate provide feedback to you in terms of the flow of the explanation, how much depth it gives, and your conviction in explaining it. Then, present that information to someone not in the class and who has never gone to therapy. What does that person say about what they would think if this was the explanation they were given?

missed sessions fee), length of sessions, how to contact the therapist, emergency procedures, and an estimation of how long therapy will take (Wiger & Huntley, 2002). Therapists should have a sense, based on their previous experience with other clients as well as on the current client's problem and the severity of that problem, of the number of sessions that might be necessary. Ethically, therapists must get clients to sign the informed consent form as early in the therapeutic encounter as possible.

Informed consent puts the client in a decision-making position (Wiger & Huntley, 2002). Clients get to choose certain aspects of the therapeutic process, primarily their role, which keeps them informed about the process so that they become more involved participants. Further, the informed consent form is a contractual agreement, which implies that they have an active role in the process and consequently the outcome.

Usually, in agency settings, clients might sign the informed consent when they fill out all of the initial paperwork. In private practice, the therapist's style usually determines how and when the informed consent is discussed; however, it should be from the very get-go. When it is not discussed at the very outset of the therapy encounter, the therapist is opening herself up to ethical problems because the client wasn't fully informed about the risks and benefits of the relationship. Case Scenario 4.1 describes an initial session where not having the informed consent signed at the very beginning of therapy was potentially problematic.

Confidentiality

The informed consent form has a section that addresses confidentiality. As with all aspects of the informed consent, the therapist should verbally discuss them to ensure that clients fully understand the parameters of the therapy situation. One

CASE SCENARIO 4.1

In my very early private practice career, I had a first interview with a husband and wife who were extremely upset because the local child welfare agency had taken their three-year-old daughter because of violence between the couple. I met them in the waiting room and brought them into my office. Before I had a chance to go over the informed consent with them, they began explaining the situation that brought them into therapy. They were quite animated and emotional. Although I wanted to have them sign the informed consent, I hesitated because I didn't want to interrupt the flow of the conversation, as I thought that might be disrespectful, and I wasn't confident yet in leading a session. This was a problem of being a new therapist and not having faith in myself to guide the structure of the session. This case was a very good learning tool for me to be more assertive in the therapy room when it came to more standard procedures, especially procedures put in place to protect the client and myself.

of the most important aspects of the informed consent is that of confidentiality. This is the notion that whatever is said in the therapy room is privileged information, which the therapist will not share with anyone without written permission from the client. However, there are exceptions to the rule of confidentiality. Wiger and Huntley (2002) described the following circumstances in which a therapist may need to break confidentiality:

- Duty to warn and protect
- Abuse of children and vulnerable adults
- Prenatal exposure to controlled substances
- Death of the client
- Professional misconduct
- Court orders/IRS/other government mandates
- Guardianship of minor or other person
- Collection agency involvement
- Third-party payer involvement
- Medical emergency
- Case consultation
- Research

During the discussion of confidentiality, therapists should inform clients of when they would need to break confidentiality. Further, if, later in the course of therapy, there is a time when therapists do need to breach confidentiality, they should explain to the client why they will be breaking it and what type of information they will relay to the other person. One possible explanation of confidentiality might be the following:

> *Therapist:* I just wanted to go over a few things about what you say in here and whom I can tell. Unless you give me written permission to tell someone, everything that we talk about here in the therapy room will be just between the two of us. However, there are a few times when I would have to tell someone else, such as if you were talking about seriously harming yourself or someone else or if there is discussion of someone, especially a child, being abused. There are a few other times that I listed on the informed consent form that I gave you a copy of. I just wanted to be upfront with you so that you know that most everything we talk about will be kept in confidence.

Beginning therapists will have supervisors, sometimes multiple supervisors, to whom they will be disclosing what was discussed in the interview. Therapists-in-training should have a section of the informed consent that explains they are therapists-in-training, who their supervisor is, and the reason for disclosing information that occurs in session. They should also explain this verbally to the client.

Therapist: As you know, I am a therapy intern. I have a supervisor who I discuss all of my cases with so that I can get further training to be more helpful for the people that I work with. I will be discussing the main points with my supervisor who will help me figure out better ways of helping you.

Therapeutic Distance

From the very beginning of therapy (even before formal therapy starts, when the therapist is talking to the potential client on the telephone), the therapist is setting the stage for the relationship. As discussed in Chapter 1, the therapeutic contract brings two or more people together into a professional relationship in which one person is self-disclosing personal information about a problem while the other person's role is to help see how to bring that issue to a productive resolution. Rules of the relationship help define the parameters of actions taken; many of these are depicted in the various ethical codes. There are also more implicit rules that lead therapists to act in certain ways with their clients.

Self-disclosing to someone usually brings a person closer to that other person. Just by telling the therapist their personal issues, secrets, and thoughts, clients usually feel a connection, sometimes a very intimate connection, to the therapist. Therapists want to show that they truly do care for the client, but not in the same way that they might care about their family or friends. Thus, they need to balance how much intimacy they feel or show and how much detachment they feel or exhibit. Too much businesslike distance might lead the client to feel unconnected in the interview. Too much caring or intimacy might frighten the client or lead to the client's thinking that the relationship is more than just a therapeutic one. Presbury, Echterling, and McKee (2002) stated, "By maintaining a proper therapeutic distance (a term we prefer to detached concern), you avoid exacerbating the client's problems" (p. 47).

Therapeutic distance is a balance for therapists between their own experience and that of the client. Leitner (1995) discussed the notion of optimal therapeutic distance and defined this as "being close enough to the other to experience the other's feelings while being distant enough to recognize them as the other's feelings—not the therapist's own" (p. 362). This is a difficult balance to maintain because the therapist should not be a therapeutic stranger (being very distant from the client) but also should not develop a therapeutic unity (excessive closeness by the therapist).

In people's normal close relationships, they do not feel detached. They become angry when someone insults or harms the person they care about, they become frustrated when they think the person is not making the right choices for his or her life, and they feel happy when good things happen to the person. This is a natural process that occurs for those close to us. Therapy is a curious process wherein, based on the intimate nature of the material being discussed, the two people in the interchange feel close and connected to each other in a unique way.

Reflection 4.1

Think about how you feel when someone very close to you gets emotionally hurt. What happens for you internally? How do you react toward the other person? Is this the same feeling that you get when you see a total stranger in the same situation? How do you think you would respond to a client in that situation? Imagine that you have been working with that client for six months and have had twenty sessions with him. What might your reaction be toward him?

Sometimes therapists lose their understanding that the client is different and should be treated differently from their loved ones.

Door Openers

Clients come in with one or more issues they want to change in their lives. We can use the metaphor that each of these issues is a room in that person's experience, and that there are thousands of these rooms, some containing what the client views as problems and some containing strengths, resources, and issues the client thinks are going well in his life. The therapeutic interviewer can use a door opener to start to explore a particular client concern. If a client's psychological world is viewed as a multi-roomed expanse where each room is a client concern and where some rooms interconnect with one another, the door opener can be seen as the entryway into one particular issue. Young (2005) defined door openers as "more than a passing social response or greeting, the door opener signals availability on the part of the listener and encourages exploration and discussion" (p. 107). The door opener initiates the conversation for client and therapist about a particular client concern.

Door openers are nonjudgmental ways to begin a conversation. They can be based on some previous knowledge, perhaps from an intake or a phone conversation. Therapists can also use client nonverbals as a way to initiate a door opener, as in the following:

- "On the phone when you made the appointment, you stated that you were really concerned about your child. Could you tell me about that?"
- "I see that you've been crying. What's going on?"
- "Tell me what brings you in today."
- "What brings you in to talk to someone like me, a therapist?"
- "What was it that led you to make this appointment?"

Going back to the multi-roomed environment, rooms are client issues. These issues do not exist in isolation from one another. Some issues are connected to and lead to other issues. Thus, once a door is opened into one room, another door in that room may open into an associated room, containing an issue that is connected somehow to the first issue. This is where exploration by the client and therapist

CASE SCENARIO 4.2

I worked with a young woman who was coming to therapy because the child protective agency had threatened to take away her son because the son had witnessed domestic violence between this young woman and her boyfriend, who was currently in jail. I started the first therapeutic interview explaining my role and the connection (and disconnection) I had with the child welfare agency. I used a door opener to talk about what occurred between her and the boyfriend that got the state child agency involved in their lives. We talked about this for awhile when she stated that part of what they were fighting about was what to do with her son, who was not doing well in school. This led to me asking a door opener about the son's school experience. The fighting between the partners and the son's school issues were not two mutually exclusive events. They were two rooms that adjoined in some fashion. This allowed me to understand how the various problems this client was dealing with overlapped. I was able then to make interventions that included each of these issues and how they might impact each other.

leads to some possibly unexplored issues. Case Scenario 4.2 describes how multiple client issues can be connected to one another.

Just as there are door openers there are door closers (Young, 2005). These are attempts made by one person to engage in a conversation with someone else, but are done in a judgmental way that closes off conversation.

- "Oh, it's you again. What do you want this time?"
- "You don't want to talk about your boyfriend again, do you?"
- "My day has been miserable. What about your day?"

These types of responses do not relay to the client that the therapist is interested in or open to hearing about the client's concerns. They discourage the client from talking freely and build a rift in the therapeutic relationship. Anything the therapeutic interviewer does that might give the client the impression that she is not interested in what the client has to say can damage the therapeutic alliance.

Basic Conversational Skills

Once the conversation gets going through the use of door openers, the therapeutic interviewer then needs to use various skills to help keep the conversation going so that the client feels comfortable enough to go into greater depth. These conversational skills allow the therapist to show continued interest in what the client is saying. These basic conversational skills form the bedrock of the therapeutic interview. However, they tend not to be focused on because they are not the ones that are noticed in the change process. Yet, without them, the larger change skills probably could not be utilized with as much effectiveness.

Minimal Encouragers

One of the most basic means of expressing to clients that the therapist is paying attention to the clients' discourse and encouraging clients to continue on their verbal path is through use of minimal encouragers. These are verbal and nonverbal means of encouraging clients to keep talking in the direction they already are. Once a door has been opened to a client issue, sometimes all they need is a minimal push to continue focusing on that topic. This is similar to a person who is spinning a basketball on his finger. The first spin would be the door opener. After that, not as much effort is needed to get the ball to continue to spin. The person just needs to do minimal taps on the ball to continue its current direction. Some of the most common verbal minimal encouragers include the following:

- "Okay"
- "Go on"
- "I see"
- "Tell me more"
- "Keep going"
- "Mmhm"
- "All right"
- "Explain that some more"

Minimal encouragers can also be nonverbal. The most common are head nods and keeping eye contact with the client. McHenry and McHenry (2007) held that minimal encouragers can also consist of using a word or phrase the client has just used, such as "hurtful," "it was new," or "forgettable." For instance:

Client: I just can't get past this awful feeling.

Therapist: Awful feeling.

Client: Yeah, it has been bothering me for so long. This feeling is . . .

As with all skills presented in this book, too much use of one specific type of skill begins to be noticed by the client and becomes an impediment in the interview. Thus, therapeutic interviewers are encouraged to vary their verbal and nonverbal repertoires.

Exercise 4.3

Watch an interview on television and keep track of all the verbal and nonverbal minimal encouragers the interviewer uses. Do you think they used too many or too few? What impact do you think the interviewer's minimal encouragers had on the interview? Did the interviewer use any minimal encouragers too often? If so, how did the interviewee respond?

Exercise 4.4:　 *Using Conversational Skills*

For the following client responses, provide the type of response requested.

　　Jennie is a fourteen-year-old student coming to see her school counselor. She has been getting detentions for the past month and has just received another one.

(Provide a door opener):
Jennie: I don't know. I can't seem not to get into trouble. This time it really wasn't my fault.
(Provide a minimal encourager):
Jennie: Well, Stacey walked by me and bumped me. On purpose. So I pushed her back.
(Provide a minimal encourager):
Jennie: Why do I have to take that? It's not right that she can start something and I get in trouble. It's like this at home too.
(Provide a door opener):

Nonverbal Communication

All behavior is communication (Watzlawick, Bavelas, & Jackson, 1967). These researchers stated, "Activity or inactivity, words or silence all have message value: they influence others and these others, in turn, cannot *not* respond to these communications and are thus themselves communicating" (p. 49). Everything a therapeutic interviewer does and says in session is information the client is taking in, gives meaning to, and reacts to. Thus, therapists need to be conscious of what they say and how they say it, because both impact the client.

　　As there are guidelines for using words, there are also guidelines for using nonverbals. Welch (2003) described two guidelines for the therapist's nonverbal behavior. The first is that of awareness. This means that therapists should be aware of how their own nonverbal behavior might impact the client. One of the best means to do this is for the therapeutic interviewer to record herself conducting sessions. Usually during the interview, especially for novice therapists who are already nervous, it is very difficult for therapists to be fully aware of their own behaviors. Through videotaping, therapeutic interviewers can view, after the fact when they are not as nervous, their behaviors during the session. Although it is still subjective, they can start to get a somewhat more objective view of themselves and how they might be coming across to the client. The second guideline is congruence. Therapists' nonverbal behaviors should match the words they are saying. When there is incongruency between the therapist's verbal and nonverbal behaviors, the client might start to distrust the therapist. Think about the following example:

> *Therapist:* I'm really glad that you are bringing up this situation today (said while leaning back, arms crossed, and a tremor in the voice).
>
> *Client:* Really, are you sure I should discuss this?
>
> *Therapist:* Of course (shaking head side-to-side).
>
> *Client:* Well . . . okay . . . I guess.

Although the therapist was giving the verbal go-ahead, her nonverbals were telling the client to be cautious in proceeding.

Nonverbal messages are more believable than verbal messages (Beebe, Beebe, and Redmond, 2005). Although we listen to what people say, we really cue in to how they say it, which gives us the understanding of how truthful people are and how we should really understand what they said. Communications researchers discuss this in terms of content and process. The content is the actual words used but the process is how it is said and how it should be understood. Confusion happens when the content and the process are incongruent. Most people will pay more attention to the process, or how a message is said, rather than the actual message.

Nonverbal behaviors can be considered attending behaviors. Kottler (2000) provided four different types of nonverbal attending behaviors: body position, eye contact, facial expressions, and nonverbal gestures. He also provided an attending checklist, including the following:

- Face the person fully
- Communicate intense interest
- Give undivided attention
- Maintain natural eye contact
- Be sensitive to cultural preferences
- Make your face expressive
- Nod your head, a lot
- Present yourself authentically

Body Position. Although there is not one body position that therapists should stay in for the whole of the therapeutic interview, there is a basic sitting position therapists can use as the foundational position when working with clients. The primary body position for the therapeutic interviewer is with an upright posture, shoulders square to the client, soles of the feet on the floor, hands resting on legs, legs slightly apart, and leaning forward, just slightly.

Egan (2006a) provides an acronym that therapists can use as a framework of proper body position: **SOLER**.

S stands for the therapist facing the client squarely.
O stands for an *o*pen posture.
L refers to *l*eaning forward.
E stands for *e*ye contact.
R refers to being *r*elaxed.

This acronym helps therapists to remember to get into a comfortable physical position so they can more easily attune to clients. This can facilitate the therapeutic relationship by sending a message to the client that what the client has to say is important and that the therapist is interested in it.

If therapists were to maintain solely this body position through the whole of therapy, clients would feel uncomfortable talking with someone who physically was similar to a statue. Therapists change positions many times during the therapeutic interview, and many different body positions are quite appropriate. However, there are several that should be avoided, including sitting Indian style on the chair or relaxed so much (perhaps considered like slouching) that they meld into the chair. Many times therapists try to use a body position that is similar to the client's. However, the therapist should not mirror the client. This could be seen in an absurd manner if, every time the client moved, the therapist moved immediately after into the same position. After two or three times of this occurring, the client would notice and become embarrassed or insulted.

Therapists should try to maintain open body positions, including not crossing their arms or their legs. It is generally thought that when a person crosses their arms they are distancing from the other person and putting a block between the two. It is not only crossed arms that can give off a negative signal to the client. Some beginning therapists, when nervous, do what I call the pretzel. They take one leg and twirl it around their other leg so that both of their feet face forward. Besides looking like an extremely uncomfortable position, this sends a message to the client that the therapist is uncomfortable and nervous. Beginning therapists also have a habit of sitting on their hands. This may be because they are unsure what to do with their hands during the therapeutic interview. To stress certain points in the conversation, therapists should use their hands to help illustrate what they are saying. When therapists use their bodies as they do in normal everyday conversations, they help to make the therapeutic interview more relaxed and comfortable.

Beginning therapists, especially those practicing in university clinics, tend to bring the client's chart into the therapy room. They usually hold these to their chest, but hardly ever open them during the session. This then becomes problematic for several reasons. First, the client gets the impression that the therapist is scared or uncomfortable. Second, it is awkward for the client seeing his chart but not knowing what is in it. This also applies taking notes during therapy. If the therapist takes notes but does not show the notes to the client, this can be quite off-putting for the client. The client will be spending time during the session wondering what the therapist is writing. It is recommended that therapists not take notes during session but instead audio or video record the session. If the therapist finds it useful to take notes, she should frame it in an open manner and offer the client the opportunity to take a copy of the notes home at the end of the session. This puts the client in a more equal position and suggests that the notes are not to help pathologize the client, but to help organize the session to assist the client better.

Physically, there should be an open space between therapist and client. Thus, the therapist should not be behind a desk while the client is sitting in a chair on the opposite side. With a desk between them, a hierarchical relationship is established wherein the client is on the lower end of the hierarchy. Sometimes therapists might have something such as a small ottoman or coffee table. This is better than being behind a desk as it gives more of a living room feel rather than that of a doctor's

CASE SCENARIO 4.3

I was working with a sixteen-year-old client who was coming to me because he was having difficulties in his relationship with his mother. Further, he wanted to stop using alcohol and marijuana, which he had been using almost every day for the last couple of years. This client had issues with authority and was not looking for another adult authority figure to tell him what to do. When he would come into my office he would lean back in his chair and put his feet up on my coffee table. Instead of taking a more rigid stance, I leaned back in my chair, put my feet up on the coffee table also, and had a conversation with him on a person-to-person basis. I believe this body position, which felt very natural to me, helped connect me with the client.

office. Case Scenario 4.3 depicts how a therapist can connect with a client by utilizing a similar body position.

Part of body position is proxemics, or the use of space. Edward Hall (1966) identified four spatial zones of interpersonal communication. The first is intimate space, which is approximately zero to one-and-a-half feet. Individuals in this zone usually know each other extremely well, such as spouses. The second zone is personal space, which is one-and-a-half to four feet. Communication between family and friends usually occurs in this space. The third zone is social space, which occurs from four to twelve feet. This is the type of space usually reserved for co-workers and other types of group interaction. The last zone is public space, which is twelve feet and beyond. This zone is where public speaking occurs. Therapeutic interviewing usually happens in the middle realms of personal space. If a therapist gets too close (intimate space and the shortest range of personal space), they may begin to invade the client's space and have the client become uncomfortable with someone being too close to him. If the therapist moves into the farther reaches of social space, perhaps six feet and beyond, she runs the risk of putting too much distance between herself and the client. This would then leave the client potentially feeling disconnected to the therapist. An appropriate distance is about three to five feet between therapist and client. When working with children, this space might be slightly reduced.

Exercise 4.5

With a partner, practice how comfortable each of you are at various distances from one another. Move very close so that your faces are almost touching. How comfortable are you? How much do you think you would be ready to listen and hear the other person? If you were a client, how comfortable do you think you would be? Then, move to the other side of the room. Answer the same questions about comfort. Then move your chairs closer or farther away from each other until you come to a distance that you both find comfortable. One thing you might notice is that you and your partner have somewhat different comfort levels when it comes to interpersonal space.

Eye Contact. Eye contact is a very important attending behavior. People can usually tell how much someone is paying attention to them based on the amount of eye contact they are receiving from the other person. Most people, when they are speaking to someone, want the other person to look them in the eyes. However, they do not want that person to be *staring* at them. Therapists should maintain eye contact with an appropriate amount of times to look away so the client does not feel under the microscope. What might the appropriate amount of eye contact be? One way to gauge this is for the person to see what they are comfortable with and do the same to others. (Do Exercise 4.6.)

Eye contact can also be cultural or age-related. In some cultures, it is disrespectful for someone who is younger to maintain eye contact with someone who is older. For instance, in general, people from Arabic countries give more eye contact than Americans, while Americans give more eye contact than Asians. This issue of how much eye contact one is giving can be quite problematic, in either direction (therapist perceiving the client is not looking at them as much as they should or the client perceiving the therapist is not looking at them as much as they should). People tend to make negative attributions to those people who do not look at them as much as they expect the other person to (Matsumoto, 2000). Further, some people who have low self-esteem might not keep as much eye contact as might be expected as normal. Therapists can check in with clients to see how much of the client's behavior is based on cultural standards.

Voice Tone. Paralanguage is the language of the voice. How a voice comes across gives a lot of information to the listener. People can tell if the speaker is scared or assertive, nervous or confident, hesitant or forthright, along with a variety of other perceptions. Therapists do this by trying to figure out what the client is saying, and by "being there" in the moment, their voice reflecting this intensity. Further, therapists might match the voice tone of the client. If a client is talking about the possibility of a very big promotion at work and is saying this in a very excited manner, the therapist can give the client some type of congratulations in a more excited manner than usual. Usually, a therapist does not want her voice tone to be too monotone or too excited. Having it somewhere in the middle would seem to be safer, and then to alter it based on certain specifics (for example, softer if something sad is being talked about, more excited if something happier is being talked about). However it occurs, the voice tone should be genuine for the therapist's current experience in the interview.

Exercise 4.6

Go to a location where many people interact. Pay attention to how much eye contact each individual in a conversation gives to the other when they are actually facing each other. How often do the individuals look away? Do an experiment in which you talk to a friend and never remove eye contact. Pay attention to what your friend's reaction is when you do this. At the end of the experiment, debrief your friend and ask what it was like to have someone maintain constant eye contact through the whole conversation.

Attitude. The therapeutic interviewer's attitude is an extremely important component to the effective or ineffective outcome in a session. Given that 30 percent of positive outcome in therapy is predicated on the therapeutic relationship, clients want to feel comfortable with their therapist. If they perceive that the therapist does not like them, is annoyed by them, or does not care about them, they might not be able to engage the therapist, which might hinder the clients' progressing toward their goals.

Therapists need to be present in the therapeutic relationship. They need to express to the client that they are there for the client, giving their undivided attention. They should display an attitude that is guided by a sense of the client's worth and significance (Rogers, 1951). Out of all of the nonverbal attending behaviors, therapist attitude might be the most problematic. All of the other attending behaviors can be easily taught. Attitude is the one least conducive to being taught. It might be pointed out to a novice therapist what type of attitude seems to be coming across, but just noting it does not change it. A person's attitude has developed over years, and although change can happen very quickly, it usually comes over time through motivation. Therapists should be open to the possibility that the way they are with clients might be altered in various ways. One of the best ways to determine whether one's attitudes are conducive for the therapeutic process is to videotape a session and view it with a supervisor, looking specifically for body and voice messages that might be relayed to the client.

Note Taking. Many novice therapists, especially those who work from a diagnostic and clinical perspective, tend to take notes during sessions early in their career. Note taking has many beneficial aspects, such as being able to document the important points of a client's discourse and as a reminder to help prod therapists to focus on certain aspects of what the client has said. Yet, having someone take notes can be somewhat disconcerting for the client. One way to assuage this is to be clear with the client about what is going in the notes and how the notes will be used. Leon (1982) stated that most people who go to a doctor expect that some type of notes are going to be taken, and that once the therapist explains that everything in the chart is confidential, the client will not be disturbed by the note taking. However, it is recommended that unless it is imperative for therapists to use the notes, they should stay away from taking them during the session.

Having a notepad on one's lap puts distance between therapist and client. Anything the therapist has, including a pen, mug of coffee, or notepad, is a barrier to the open flow between therapist and client. When taking notes in session, therapists should allow the clients to see what is being written or offer the clients the opportunity to take the notes home with them. Otherwise, note taking becomes a situation in which the client can think that the therapist is "analyzing" them, which puts distance in the relationship. Brems (2000) stated, "Note taking is appropriate only in settings where therapeutic rapport is not an issue; when a relationship is to be established, note taking interferes" (p. 16). This is somewhat of an extreme stance. However, therapists should consider the impact that taking notes might have on the client as it may lead to the situation in which the client is taking time in the session wondering what the therapist is writing on the notepad, rather than moving toward his goals. If therapists are going to take notes, they can introduce the idea to the client in a way that makes note taking seem collaborative rather than secretive.

Therapists are encouraged to take very detailed notes of what occurred in the session immediately after the session. Many insurance companies have now accepted forty-five or fifty minutes to be the expected amount of time for a session. This is partly based on the allowance for the therapist to take a break between sessions (if seeing clients on the hour), to utilize the bathroom if needed, and to write the notes for the case just seen. Many therapists wait until the end of the working day to write all of their notes for the cases they saw that day. This is potentially problematic for several reasons. First, many times therapists are so tired by day's end that they put off doing the notes until the next day. This is especially problematic for those therapists working with groups where a case note has to be made for each client in the group (and some groups can have twenty members). Secondly, even if done at the end of the night, the longer therapists wait to write down what occurred, the more chance they will not remember specifics and particulars of each case. Below is one possibility of how to introduce note taking into a session that could be productive for the therapist and respectful of the client as well as actually enhancing the relationship between therapist and client.

> *Therapist:* I am going to take some notes just to make sure I am getting all of the important points. If, at the end of the session you would like, I can make a copy of them for you.

This puts the client in a more respected position, where the therapy process is more open. Therapists can even, at the end of the session, collaboratively write the session's progress notes with the client. This puts the client in an even more respected position, where the client knows exactly what is being written and put into the chart.

Listening

Therapeutic interviewers are expected to hear and listen to their clients. Listening is not the same thing as hearing. Beebe, Beebe, and Redmond (2005) distinguished between the physiological process of decoding sounds, which they referred to as hearing, and the process of making meaning of those sounds, which entails listening. Although people may hear, they may not be listening. Therapeutic interviewers pay attention to client messages, both verbal and nonverbal, and attempt to make sense out of what the client has said and done, based on the context of the client's situation and problem. Listening is perhaps the therapist's primary therapeutic tool. Given that many people hold that interviewers should do only 20 to 30 percent of the talking in an interview (Barone & Switzer, 1995), therapeutic interviewers will be spending approximately 70 to 80 percent of the time in the interview actively listening to the client.

There are five basic types of listening (Long, 1996). Nonlistening refers to the notion that someone may physically hear the sounds from another person but not consciously become aware of what the other person is saying. Pretend listening occurs when the person who is supposed to be listening looks as if he or she is listening (that is, the person is facing the speaker, providing eye contact, nodding, and so forth) but the person's conscious awareness is elsewhere. This might happen when the person is daydreaming or thinking about something other than what the speaker is talking about. Selective listening refers to paying attention to only bits and pieces of what the speaker is saying. The listener hears only a part of what is being said, perhaps only the positive messages or conversely only the negative messages. Some listeners will filter out anything that might cause anxiety for them. The fourth type of listening is self-focused listening. It happens when the person who is listening does so through a lens that is so self-focused that the person has trouble being able to take the perspective of the other person. Empathic (other-focused) listening is being able to hear what the other person is saying along with that person's perspective. It is the type of listening that effective therapeutic interviewers engage in during a therapy session.

Listening Barriers

There are many potential barriers to effective listening. These can be environmental, psychological, or cultural. Any type of occurrence that hinders the therapist from fully listening to the client and making sense of the client's communication can potentially negatively impact the therapeutic interview. Therapists can attempt to listen by tuning in to each of these potential barriers and doing their utmost to prevent them from impacting the process of the therapeutic interview.

The setting in which an interview occurs can present several potential barriers to effective listening. Barone and Switzer (1995) highlighted some of the environmental obstacles that listeners should try to manage. There might be problems with lighting, where the room is too dark, too bright, too glaring, or too harsh. Therapists should ensure that light bulbs are replaced if broken or dimmed if too bright. There might also be problems with seating if the chairs are uncomfortable, the furniture is noisy (squeaks), or the furniture presents a barrier between the parties. Further, there might be issues based on spatial arrangements, with furniture being too close or too far apart. Other environmental obstacles include problems with room temperature and sound. A therapy room that is too cold, too hot, too muggy, or smells can negatively impact both the therapist and the client. Clients and therapists might also be distracted visually. If there are cluttered desks, distracting objects, or other types of movement (such as through a window, although window shades/blinds should be used to protect client anonymity from someone looking in from the outside), people may focus on these rather than the person talking. It is recommended that offices not be overly cluttered with objects as this may distract the client's attention. Although Sigmund Freud's office was full of objects he collected from all over the world, this is probably not a good idea as it may lead to overstimulation (especially for younger clients or those easily distracted).

Therapists can become distracted from listening to clients based on many psychological and internal issues. Hunger is a primary issue that impedes therapists and can cause an awkwardness during the interview. When people are hungry, they tend to focus on what and when they might be able to eat. A rumbling stomach can be a point of distraction in the session. Most people have had the experience of having their stomach rumble while in a conversation. This usually leads to a feeling of embarrassment and a pause, even if only for a second or two, of the conversation. Having to eliminate is also a primary issue. Nothing distracts therapists more from their clients than a full bladder. Therapists should manage their time so that these bodily needs do not detract from their focus during sessions. Therapists might also experience what can be considered psychological noise. This is when some type of internal thought or feeling is intense enough to shift the therapist's focus from the client's talk to something internal to the therapist. Psychological noise might arise based on something the client said that upset the therapist. For instance, if a client talked about killing an animal and the therapist is a member of P.E.T.A., the therapist may become angry and not be able to keep full attention on the client's continued discourse. If the client is angry and calls the therapist a negative name, such as "bitch" or "jerk," the therapeutic interviewer might become angry in response. Therapists might also be distracted from listening because of physical problems (such as headaches, soreness, or other discomforts). It can be difficult to give someone full attention when internal processes are off-kilter.

Culturally, therapists might experience language obstacles, such as different languages, accents, or colloquialisms. People might talk at a different pace from that of the therapist—either too fast so that the therapist cannot keep up or too slow, so that the therapist starts to drift because her understanding is ahead of the client's speech. If a therapist focuses too much on trying to pay attention and decipher what the client is saying, the therapist will find it difficult to get to the deeper layers of the client's story.

Responding

Therapeutic interviewers need to be able to take the client's perspective to be able to better understand the client's unique context. Responding is the final part of the listening process (Beebe, Beebe, and Redmond, 2005). If the therapist does not respond to the client and let the client know that she heard the client's message, she will send her own message that she is not present in the interview (a type of disconfirming response). Long (1996) explained that therapists may exhibit one of several different types of response styles. The *one-upper* is the type of listener who responds by expressing her own situation and how it is either better, or worse, than the speaker's. The *discounter* responds in a way to make the speaker feel as if his thoughts, feelings, and experiences do not really matter. The *expert* attempts to show how superior she is by expressing commands. The *advice-giver* listens for openings in which she can then offer suggestions of how the person can change his situation, usually through "You should . . ." or "Why don't you. . . ." The *cross-examiner* listens by asking questions. Talking with them seems to be like an interrogation in which question after question is thrust at the speaker. The *"canned"* counselor can produce some of the stock therapist responses (for example, "How does that make you feel?" or "What makes you think that?"). What makes the canned counselors problematic is that their attitude is that of being more focused on their own perspective, ready to evaluate the client rather than truly understanding the client. The *problem-solver* attempts to figure the client out without allowing the client the opportunity to do so. The last type of response style is the *empathizer*. This type of listener focuses in on the client's perspective and relays their understanding back to the speaker so that the speaker can explore his perspectives better. Effective therapeutic interviewers operate primarily from the empathizer response style. The other styles are for the most part problematic. However, there are times, especially in a crisis situation, where the advice-giver can be useful. As a default setting, therapists should work from the empathizer position.

Silence

Silence is golden sometimes. Most beginning interviewers have some of their most difficult times in dealing with silence during the therapeutic interview. Having supervised student therapists during live supervision from behind a one-way mirror, I understood quite quickly that when a silence occurred, the next thing the therapist said was usually not productive. This is because it came from a place of anxiety rather than therapeutic thoughtfulness. Especially in the beginning of a therapist's training, the length of silence might seem to grow exponentially with every additional second of silence that occurs in the room. The longer the silence grows, the more the therapist begins to doubt her skills and whether she is being productive with the client. The anxiety from the silence seems to build on itself so that the therapist wants to say something, anything, so that the silence is broken.

Silence can be an excellent tool to utilize and is appropriate in many instances during a therapeutic interview. On the surface, it might seem that when the therapeutic interviewer is silent, she does not know what to do. However, the use of silence can demonstrate to the client that the therapist is attending to the client's story (Doyle, 1998). When a significant reflection or idea has been introduced in the conversation, clients may need time to digest it to see how it impacts them. Silence is useful when there is a lull in the conversation, as it puts the onus of direction onto the client. Silence is also useful after a client has hinted at something important. By maintaining the silence, the therapist is sending a message for the client to go into greater depth about that topic.

Most therapists hold that the interviewer should wait out the silence. The therapist's fear is that the silence will become a challenge, similar to the scene in *Good Will Hunting* where Robin Williams, the therapist, gets into a silence match with Matt Damon, the client. Williams tells Damon's mentor, who needs to ensure that therapy is being productive, that the two sat in silence the whole session. He further states that he cannot talk first because he needs to set a precedent in the therapy interview. This type of situation might occur with adolescents who are being

Exercise 4.7

With a fellow classmate, sit across from each other, approximately three to four feet apart. Adopt a comfortable therapeutic interviewing position (feet on the floor, facing each other, shoulders squared, nothing crossed, arms on thighs, and leaning slightly forward—remember, SOLER). With your attitude and body, give the impression that you are ready to hear whatever the other person wants to talk about. Sit there, demonstrating your comfort and readiness to listen, while taking in the other person's readiness to talk. However, instead of talking, neither person should say anything. Spend five minutes in silence until you are comfortable not saying anything to your partner.

forced to go to therapy. Usually silence is not a game between therapist and client, but is used so that clients can think out an issue they are currently experiencing.

Just as therapeutic interviewers use silence strategically, so do clients. Doyle (1998) described four states in which a client might use silence. In the resistive state, the client might not want to talk about something because of the uneasiness of it, such as pain or embarrassment. In the reflective state, clients are silent because they are thinking about what has been discussed in the interview. In the inquisitive state, the client is silent because he is waiting for the therapist to give the interview and conversation direction. In the restive state (also known as the exhaustive state), the client is emotionally spent and needs time to recuperate. Therapeutic interviewers should keep in mind that in-depth emoting is emotionally and intellectually exhausting and that clients might need some silence to regain themselves. Below is an example of how silence can be useful in an interview:

> *Therapist:* Could you talk more about what that was like for you when you were having that argument with your wife? (door opener)
>
> *Client:* I just couldn't believe it.
>
> *Therapist:* Go on. (minimal encourager)
>
> *Client:* It was like I was having an argument with my mother when I was younger.
>
> *Therapist:* Mmhmm. (minimal encourager)
>
> *Client:* I just couldn't believe that I was in the same situation with my wife as I had been with my mother.
>
> *Therapist:* (silence)
>
> *Client:* (after twenty seconds of silence). Holy cow. I'm scared to confront my wife because I couldn't confront my mother. It's the same thing.

Silence in this situation allowed the client to get better connected to the feelings he was bringing up. By not saying anything, the therapist allowed the client to make connections and to really experience what was going on for him.

Using the Client's Language

Every person speaks in a unique way. Although there are significant commonalities among people, there are also distinct differences. When there is too much of a difference between the way that people communicate, or the specific use of language that people use, they tend to make note of these differences. This then distinguishes the people as different, leading to one type of disconnection between two people.

O'Hanlon and Wilk (1987) held that one of the most important ways of building rapport with a client is to utilize the client's preferred terminology or phrasing. Therapeutic interviewers can get in tune with a client by incorporating the client's phraseology into their own talk. By picking up on key phrases or patterns of speech, the therapist can get into a verbal rhythm with the client. However, this is not a full-fledged guarantee for connection. A caution in doing this is that it needs to come across as natural. This is especially the case when working with adolescents, where the use of teenagers' colloquialisms may come across as forced when spoken by an older therapist.

In order to be able to shift from one's own use of language to that of another person requires the therapist to become somewhat of a linguistic chameleon (Watzlawick, 1978). Since the therapist's job is to work from the client's perceptual framework, the words used need to be relevant and meaningful to the client, more so than to the therapist. When therapists work from their own verbal understandings, the meanings might not resonate for the client. Those words then might have been meaningless and useless.

A subset of using the client's language is using the sensory modality language the client is using (Watzlawick, 1978). Thus, if the client talks mainly in the visual modality (for instance, "I see what you mean," "It was right before my eyes"), the therapist can then shift her language to a more visual manner, especially in the use of reflections (for instance, "You are seeing the situation as being somewhat hopeless").

Using Obscenities

One special case of using the client's own language is when the client uses curse words and obscenities. Many clients will use obscenities and curse words to help explain their problematic situation. There is usually no regulation from the therapist on whether they should or should not use this language, unless they are becoming offensive and abusive. For the therapeutic interviewer, cursing is dependent on the context. It would seem that with children and most minors, cursing would not be appropriate. However, when working with an adolescent who is using a lot of expletives, cursing by the therapist, not at the client, but in descriptions and explanations, might help connect the two. A caution here is that the adolescent might conclude that cursing in other contexts with other adults is acceptable. Thus, the therapist's use of cursing should only come after the adolescent client's first usage.

Therapists are trained to use the client's language. If the client uses curse words to describe his situation, the therapist can use the same or similar curse words. One therapist who became extremely famous for his use of curse words in therapy is Albert Ellis. However, although he would use curse words as a description of what might be going on for the client, he would also sometimes use them in a very confrontative manner. Ellis is very comfortable in his use of slang when talking with a client. Part of his use of such words comes from his theory, rational emotive behavior therapy, in which he attempts to help clients, and himself (or therapists), transcend *must* and *should* commands they might tell themselves, such as "One should not curse."

Ellis isn't the only therapist to utilize curse words. Many have at some point in their careers. Therapists such as Carl Rogers may swear in session, using words such as "damn" and "hell." Although these might not be viewed as negatively as some other curses, they can be quite powerful. They also might be offensive to a client from a more puritanical background. Therapists should be cautious and gauge how their use of cursing during the therapeutic interview will be received by the client.

Although there are potential negatives of cursing in session, there are also potential advantages. The use of curse words can be a joining mechanism for people. Swearing can help increase a sense of intimacy, which then signals a certain connection between people (Winters & Duck, 2001). When the therapeutic interviewer swears, a wall of formality and distance can be broken so that two people are simply engaged in a conversation. Since swearing usually signifies informality (Winters & Duck, 2001), by swearing the therapist sends a message that things can be talked about during the therapeutic interview in any manner the client deems acceptable. Sometimes clients will hold back swearing because they do not want to offend or shock the therapist, yet if the therapist has used some of these swear words, the client can more freely use them. However, the standard is for the therapist to hold off until the client uses that type of language, unless the therapist believes that the use of curse words will help push the client more quickly and more effectively toward his goal.

Use of Humor

Humor can be found in every social context (Lynch, 2002). As one type of unique context, therapy does not have to be a completely solemn affair, or even a mainly solemn affair. Unfortunately, the field of therapy has looked at those therapists who use humor in the helping process "as being callous, uncaring, heartless, and indifferent" (Kisthardt, 2002, p. 175). Some people hold that there are some things that should be joked about and other things that should never be joked about. The use of humor in therapy seems to be on the fence with people in both camps. Perhaps it is not a case of whether joking and humor should be used in therapy, but *how* it should be used.

Humor is becoming more commonplace in psychotherapy (Fry, 2001). Therapeutic interviewers can inject humor into the session to join with a client, to show the client that life does not have to be taken so seriously, and to reframe situations. One of the main proponents of humor in therapy, Albert Ellis, developed slogans, songs, and various other ways of getting clients to change. Ellis (1977) explained the rationale for the use of humor in psychotherapy when he said, "Why not poke the bloke with jolly jokes? Or split their shit with wit?"

One of the primary reasons that people use humor is to relieve tension (Lynch, 2002). It shifts the context from being excessively serious without room for difference to open up possibilities of viewing self, other, or context differently. Greenwald (1987) explained, "A humorous context can help create a therapeutic atmosphere of freedom and openness" (p. 43). One of the keys of humor is that it creates conditions for connection and change. Humor helps to prevent people from taking themselves too seriously (Borcherdt, 2002). Besides the emotional benefit, a good sense of humor has been associated with positive physical health and well-being (Boyle & Joss-Reid, 2004; Goldstein, 1987).

Through the use of humor, therapist and client can develop a relationship that is more flexible than a typical business relationship. They can be serious, they can joke, and they can be anywhere in-between. People in joking relationships tend to have higher intimacy rates, both knowing that the jesting between them is a sign of a connected relationship. Just because two people in a conversation are laughing together does not mean that they are not focused on the business of the interaction. Corey (2005) stated, "It is important to recognize that laughter or humor does not mean that work is not being accomplished" (p. 32). Corey cautioned, however, that sometimes laughter can be used to cover up anxiety or experiencing. Therapists should learn to distinguish between useful and non-useful laughter.

The use of humor and the ability to laugh can be extremely therapeutic. Milton Erickson stated that "you need to teach patients to laugh off their griefs and to enjoy their pleasures" (Gordon & Meyers-Anderson, 1981, p. 29). Franzini (2002) provided the following types of humor that therapeutic interviewers might use with clients including jokes, puns, therapist self-deprecation, comical observations, discussing absurdities, parapraxes, and illogical reasoning, among others.

Exaggeration.   One common type of therapeutic humor is the use of exaggeration (Young, 2005). Exaggeration is taking a situation and making it bigger than it is. It pulls at the corners of truth and includes some type of silliness. Albert Ellis (1971) often used this approach. The following is a transcript of his work with a twenty-three-year-old woman:

> *Client:* I was brought up to think that I mustn't be selfish.

> **Ellis:** Oh, we'll have to knock *that* out of your head!

> **Client:** I think that that is one of the basic problems.

> **Ellis:** That's right. You were brought up to be Florence Nightingale—which is to be very disturbed! (p. 227)

Therapist Self-Deprecation. Therapists can set the stage for the use of humor in therapy by making fun of themselves. By engaging in therapist self-deprecation, the therapist is sending a message to the client that a person can be okay and still poke fun at herself. Many times, clients have problems with being able to critique themselves. They might take themselves too seriously. Having the therapist as a model of how one can poke fun at oneself while still having self-confidence can be a very powerful experience in therapy.

> *Client:* I can't seem to get things right in relationships.
>
> *Therapist:* Be thankful you're not dating me, or things would be even worse!

Absurdities. Carl Whitaker is perhaps best known for his use of absurdities in psychotherapy, even sometimes calling his approach a "therapy of the absurd." He used absurdity to get people to realize the absurdity of their own questions or ways of being (Whitaker & Bumberry, 1988). The following is an interchange between Whitaker and an adult woman:

> *Client:* So, Carl, I don't know where I am with my boyfriend problem. I don't know what to do!
>
> *Whitaker:* Did you expect to have a solution?
>
> *Client:* Well, yes. I kind of want some kind of solution.
>
> *Whitaker:* Oh? Merry Christmas! (p. 149)

By making an absurd answer, Whitaker demonstrated the absurdity of the client's question. In his view, since we can never remove ourselves from problems and will need to live life, an attempt by a client to live problem-free is absurd. His response helps to showcase this.

Although the use of jokes and humor can be appropriate with certain clients, therapists should be cautious using humor with clients from a different cultural group (Fabian, 2002; Maples et al., 2001). When therapist and client are from the same culture, the use of inoffensive jokes, therapist self-deprecation, and references to commonly held humorous situations can be acceptable (Maples et al., 2001). However, different cultural groups value humor to varying degrees. When working with clients from a different cultural group, therapists should avoid using sarcasm (especially when directed at the client) and should hesitate to use jokes with individuals from certain cultures, especially Middle or Eastern Europeans, or with those whose language is different from the therapist's, as jokes sometimes do not translate appropriately (Fabian, 2002). Given that the therapeutic interview is a conversation between two people, the therapist should gauge the reaction that her use of humor will probably have on the client. Things to think about for the therapist are the sense of humor of the client, the tone of the current conversation, what type of humor the therapist will use, and what might offend the client.

Part of what leads the therapist to decide how to use humor is what the focus of the humor is. Turner and Hersen (1987) explained, "The key is that one does not laugh *at his or her client*, but *with his or her client*" (p. 19). In a therapist's nontherapy role, perhaps as friend or family member, sarcasm can be a primary means of humor. A lot of sarcasm can be put-downs. In therapy, the therapist should be careful to shift the sarcasm from being about the other person to being about the situation the person may find himself in. The use of humor in therapy should also be spontaneous, rather than contrived (Mindess, 2001). When the therapist has to preplan jokes, the jokes tend to come off as forced or not fully relevant to the client's particular sense of humor or clinical situation. Spontaneous humor occurs within the flow of a relationship, based on the specific context of the therapeutic interview.

It has even been proposed that therapists-in-training take a course on humor (Franzini, 2001). Learning this skill would assist therapists in knowing when humor is appropriate, how to utilize their own sense of humor, and assessing the client's reaction to the use of humor. Case Scenario 4.4 describes how a therapist can use humor to make inroads with a client, specifically one dealing with depression.

Confrontations

It might seem that the therapist should be all-accepting of the client. However, sometimes client talk is not grounded in what is actually going on in the client's life. At these times, it might be useful for the therapeutic interviewer to confront the client about the discrepancy between what the client is saying and what actually is occurring.

In the field of counseling, confrontations have had a negative connotation, primarily because of their use in the field of substance abuse counseling. The old model of working with people dealing with addictions was to confront them in a somewhat aggressive manner until they admitted that they were addicts. This in-

CASE SCENARIO 4.4

I was working with a sixteen-year-old client who was severely depressed and suicidal. I was leaving the agency where I was seeing him, so I set up a transfer session with his new therapist. The client was a musician and had toured with religious church orchestras. During the transfer session, when he was explaining this to the new therapist, I asked him if, during the tour of performances in different cities, he would go to the front of the stage and act like most rock groups, saying something like, "Hello, Chicago! How are you tonight?" The client, the new therapist, and I laughed at this image. At *that* moment, the client wasn't as depressed as he had been. By infusing this type of humor into the session, the stage was set for the client to accept that he didn't always have to be depressed and could have fun and find humor in things. Further, it eased the transition from his working with me to his working with this new therapist. He saw that the new therapist could laugh and was a real person.

your-face type of confrontation pitted therapist against client. Substance abuse counselors found that their confrontations to a client about the client's substance use were insufficient, so they recruited the client's family and friends into this confrontation, a process which has been called intervention.

In today's counseling culture, confrontations have a different meaning. Given that therapists are trying to understand the worldview of the client, they use confrontations when the client is exhibiting discrepancies. Confrontation can be necessary when a discrepancy makes understanding the client, difficult. Many authors have discussed using confrontations when the client displays any type of discrepancy (Ivey & Ivey, 2003; Kottler, 2000; Young, 2005). Ivey and Ivey defined confrontation in the following way:

> Confrontation is *not* a direct, harsh challenge. Think of it, rather, as a more gentle skill that involves listening to the client carefully and respectfully and then seeking to help the client examine self or situation more fully. Confrontation is not "going against" the client; it is "going with" the client; seeking clarification and the possibility of a new resolution of difficulties. Think of confrontation as a supportive challenge. (p. 225)

Some of the common discrepancies a therapeutic interviewer might see, along with how the therapist can use confrontation, are included in the following list:

- Incongruity between what a person is *saying* versus *doing*

  "You say that you only want to be with Sheila, yet you are going out several times a month and having one night stands with other women."

- Incongruity between what a person *says now* versus what was *said earlier*

  "I'm a bit confused. In previous sessions, you said that you don't want anything to do with George. Yet now you are saying you want to see how things can work out. Could you explain this?"

- Incongruity between how a person *behaves now* versus how the person *behaved earlier*

  "Last week you were working toward not drinking anymore. Now this week you are drinking."

- Incongruity between what *the person reports* versus what has been *reported by others*

  "You are telling me that things are going great in your family. But when I talked with your parents, they said that things are worse now than ever."

- Incongruity between *verbal* and *nonverbal messages*

  "You say that you are doing fine, but your voice is so sad when you say it."

- Incongruity between *values* and *behavior*

  "For you, you hold honesty to be one of the most important qualities for someone. And you've been lying to your wife about what you are doing when you go away on business."

- Incongruity between *experiences* and *plans*

  "You've had people tell you that you can definitely move up in the company, but you want to quit because you think there's no room for advancement."

Confrontations should not be used as a way for a therapist to "get after" a client. They are used with a sense of empathy when the therapeutic interviewer has difficulty making sense of the client's situation because of the discrepancy. Minuchin, Nichols, and Lee (2007) provided an interesting way to present a challenge to a client, "We often say `That's interesting . . .' before pointing something out, in order to make it an object of curiosity rather than an occasion for defensiveness" (p. 7).

Another type of confrontation during the therapeutic interview occurs when the therapist uses immediacy, actively discussing a process occurring between therapist and client. For instance, if a client is being secretive and not engaged during a particular therapeutic interview, the therapist might say, "Alan, I'm not sure what's going on for you, but you seem to be holding back right now."

Given that the therapist is the professional in charge of the interview, she needs to be aware of what is occurring in the therapy room. The therapist should pay attention to what is immediately happening in the interview and give appropriate feedback to the client when it seems that the interview is not progressing in a productive fashion. One means of doing this is for the therapist to let the client know that what is transpiring is not comfortable for her.

> *Therapist:* Jerry, I wanted to let you know that I am not feeling 100 percent comfortable in this interview. Several times you have asked me for certain things I couldn't give you, such as a letter stating that you were disabled or for me to give you medications. Each time, when I told you I couldn't fulfill your request, it seemed you became very upset. You also changed your body behavior in an aggressive manner that made me physically uncomfortable. I'm wondering what your thoughts are on this.

By confronting the client in this manner, the therapist is owning her own perceptions and role in the transaction.

Confrontation can also be used when the client is engaging in unethical, unsafe, or otherwise destructive behavior. Kottler (2000) discussed these types of confrontations as feedback. He provided four guidelines for giving feedback to clients:

1. Include both supportive and critical features.
2. Be specific.
3. Provide supporting examples.
4. Be sensitive.

Young (2005) noted that receiving feedback is a tool for self-growth for clients, "Clients need accurate feedback in order to confront inconsistencies in their own attitudes and to know how they are affecting others. Most problems that people face are 'people problems'" (p. 177).

One of the difficulties of giving feedback to a client is that it usually comes across much better when it is housed with an already existing supportive relationship. Confrontation should not be used early in the therapeutic relationship as it can be perceived as too domineering and rude. Therapists should first support the client and then challenge the client through a confrontation (Neukrug & Schwitzer, 2006). When the therapist tries to make sense of a client's discrepancies in this way, both therapist and client are able to better understand the client's worldview and experience.

Ivey and Ivey (2003) suggested that confrontation can be viewed as having three steps. The first one is to identify what incongruity the client is exhibiting. The second step is discussing with the client, in a clear and overt manner, what the-incongruity is and then helping the client to resolve the discrepancy. The third step is evaluating whether the confrontation helped the client to move toward growth.

Exercise 4.8

For the following client statements, develop a response that is a confrontation, noting the discrepancy in the client's statement.

1. All I do is sit around the house and mope. I must be the most pathetic guy on the planet. I watch TV and see other people having these great lives while I'm pretty much a bum. The other day, when I was at the library, I overheard these people talking about going kayaking. I want to do stuff like that, but I just won't leave the house.
2. This guy was hitting on my sixteen-year-old sister the other day. I almost beat him to a pulp. All guys want to do is to get into girls' pants. So I'm not gonna allow any guy near my sister. I told this to the girl I'm dating currently. We talked about how our relationship is based on friendship, not sex.
3. I don't know why the judge said I have to come see you. Yeah, I hit my wife a little bit, but it really wasn't anything serious. If it was serious, she would have been in the hospital. I would never do that. It was only a couple of bruises.
4. Why was I born so ugly? I want to go on one of those extreme makeover shows. Maybe then they could work on me so someone could actually look at my face without revulsion. My last three boyfriends would lie to me and tell me I was attractive, but I could see through that.
5. I am a family guy. I love my family. They mean the world to me. When I get home from work, I make sure I give them thirty minutes of my full attention. Then I get together with some of my friends and play pool at the corner bar for the rest of the night.

Summary

Beginning a therapeutic interview requires a combination of comfort and seriousness. The therapist must join with the client so the client can feel at ease and comfortable talking with the therapist about the concerns that brought him to therapy. The therapist must also demonstrate that the client's concerns are meaningful. Once an initial connection is made, the therapist can use various conversation skills, such as door openers, minimal encouragers, using the client's language, humor, obscenities, and confrontation to maintain the connection with the client and explore the client's story in greater depth.

Exercises

1. Pay attention to your normal conversations. Which of the basic interviewing and conversational skills are you using? How do you think these skills impact the other person's participation in the conversation? Play around with your use of these skills to observe what impact it makes on the conversation when you change your own use of listening and responding techniques.

2. Role-play a therapeutic interview with a fellow student. For the client, try to come up with as many different discrepancies as possible. For the interviewer, try to notice what the different discrepancies are and reflect these back to the client.

5

Reflecting Skills

Exploring Content, Feelings, and Meanings of the Client's Story

The previous chapters discussed who clients are, who therapists are, and how to begin a therapeutic interview and keep it flowing using door openers, minimal encouragers, and other basic conversational skills. Once a therapeutic interview begins, therapists must utilize additional skills to be able to contact a client and the specific issues bringing that client to therapy. This chapter explores reflecting skills, which the therapist uses to follow along with the content of what the client is communicating (paraphrasing) as well as the feelings (reflecting) and meanings (advanced reflecting). These types of conversational skills are more advanced than the basic conversational skills and are usually the ones that most people do not use in nontherapy situations. However, they are some of the most significant and powerful communicational responses therapists can use with clients. This chapter provides an overview of each type of reflecting response, providing many exercises for the reader to practice developing these important skills.

Exploring Content

Client Stories

People understand their lives and talk mainly in stories (White & Epston, 1990). The stories that people tell give the listener a window into those people's worlds. Their worlds contain what occurred for them, their feelings, hopes, dreams, disappointments, and everything else that makes them who they are. The stories that people tell about themselves flow into a coherent whole.

Most people, including many of those who enter therapy, are not aware that they explain their lives in stories. Some stories are quite simple (for example, "I went to work today and came home late"), while others are much more complex (for example, a biography). Once telling the tale, however long it might be, people want to know that the person listening is following along with the plot. If not, this could be very frustrating and lead to the storytellers' feeling unheard and devalued. Imagine if Homer had to keep pausing or retelling certain passages in his telling of *The Iliad* if the people listening weren't following along and understanding who was who, what they did, and what they thought. It would have taken Homer a lot longer to tell this tale, or he might have given up telling it altogether, if he thought that people weren't following along with what he was saying.

There probably are not too many people who enjoy talking for the sake of talking without the listener's acknowledging and ensuring that they understand the plot. This is where the skill of paraphrasing comes in during the therapeutic interview. By letting the client know that the therapist has understood the content of the communication, therapists acknowledge the client, demonstrate that they value the client's communications, and push the client to go further with the story and deeper into the conversation.

What Is Content?

When clients communicate their understanding of their life story (most likely a chapter or subchapter in their life that contains the conflict bringing them to therapy), they do so on three main levels. The first level is the content, the second is the feelings, and the third is the meaning. The content is the story the client is telling (who, what, where, when, and how). These are the "facts" as the client knows them. They do not have to be "truths," but are simply what the client says occurred. The content refers to the client's actions and thoughts. For instance, if a client stated that she was the president of the United States during last year but has now retired, these are the content (she was president of the United States and has now retired) even though the therapist knows these are not true. At this point in the beginning of therapy, the client does not have to be confronted about the truth of the content. The therapist can just paraphrase the content and return to the veracity of the statement once a connection between therapist and client has been made.

Most people, when they begin to express themselves and tell their story, begin at the content level. It is usually when someone is extremely upset that they begin at the feeling level, perhaps with "I am so mad right now, I am about to burst." It is rare for someone to begin a conversation at the meaning level as it takes time to explore both the content and the feeling to get to the meaning. Further, many people are not as in touch with the meaning level as they are with the content and feeling levels.

People are very accustomed to explaining the content of their story and their lives. Think about the things that others say when a spouse or family member arrives home from school, work, or simply being out.

- "What did you do in school today?"
- "How did your job interview go?"
- "Tell me what it was like at work today."

Each of these door openers leads to the person beginning to relate the things that happened in that person's day. Although other levels are involved (feeling and meaning), people usually begin with the content. Here is a typical conversation between parent and child at the end of the school day:

Parent: How was school today?

Adolescent: It was alright.

Parent: What did you do?

Adolescent: Well, in first period, we had a quiz. Then in second period, we watched a movie about the American Civil War. And in third period, we listened to a boring lecture on differential equations.

Parent: Do you enjoy math class?

Adolescent: Not really. The teacher is so dry. He doesn't make the material exciting. So me and my friends work as a group together to learn the material.

This conversation could proceed in the same direction, with mainly the surface happenings of the adolescent's life being talked about. Although some feelings were touched upon (feeling bored), the brunt of the conversation focused on what happened and who did what.

What Is a Paraphrase?

A paraphrase is a restating, in the therapist's own words, the behaviors, thoughts, and facts of what the client has just said. The therapist does not give his own opinion of what is right, wrong, good, bad, or proper. The therapist is not giving advice to the client or trying to sway the client. It is a means of trying to follow along and understand the client's story. The paraphrase is a nonjudgmental statement of what the client has just said.

It is important that clients know the therapist is following along with what is being said because if not, the client will keep repeating the story so that the therapist knows what is going on. Take the following interchange:

Client: I told her over and over that I didn't want to go with her. But she kept on saying I had to or else she'd feel so alone. But there were going to be people there that I didn't want to see.

Therapist: She kept on trying to get you to go.

Client: Yes, and I kept telling her I didn't want to go. That's not my scene. She's my friend, but those people aren't.

Therapist: You don't want to hang around with those other people.

> *Client:* No, I told her I didn't like them. But she didn't listen. I don't know what I needed to say to her to get her to hear me.
>
> *Therapist:* She didn't hear you.
>
> *Client:* No, she didn't. I told her over and over, but she didn't.

This situation could have been enhanced by the therapist letting the client know that he had heard the main points of the story, especially the point about the client having told, many times, the other person that she did not want to go. Once the client knows that the story has been heard, she can then move to the next phases of describing her experience—the feelings and meanings. There are some additional benefits of using paraphrasing. It helps clients stay on target with the main points they are trying to communicate. Another benefit is that it allows clients to think about what they said and potentially to add any missing pieces that they didn't consider before or that the therapist might not have understood. Further, by hearing how others are hearing them, clients become better storytellers.

From the first utterance, clients are communicating on all three levels. However, it is much easier and safer to move from the less intense to the more intense. Content is the most surface level communication, feelings the next level, and meanings the deepest level. When people self-disclose, they tend to disclose less personal information when they first meet someone, building up trust with the other person until they are self-disclosing very intimate details of their hopes, fears, and self-understanding once a relationship has developed. When therapeutic interviewers focus too quickly on the intense feelings and meanings of the client, the client can become overwhelmed, scared, embarrassed, or hesitant. This might slow the client from focusing on the issue.

Therapeutic interviewers must be able to decipher the various levels of the client's communication. For instance:

> *Client:* This job is so confusing for me, I'm not sure I can handle it.

The content level is that the client has a job and is having difficulty dealing with it. There are other things going on in this statement (such as how they feel about the job and what it means for them that they doubt whether they can handle the situation). These higher levels of communication will be addressed later in the chapter.

Therapists should not interrupt the client to provide a paraphrase. It should come in the natural flow and breaks in the conversation. Sometimes clients will give a one- or two-sentence statement and then stop, not providing the therapist much information to give a paraphrase. At other times, clients will talk for five to ten minutes straight (sometimes the whole session, although this is usually not helpful for the client as they are going to the therapist for more than just venting). Either way, therapists should be picking out the most important points of a client's communication and then feeding these back to the client so the client knows the therapist is following her.

For instance:

Client: Today, after I woke up, I went shopping for food and called my boyfriend to see if he wanted to come over. He said that he was too busy tonight but that we could get together tomorrow night.

The content of what the client said was:

- She woke up today.
- She went shopping for food.
- She called her boyfriend.
- She asked if he wanted to come over.
- He said he was busy.
- He asked if she wanted to meet tomorrow.

In this case, the therapist would not want to restate everything the client said because not everything is important to the reasons why the client is in therapy. The main points the client was trying to relay in this example were that she called her boyfriend who couldn't come over tonight but wanted to come tomorrow night. Unless the client is coming to therapy because of issues of sleeping too much (perhaps if dealing with symptoms surrounding depression), it is not important to relate back to the client that she woke up. The food shopping also does not seem to be the primary issue going on (unless the client has been dealing with issues of not taking care of her basic needs). Thus, a paraphrase for the client's statement could be, "You called your boyfriend today so that you might spend time tonight, but since he was busy, you arranged for tomorrow night."

When paraphrasing, therapists take in what the client said and then, using their own words, state back to the client what they heard. Sometimes therapists will use the client's own language, but generally they will want to frame it themselves. This allows clients to hear how other people are hearing them.

Building Paraphrases

There is no one set way of developing and building paraphrases; they can take many different forms. They should not be overly formulaic as they would then not fit the therapeutic interviewer's usual way of communicating. Paraphrases should be a natural outgrowth of how the therapist communicates, but geared toward this specific context, counseling. However, there seems to be a general way of preparing them. Poorman (2003) identified four stages to building an effective paraphrase response:

1. The therapist remembers the client's communication.
2. The therapist identifies the content of the communication.
3. The therapist puts the client's communication into the therapist's own words.
4. The therapist relays this understanding back to the client.

Exercise 5.1 Identifying the Main Points of a Client's Statement

For the following client statements, write down what the most significant points are of the client's communication.

1. I think my husband is having an affair. I walked into his home office the other night, and he quickly closed a window he was working on at the computer. His face flushed, and he was acting very odd. When I asked him what was going on, he said, "Nothing." I know that something was going on.
2. Why does he keep bothering me? My brother never lets up on me. Yesterday, he called me stupid and said that I'll never pass fourth grade. Just because he's two years older than me, he thinks that he's better than me. I'm going to pass fourth grade! I should tell Mom and Dad that he's picking on me.
3. Last week, my friends and I were driving around in one of my friend's cars. We had been drinking a little bit, and my friend really shouldn't have been driving. When we went to park at the fast-food place, my friend hit a parked car. He then drove away, but I could see that it did a lot of damage to the other car. I feel bad that I was involved with that. My parents asked me how the evening went, and I told them nothing big happened.
4. I have a cat, Boots, who I've had for eighteen years. She's been really sick lately so I took her to the vet. The vet did all sorts of tests and told me that Boots has late stage kidney failure, which she said was the number one killer of cats. She then said Boots only has a couple of days left to live and wanted to know if I wanted to put her to sleep. I don't think I could put her to sleep. I want her to pass away at home, with people who love her.

The particulars of developing and presenting a paraphrase back to a client are a bit more difficult. They entail an understanding of context, not only in the client's communications but also between therapist and client. Therapists pay attention to the main points of the client talk and relay back their understanding of this. Further, this interchange is housed within the larger frame of a therapist-client interview. Thus, proper paraphrases occur based on client talk, therapist perception, therapist personality, and what has occurred so far in the therapist-client relationship.

General and Specific Paraphrases

When therapeutic interviewers paraphrase, they can try to encompass everything the client has stated in a general manner or can give the specifics of the client's communication. Each way of paraphrasing provides the client the sense that the therapist is following along. The specific paraphrase clearly articulates that the therapist is getting the "nitty-gritty" of the client's story, while the general paraphrase conveys that the therapist is getting the "gist" of the message.

Exercise 5.2 Constructing Paraphrases

For the following client stories, identify the main points of the story, put the story in your own words, and construct a paraphrase to state to the client.

1. My girlfriend told me last night that she wants to start to see other people. She thinks that three years is long enough in this relationship and that she wants to see what else is out there. I am thinking of breaking up with her because I don't want to have one of those types of relationships where the person doesn't want to be with you.
2. I saved up for three years to put a down payment on a house. When the hurricane hit this year, it wrecked a lot of my apartment, and I had to pay a lot out of my pocket. My roommate then moved out, leaving me to handle the brunt of the bills.
3. All my life I've wanted to be a doctor. But my grades were never good enough. I thought maybe I would be a science teacher. But I just can't see myself teaching for the rest of my life. I'm looking into physician's assistant school or maybe radiology technician.
4. My parents are going through a divorce now. When I'm at my father's house, he asks questions about my mother, like if she is "spending time" with anyone. When I'm with my mom, she doesn't want to hear anything about my father.
5. My band finally got a gig. When I got up on stage, I just froze. I couldn't remember the chords for the first song, and I made a bunch of mistakes. Everyone in the band was mad at me at the end of the performance.

If a therapist only utilizes general paraphrases, clients might feel belittled that their full story wasn't being taken into account. If a therapist only utilizes specific paraphrases, clients might be slowed down because the therapist would be doing a significant amount of talking and focusing on all of the details of the client's story rather than the main direction of the story. As with all skills discussed in this book, too much use of any one skill can become awkward and slow the flow of the interview.

Therapists should use both general and specific paraphrases during a therapeutic interview to allow the client to know that the details are being understood while the big picture is also heard. However, there is not a clear distinction of when to use one versus the other. Both should be utilized. Perhaps one rule of thumb is that, when the client expresses something the therapist deems as very important, the therapist should consider using a more specific paraphrase.

People want to know that others have a good sense of their whole story while also paying attention to the fine details. The following example illustrates the differences between a general and a specific paraphrase.

> *Client:* Can things get any worse? Today, I woke up and stubbed my toe on the way to the bathroom, the hot water was not working for the shower, I cut myself while slicing a bagel, I got caught in traffic for an hour and was late for work, and then at work I forgot to bring in the report that was due.

After work, I got takeout for dinner, and after I drove away, I realized that they gave me the wrong order.

Therapist: Wow, it seems like it was a rough day. (general paraphrase)

Therapist: You stubbed your toe and cut your hand. Traffic was so bad you were late for work, and to boot, you left a work project at home. Then to top it off, they gave you the wrong food order. (specific paraphrase)

As can be seen, there is a big difference between the level of depth given between the general and specific paraphrase. Therapists can vary the level of depth to match what they think the essence is of the client's story—that part of the story that is most important and will help the client move forward toward her goals. (Do Exercise 5.3.)

Nonjudgmental Paraphrases

Therapists listen to the client's story and try not to be judgmental. Being judgmental would be taking one side versus another. Judgment can be made against the person(s) the client is talking about or about the actual client. When a therapist, even in a subtle way, provides a judgmental paraphrase, the therapist might give the client the wrong message that he agrees with her when he actually does not or that what the client is doing is wrong.

When a therapist paraphrases with a judgment agreeing with the client, the client may think she is right in the way she thinks and that the therapist supports this. For instance, consider the following exchange:

Client: I loaned Stacey a book. She said that she lost it. I'm not sure I believe that, but she hasn't offered to buy me a new one.

Therapist: Stacey lost the book she borrowed from you, or maybe even something more than lost, but now won't buy you a replacement.

Here, the therapist has implicitly agreed that Stacey might be engaged in some type of shady business surrounding the book. A nonjudgmental paraphrase might look like the following:

Therapist: You let Stacey borrow a book and now you're not sure what is going on or whether she will reimburse you for it.

Although it is a subtle difference between these two therapist responses, in the first one, it is assumed that Stacey lost the book and isn't replacing it. In the second

Exercise 5.3 General and Specific Paraphrases

For each of the client statements in Exercise 5.1, provide a general and a specific paraphrase.

response, there is more ambiguity about Stacey's position, as she is not there in the therapy room to make her position known.

Therapists can help avoid judgmental paraphrases by assuring that clients know that the response, and the therapist's understanding of the situation, is the client's understanding of the situation rather than the therapist's. This can be fostered through certain phrases such as the following:

- In your mind
- For you
- You think that
- It seems to you
- You get the sense that

Here are some examples:

- "In your mind, your wife is the one with the problem, not you."
- "For you, he's not treating you the way you think he should."
- "You are finding that your boss is asking a lot of you recently, and you think that she is too demanding."
- "It seems to you that he should take your thoughts into consideration more."
- "Things have been kind of different at work, and you get the sense that the upper administration is planning something."

Although the use of these types of phrasings can help to provide a nonjudgmental paraphrase, it does not ensure that the client will hear it the way it was intended. Therapeutic interviewers should be attuned to when clients may be receiving a message in ways that might not be helpful for them.

Exercise 5.4 *Keeping the Paraphrase Nonjudgmental*

For the following client statements, create a paraphrase that captures the main points, while also maintaining a nonjudgmental stance.

1. My girlfriend had to sabotage my computer. All my files are gone—the important files that I needed for my dissertation. I think she's upset because I was flirting with another girl last week.
2. My child is out of control. She sneaks out of the house every night, and I think she is having sex with boys. She's making my life miserable.
3. I got reprimanded today at work. But I really didn't do anything. My boss was rambling on and on, so I asked him what the point of his talk was. He wrote me up for having an "attitude." He's such a jerk.
4. I can't believe my mother is so controlling. I brought home this guy for her to meet. After ten minutes with him, she brought me in the kitchen and told me he wasn't right for me and that I shouldn't see him again. The nerve of her!
5. I couldn't sleep last night. My neighbors are so disrespectful. They had a party last night and were blasting their music all night long. What's wrong with them that they're so inconsiderate?

Rating Paraphrases

Therapists, no matter how good they are, are not always accurate when constructing a paraphrase. Although it is usually more difficult to construct an accurate reflection of feeling or meaning, building an appropriate paraphrase takes hard work from the therapeutic interviewer. Therapists should continually try to gauge how well they understand the client's messages and how well they are helping the client move toward her goals. Young (2005) provided a quick means of assessing the effectiveness of a therapist's paraphrase. He utilized a depth scale that is based on -1, 0, or +1. A paraphrase of -1 actually moves the client to a more superficial discussion, away from the main points of why the client has come to therapy. A paraphrase of 0 shows that the therapist accurately rephrased the content and thoughts. A paraphrase of +1 demonstrates that the therapist has heard the unsaid part of the client's statement and relayed this back to the client. The following dialogues exemplify each of the levels.

–1 Paraphrase

Client: My father told me off last night. He said he is tired of me not working or contributing to the house. But I just can't seem to get a job.

Therapist: Things don't seem to be going your way.

0 Paraphrase

Client: My father told me off last night. He said he is tired of me not working or contributing to the house. But I just can't seem to get a job.

Therapist: Your father and you had an argument last night about you not contributing as much as he wants you to.

+1 Paraphrase

Client: My father told me off last night. He said he is tired of me not working or contributing to the house and that I was pushing my luck with him. But I just can't seem to get a job.

Therapist: Although you are trying to get things going, it seems that it isn't at the level that your father is expecting from you. This has been a huge issue between you and him for a while.

Connecting Paraphrases with the Basic Conversational Skills

Paraphrases do not occur in isolation. They are just one part of the therapeutic interview. We have already discussed how to start an interview and ways to keep the conversation moving. Paraphrases build on the foundation of connection made between therapist and client to move the client to a deeper level of expression and experience. They are designed to allow the therapeutic interviewer to keep track of

Exercise 5.5 Rating Paraphrases

Rate the following paraphrases on the depth scale of -1, 0, or +1.

1. *Client:* My husband doesn't listen to me. I've asked him a hundred times not to leave dirty dishes in the sink, yet he still leaves them there. I'm ready to pull my hair out of my head.
   Therapist: It seems like this is the same thing over and over, telling him but him not listening to you.
2. *Client:* I got into a car accident this morning, nothing major. But it made me very late for work. When I finally got in, my boss asked to talk with me. She said that I "wasn't dependable" and that she was letting me go.
   Therapist: You were late and now you have been fired.
3. *Client:* Things must be changing for me. I went to this music concert the other night. It was awesome, thousands of people there, all rocking out together. I actually met someone there, and she and I are going to go out next week.
   Therapist: It sounds like your life is taking a different, more positive direction than in weeks past.
4. *Client:* At my construction job, I was using the circular saw. Some idiot bumped me from behind and my hand hit the saw. My pinky was cut off, and now I have to go to a lot of surgery and have tons of rehabilitation.
   Therapist: Some guy bumped into you at work and injured you.
5. *Client:* My children are out of control. One was just arrested for killing a cat in the neighborhood. The other was suspended from school for getting into a fight. My daughter is thirteen and having sex with boys. I wish I could just leave and go somewhere alone.
   Therapist: It sounds like all of these troubles are attacking you at once and you're not sure how to cope with all of it.

the client's story and to inform the client that the therapist is following along and understanding. When this occurs, the therapeutic alliance is strengthened.

Once the therapist has begun to join with the client (remember that joining is a continuous process throughout the whole of therapy), a conversation occurs about the particular issue(s) that brought the client to therapy. Therapists use door openers to get this conversation going. While a client begins telling her story, the therapist uses verbal and nonverbal minimal encouragers to let the client know the therapist is following along and to probe for more information. When the client has provided sufficient information for the therapist to understand the what, who, how, when, and where of the client's story, paraphrases can be used to reassure the client that the therapist is following along. They can also be used to let the client know that she can go to deeper levels of her experience. The following therapist/client exchange demonstrates all of these components put together:

Emma (Therapist): Welcome to therapy, Barry. We didn't get a chance to talk much over the phone when you were setting up the interview. Could you tell me a little about yourself? (*beginning of the joining process*)

Barry (Client): Well, I was born in St. Louis but really grew up in Kansas City. I'm an accountant, have a wife and two children.

Emma: How old are your children? (*Continuation of joining*)

Barry: One is seven and the other is five.

Emma: What's it like to have two young ones? (*continuation of joining*)

Barry: It's great. They are both girls and I love them to death. I just wish I could spend more time with them.

Emma: Yes, it can be tough when work and home life collide. (*general paraphrase*) You mentioned it briefly on the phone, but could you talk about the concerns that led you to make this appointment? (*door opener*)

Barry: Well, for some time now, I haven't felt satisfied in my life. I'm an accountant, and I think I'm good at what I do, but it isn't really fulfilling.

Emma: O.K. (*minimal encourager*)

Barry: I don't want to be doing this for the next twenty years.

Emma: Tell me some more about that. (*minimal encourager*)

Barry: I'm bored in my job.

Emma: Talking about boredom, what about in other areas of your life? (*door opener*)

Barry: It's tough for me to say, but I'm a bit bored in my marriage.

Emma: You've been finding that in your work life it is not as rewarding as you would want it and have also been finding that some of those feelings are in your marriage. (*specific paraphrase*)

Barry: Yes. I haven't told my wife, but I think she can sense something.

Emma: Go on. (*minimal encourager*)

Barry: We used to laugh a lot together and be playful with one another. Now, it's pretty much work and kids and there isn't much romance between us.

Emma: Your relationship with your wife has switched from playfulness to something that sounds like you think it is more mundane. (*paraphrase*)

Barry: Yes.

Use of Metaphors

Therapists have been using metaphoric language from the very first therapy session in which a therapist tried to understand a client's experience (Wickman et al., 1999). The use of metaphors in therapy can be a very powerful way of understanding and relaying back to the client the therapist's perception of the client's situation. Metaphors produce a vibrant picture that can pique a client's interest and ensure the client knows the therapist has a good grasp of the situation. Therapist use of metaphors can also enhance the therapeutic alliance (Stine, 2005). The

Exercise 5.6 Connecting Paraphrases and Basic Conversation Skills

For the following client/therapist dialogue, supply the appropriate type of response for the therapist.

Client: This is the first time that I've ever come to a therapist. I'm not sure what I'm supposed to be doing.
Therapist: (*Provide a joining response*)
Client: Well, I'm sixty-three years old. My husband passed away three years ago. I'm retired. I was a school teacher.
Therapist: (*Provide a joining response*)
Client: I love children. They kept me young all of these years.
Therapist: (*door opener*)
Client: I'm just feeling really down lately. I don't think I would say I'm depressed, but I'm definitely not happy.
Therapist: (*minimal encourager*)
Client: It's been like this for the past year or so. I thought it might be grief about my husband's passing away. We had been together for thirty-three years. But it's been three years since he passed away, and I think that I should be over it by now.
Therapist: (*paraphrase*)
Client: Yeah, my friends are trying to set me up with people to go on dates with, but I kind of don't want to.
Therapist: (*minimal encourager*)
Client: I don't think I want to start a relationship with someone else right now. Most of these guys are older than me. I already buried one husband. I don't want to start feeling for someone else and then have to bury them.
Therapist: (*paraphrase*)

metaphors used between therapist and client become a symbolic shared language between the two.

Metaphors have been used in poetry to get across emotions that might be harder to explain in a straightforward manner. To express being in a stagnating relationship, someone might say, "It's like flotsam in the ocean, bobbing up and down, but going nowhere." This would actually be a simile (a comparison). The person might also express this as a metaphor, "This relationship is a really long and slow torture." For the purposes of this book, we will use metaphor, simile, and analogy interchangeably and discuss them all as metaphors.

Metaphors can be initiated by either the therapeutic interviewer or the client. When therapeutic interviewers can connect with client-generated metaphors, they join with and speak the language of the client, with the reflection resonating more clearly with the client. This allows the therapist to be more empathic and respectful. Therapeutic interviewers can also generate metaphors, which can also enable the client to experience the discussion more vividly. Wickman et. al. (1999) stated,

Exercise 5.7 *Constructing Word Pictures/Metaphors*

For the following client statements, construct a paraphrase that presents the material in the form of a word picture.

1. Today, after getting off of work, I went down to the beach. I sat there watching the ocean for hours, trying to figure out what to do with my life. The path I'm on does-n't seem to be getting me anywhere. I'm miserable at my job and not having a rela-tionship.
2. My boyfriend broke up with me again. This seems like the same pattern we go through. We are great for a couple of months, then something happens where he gets upset and breaks up with me. Two weeks later he comes back and apologizes and we get back together. I can't seem to get out of this pattern.
3. My boss called me in to her office today because she said she needed to talk to me. She sat me down and went over all of the things that I did this year that have helped the company. She thanked me for my dedicated service and gave me a raise. I'm really proud of myself for doing such a good job.

"This use of metaphor, created by the counselor, does not change a client's prob-lems; rather, it changes perception of the problem and allows for solutions as yet unconsidered" (p. 389). DiGiuseppe and Muran (1992) cautioned that therapists and clients will not always share the same meaning about what is being connected by the metaphor. Therapeutic interviewers should be cognizant of how the client is reacting to the metaphor and whether it seems to be understood by the client.

Metaphors can be thought of as word pictures. These paint pictures for the other person in the interchange, more vibrantly relaying information. One of the benefits of using metaphors is that they connect the current experience to under-standings and experiences that people have had previously (O'Hanlon, 1987).

Here are some examples of how therapists can use metaphors with clients:

Client: My parents said that I either have to get a job or get out of the house. I went out today to look for a job, but nothing interested me. I looked in the newspaper, but all the job ads were blah.

Therapist: It's like you were floating down a river with no interesting docks, but you knew that your boat was slowly sinking and you had to dock soon.

Client: I don't know what I'm supposed to do. I have to work to keep food on the table for my family. I have to take care of my parents because they are getting older. My younger sister is having problems with drugs, so I'm trying to help her out. And at work, they expect me to do everything.

Therapist: It's like you are trying to juggle five different knives and there seems to be too many of them and they are starting to slice you and give you pain.

Client: I think I'm a pretty nice person. That's how I view myself. But sometimes I do some pretty mean things. I can't believe that I do things like that.

Therapist: It's as if you are looking in the mirror but the reflection is someone who you don't know.

Advanced Reflecting Skills

Advanced reflecting skills serve multiple purposes in a therapeutic interview. They require more skills of the therapeutic interviewer than the basic reflecting skills of minimal encouragers and paraphrasing. Although they will be discussed in this chapter as somewhat isolated skills, good reflections cannot be constructed without the use of all of the microskills previously discussed. Further, these skills need to be integrated into the person of the therapist. They are all simply techniques; however, once the therapist brings himself into the therapy room, these skills assist in conducting an effective therapeutic interview. Reflections, when given from a genuine stance, greatly assist in the progress of therapy.

Reflection of Feeling

As discussed previously in the chapter, paraphrasing the client's story allows the client to know the therapist is following along with the facts of the situation. When clients do not think that the therapist understands the *what* of the situation, they tend to continue to explain it until they have a sense that the therapist *gets it*. After reflecting the content of the client's statements, there is greater room to explore the depth of the client's experience. At this point in the process of therapy, the therapeutic interviewer has joined with the client, opened up room for the client to discuss the concerns bringing her to therapy, and has used minimal encouragers and paraphrases to allow the client's story to unfold. The next step in the process is to reflect the emotional content of the client's communication. By reaching the feeling level of the client's discourse, client and therapist can both try to achieve a richer understanding of the client's contextual frame for the problem.

Defining Empathy

Empathy is the combination of accurately reflecting content, feelings, and meanings, along with a therapist mind-set of perceiving the client's phenomenological worldview. Most theoretical orientations hold empathy to be an integral component of the therapeutic process. Empathy can be conceived as being able to perceive, understand, and experience what the client is experiencing, however, the therapist understands that these are not his feelings, but rather the client's. Carl Rogers (1951), who perhaps more than any other therapist espoused the importance of accurate empathic understanding, provided an explanation of how the therapist will need to decenter himself socially so as to understand the client's phenomenological frame:

> It is the counselor's function to assume, in so far as he is able, the internal frame of reference of the client, to perceive the world as the client sees it, to perceive the client himself as he is seen by himself, to lay aside all perceptions from the external frame of reference while doing so, and to communicate something of this empathic understanding to the client. (p. 29)

The exercises in this chapter are designed to help the therapeutic interviewer to move closer to understanding the client's frame of reference and relaying this back to the client.

Empathy is an extremely important process on many levels of the therapeutic encounter. Empathy is useful to the client, the therapist, and the therapeutic process. Johnston, Van Hasselt, and Hersen (1998) provided the following description of the usefulness of empathy: "(a) assists in building the client-therapist relationship, while providing support to your client, (b) encourages client response and exploration, (c) assists the therapist role by providing methods to clarify client response, and (d) provides the foundation for the use of other interventions" (p. 48). By providing the client with an accurate empathic understanding, the therapist conveys an attitude of connection and acceptance that helps the client.

Empathy can be broken into two complementary aspects; one internal, the other external. The external aspect is more overt in that the reflection not only of the content, but also more importantly, of the client's feelings and meanings is given back to the client. The second level of empathy, the internal aspect, refers to a mind-set of the therapist. It consists of being able to understand another person's internal experience. These two complementary aspects can be seen as the technique and attitude of empathy. The skills and techniques presented in this chapter are a building block to begin to develop the therapeutic interviewer's own style of relating to clients. Having a beginning guide with which to come in contact with clients aids the therapeutic interviewer to focus on what is going on for the client.

Empathy in Practice

Although the ideas behind accurate empathic understanding may seem easy, they tend to be difficult to put into practice. Therapeutic interviewers need to continuously assess if they are in the proper mind-set to utilize their listening skills. This entails listening to the client in a way that not only the overt story, feelings, and meanings are heard, but also those that are underneath the surface, hinted at, or not yet recognized. The client's underlying messages should come forth in the conversation.

Empathy is more than just saying the words involved. It is an attitude on the part of the therapist. Turner and Hersen (1987) explained that "interviewers must communicate to clients that they *understand* how they feel, that they *appreciate* their frustrations, and are *fully aware* of the intricacies of their lives" (p. 17). Therapists must "be present" during a therapeutic interview to be able to connect to the material and processes occurring in the therapy room. There is a difference between emotional empathy and cognitive empathy (Young, 2005). In *emotional empathy,* the therapist gains an understanding of what the client's feelings are and responds to the client so that this understanding is known. In *cognitive empathy,* the therapist gains an understanding of the values, worldview, and intentions of the client and responds so that this understanding is known. This chapter will discuss the specific techniques of how to respond once the therapeutic interviewer is connected to the client's experience. Therapeutic interviewers should continually monitor their own attitude in terms of how present they are in the therapy room so that the skills of reflection develop through a genuine stance.

One of the difficulties of empathy is when and how much to use during therapy, especially during the first session(s). An effective therapist will be able to gain a depth of understanding rather than just doing the skills, especially in the early stages of therapy (Carkhuff & Berenson, 1967). These authors suggested that too much empathy in the beginning of the therapeutic relationship might overwhelm the client. They also suggested that it might be possible for the therapist to use too little empathy, which would then decrease the amount of psychological tension necessary for a client to use in the process of change.

Curiosity

As we've seen, the skill of reflection is linked to the attitude of the therapist. Most therapists come into the field of counseling because they are curious about how they can be helpful to other people. Curiosity is a very important skill for a therapeutic interviewer. In this book, curiosity relates to the therapist's interest in what is going on for the client at the present moment. This curiosity should not be confused with voyeurism. The latter is finding out information to justify a need within the therapist that is not designed to help the client. For instance, if the client stated, "You'll never guess what sort of perverted act my husband wanted to do last night," the therapist might want to know what the perverted sexual act was to satiate his own curiosity. However, knowing this information is probably not as important for the client as exploring how she felt about the husband wanting to perform the act and what that says about the relationship for her.

Curiosity can be a very good thing. The therapeutic interviewer should be curious about how the current situation makes sense for the client. This is a very important goal for the therapist (perhaps one of the most significant): to get to the point where it makes sense *for the therapist* that *the client* is thinking, feeling, and behaving in the ways that she is, regarding the situation. The therapeutic interviewer does not have to agree with the client's beliefs, behaviors, or feelings, but should understand how these make sense for her. When therapists reach this point, reflections will better hit the mark and therapeutic interventions will have a greater likelihood of being useful.

The skill of reflection is one means of contributing to the quality of the therapeutic relationship. If a therapist continuously reflected just the content, the client would be able to tell her story, but she would not be able to get to the more mean-ingful parts of the discourse. These are the parts that lead to change. Content is readily available in most people's conversations. People will talk about what they did, who they did it with, when they did it, how they did it, when they think they'll do it again, and so on. However, it is when therapists reach the point of understanding how the client is impacted by what occurred that change can more readily happen.

Content and Feelings

A wife tells her husband, "I love you." A friend tells another friend, "I love you." A child tells her doll, "I love you." A woman tells her cat, "I love you." A daughter sits in front of the tombstone of her mother and says, "I love you." A husband, in an exasperated voice, tells his wife, "I love you!" Each of these scenarios contains the same exact words, but a different *expression* of feeling, which leads to a differ-ence in the way in which the sentence is meant and perceived.

Within each utterance a person makes, there are multiple levels of expres-sion. There is the *content* of what is said, the *feeling* that the person has about the content, and the *meaning* of what it says about her as a person that she felt this way about this situation. The content is usually the easiest of the levels to ascertain. The feeling level is the next difficulty level to understand. The meaning level is the hardest level to perceive and can usually be reached only after gaining a better understanding of the context of the situation and the person. The distinction between content and feelings is similar to that between the cognitive (thoughts, ideas, beliefs) along with the behavioral (what someone did) versus the emotional aspect. The distinction between feeling and meaning is similar to that between what the person felt about what happened and why they felt this way. One of the first skills that a new therapist will need to master when conducting therapeutic interviews is to be able to move back and forth between the content and feeling levels of communication. Exercise 5.8 provides practice on distinguishing between the content and feeling levels of communication.

Being able to detect the differences between the content and the feeling levels of communication is one of the first steps to gaining an understanding of the per-ceptual and phenomenological world of the client. It takes skill to gain a sense of what is going on for the client on the multiple levels of complexity in a client's world. Therapists put a lot of effort into trying to gain as full an understanding of the client's perspective as possible. It usually takes years of practice to be able to work at the multiple levels.

What Are Feelings?

What exactly are feelings? Feelings are our emotions along with our ability to experience an emotional arousal. One of the keys to reflecting feelings is to be able to grasp the client's feeling(s) and respond to the client with an understanding of her emotional experience. Clients may not be fully aware of how they are inter-

Exercise 5.8

In the following statements, decipher what the content of the client's statement is along with the feeling that is attached to it.

Example: The doctors say that my child has autism. I'm not quite sure what that is, but it doesn't sound good.

> *Content:* Child was diagnosed with autism and parent does not fully understand the diagnosis.
>
> *Feeling(s):* Confused and scared

1. I had to have dinner with my family again, even though I didn't want to. I don't know why I keep on saying yes to them. All they do during dinner is berate me about being a waitress and not going to school.
2. For some reason I can't understand, I keep doing this same thing over and over again. I've tried to stop. But every time I pass by the bar, I can't seem to not go in. And when I'm in the bar, I can't not drink.
3. I think I might have a sexually transmitted disease, and I don't know what I'll do if my blood test comes back positive. Would anyone else ever want to have sex with me again?
4. I just found out my wife has been cheating on me. I'm thinking of divorcing her.
5. I sat down with my partner the other day, and he and I worked things out, finally. I really think that we've gotten things back on a good track.
6. My partner has been physically abusing me, and I think he'll keep doing it. I know I bring it on myself because I keep harping at him to get a better job and stop drinking.
7. I haven't been able to get out of bed for a week, and I'm not sure if that's normal. This is the worst that things have been, and I'm starting to think that something is really wrong with me.
8. I have been dating this woman for six months now, and I really think that this relationship can work out. I've been disappointed in relationships in the past, but I have a certain feeling about this one.
9. I just buried my husband after thirty years of marriage. He had a heart attack, and I don't think that my life will ever be the same. He was not only my husband, but my best friend.
10. My son has been bullying other kids in school, and I think this might impact his schooling. The principal is saying that if he does it again, he will dismiss him from the school.

nally or externally emoting. Many people can let you know some of their surface emotions, such as anger, happiness, and sadness, yet they may have difficulty moving beyond that and getting in touch with the nuanced way they are experiencing their emotions. Gordon (2001) suggested that "people are conditioned almost from infancy to think of feelings as bad and dangerous—enemies of good human relationships" (p. 81). In most professions, people are trained to put aside their "feelings" and operate based on cognitions rather than affect. This is especially true for males, where expressing feelings—especially fear, sadness, and anxiety—can be signs of weakness. Thus, many people might have learned not to express their feelings to another person. This makes it even more important for therapeutic interviewers, in a safe environment, to connect with clients' feelings.

Why might some clients either not be aware of their feelings or be hesitant to discuss their feelings with the therapist? Family background, culture, and/or gender may play a role in the expression of feelings (Young, 2005). People from some cultures, such as Asian, may be hesitant to go to a therapist, or if in therapy, not be as emotionally expressive as people from other cultures, such as Hispanics. Regarding gender, many men may base their emotional expression on the "cowboy syndrome," believing that they have to always be strong. Men following this gender role may feel that they are weak when they express emotions—especially those regarding fear, doubt, and loneliness.

There are many ways to respond in a reflection to let the client know the therapist heard the emotive expression. When the client provides her own feeling word, the therapist then has a choice of using this word in the reflection or choosing a different word. A rule of thumb is for the therapist to take the essence of the client's feeling and put it into his own words. However, there are times when it is more powerful to reflect the exact (or close to exact) wording back to the client. For instance:

> *Client:* I am just so angry, I can't believe it.
>
> *Therapist:* You are very angry.
>
> *Client:* Yes, I can't believe he did this to me.
>
> *Client:* This is such an awful feeling. I am completely depressed.
>
> *Therapist:* You are completely depressed.
>
> *Client:* Yeah, it is so overwhelming.

However, using the client's words too often in reflections might lead the client to perceive this as disrespectful. Clinicians define this as mirroring. Too much mirroring can be harmful for the therapeutic relationship. Clients will then become aware that the therapist is using "techniques" on them instead of "being" with them. Repeating clients' words in too many reflections does not move the client to gain a richer and deeper sense of self. Further, it usually alienates the client from the therapist. Thus, using the client's own words should be done sparingly, when the therapist believes that it will have the most impact in the therapeutic interview.

Intensity Levels of Feelings

If using the client's own words too often can hamper what is occurring in the therapeutic interview, how might a therapist move around this and be helpful to the client? The therapeutic interviewer is one person in an interchange between two people. Thus, the therapist should be bringing something to the table himself. The therapist's own way of understanding clients is important. One thing that new therapists will need to do is to start practicing changing the words of the client into their own words. Thus, the therapeutic interviewer will be acting like a thesaurus, taking in the client's language and transforming it into his own language while still maintaining the essence of the communication.

To do this, therapists will want to find feeling words that are close to the client's expressions and experiencing. In the process of reflecting, there are three levels of intensity: higher, lower, or equal intensity. Each level can be used therapeutically to raise or lower the emotionality for the client. The following exchange shows how a reflection can be slightly altered by changing the intensity of the feeling being reflected:

> *Client:* I am angry about what happened.
> *Therapist:* You are perturbed about what occurred. (lower intensity)
> *Therapist:* You are mad about what occurred. (same intensity)
> *Therapist:* You are furious about what occurred. (higher intensity)

Each of these responses moves the client in a certain direction. The lower intensity reflection attempts to lessen the severity of the client's response. This is used when the therapist intuits that the client is overstating what is going on for her. The same intensity reflection attempts to get the client to focus further in the place that she is in. The higher intensity reflection pushes the client to take a step further to connect to a stronger emotional experience. The level of intensity the therapist uses is dependent on the context of the client's statement. One thing that therapists should keep in mind is that feelings tend to be transitory (Gordon, 2001). People do not maintain a certain feeling indefinitely; there is fluctuation in the intensity of feelings throughout each day of people's lives. People connect better with what is going on for them when another person accepts and responds to their feeling. The person will usually deintensify the feeling when someone engages in empathic understanding. For instance, a client might come into a session saying, "I'm so upset at my wife, I could choke her." The therapist can connect with that initially intense feeling and respond back to the client, perhaps with "You sound like you are extremely angry with her." The client might then come back with, "Yeah, I don't want to divorce her or hurt her, but this has really annoyed me." When people feel heard and listened to, they tend to be able to process their feelings and thus not be as dominated by them as they might be if the feeling wasn't processed and was allowed to boil over.

Based on what the client has said previously, the nonverbal way in which the response is said, and the therapist's own intuitive sense, the therapeutic interviewer will use a level of intensity he believes best matches the client's truest intentions. Table 5.1 presents how feelings can be understood at various levels of intensity.

There are times when clients might overstate or understate what they are feeling. Therapists can help clients better articulate their inner experiences by

TABLE 5.1   *Intensity Levels of Feelings*

Feeling	Lower Intensity	Same Intensity	Higher Intensity
Happy	content pleased glad	cheerful joyful delighted	ecstatic exultant blissful
Sad	down blue low	upset unhappy glum	miserable depressed dejected
Worried	bothered apprehensive	nervous concerned	anxious scared
Hopeful	encouraged rosy	optimistic positive	buoyant confident

reflecting the appropriate level of intensity of the feeling. Sometimes, in the beginning of therapy, therapists might tend to "play it safe" and shoot for a lower intensity so they do not make more out of a problem than the client is actually experiencing. This is an especially important tactic when the client is very hesitant to express feelings. When the therapist gets the sense that a client is willing, but for some reason unable to fully get in touch with her feelings, he can raise the intensity by reflecting at a higher intensity level. Carkhuff and Berenson (1967) held that it is the therapist's ability to move the client to ranges not fully explored that is the key to therapy. They stated that a therapeutic interviewer's goal is "movement to levels of feeling and experience deeper than those communicated by the client, yet within a range of expression which the client can constructively employ for his own purposes" (p. 27). Exercise 5.9 provides an opportunity to practice working at the three levels of emotional intensity.

Designing Reflections

One of the first steps in designing reflections of feelings is figuring out what the various feelings are that the client is experiencing. Sometimes clients will express multiple feelings at a time, depending on the length and complexity of their communication. Therapeutic interviewers do not need to reflect every single feeling the client expresses. By highlighting what seems to be the primary feeling(s), therapists are getting to the essence of the client's experience. The key is to try to figure out what the *main feeling* is that the client is trying to express. Once this occurs, the therapeutic interviewer has a therapeutic decision. He must decide how much reflecting the other multiple feelings will assist the client.

Exercise 5.9

After each word in the list, choose a corresponding feeling word that is (a) at a lower intensity, (b) at the same intensity, and (c) at a higher intensity.

Example: happy

>Lower intensity: upbeat
>
>Same intensity: joyed
>
>Higher intensity: elated

>1. angry
>2. revolted
>3. lonely
>4. anxious
>5. embarrassed
>6. guilty
>7. depressed
>8. surprised
>9. fearful
>10. disappointed

The following exchange is an example of choosing the feeling that is most salient to the core of what the client is trying to express.

>*Client:* This day has really sucked. Some idiot cut me off and then at work, I forgot to bring in the report that I was working on. Everyone in the meeting knew that I didn't have it.
>
>*Therapist:* It seems that was quite embarrassing for you, not having the report at the meeting.

The client mentions being angered at a person who cut her off, but the embarrassment at work seems to be the essence of what the client is talking about. Highlighting the annoyance of someone cutting her off would probably not add as much

Reflection 5.1

How aware are you of your own feelings? Which types of feelings tend to be more on the surface? Which take a bit more time to get in touch with? What types of things evoke more feelings for you? Set aside one day and do a feeling journal. Periodically, throughout the day, check in with yourself and write down what you are feeling at that time and what prompted that feeling. At the end of the day, take some time to reflect on how you are impacted by the feelings that you had.

intensity to the disappointment in self of forgetting the report. On other occasions, therapists might want to reflect the multiple feelings:

> *Client:* I waited all weekend for a friend to call me. I don't know why I didn't try to call someone. I wish I was a different person sometimes.
>
> *Therapist:* You were lonely this weekend, which led to you feeling disappointed in yourself for not making a more active effort at connection.

In this example, the client's two feelings of loneliness and disappointment are equally important to her experience. Leaving either one out would not let the client know that the therapist has a full grasp of what she is going through.

Within clients' communications, especially when they are very talkative, therapeutic interviewers will need to hear their full discourse and decipher which material is of the highest priority, medium priority, or not fully relevant to the therapeutic endeavor. Not everything the client says in the therapeutic interview is relevant to what brought them to therapy. Clients might talk about how they felt during a movie they went to, while eating at their favorite restaurant, or while watching their favorite television show. Although these might be important to talk about for joining purposes, they usually do not add to the depth of personal exploration in the interview. Exercise 5.10 provides an opportunity to prioritize the importance of the different feelings a client conveys in communication.

Responding with Reflections

The first step in the reflection of feeling process is getting into tune with the client's experience—how the client is currently feeling about the situation. The second step is for the therapeutic interviewer to let the client know that her emotional position is understood. This is done by taking the client's communications (both verbal and nonverbal) and communicating these back to her. The most basic way of doing this is to use the following phrase, "You feel _____." Exercise 5.11 provides the opportunity to formulate basic reflection of feeling responses.

The emotions identified by the therapeutic interviewer allow the client to know that the therapist is in tune with her. However, therapists can take a step further by connecting the client's feeling with the situation that prompted those feelings. A standard when learning how to reflect feeling is to use the following phrase: "You feel _____ because _____" where the first blank would be a feeling word and the second blank would be the content related to why the client feels as she does. For example, if a client said, "I've just had it up to here with the way my parents are treating me," a reflection could be, "You feel frustrated because you don't think your parents are treating you right." As with all therapeutic responses, too frequent use of this wording could become a detraction from the therapeutic process. New therapists might practice this phrasing in the very beginning of their training to improve their skill at detecting and responding to content and feelings; however, they should try to augment the various ways in which they word reflections. As with all therapeutic maneuvers, they should be genuine. Exercise 5.12

Exercise 5.10

For the following client statements, figure out what the various feelings are that the client is expressing. Then rank these in terms of the significance/importance of each of the feelings based on what the client is saying.

Example: I came out to my parents yesterday. They freaked. They said they didn't want a son that was a "fag." I thought they would handle it better than they did. I had more faith in them than that and they let me down. I don't want them to think bad of me. I don't. This is who I am and I'm happy with who I am. It's upsetting when people say stupid things to me and do nasty things to me, like spit at me.

Feelings: Contentment (with self)
Disappointment (in parents)
Anger (at the people being discriminatory)

1. Yesterday, I found out that I was not accepted to graduate school. I knew that I wasn't a sure bet to get in, based on my g.p.a. and GRE scores. However, I thought I had an excellent vita in terms of research and extracurricular activities. I only wanted to go to this one school, so that was the only one I applied to. I know that if they accepted me, I would be a really good graduate student. I am much more motivated now than I have been in the past. I don't think I can tell my parents. I just don't want to see the looks on their faces.

    Feelings: _____

    _____

    _____

2. Things with my husband haven't been going that great. We've been married for seven years and at first, things were good. However, over the last three years, we've pretty much drifted apart. I'm not quite sure how much I want to reconnect. But my religion says that divorce is not right. And then at work I have been flirting with someone. I look forward to going to work because I finally feel that spark again—just not with my husband. At times when I'm flirting with this other guy, I don't think too highly of myself.

    Feelings: _____

    _____

    _____

3. I've been picked on in school this past year by this bully, Derek Morse. Almost every day he pushes me, calls me names, and steals my money or something from my backpack. He's bigger than me and I think that he'd hurt me if I tried to stand up to him. I don't want to tell the principal because they usually don't do anything anyway. I would tell my parents, but they already think poorly of me. I guess this just goes to show that I'm a loser.

    Feelings: _____

    _____

    _____

Exercise 5.11

For the following client statements, reflect the main feeling of the response by using the phrase, "You feel _____."

Example: I can't seem to stop drinking. Although I want to stop, I seem to always wind up with a beer in my hand.
  "You feel frustrated."

1. I'm not really good at anything. Nobody likes me. At times, I don't even like me.
2. My house just got foreclosed on. Now I have nothing.
3. Although relationships haven't worked out for me in the past, I think that this one will be different.
4. When I got up in the front of the room to do my presentation, I couldn't remember anything. I flubbed the whole thing in front of all those people.
5. I was hoping that my friend would help me out this week. I really needed her help. She told me she would call me back, but she never did.

provides an opportunity to practice phrasing reflections in the "You feel _____ because _____" format.

Ownership of Feelings

Some people have a tendency to talk in a way that does not fully own their feelings. They might say things like "Most people get angry when they're fired" when they are angry about being fired or "One wouldn't want to talk to one's mother like that if one didn't want to have an argument" when they are upset at how their

Exercise 5.12

Respond with a reflection of feeling in the "You feel _____ because _____" format for the following client statements.

Example: I failed another class and I'm getting kicked out of school. I thought I could pull my grades up, but I guess I didn't do as well as I thought.
  "You feel disappointed because you thought you could improve your grades."

1. I don't think that she'll go out with me. Every time I try to talk to her, she goes to find someone else to talk to.
2. Things seem to be going my way today. The doctors say that they are releasing me from the locked unit in two weeks.
3. This shouldn't be the way that things are. I lock myself in my room all day and I miss contact with people.
4. How could this happen? When I got home from work today I found that my dog had died. I loved that dog.
5. I'm going to tell my parents this weekend that I'm gay. I think they'll take it pretty badly, but I want to be honest with them.

child is talking to them. Virginia Satir (Satir & Baldwin, 1983) called this the communication stance of the super-reasonable or the computer. Through this communication stance, people intellectualize their situation rather than experiencing their emotions. One possible reason for this is that the feeling is too overwhelming for them, so they push emotionality to the side and try to intellectualize. In this way, they will not be hurt by their emotions.

Reflection of feelings is extremely important to starting the process of acceptance and ownership. A rule of thumb with someone who tends to intellectualize rather than emote is to start reflections with a lower intensity level. Reflecting at too high an intensity level, the client might be too overwhelmed and not be able to connect those feelings to self. Starting at a lower intensity level allows room to shift to a higher intensity level, if that higher level intensity is more appropriate for what is going on for the client.

When the therapist reflects the feeling of the client's statement, the client can experience the reflection to check in with herself and see if the reflection is accurate and fits. If it does not fit, the client will let the therapist know.

> *Client:* I don't know about this new position. I'm not sure I'm ready.
>
> *Therapist:* It sounds like you're feeling anxious.
>
> *Client:* Not exactly. It's more like I am feeling scared rather than anxious.

Here, although the therapist attempts to relay his understanding of the client's experience, he is a bit off target. It is acceptable to not be accurate, as long as the therapeutic interviewer is willing to really hear the client and attempt to get a better sense of the client when she states that the reflection is not quite on target. With more practice listening to clients, the therapist will make fewer errors.

When the therapist articulates feelings that might not be as overt to the client as they are to the therapist, the client can then take time to explore her own perspectives. This gives the client the space to delve into topics and feelings she has probably not explored in the depth that she is during the therapeutic interview. Sommers-Flanagan and Sommers-Flanagan (1999) described this process as interpretive reflection of feeling. They defined these types of therapist responses as "feeling-based statements made by interviewers that go beyond the client's obvious emotional expressions. The goal of interpretive feeling reflections is to uncover client emotions" (p. 90). In order to produce productive interpretive reflection of feelings, the therapeutic interviewer attempts to read into the client's narrative and gain a deeper sense of how the client might be feeling at the present time. This is done by the therapeutic interviewer understanding the context of the client (age, race, gender, sexual orientation, ethnicity, socioeconomic level, and so on) and trying to put himself into that position to see what he thinks that person would be feeling. Consider this example:

> *Client:* I don't think I want to be with my wife anymore. I can't stand her. I can't take going home at night knowing that I'm going to have an argument with her.

>*Therapist:* You're angry at your wife and frustrated at having all these arguments with her.
>
>*Client:* That's right. Why does she keep attacking me?
>
>*Therapist:* I get the sense that there is something more going on for you. Maybe it is that you are disappointed in how things are working out in the marriage.

Here, the first therapist reflection is a basic reflection of feeling based on the client's first statement. The second therapist reflection attempts to take a step forward and go for a deeper level of feeling of the client.

This distinction can be viewed in terms of primary and advanced levels of empathic understanding (Egan, 1994). At the primary level, the therapeutic interviewer is able to gain an understanding of what the surface feelings and meanings are for the client and let this understanding be known to the client. At the advanced level, the therapeutic interviewer not only understands the surface emotions and feelings, but also can go beyond these to the more hidden and unknown. The interviewer then provides a reflection or statement that lets the client know that her worldview was understood.

It is important to use both basic reflection of feeling responses and interpretative reflection of feeling responses. Combined, these types of responses allow the therapist to help a client gain a better understanding of what she is presently experiencing. Sometimes, having someone else give us feedback about how we are coming across, along with the deeper layers of what we are expressing, allows us to explore that feeling in a greater depth.

Phrasing Reflections

There are many ways to phrase reflection of feelings. A key is to vary the reflections so the therapist is not reflecting in the same way every time. The client would pick up on this tendency, and it could start to hamper the connection made between the two. As stated previously, in the beginning of training, new therapists may be using more of the formulaic ways of responding in their reflections. This is perfectly acceptable. By practicing how to do some of the standard reflections, therapists are also learning how to tune themselves in to the story, feelings, and worldview of the client. Once this skill becomes part of the normal behavior during a therapeutic interview, therapists will not have to think about what words to use; they will just flow. A therapist's typical way of speaking will come out so that a more genuine two-person interchange occurs. In the meantime, here are some other ways of phrasing reflections:

- "It seems that . . ."
- "I hear that you feel . . ."
- "(Feeling) seems to be a big issue for you right now."
- "This makes you (feeling)."

- "You get anxious when test time comes around."
- "Fear seems to be the major thing for you right now."

Another way of constructing reflections of feeling is to word them in the first person, as if the therapist is the client. For instance, the client might state, "I can't seem to make a connection with my mother. She has always been distant to me, and I have always wanted to please her." The therapist could then reflect, "Although I have tried to connect with my mother, I'm frustrated that I can never really be close to her." Using this voice for reflections comes when the therapist is truly "in there" with the client and focusing totally on the client's perspective. There is a potential to offend the client if this type of reflecting is taken as a therapeutic ploy instead of a true attempt to "get in there" with the emotional experiencing of the client.

Statements or Questions

Reflections are therapeutic interviewers' understandings of client statements and meanings. Based on the context in which clients express themselves, therapeutic interviewers perceive certain overt and covert feelings, ideas, and meanings. When reflecting these perceptions back to the client, therapists should use a more declarative tone rather than a questioning tone. For instance, if a client stated, "I don't even want to go out of the house anymore because I don't know what people would think of me," the therapist, hearing this, can reflect back, "You are hesitant to leave your house because you're embarrassed how other people will view you." At the end of the reflection, the therapist can keep his tone constant or raise the inflection to signify a question. Reflections should be declarative statements of the therapist's understanding of the client; there should not be a raised inflection at the end.

A questioning tone at the end of reflections tends to imply that the therapist does not quite understand everything the client is saying and needs further clarification. Although it does represent an attempt by the therapist to understand the phenomenological world of the client, listening and responding in sentences rather than questions allows the client to know the therapist is following along in the conversation. Therapeutic interviewers also own their reflections by making them as statements rather than questions.

Paraphrase or Reflection

Reflections differ from paraphrases in that paraphrases focus on the content (story, thoughts, ideas, beliefs, situations), while reflections focus on the feelings the person experienced. Most people are comfortable talking in the content realm of communication. We tell each other the stories of our lives all the time. When we first meet someone, we might tell them where we were born, what type of work we do, what our favorite music is, and other such details. However, we tend not to tell them how we feel about the type of work we do, what we are currently angry about, hopeful about, scared, and so on. Being able to distinguish between the content and the feeling of a response is an extremely important skill. The more therapists can hear the multiple levels in the client's communication, the better the chance that they will be able to address the client's most pressing concerns. Building from this skill, therapeutic interviewers should also be able to provide both paraphrases and reflections of feeling. The more they can distinguish between the two and operate comfortably at both levels, the more options are available to work with clients. Exercise 5.13 is good practice in distinguishing between the two.

Reflection of Nonverbal Feelings

Clients are overt and covert in their expression of feelings. Sometimes they will be forthright and on target with how they are feeling. For example, the client might state, "I am very angry at my son today." The feeling is there and present and the client is aware that she feels this way. Sometimes the feeling is more hidden. If a client was in a romantic relationship and the other person broke up with her, she might state, "Well, I don't think I would have done it so harshly." This gives the therapist a clue that the client was hurt by the ending of the relationship.

Exercise 5.13

For the following client statements and therapist responses, choose which therapist response is a paraphrase (content) and which is a reflection of feeling. Answers are at the end of the chapter.

1. "I had the worst day in years. I'm being evicted from my house and I don't know where I'll go."
   a. You're scared because your future is uncertain.
   b. You have to move out of your house and you aren't sure where you can go.
2. "My parents refuse to talk to me anymore. They say they're tired of bailing me out of jail. Maybe they're right about me and that I'm no good."
   a. Your parents have helped you in the past with troubles, but not this time. And now you're thinking about if you agree with them.
   b. You seem to be a bit disappointed in yourself.
3. "I sat home alone on Saturday. No one called me. I didn't call anyone."
   a. You stayed home and didn't talk to anyone.
   b. It sounds like you were lonely.
4. "How long will I have to keep on grieving. It has been six months since he died and I'm still crying every day."
   a. You're concerned that this feeling will stay a long while.
   b. After what seems like a long time for you, you are still having the effects of the death.
5. "I told Becky that I couldn't stand being around Susie. Then Susie came to me saying that Becky told her what I said. I can't believe Becky would do that."
   a. You told your friend a secret, and she told the other person what you said.
   b. It seems like you're angry that your confidences were betrayed.

Reflection 5.2

Think about your own personal theories of what certain nonverbal behaviors mean. What attributions do you make when a person keeps her head tilted down? Continuously plays with her fingers? Has a quivering voice? Bites her lip? Quickly kicks her legs? What might be some alternative explanations for each of these behaviors?

The therapist can also pay attention to how a client behaves in the therapy room. People's nonverbal behaviors are a form of communication. As Watzlawick, Bavelas, and Jackson (1967) explained, a person cannot not behave. Further, all behavior is a type of communication. This means that a person cannot not communicate. Thus, a therapist should be cognizant of the nonverbal expressions of the client and then attempt to determine how these nonverbals complement or contradict the verbal messages the client is expressing. Being aware of the internal and external experiences of the client allows therapists to better come into contact with the client's full experience.

As with verbal responses, some nonverbal behaviors are easier to read than others. For instance, if a client comes in with red puffy eyes and tear streaks down her face, the therapist can assume that the client is upset about something. Although there might be other reasons for the nonverbal behaviors (perhaps eye allergies or having recently been sprayed in the face with pepper spray—yes, a bit extreme, but there are varying explanations for behaviors), therapists make the best guess of what is going on for the client based on the information they have at the present moment. Yet therapists should think of their understanding of the client's perspective as an hypothesis. Hypotheses can be wrong. The therapists' job is to continuously try to hone hypotheses to try to be as accurate as possible. However, accuracy tends to be determined by the client, not the therapists. Therapists should check in with their client to see if their understanding of the client's experience is accurate. This can be accomplished through perception checking:

> *Therapist:* Jim, I'm getting the sense that this situation with your friend is really getting you to question your definition of loyalty. Does that sound right for you?

Further, being aware of nonverbal signals that clients give while delivering a reflection is important to therapists in gauging how accurate they are. Behaviors such as head nods, "mm-hm"s, and shaking of the head give clues as to whether the therapist's interpretations of the client's worldview and experiences fit the client's own frame.

When a client turns away from the therapist, lowers her voice, pulls her arms in to her body, or does any of a million other behaviors, these might be clues for the therapeutic interviewer of how the client might be feeling at the moment. If the discussion in the session is about a past trauma and the client's body starts to curl into a ball, the therapist might get a sense that the client is having a difficult time thinking or talking about this. The therapist can reflect, "This is still upsetting you today, right here."

Keeping the Focus on the Client

When telling their stories, many clients have a tendency to shift the focus away from how what happened impacted *them* to what *other people* did to cause them to behave or feel in the way they are in the present. If the therapist followed this lead, much time would be wasted on complaining about a third person. This does not enable the client to explore how whatever the other person did is impacting her. Thus, it is the therapist's job to keep the client focused on herself.

The client comes into the therapeutic interview, usually discussing what those around her have been doing that she does not like. A skilled therapist will hear beneath this level of content to what the client is experiencing at the moment. Imagine a ball of dough on a kitchen counter. The baker rolls out the dough and then folds the ends back into the middle to start the process over. If the center of the dough is the client's internal experience (feelings and meanings), clients tend to roll the dough out to the periphery (a focus on other people). The therapist then takes what has been talked about in terms of other people and brings it back to the client. By continually folding the dough back into itself, the therapist pushes out the complexities of the client's situation and provides for a richer and deeper process. For instance, take the following therapist–client interchange:

> *Client:* I can't believe my boyfriend, after three years of being together, decided that he wants to see other people.
>
> *Therapist:* Your boyfriend wants to see other people.
>
> *Client:* Yes, he says that he needs to experience life more than he has. He says that he's been stifled and that by dating other people, he'll be able to grow.
>
> *Therapist:* He's not content in the relationship and thinks that there is more for him out there.
>
> *Client:* I don't know how he can do this. Yes, he was in a five-year relationship before we started dating, so he hasn't been on his own in eight years. But still.
>
> *Therapist:* You think that he hasn't been independent in a long time.

This conversation is moving further and further away from how the situation is impacting the client toward talk about a third person, her boyfriend. Instead of keeping the client in the here-and-now, the talk in the conversation is speculation about why this third person is operating in the way that he is. Even if a conclusion is made, that third person is not in the session to receive this feedback.

Although this might be helpful to the client in terms of her being able to vent, it is not really productive in getting the client to explore how she thinks and feels about the situation. Here is the same conversation, with greater focus on the client's experience:

> *Client:* I can't believe my boyfriend, after three years of being together, decided that he wants to see other people.
>
> *Therapist:* This seems to be a shock to you.
>
> *Client:* Yeah, I thought things were going well. But he told me that he's been stifled and that by dating other people he'll be able to grow.
>
> *Therapist:* It seems as if you felt good in the relationship, that things were going in a positive direction. Now, you are confused as to what happened.
>
> *Client:* How can we have been together so long and had such different experiences in the relationship? I thought I was treating him so well.
>
> *Therapist:* You are feeling upset because you seem to want this relationship.

Through keeping the focus on the client, the client is able to focus more clearly on how she is being impacted by what the other person is doing. The therapist and client could spend the whole session talking about what the third person did and how it was bad, wrong, inconsiderate, selfish, and so on. Yet, all of these things are impacting the client in some way.

During the course of the therapeutic process, when the therapist has provided reflections that keep the focus on the client, clients tend to stop talking about other people and begin focusing more on what is going on for them. This inward focus helps move the client toward an internal locus of understanding and evaluation rather than an external perspective. Exercise 5.14 (page 126) provides practice in developing reflections that keep the focus on the client.

Reflection of Meaning

The first two levels of a client's statement are content and feeling. Usually, clients want to know that the therapeutic interviewer has heard their story first before they are more open to exploring how they felt about that situation. The third and deepest level of client statements is that of meaning. Meaning expresses how the client views herself based on what happened and what she felt about what happened. This tends to be the most important level to work at because when meaning is explored, the client has a richer and deeper sense of herself. Change is more likely to occur through the meaning level. Ivey and Ivey (2003) explained, "If you help your clients find a *why* through exploration of meaning, they will often find their own *how* or way to achieve their objectives" (p. 282). However, it takes time in the therapeutic interview to gain a good sense of the client and the importance that the situation and her reactions to that situation have for her. This requires listening

Exercise 5.14

For the following client statements, provide a reflection of feeling where you keep the focus on the client instead of a third party.

1. I'm fed up. I can't take living with Sylvia any longer. She leaves her stuff all over the house, never offers to clean, and plays her music too loud.
2. I'm worried about my sister. She just broke up with her boyfriend and she has been locking herself in her room all day and night. She cries all the time and doesn't seem herself.
3. Frank's parents keep on yelling at him. He tells me that he can't do anything right in their eyes. Every time he tries to help out, they yell at him for doing something wrong.
4. He did it to me again. I don't know why he keeps on calling me up and asking me out and then breaking the date. People said he was a bit flaky.
5. My daughter has another cold. I took her to the doctor, but they can't figure out what is wrong with her. I made another appointment at a new doctor for her for tomorrow.

to what is occurring below the level of the client's statements. Reik (1968) defined this as "listening with the third ear."

Reflection of meaning gets to the essence of why the problem is significant for the client. At this level, the client gains a better sense of what is going on for her. The meaning level can be understood through associated terms such as values, beliefs, unconscious motivators, and making sense of things (Ivey & Ivey, 2003). There are two main ways of getting to the meaning level of client experience. The first is a straightforward approach in which the therapist asks the client what the meaning is for her. Some possible questions would be, "Why is this so important for you?" "What does this mean to you, that this is going on?" and "How do you understand yourself based on what occurred?" Sometimes the client can explain how the situation is meaningful. However, people usually are not aware of the meanings they are dealing with, so the therapist needs to be extremely skilled at listening to the unsaid and making it more overt. This is where the therapeutic interviewer might have to take a step, or two, or three, ahead of the client and base his perceptions on intuition and therapeutic hunches. When reflecting meanings, it is important for the therapist to be somewhat hesitant in case his intuition does not resonate with the client.

Meanings of clients are tied up in their worldviews and values (Young, 2005) as well as in significant events that have occurred in their lives (Ivey & Ivey, 2003). Clients have a sense of who they are that is usually based on a story they have created regarding their place in the world. Young delineated four different perspectives that client worldviews might take. The first is their *view of self*. Clients may think they don't deserve to be treated well, that nothing right will happen for them, that they shouldn't even try because they'll only fail again, or some other type of story that then filters into how most situations they encounter impact them. The second perspective is a client's *view of others*. They may have a sense that "women cannot be trusted," "adults are out to get you," "skinny people look down on overweight people," or some other such notion. The third perspective is the belief about the *environment or the world* in general. This can usually be gleaned from people's phrasings, such as "It's a dog eat dog world," "You have to fend for yourself," and "One step forward leads to two steps back." The last perspective is that of *values*. These are usually grounded in a notion of what "should be." For instance, clients might think that you should always "turn the other cheek" or you should never betray another person. Based on what the client's worldview is (and clients have a countless variety of worldviews), the therapist has a better sense of why whatever is happening is significant for the person.

One way of trying to decipher what the meaning is for someone is to keep asking yourself, "Why is this important to her?" When exploring someone's meaning in this fashion, the answer to why is usually in the content of what happened. Therapists will then need to ask themselves this question again. The next answer is still probably content. This process needs to continue until the therapist arrives at the meaning level. For instance, take the situation of a client who is debating whether to break up with his girlfriend because he is Jewish and she is Catholic and his parents have told him that they would disown him if he married her. In trying to assess the meaning, the therapist might think that it is the client being torn between staying in a relationship with someone he loves and breaking up with her because of his parents' desires. This explanation is only at the content and feeling levels. If the therapist asks himself, "Why is this important to the client?" he might come to the understanding that the client wants to have a happy marriage. This still stays at the content level, although it is movement away from the specifics of what happened toward what the person wants and desires. Another round of asking about the importance is necessitated. This might lead to an understanding that this is important to the client because he holds "family" very dearly. The situation then leads to a major difficulty in that he is trying to determine how to develop his own family while also respecting the wishes of his family of origin.

When reflecting back the meaning to the client, therapists can use phrases similar to that of reflection of feelings, using the same reflection base, "You feel _____ because _____," where the first blank is a feeling word and the second blank is why it is important for the client (what it means for them). This does not have to be the only way that meanings are reflected back to clients. As always, therapists should alter their style throughout the interview so that they do not become too predictable or redundant. Here are some examples of therapist reflections of meaning:

- You feel frustrated because you had put so much into this, thinking that this would show everyone that you are not a failure.
- This situation is so overwhelming to you because you want so much to be a good father and don't think that you are being one.
- The end of this relationship is devastating for you, since you never thought you were pretty enough or good enough. And now, this guy has left you for

someone else and you are thinking that this is confirmation of what you had thought.

- For you, being who you are and still being accepted is extremely important. You want so much for people to respect you for who you are.

Putting It All Together

The skills discussed so far in this book are used in conjunction with one another to provide a means of contacting clients, allowing them to tell their stories, and then getting them to focus more deeply on their own experience and how they are

Exercise 5.15

For the following client statements, decide what the client is saying about him- or herself (the meaning of the client's statement).

1. All my life I have wanted to be a doctor. My parents have told me that is their dream for me. I went through undergraduate as a pre-med major to become a doctor. I got into medical school and started; however, I don't really like it. I know I would make a lot of money and be respected. But I don't think I would respect myself. In college I took some classes in engineering and that seemed to really mesh with me. Yet, I think if I told my parents I want to quit medical school, they'd kill me.

2. I went away on a business trip to Las Vegas and went to the casino. Did you know they give you free drinks while you're playing? So I played and drank. And drank and played. I don't remember how much money I lost, but when I woke up in the morning, there was some strange woman in my bed. I woke her up and told her to leave. Then I looked down at my wedding ring. I've always been faithful to my wife and thought of myself as a good husband. I don't know what I'm going to do now. I don't even remember what happened, I was so drunk.

3. Growing up, I was always an outgoing person. I had tons of friends and felt connected. Then I moved away to college and something happened. I couldn't find a group of friends to get in with. I lost touch with my friends at home and now I feel very alone. I always thought I was an extraverted person, but now I'm having a very different view of myself and I don't think I like who I am becoming.

Exercise 5.16

For the client statements in Exercise 5.15, provide a reflection of meaning.

being impacted by everything. There is a general pattern that can be used when practicing the microskills of empathy:

1. Start with a door opener.
2. Use minimal encouragers to get the story going (and to keep it going throughout the whole of the therapeutic interview).
3. Begin with paraphrasing the content of the client's talk.
4. Reflect the feelings the client brings up.
5. Reflect the meaning for the client.

However, this pattern should not be followed so strictly that it becomes a rule. The therapist might start with a reflection of feeling, based on whether the client goes in that direction from the start of the interchange. Or he might start with many minimal encouragers if the client is quite talkative and has a lot of content to talk about. Further, he will want to move back and forth between content and feeling, fleshing out the client's story through use of minimal encouragers (and possibly questions, which will be discussed in Chapter 6). One of the last parts of this process is to reflect the meaning of the client's contents and feelings. The following is an extended transcript demonstrating how a therapeutic interviewer can use all of the skills presented to work with a client:

Omar (therapeutic interviewer): It has been two weeks since we last talked. What is most pressing for you to talk about today? (door opener)

Tori (client): I guess I'm concerned about my relationship with my mother.

Omar: Okay. (minimal encourager)

Tori: She can be so overbearing sometimes. She tries to control my life.

Omar: Tell me more. (minimal encourager)

Tori: For my whole life, my mother has been trying to direct what I do. I went into law school because she wanted me to be a lawyer, not because I wanted to be one. I've always listened to her, and I'm tired of it now.

Omar: You realize that you don't want your mother to have control of your life. (paraphrase)

Tori: That's right. It's gone on for too long. I'm my own person. I can make my own decisions. I'm twenty-three. Aren't I supposed to be an adult?

Omar: You're frustrated that you are being treated like this. You're an adult now and want to be treated like one. (reflection of feeling)

Tori: Yes, I do. Other people let me live my life, why can't my mother? I feel dominated by her and I've never shown the strength to stand up to her.

Omar: Go on a bit more about that. (minimal encourager)

Tori: Since I was young, I've always wanted to make her happy. Even when she wanted something from me that I didn't quite want to give, I did it for her anyway. But how long do I have to keep giving?

Exercise 5.17

For the following client-therapist interchange, develop a therapist response that will help the client explore the situation more deeply. Base your statement on the type of response requested.

Client is a seventeen-year-old female who is coming to see you in your role as a school guidance counselor.

Therapist: (provide an opener)
Client: Well, I just found out that I am pregnant. I am only a junior and was thinking that I would go on to college.
Therapist: (provide a minimal encourager)
Client: But I don't know what to do now. I told the father of the baby, but he said I should get an abortion, and if not, he doesn't want anything to do with either of us. But I'm not sure I think having an abortion is right.
Therapist: (provide a reflection of content)
Client: Yeah, I'm struggling to figure out what's right. I don't want to think that I killed someone, even if it is a fetus that is only eight weeks in development. Plus, I've never had a surgical operation before. I've heard sometimes after the procedure, you can't have any more children, and I do want to be a mother.
Therapist: (provide a reflection of feeling)
Client: I've always been on the right track. If my parents find out about this, I think they'll kill me. I would kill me if I was my parents. This just isn't like me, to not have protected myself. I thought I did, but not as carefully every time as I should have. I've always been the good girl. Now what will people think of me.
Therapist: (provide a reflection of meaning)

Omar: For the longest time, you've tried to please your mother. Now, it seems like you are making a decision that the person you want to please most is yourself. (reflection of meaning)

Tori: Yes, I want to be happy!

Exercise 5.17 provides an opportunity to practice building a coherent format of fully engaging a client on each of the levels of client experience.

Through using the method of paraphrasing and reflections, clients are provided a comfortable environment to explore more deeply how they are being impacted by the present situation.

Summary

The skills of reflection of feeling and reflection of meaning, in conjunction with paraphrases and minimal encouragers, provide the foundation of therapeutic interviewing. These skills allow clients to connect and feel comfortable with therapists, to explain the story of why they are coming to therapy, to experience how their story is getting them to feel, and most importantly, to become more aware of how they perceive themselves based on everything discussed in the session. Therapists need to learn reflecting skills so that they become second nature. Therapists can then build on these skills to work with clients in the most effective manner. Not every theoretical orientation utilizes this process to contact and engage clients. Yet, as a foundational skill that transverses most, if not all, therapeutic approaches, this format allows therapists and clients to explore client issues in depth.

Exercises

1. Go to your university or public library and find as many psychotherapy/counseling videos as you can. Watch the videos with a notepad/computer in front of you and write down the exact wording the therapist uses for opening skills, minimal encouragers, paraphrases, reflections of feeling, and reflections of meaning. Compare how the various therapists word their responses and see which therapist resonates most with your own style.

2. With two partners from class, role-play a first session between a client and a therapeutic interviewer. One person role-plays the therapist, one person the client, and a third person acts as a judge. The therapist should use opening skills, minimal encouragers, paraphrases, reflections of feeling, and reflections of meaning. However, there should be no questions asked. The third person might have a buzzer to use if the therapist does ask any questions.

3. Have someone role-play a client while you conduct a therapeutic interview. Record the interview and then transcribe the interview using the following format. Write what the client said. Stop the tape and then write what you think the client was *really* trying to say to you (the main essence of the client's statement). Then play the tape and transcribe what you said. Stop the tape and write a new and better response once you really think about the client's main point.

Answers to Exercise 5.13

1. a. reflection of feeling
   b. paraphrase

2. a. paraphrase
   b. reflection of feeling

3. a. paraphrase
   b. reflection of feeling

4. a. reflection of feeling
   b. feeling

5. a. paraphrase
   b. reflection of feeling

6

Questions and Goal-Setting Skills

Asking Purposeful Questions and Developing Collaborative Therapeutic Goals

So far in this book, the emphasis has been on *not* using questions during the therapeutic interview (outside the realm of joining and perception checking). This is because there are many other ways to establish a therapeutic relationship with clients in order to help them explore their own perceptions about problem situations. This chapter addresses the use of questions in therapy and will present different types of questions that can be helpful during the therapeutic interview. Questions will then be explored to see how they can help therapist and client develop mutual goals.

As discussed in Chapter 1, one of the main components of interviewing is the use of questions and answers. Different theories employ specific questions unique to them, while others might not utilize questions at all. This chapter is designed to provide the therapist with an overview of the potential use of questions, regardless of theoretical orientation. Although it might seem easy to ask someone questions, it is actually harder than first thought. Because of their potential pitfalls, questions should be used in moderation during an interview. Donaghy (1984) suggested that only 20 to 30 percent of the interview should be spent on questioning.

Questions in the Therapeutic Interview

Why Use Questions?

Questions can be an important component of the therapeutic interview. They help get the client to give information or to think about issues being discussed. Questions enable the therapist to gain enough information to make an effective assessment of the client's issues (Ivey & Ivey, 2003). Questions can also impact the level of rapport between the two people in the interview. This usually happens during the joining stage of therapy. People like to know that the other person is interested in them. Interest is conveyed by asking questions about the other person and being curious. Questions can also help clients gain information about themselves that they forgot or never knew (Donaghy, 1984).

On first thought, it might seem that questions should be the mainstay of the therapeutic interview; however, this is not the case. One problem with questions is that they tend to be overused. To make matters worse, therapists tend to use them without purposeful inquiry. When novice therapists work with clients for the first time, or during role-plays in classes, they tend primarily to ask questions. These questions, although coming from a place of curiosity, tend not to be very therapeutic. This is because the curiosity is sometimes not as client-focused as it is therapist-focused. The therapist is more interested in the story than how the client makes sense of the story. Here is a typical interchange that I hear from my beginning students during the first role-play we do in class (in which I ask them, without any direction, to have a first session with a client):

> *Student Therapist (ST):* What would you like to talk about?
>
> *Mock Client (MC):* I'm having some problems with my girlfriend.
>
> *ST:* What sorts of problems?
>
> *MC:* Well, she is kind of friendly with other guys.
>
> *ST:* Do you mean she is flirting with other people?
>
> *MC:* No, not really. Just that she's a nice person and talks to a lot of people. Since she's attractive, a lot of guys come over to talk to her.
>
> *ST:* Do you love her?
>
> *MC:* Yes.
>
> *ST:* Does she love you?
>
> *MC:* Yes.
>
> *ST:* Then what is the problem?
>
> *MC:* I don't like it.
>
> *ST:* How does it make you feel when you see her talking to another guy?
>
> *MC:* My stomach turns over.
>
> *ST:* So you're jealous?
>
> *MC:* No, I'm not jealous. I just don't like it. I don't know why she has to talk to everyone.
>
> *ST:* Have you talked to her about not liking it?
>
> *MC:* Yes.
>
> *ST:* And what did she say?

MC: She said that it's just part of her personality and that I should trust her.

ST: Do you trust her?

MC: Yes.

ST: Then what is the problem?

MC: I know that she's not doing anything, but it just bothers me.

ST: Have you had a girlfriend in the past who cheated on you?

MC: Not that I know of. Rationally, I know that it shouldn't bother me. She loves me. She's not talking to them to try to hook up, but for some reason I just can't get past this.

ST: What have you tried to get past it?

After teaching an introductory foundations of interviewing class many times on both an undergraduate and graduate level, I have found this conversation is not only typical, but also almost the rule. Deviance from it comes when the student has had some previous training in counseling skills. As can be seen from this transcript, the therapist is quite detached from the client's perspective. The questioning is used to try to get to the meat of the issue without a way of connecting to the client and connecting to the story in a coherent fashion to open it up for exploration. Further, the student's personal biases tend to come through (that is, assuming that the problem might stem because of a past girlfriend who cheated on him).

Questions help to make the session seem as if the conversation is moving forward, especially when the interviewer believes it is not moving anywhere. Novice therapists tend to ask clients questions because they are not sure what else they should be saying; they think that if they ask another question and get the client talking, they are being productive. Too much time spent questioning takes away from time moving toward change. Egan (2006a) cautioned that some therapists ask questions as if the goal of therapy is to get information instead of helping the client move toward change.

The purpose of questions, as with paraphrasing and reflections, is to help the therapeutic interviewer better understand the client's worldview while also setting the stage for the client to move toward change. Good questions help both

Exercise 6.1

Conduct a role-play therapy interview with someone acting in the role of a client. From the beginning until the end of the interview, do not use a question. Sometimes we are unable to be as observant of our own words so you might consider doing this in a triad where one person is the interviewer, one the client, and the third pays attention to the therapist to ensure that no questions are being asked. Only use the skills that have been discussed thus far. How was it for you conducting an interview with no questions? What information did you want to know that wasn't addressed during the interview? After doing this exercise, conduct another role-play where you *only* ask questions. What difference did you notice between the two sessions?

client and therapist understand what is going on for the client. Further, they enable the therapist to help move the interview one small step forward toward getting the client to accomplish the goals of therapy.

Functions of Questions

Questions can do many different things during the therapeutic interview. Sometimes they are used to start a conversation, sometimes to end an interview. Other times they are used to infuse humor into the interview. Some therapists use questions as interventions while others use them to perception check. Ivey and Ivey (2003) explained eight major functions of questions during a therapeutic interview:

1. *Questions help begin the interview.*   Most therapeutic interviews begin with a question from the therapist to the client. It is an easy and common way to start an exchange. Clients expect that in the beginning of an exchange, the other person will ask them what it is they want. Think about various service professions and what occurs during the first moments of that conversation. In fast food restaurants, the cashier asks, "Welcome to _____, what can I get you today?" At a doctor's office it might be, "How are you feeling today?" In the beginning of the therapeutic interview, either when the therapist and client first meet, or during a specific interview, there is typically some type of question to the client to check in on the client's status. These usually come in the form of one of the following:

- "What brings you in today?"
- "How can I help you?"
- "How have things been since the last time we met?"

Most of the questions asked in the beginning of an interview are open-ended, intending to give the client room to explore and talk about what he is interested in. However, if the therapist is conducting an assessment interview, more closed-ended questions might be used.

2. *Open-ended questions help elaborate and enrich the client's story.* Open-ended questions, more than closed-ended questions, provide the client room to explain what is going on for him. Given that one of the main components of a therapeutic interview is for the therapist and the client to gain a deep and rich sense of the client's perspective, the therapist needs to ask questions in a way to get to the client's worldview. Open questions, more than closed questions, allow the therapist to do this. Open and closed questions will be explained in greater depth later in the chapter.

3. *Questions help bring out concrete specifics of the client's world.*   Therapists work between a client's general overall experience and the specifics of an individual event. Questions allow a therapist to move back and forth between the two. They aid the therapist in getting to the specific details of the client's life while understanding these within the larger scope of the client's world. Ivey and Ivey (2003) explained that perhaps the most useful question interviewers have at their disposal is "Could you give me a specific example." This could be asked to a client with any type of presenting complaint at any intensity level. Therapists can also ask clients to walk them through how a typical problem cycle happens. Fisch, Weakland, and Segal (1982) explained the type of adequate information they try to obtain from clients, "By 'adequate' we mean information that is clear, explicit, and in behavioral terms—what specific individuals say and do in *performing* the problem and in their attempts to deal with it, rather than general statements or explanatory interpretations" (p. 69). This is what O'Hanlon and Wilk (1987) discussed as "video description," which is an attempt to get the client to relay the facts of the situation rather than the meanings attributed to those facts.

4. *Questions are critical in assessment.* Most assessment and diagnostic interviews are filled with questions, which enable the therapist to gain enough information about the problem context to understand what is going on. Clinicians need to rule in certain potential problems and rule out other potential problems. Questions are a quick way to determine what the clients' primary problem areas are and the duration, intensity, frequency, form, course, and consequences of these. Although an assessment might be able to be made hypothetically without the use of any questions, the process would be extremely difficult and awkward to conduct. For those therapeutic interviewers who conduct intake and assessment interviews, questions are one of the main modes of collecting information. This will be discussed more in Chapter 10.

5. *The first word of certain open questions partially determines what the client will say next.* Therapist and client mutually influence one another. What one says informs what the other says. The question that a therapist asks informs how the client phrases his answer, which then informs how the therapist phrases her next question or response. Ivey and Ivey (2003) explained that *What* questions tend to lead to facts, *How* questions to discussions of sequences, *Why* questions to reasons, whereas *Could* questions give the client more freedom to participate or not and to answer in his own manner. The following therapist responses demonstrate the impact that the therapist's wording has on the client's response:

> *Client:* I know that I've been different for a lot of my life. Some people recently asked me if I'm gay. I didn't know what to tell them. I have been keeping this to myself for so long.
>
> *Therapist:* What has been preventing you from saying something to someone?
>
> *Client:* I didn't want them to hate me.

> *Client:* I know that I've been different for a lot of my life. Some people recently asked me if I'm gay. I didn't know what to tell them. I have been keeping this to myself for so long.
>
> *Therapist:* How do you plan on dealing with this in the future?
>
> *Client:* I don't want to keep restricting myself and feeling bad about who I am. So perhaps I will begin by telling those people who are closest to me.

Client: I know that I've been different for a lot of my life. Some people recently asked me if I'm gay. I didn't know what to tell them. I have been keeping this to myself for so long.

Therapist: Why have you kept this so private?

Client: I don't know if people could accept me. I don't want to lose those people I am close to.

Client: I know that I've been different for a lot of my life. Some people recently asked me if I'm gay. I didn't know what to tell them. I have been keeping this to myself for so long.

Therapist: Could you tell me about what you were thinking when they said this to you?

Client: I was a little shocked. Then a little upset at myself that I didn't tell them.

6. *Questions have potential problems.*   Questions are extremely useful in a therapeutic interview, when they are used properly and effectively. However, many therapists use questions in ways that help to lead to problems in the therapeutic relationship and process of therapy. Questions can lead the client to feel bad about himself. They can also show the therapist's bias. If using too many questions, they can come across as inquisitorial. Questions can also make clients feel defensive. These potential pitfalls of questions will be discussed later in this chapter.

7. *In cross-cultural situations, questions can promote distrust.*   Because the person who uses questions is usually the person in power in a relationship (Ivey and Ivey, 2003), questions tend to put the other person on edge. Depending on the cultural heritages of the therapeutic interviewer and the client, a majority culture therapist might come across as too authoritarian if she asks too many questions to a minority client. This distrust can also happen in situations in which the therapist is from a higher social class than the client or when the client is involved with therapy because of legal troubles. One way to get around this potential problem is for the therapist to use questions in a way that connect with clients, especially for joining and finding out more about that person's culture.

8. *Questions can be used to help clients search for positive assets.* Questions in themselves are not positive or negative, useful or not useful. It is the way in which they are used that leads to their effectiveness. Students who are first learning how to conduct therapeutic interviews tend to ask questions to get to what is going wrong. This is also usually the case in assessment interviews (although a good assessment will cover what is going wrong as well as what is going right in the client's life). Questions do not have to be used solely for finding out what the problem is. They can also be used for finding out what the problem is not. Therapeutic interviewers can use questions to look for the strengths, competencies, and resources of clients. This issue will be addressed in much greater depth in Chapter 9.

Open and Closed Questions

There are two main generic types of questions: open questions and closed questions. Open questions allow room for the client to express himself in the ways that make sense to him. They tend to get clients to talk about the situation and give clients the possibility of exploring the situation at a deeper level. Open questions usually generate a wide variety of information.

Although there are potential disadvantages to open questions, the advantages outweigh them. Most of the questions asked during a therapeutic interview should be open-ended. Since one of the primary intents of a therapeutic interview is to gain the client's perspective, open questions allow the client to express himself in his own words and in ways that he feels are justified.

Open questions are two types: highly open and moderately open (Barone & Switzer, 1995). Highly open questions provide very few restrictions and leave the field very open (for instance, "What would you like to talk about today?"). Moderately open questions tend to have a somewhat narrower focus than highly open questions along with a briefer response from the interviewee (for example, "What about work would you want to talk about today?"). Both of these types of open questions are useful at different points in the therapeutic interview. Highly open questions are good at the beginning of the first or subsequent interviews. Since the therapist does not know what issue(s) the client is coming in with, a highly open question gives the client room to go anywhere.

> *Therapist:* It has been two months since we last met. What is going on for you now?

Moderately open questions are good once the client starts down a certain path, so that the therapist can help structure the interview for the client to stay on that path, but still have freedom to explore.

> *Therapist:* You've been talking about what it was like growing up with a mother who was so controlling of you. What of that situation is still impacting you today?

Closed questions ask for a specific response. Many times, they are a forced choice type of question ("yes" or "no"). They usually do not lead to more depth of focus for the client. However, they are used by clinicians during assessment interviews or other therapy interviews to determine whether something occurred or did not occur or for factual information (for example, "What is your age?" or "Where were you born?"). For instance, if a therapist is assessing a client about suicide, closed questions can be more effective in determining whether the client is suicidal or not.

> *Therapist:* What are your thoughts about suicide? (open question)

> *Therapist:* Are you currently thinking about harming yourself? (closed question)

With the open question, clients can talk about their views of suicide without ever answering whether they are currently thinking about killing themselves. With the closed question, clients are forced into a "yes" or "no" answer, giving the therapist a much better sense of the need of further exploration around this issue. Although the client says "no," it does not mean the therapist should not continue exploring this issue. However, the client's response helps determine how much further into the assessment they should go.

Questions that start off with "Did," "Are," and "Do" tend to be closed questions. "Why," "What," and "How" are usually open-ended questions.

Examples of closed questions:
- Did you react when your boyfriend called you that name?
- Are you willing to make a change in your life?
- Do you ever go outside the house when you are upset?
- When did this problem start?
- Who are you closest to in your family?

Examples of open questions:
- Why are you coming to therapy at this point?
- What are you hoping to get out of these meetings?
- How do you normally react when you are being called those names?
- What sorts of things occur when you are feeling down?

To compare how the same issue can be addressed with open and closed questions, read the following pairs:

- "Are you doing okay today?" (closed)
- "How are you doing today?" (open)

- "Do you get along with your mother-in-law?" (closed)
- "How do you get along with your mother-in-law?" (open)

- "Do you have hobbies you do on your days off?" (closed)
- "What types of things do you like doing on your days off?" (open)

Closed questions are best used when specific information is needed. If the therapeutic interviewer needs to know whether the client is married, a simple closed question, "Are you currently married?" can suffice. Closed questions are typically asked during intake and assessment interviews because these types of interviewing focus more on information gathering than client change. Since they give room for elaboration, open questions tend to be preferred by clients, therapists, and therapy instructors.

Several potential problems arise when many closed questions are used (Hutchins & Vaught, 1997). First, if the therapeutic interviewer starts the session asking several closed-ended questions, the client might think that the therapist will take charge of the whole session. This could lead to the client taking a more passive role in the interview than that of co-collaborator. Secondly, the more that closed questions are used, the higher the probability that the therapeutic interview might come across as an interrogation. Not too many people like question after question being posed to them. Third, closed questions usually do not work well with a client who is not very verbal. This can be especially troublesome with a client who does not fully want to be in therapy, as the following transcript demonstrates:

> *Therapist:* Jim, did you do the homework that I assigned last week?
>
> *Jim:* No.
>
> *Therapist:* Did you think about doing it?
>
> *Jim:* Not really. I forgot.
>
> *Therapist:* Do you want me to repeat what it was?
>
> *Jim:* If you want.
>
> *Therapist:* I'm getting the sense that you're not fully engaged with what we're doing here.

The therapist in this scenario is coming across in a forceful manner. The therapeutic alliance is probably being hurt because the therapist is pushing the client too much in a direction the client does not want to go in the present moment. An alternative way of working with this client could be as follows:

> *Therapist:* Jim, I was wondering what the status is of the homework for you to do this past week.
>
> *Jim:* I didn't do it.
>
> *Therapist:* Okay. What do you think occurred this week that prevented it from happening?
>
> *Jim:* I kind of forgot about it.
>
> *Therapist:* Then perhaps it wasn't the best homework assignment as it wasn't really that memorable. Perhaps we can think of an alternative that catches your eye a bit more.

In this second scenario, the therapist does not force the client into that specific homework assignment. Further, she doesn't make him feel bad for not completing the homework, but attempts to normalize it.

Thus, open questions have a lower probability of being detrimental to the therapy process. One of the biggest skills for a novice therapist is to be able to take a closed question and reword it into an open question before it ever gets asked. Exercise 6.2 provides the reader an opportunity to practice this skill.

Swing Questions

The two main types of questions, open and closed, allow therapeutic interviewers not only to gain information from clients, but also to challenge clients to think about certain issues, while also helping in the joining process. Sommers-Flanagan and Sommers-Flanagan (2003) proposed a third type of question: swing questions. These are questions that can be answered with a "yes" or "no" answer, but are really intended to get clients to respond with a lengthier answer. These questions

Exercise 6.2   *Developing Open Questions*

For the following closed questions, reword them so that they

Example: "Do you want to go to the movies this weekend?" (c

"What are your thoughts on going to the movies this weekend

1. "Are you willing to change?"
2. "Is not being around your stepfather the main thing you want?"
3. "Did you do anything about your depression?"
4. "Do you realize the connection that you and your mother have?"
5. "When did this problem start?"

attempt to gauge whether clients want to answer the question. Swing questions tend to start with "Could," "Would," "Can," and "Will."

- "Could you tell me about what you were thinking when you found out your wife was cheating on you?"
- "Would you talk more about what that was like when you were in that confrontation?"
- "Can you describe what you did when you found out that she had betrayed you?"
- "Will you discuss what you did last week to work on your problem?"

Exercise 6.3   *Distinguishing Open, Closed, and Swing Questions*

For each of the following questions, determine whether it is an open, closed, or swing question. Answers are provided at the end of the chapter.

1. How is your mother feeling today?
2. When is your birthday?
3. Can you tell me about the movie?
4. Did he ever call you for a second date?
5. What was it like growing up in your house?
6. Would you care to elaborate on your perspective?
7. Are you sure that is what she said?
8. Could you tell me more about your cats?
9. Do you still think about your ex-wife?
10. What is a typical day for you at work?

Phrasing Questions

How a question is worded and phrased impacts not only how the client answers the question (if at all), but also the quality of the therapeutic relationship. Poorly worded questions can turn a client off or get them to be defensive. Donaghy (1984) discussed various question-phrasing problems including long, short or precise, double-barreled, negative, sharp, direct, and leading.

Long questions are ones that seem to never have an end. The therapeutic interviewer asks a question that seems to take five minutes to get out. The longer a question, the more chance there is that the client will get lost within the question and be unsure of how to answer it. This is especially true for younger clients. Take the following example:

> *Therapist:* I wanted to ask you a question, because I've noticed now that you tend to do this a lot, and I was thinking that this might be helpful for you to talk about, because when we first met you said that this was an issue for you. So I thought it might be important since it cuts across several areas of your life, and this issue of attachment seems to be key for you, and I was just wondering what you thought about it.

This question is too long and rambles too much. At the end of the question, the client isn't quite sure what the therapist asked.

Short or precise questions seem to be the counterpoint to the long question. These questions are so short or precise that they act like a jab in boxing. Because they are usually not framed properly, they come out of the blue and take the interviewee off balance. Short questions can be something as simple as, "What's up?" This question tends to get a generic response of "Nothing." Precise questions ask the client for such specific information that the client usually doesn't have that information. An example of this type of question is, "How many times during the last year have you felt a bit down?" Clients who have felt down have probably felt that so often that they have no clue about the precise number. They just know that it is much more than they want.

Double-barreled questions are when interviewers ask two questions at the same time. Many people tend to ask double-barreled questions without even knowing they are doing so.

> *Therapist:* How much do you like your teacher and school?

This question actually asks two questions. The first is "How much do you like your teacher?" The second is "How much do you like school?" Clients are put in a tough position when asked double-barreled questions because they are not sure which one to answer. Further, the therapeutic interviewer might have a difficult time fully understanding the client because the client might have responded with something such as, "Somewhat." The therapist now has three options. The client might somewhat like the teacher, but did not answer about school. The client might somewhat like school, but did not answer about the teacher. Or the client might somewhat like the teacher *and* somewhat like the school. The therapist can avoid this potentially ambiguous situation by asking two separate questions:

> *Therapist:* What do you think about your teacher?
>
> *Client:* I really like her. She's very nice and really listens to me.
>
> *Therapist:* How do you like your school?
>
> *Client:* Well, the school itself isn't that great. There are some students there that cause trouble, so I try to stay away from them.

Negative questions use a phrasing that tends to lead to defensiveness in the client. They focus on what is not going well instead of what is going right. Negative questions ask the person about things in a way that addresses what might seem like the "bad" things in life. When asked negative questions, clients may try to qualify their answers since they may not want to take such a firm stance on what is going wrong or what they do not like. The following are examples of negatively phrased questions:

- What's wrong with . . .
- What do you dislike about . . .
- What is your least favorite aspect of . . .

Negative questions should be reworded to a positive. For the questions previously presented, they could be reworded as:

- What is right with . . .
- What do you like about . . .
- What is your most favorite aspect of . . .

Sharp questions use some type of wording that, instead of the jab from the boxer, seem to be a prick from a knife when they are asked. Examples of this type of question follow: "Are you sure about that?" "Would you say you are jealous?" and "C'mon, tell me the truth. What's going on?" Donaghy (1984) recommended that interviewers use qualifiers to soften these questions, such as "might," "perhaps," or "somewhat."

- How might that thought be inaccurate?
- Perhaps there is more to the situation than that?

Direct questions are usually appropriate to ask during the therapeutic interview. Many clients come to therapy ready to talk about what is going on for them. However, there are some clients who come to therapy, perhaps who are court-ordered, shy, or embarrassed, who might be hesitant to answer questions when they are asked in too direct a manner. Therapeutic interviewers can try to ask questions more indirectly if they believe the client is taking offense or being defensive to a more direct line of inquiry.

Reflection 6.1

What type of information about you and your life would you be hesitant or unwilling to divulge to the therapist? How would you feel if someone asked you directly and straight out about your sex life, why your relationships ended, or other such topics? How would you prefer for them to ask you?

Pitfalls of Questions

Although they can be extremely helpful, questions are not always useful in the therapeutic interview. Sommers-Flanagan and Sommers-Flanagan (1999) held that "Questions are the most commonly used and abused clinical interviewing technique" (p. 96). Since many of the questions asked in the therapeutic interview are spontaneous, therapists might not fully think about the implications of their questions. This section explores some of the major pitfalls of questions so that therapists can stay alert to ensure they do not make these or other types of mistakes during the therapeutic interview.

The questions therapists ask should have a purpose. Unfortunately, this does not always occur. Therapeutic interviewers sometimes use questions as a crutch to avoid moving clients into a deeper connection with their own experience. They do not do this on purpose, but when they are unsure of where to go or afraid of the path the client and story are currently on. When questions keep things on a surface level, clients tend not to be moved. One of the problems with this is that when the therapist does not know where else to go in the interview, the next question asked is usually out of desperation instead of a logical movement to help the client move toward his goals. This desperation leads to a question being asked that is probably not going to be useful. It also will be a signal to the client that the therapist is unclear, scared, lost, or anxious.

Another potential pitfall is when questions are asked one after another. When questions are asked in a rapid fire manner, clients tend to be put off and feel like they are being interrogated. A pattern of question–response, question–response, question–response occurs when the client then awaits the next inquiry and provides the appropriate response. The image of a lawyer and a person on the witness stand comes to mind, whereby if the person on the stand is for the opposing side, the questions can seem to be accusatory and interrogational. If the person on the stand is for the same side, the lawyer might come out in what seems to be a nicer tone; however, being up on a witness stand or in a therapist's office is still anxiety provoking.

When therapists ask questions, they come from the therapist's perspective of what will be important to know or important to get the client to think about. Questions are based on the therapist's ideas of what is important and might not mesh with the client's worldview. Thus, some questions might distance the client as the client might not think they are important. This would lead to the phenomena of the client saying, "Why are you asking me about that? I'm here about _____ and you are talking about _____."

Therapists might also infuse their own biases into questions. This is when, instead of asking a question, they actually make a statement. An example of this is when an interviewer asks, "You know, I just had a thought. What would you think if instead of yelling the next time you get mad, you walked into the other room and hit a pillow instead." This is more of a recommendation from the therapist than a question intended to explore a client's perceptions. The "What would you think" at the beginning of the question has a tendency to get lost in the delivery. Therapeutic interviewers can attempt to avoid the impact of these biases by checking with the client at the end of a recommendation. For instance:

> *Therapist:* You know, I just had a thought. Perhaps instead of yelling the next time you get mad, you walked into the other room and hit a pillow instead. What do you think about this idea?

Interviewers sometimes use the question pitfall of "the leading push" (Stewart & Cash, 2003). This is when the therapeutic interviewer suggests to the person what they should answer. This usually occurs based on the vocal inflection the interviewer uses, as in the following: "You really want to get along with your brother, right?" Barone and Switzer (1995) explained leading questions as providing "hints to the interviewee about what answer the interviewer wants to hear or considers correct" (p. 108). The leading question might be the type of question that introduces the most bias into the interview (Donaghy, 1984).

> *Leading question:* You care about your mother, don't you?
>
> *Non-leading question:* What are your feelings toward your mother?
>
> *Leading question:* Are you really looking for love with these different women?
>
> *Non-leading question:* What attracts you to these different women?
>
> *Leading question:* How can you think that it's okay to treat someone that way?
>
> *Non-leading question:* What are your views on how people should be with one another?

Interviewers might also find themselves using the guessing game (Stewart & Cash, 2003). This is when interviewers ask questions in such a way that they appear to be guessing at the answer. Some common examples of this follow:

- Was it the thrill of it that made you cheat on your wife?
- Is your teacher the reason you don't want to go back to school?
- Did you think that she didn't like you?

This type of questioning is done primarily with children, who tend to be less verbal. The problem with the guessing game is that it begins to limit the client's

Exercise 6.4   Correcting Pitfall and Phrasing Questions

For the following questions, identify which type of wording/pitfall they represent and then change them into more appropriate questions. Answers are provided at the end of the chapter.

1. When are the times that you don't want to be around your spouse?
2. What needs to happen here in therapy, after you talking about your anxiety about work and not knowing whether you want to continue on in this career path, so that, when you think back in five years, you are comfortable with what happened to help move your career in the direction that you want it?
3. What seems to be going on at home and at work?
4. You really want to stop doing this, don't you?
5. Why don't you try to keep out of his way the next time he comes home drunk?
6. So, you got dumped by your girlfriend?
7. Was it the yelling that made you want to leave the relationship?
8. How many times have you thought about quitting your job in the last year?
9. What do you think about your performance in this class and how you will do overall?
10. What do you like least about your significant other?

responses instead of opening them up. Also, if the therapist often uses this type of questioning, and is often wrong in her guesses, the client can begin to lose regard for her. Clients do not want to go to therapists who are consistently wrong in their perceptions of what is going on.

Goal-Setting Skills

Once the therapeutic interviewer and client have discussed the issue(s) that brought the client to therapy, they can collaboratively work on goals to make the therapeutic encounter useful. This is one of the areas that distinguishes the therapeutic interview from other types of interviews or talking with friends. When discussing problems with friends, the end result is usually a dictum, which might not fully be what the person wants. For instance, a friend might say, "He cheated on you. Get rid of him" or "Why did she lie about you? Don't ever talk to her again." This result is what the *other* person thinks is best instead of the person with the problem. The advice that friends give is usually not followed because it tends not to mesh fully within the client's worldview. Therapeutic interviewers work with clients to help them develop goals that are personally meaningful for them and are what they desire for themselves.

Are Goals Necessary?

Clients tend to come to therapy because the path they are on is not quite as they would like it. They usually have a good sense that there is something going on that is bothersome to them. However, they might have difficulty fully defining what it is that is a concern for them or what to do about it. Because many clients are unclear about where they want to go or how they can get there, therapists can help them to define where it is that they want to get to. Just by setting a goal, an expectation develops that the client will be different from the way he currently is. De Shazer (1985) stated, "When a goal is defined, the expectation of a different, more satisfactory future starts to develop and behavior changes in the present become possible" (p. 94).

Goals also help to motivate clients to continue on the path to where they want to go. Clients are already frustrated and upset when they come to therapy. If therapy were amorphous as to its purpose, clients might give up in their pursuit. However, by having goals, clients see that there is somewhere they are going. Further, by having a conversation about goals, therapist and client engage in a conversation about therapy and how it can be effective for the client.

Therapists can distinguish between general goals and specific goals. General goals are more global—perhaps "feeling better," "being happier," or "having a better relationship." Specific goals refer to precise things a client wants, such as "moving out of the house," "starting a job," or "getting out of bed before ten o'clock in the morning." Although each client has his own unique goals that bring him into therapy, there are some fundamental therapeutic goals that occur across models of therapy (Kleinke, 1994). These are the following:

> (1) helping clients overcome demoralization and gain hope, (2) enhancing clients' sense of mastery and self-efficacy, (3) encouraging clients to face their anxieties rather than avoiding them, (4) helping clients become aware of their misconceptions, (5) teaching clients to accept life's realities, and (6) helping clients achieve insight. (p. 32)

Although not each of these goals will be focused on with each client, they tend to find their way into most therapeutic encounters. These are general goals that can be for any client. How a general goal fits for a particular unique client will become the specific goal.

Setting Goals with Clients

There are many different ways for therapeutic interviewers to begin setting goals with clients. Some therapists use the first question in the interview to start probing for goals. Other therapists wait several sessions so that they can gain as much information as possible about the client before setting goals. To get things moving in the direction of goals, therapeutic interviewers can simply ask clients what it is they want to work on in therapy. Therapists can work on a goal for each session or for the whole of therapy. For an individual session, a therapist can ask, "How will you know that this session was helpful to you?"

If a therapist decides that goal setting in the first session is important, she can set the stage through her attitude and questioning. By understanding that there are things clients want to change in their lives, therapists can adopt a posture of understanding what is being discussed in the interview as keys to opening doors for clients to get where they want to go in life. The therapist's questions would then be informed by this attitude. Bertolino and O'Hanlon (2002) provided the following questions that help, from the start of therapy, to orient the client toward the future, change, and goals:

- How will you know when things are better?
- How will you know when the problem is no longer a problem?
- What will indicate to you that therapy has been successful?
- How will you know when you no longer need to come to therapy?
- What will be happening that will indicate to you that you can manage things on your own? (p. 91)

Each of these questions frames the therapeutic relationship as one that has the distinct purpose of getting clients closer to their goals so that the relationship can end.

There are always several goals occurring at the same time during the therapeutic interview. First, the client is trying to get certain things happening in his life so that he is happier with the way his life is going. Second, he wants things to happen so that he does not need to come back to therapy any longer. Third, the therapeutic interviewer wants things to occur for the client so that the client does not come back to therapy any longer. Each party in the interview wants all three of these goals, to happen as soon as possible. Further, there might be other goals involved, such as those by referring bodies or other individuals who desire change for the client.

Components of Good Goals

Although it would seem easy to develop goals, they are actually difficult to flesh out. Many goals that people develop, outside of therapy, tend not to be effective. This is because they are usually not thought out. They may have been developed in reaction to a situation instead of with logical thought.

Although people experience goals differently, there tend to be some general guidelines for the development of goals. De Shazer (1991) provided seven general characteristics of workable goals:

1. small rather than large;
2. salient to clients;
3. described in specific, concrete behavioral terms;
4. achievable within the practical contexts of clients' lives;
5. perceived by the clients as involving their "hard work";

Reflection 6.2

Think about some goals that you made for yourself. Perhaps these were "New Year's resolutions." How many of them did you actually accomplish? Why didn't you accomplish all of them? Keep those goals in mind while you read ths section on the components of good goals.

6. described as the "start of something" and not as the "end of something";
7. treated as involving new behavior(s) rather than the absence or cessation of existing behavior(s). (p. 112)

Walter and Peller (1992) provided some additional components of goals in that they should be in the here and now, in process form, in the client's language, and based on the client's control. Whatever goals are developed should be modifiable. Since life is never static, goals should be able to be altered to fit whatever new circumstance might arise. The following section highlights each component of good goals.

Goals Should Be Small.   Clients sometimes come to therapy wanting huge personality change. If client motivation would last years, and if managed care would agree to pay for several years' worth of therapy, this might be okay. Clients usually do not come to therapy at the first sign of discord. After the first serious disagreement, couples do not come to therapy. After the first time that someone feels depressed, they do not call up a therapist. After the first time that a child severely misbehaves, parents do not contact a child therapist. The problem(s) clients are dealing with have been building up, usually for a long period of time. Clients tend to make the therapy appointment when they are close to their "wit's end." If the therapist helps the client create a large goal, the client will probably not have the motivation to continue therapy until the end, when the goal has been achieved. However, this is not always the case. Psychoanalysis, which was the predominant mode of therapy for most of the last century, more or less held that clients would need to go to therapy for years before change would occur (some even had their clients agree that they would not make any significant changes in their lives as a prevention of defense mechanisms) and many clients stayed in analysis to try to get there. Unfortunately, many clients did not. Within the last twenty years, the brief short-term therapy approaches have been increasing in popularity, due partially to their focus on small and achievable goals.

Goals should be small—small enough that the clients might be able to accomplish a goal, or at least part of a goal, by the next session. Goals can be broken down into several smaller goals that can be accomplished in a shorter time frame. If clients reach a goal by the next session, they develop a sense of competence and accomplishment. This motivates them to continue pursuing other goals and will help remotivate them for further change.

In order to shift clients from thinking of large-scale change to thinking of small-scale change, therapists can ask clients, "What is a very small thing that will happen that will show you that things are moving in the right direction?" Through this means, goals can be broken up into smaller components so that they do not become an all-or-nothing event. One difficulty for clients is that they enter therapy thinking that the problem has to be completely gone or it is still a problem. Therapists can start to chip away at this notion by showing that each small goal that is reached not only helps to get the client closer to the larger goal, but also makes life better along the way, even before the large goal is accomplished. Further, once the change process happens, no matter how small, other changes usually follow along. Exercise 6.5 helps the reader to create small goals.

> *Bad Goal:* "My life will be right."
>
> *Good Goal:* "I will begin looking for a job."

Goals Should Be Measurable (Specific).   Many of the goals people develop, without the help of a therapist, tend to be extremely vague. Therapists and clients both need to know when clients reach their goals. If a goal is something abstract, such as "be happy," the client and therapist have a hard time knowing when the client has reached that mark. They could theoretically work together for the rest of their lives trying to figure out if the client is "happy." But if the goal is a specific action, "I will apply for a job" or "I will get out of bed before noon," therapists and clients will know if the client has met the goal. This allows them to determine whether therapy is useful and when therapy is no longer necessary.

> *Bad Goal:* "I will do better in relationships."
>
> *Good Goal:* "I will ask someone out in the next week."

Berg and Miller (1992) explained, "When goals are stated in precise terms, the opportunity develops for the client to immediately take credit for his successes" (p. 38). When clients start to move toward goals, especially when the goals are small and measurable, these small changes start to snowball and build up momentum so that the clients realize additional positive changes in their lives. Exercise 6.6 helps the reader create measurable goals.

Exercise 6.5   Developing Small Goals

For the following goals, reconstruct them so that they are small rather than large.

1. I will change careers from being an accountant to becoming a school teacher.
2. I will learn how to cook.
3. I will not freak out every time I have to do a presentation in class.
4. I will be more available to my family.
5. I will take better care of my health.

Exercise 6.6   Developing Measurable Goals

For the following goals, change them so they are more specific in order that therapist and client can measure them.

1. I will change careers from being an accountant to becoming a school teacher.
2. I will learn how to cook.
3. I will not freak out every time I have to do a presentation in class.
4. I will be more available to my family.
5. I will take better care of my health.

Reflection 6.3

Most people have experienced a situation, probably multiple situations, in which other people thought that they should change, and they did not agree with them. When this happened for you, how much did you work to achieve that change? What were your thoughts regarding whether and how you should work to make changes recommended by another person?

Goals Should Be Salient to the Client. Goals need to be desired by the client. Berg and Miller (1992) explained, "The treatment goal must be *important to the client*, and the client must view the achievement of that goal as personally beneficial" (p. 33). If clients do not care about the goal, why would they work toward that goal? Therapists should spend time with clients, working and reworking the goals to ensure that the client cares about attaining the goals that were developed. If the therapeutic interviewer told the client what the goal is, instead of it coming from the client, it would probably not be as important to the client.

> ***Bad Goal:*** "I will not go out so much because *my wife* doesn't like it."

> ***Good Goal:*** "I will come home at 5:30 pm because *I* want to spend time with my family."

Goals Should Be Realistic and Attainable. Good goals need to be realistic so that the client, hopefully sooner rather than later, will be able to accomplish that goal. Why would a therapist help a client set a goal the client could never reach? If the therapist asked the client what goal he had and the client responded, "To marry Jessica Alba," this would not be a realistic goal (especially if the client had never met her and there was no foreseeable introduction between the two). The likelihood that the client could achieve that goal would be extremely small. Thus, it would only cause more frustration to work toward that goal. The same goal is not realistic for every client. Based on education, income, family dynamics, and a host of other factors, each person is different. Therapists should work with clients to help determine what makes sense for that particular person.

> ***Bad Goal:*** "I will win the lottery."

> ***Good Goal:*** "I will open up a bank account and put in 5 percent of my paycheck every week."

Exercise 6.7   Developing Realistic Goals

For the following goals, change them so that they are realistic and attainable.

1. I will own a Fortune 500 company once I finish with this bankruptcy.
2. I will win back my ex's love so that she leaves her fiancé and comes back to me.
3. I will right all of the wrongs I have committed in my life.
4. I will be the best student ever at this university.
5. I will never have another panic attack in my life.

Goals Should Be Inclusive of the Client's Hard Work (in the Client's Control).   Goals should not be about other people, but should have steps that the *client* will be making. When a client states, "I want my wife to show me more affection," the therapist is put in a difficult position because the wife is not in therapy, the husband is. The therapist can start to get the client to focus on self by asking, "Whether she is more affectionate or not, how do *you* want to be in the relationship?"

Once the goal is based on what the client will do, therapist, client, and other people in the client's relational field can then focus their praise on the client (instead of anyone else) for the positive changes being made. Berg and Miller (1992) explained some of the reasons for acknowledging clients' "hard work." First, it helps to promote clients' sense of worth. Clients' dignity is protected because the goal is not impossible, but attainable given their hard work. Second, most clients will agree that reaching a goal includes some type of hard work. Thus, it helps them to buy into the therapy process. Third, by focusing on "hard work," the therapist and client are in a "win-win" situation. Failure does not happen. Not reaching the goal is only a sign that more hard work is needed. Exercise 6.8 helps the reader to develop client-focused goals.

> *Bad Goal:* "My child will start listening to me more."
> *Good Goal:* "I will use a token economy system to try to help my child stay on target more."

Goals Should Be the Start of Something.   Goals should be the start of something instead of the end of something. Take the following scenario. Do *not* think about a huge pink fluffy rabbit. Don't imagine that big pink rabbit hopping around. Don't visualize that huge pink fluffy rabbit eating a carrot. Were you able to not think about the rabbit? Sometimes, the more you try to end something, the more that something stays with you. This is one of the difficult aspects of counseling someone dealing with an addiction (and occurs with most of the problems that people bring to therapy). They usually tell themselves "I cannot drink. I cannot drink." But by doing this, they are always in connection with drinking.

The more that someone focuses on *what not to do*, the less they are actively working on *what to do*. Thus, instead of getting the client not to drink (have the

---

Exercise 6.8   Developing Goals That Focus on the Client

For the following goals, change them so that they focus on change by the client instead of someone else.

1. My wife will treat me better so that we don't fight anymore.
2. My son will do better in school so that he does not fail out.
3. Since there is too much stress at work, my boss will ease up on me and not be so mean.
4. My teachers will grade my papers fairly so I get the grades I deserve.
5. My cats will not make as much mess around the house as they do now.

problem), the therapist can work with the client in terms of what he wants to do that would make his life more fulfilling. Further, goals should discuss the first small steps the client will take rather than the end result. The following exchange exemplifies this process:

> *Client:* I don't want to drink anymore.
>
> *Therapist:* If you weren't drinking, what would you be doing instead?
>
> *Client:* Well, I would probably have a hobby.
>
> *Therapist:* What type of hobby would you have?
>
> *Client:* Perhaps photography.
>
> *Therapist:* What else would you be doing when you're not drinking?
>
> *Client:* I'd be getting along better with my family.
>
> *Therapist:* How would you be different with them?
>
> *Client:* I probably wouldn't be starting fights with them.
>
> *Therapist:* What would you be doing instead?
>
> *Client:* Maybe I would call them up and see if they wanted to go to a movie.

In this interchange, the therapist has helped the client create two goals: (1) developing a hobby and (2) getting along better with family members. Each of these goals would need to be further clarified to agree with all of the previous and subsequent points about the components of good goals. Yet instead of always connecting himself to the problem, the client is moving away from it and toward more positive aspects of his life. Exercise 6.9 helps the reader create goals that start something, rather than end something.

> *Bad Goal:* "My wife and I will stop fighting."
>
> *Good Goal:* "I will talk calmly when my wife and I have a disagreement."

Goals Should Be Able to Be Implemented Immediately (in the Here and Now). Good goals should allow the client to start working on them immediately.

Exercise 6.9   *Developing Goals That Focus on the Start of Something*

For the following goals, change them so that they focus on the start of some activity instead of the end or absence of that activity.

1. My wife and I will stop yelling and arguing with one another.
2. I won't have this dreadful feeling in my stomach all the time.
3. I will stop procrastinating about the things I need to do.
4. I hate that I perseverate on things all the time. I don't want to do that anymore.
5. I won't drink alcohol again for the rest of my life.

By building on the momentum from the session, clients should leave the therapeutic interview and be able to, without delay, work toward their goals. Clients have taken a huge step in their lives by setting up and attending the first session. Therapeutic interviewers should utilize the initiative that clients take by coming to the session by helping them to develop goals that, once the clients leave the therapy interview, they can immediately begin. Working toward goals is hard work. The longer that someone puts it off, the greater likelihood that they will continue to procrastinate in working toward that goal and the lower the chance that they actually will attempt it, let alone accomplish it.

> *Client:* I want to get along better with people.
>
> *Therapist:* Okay, what will be the first thing that you will do when you leave this session to try to reach that goal?
>
> *Client:* Well, I think when I go home I will thank my wife for staying with me and trying to work it out.
>
> *Therapist:* And after that, what will you do?
>
> *Client:* I will create a list of the people who I haven't treated well and then apologize to them.

> *Bad Goal:* "Next year, I'll start to treat my family better."
>
> *Good Goal:* "Today, when I go home, I will give each member of my family a compliment."

Exercise 6.10   Developing Goals That Begin Immediately

For the following goals, change them so that they motivate the client to start working on them immediately.

1. Within the next month, I will begin to look for a job.
2. The next time that my wife tries to pick a fight with me, I will be calm.
3. I will use relaxation techniques the next time I have a panic attack.
4. The next time I go food shopping, I will buy healthier foods so I can start my diet.
5. To show my wife how much I love her, on Valentine's Day, I will treat her to a very nice dinner.

Reflection 6.4

Think about some issue that you have in your own life that you want to change. Develop a goal that conforms to all of the characteristics of good goals previously presented. How does this impact the way in which you view this concern? Does the concern seem easier to resolve once you have placed the goal into this form?

FIGURE 6.1 *Characteristics of Good Goals*

- Small
- Measurable
- Realistic
- Salient to the Client
- Inclusive of the Client's Hard Work (in the Client's Control)
- The Start of Something (in a Positive Form)
- Able to Be Implemented Immediately (in the Here-and-Now)

Prioritizing Goals

Some clients might come to therapy with one, and only one, specific problem. However, most clients usually come in with multiple problems, and then through work with the therapist, develop multiple goals. Things could get a little confusing if therapist and client attempted to work on all of the goals at the same time.

Client goals are usually based on intensity levels, with some goals being more important and significant for the client. Therapeutic interviewers can help clients to figure out which are the primary goals, the secondary goals, the tertiary goals, and so on. By doing this, clients can more clearly focus on specific goals to see them through to completion.

> *Therapist:* What are the things that bring you in to see me?
>
> *Jon:* My life is really a mess. I've been pretty much in a rut for several years now. I work in a computer company handling the inventory and that's pretty much it for me in terms of advancement.
>
> *Therapist:* Okay, so your job is one area you would like to change. What else?
>
> *Jon:* Well, I'm pretty lonely. At work, I'm on the computer all day in my cubicle in the back of the office. I really don't interact much with people at work. Then when I get home, I usually heat a microwave dinner and sit and watch television. I don't really have friends that I hang out with, and I'm not happy about that.
>
> *Therapist:* You'd like to have more friends and be more social.
>
> *Jon:* Yes. I'm pretty lame right now.
>
> *Therapist:* Are there other things that you'd like different in your life?
>
> *Jon:* I've been thinking that maybe I could go back to school. I've really been thinking that I want to be a pharmacist. It seems to be the hot job now. I've done some research, and it would really take me a lot of science courses in order to get into pharmacy school. But I think I would really enjoy that.
>
> *Therapist:* So, going back to school and getting into a new career is a possibility.
>
> *Jon:* Yeah.
>
> *Therapist:* Jon, we've talked about your desire to get a new job, to become more social, and to go back to school. Which of these would you want to work toward first?

One issue with goals, especially if they have been developed in one of the beginning interviews, is that clients may not have discussed all of the concerns that brought them to therapy. Sometimes clients need to feel a connection to the therapist before they can trust the therapist with some of their most secret information. Thus, goal setting is a continuous process throughout the whole of the therapy endeavor. Therapists should check in with clients to see if other issues have emerged that might be pertinent for the client to work on in therapy. The more goals the client has, the more the client realizes that there are many different pathways toward improvement in life.

Incorporating Goal Characteristics

The following extended transcript presents a negotiation between therapist and client on how to set client goals so that they meet all of the characteristics of good goals:

Therapist: What seems to be going on for you? (door opener)

Client: Things have always gone against me in life. My brother was my parents' favorite child. I didn't really take to school. I haven't been able to maintain a job for longer than three months. And now I just found out that I have diabetes.

Therapist: Wow, it sounds like you are thinking that you don't measure up. (paraphrase)

Client: Yeah.

Therapist: Tell me more about that. (minimal encourager)

Client: My brother is better at me in so many things.

Therapist: But I hear you also saying that you don't think you measure up in general, even more than just with your brother. (paraphrase)

Client: Well, I never felt like I fully belonged. I had a couple of friends but not great friends. I dated some people, but nothing where we were both in love.

Therapist: I get the sense that you think you missed out on a lot in life, and you're feeling lost and lonely. (reflection of feeling)

Client: Yes. I wish my life was different.

Therapist: How would you want it to be? (question to get toward goals)

Client: I want to be happy. I want to be loved. I want to feel needed. I would like for my parents to appreciate me for who I am, for my brother not to look down on me and see me as the black sheep of the family.

Therapist: Those are some great long-term goals. Out of all of those, what would be the one that you would like to work toward first? (prioritizing goals)

Client: I guess being happy would be an important one.

Therapist: Okay, so let's break that down a little bit because "being happy" is such a huge thing. When you say "happy," what do you mean by that? (making goals more specific)

Client: That I feel good. That I'm glad that I'm alive. That I'm doing things, instead of just staying in the house and watching movies.

Therapist: It's tough sometimes to know when someone else, or even yourself, is happy. What would I see you doing that would let me know that you were happy? (making goals measurable)

Client: Perhaps I would be going out of the house more.

Therapist: Great. Where would you be going? (getting specifics)

Client: To the movies. To dinner. Museums. The beach.

Therapist: Who would you be going with?

Client: I have a friend, Frankie, that might go with me.

Therapist: All right. What if Frankie wasn't home? How willing would you be to go to one of these places on your own? (ensuring that it is inclusive of the client's hard work)

Client: I feel kind of awkward going to dinner or a movie by myself.

Therapist: Where would you feel comfortable going to by yourself?

Client: I would probably go to the museum or to the park. Maybe for lunch I would go by myself, but dinner would be weird. I'd also go to the bookstore by myself.

Therapist: All right, we're making progress. Where, after you left the office today, could you go to that you would feel comfortable and, more importantly, that you'd probably enjoy? (getting the client to immediately work on the goal)

Client: I think if I went to the bookstore and got a coffee and browsed some of the books—that would be enjoyable.

Therapist: What is the likelihood that you would go do that right when we finish? (assessing motivation for this goal)

Client: I do have the afternoon free, so I could do it.

Therapist: Yes, you could do it. But what's the likelihood that you *will* do it? (challenging the client to engage in the target behavior)

Client: Pretty good. I want to start getting better, and I think this could be the first step toward that.

The therapeutic interviewer has now worked with the client to develop a small, measurable, realistic, salient goal that includes the presence of something instead of the absence, the start of something, the client's actively doing something for it, and the capability of being started immediately. The likelihood that this client will begin movement toward this goal is much greater than if they had agreed on a goal of "making my life happier," as the latter is too overwhelming. Further, that

Exercise 6.11   Establishing Good Goals

For the following client goals, change them so that they meet the characteristics of good goals.

1. "I want to stop worrying so much about the future."
2. "I can't stand my neighbor. I wish he'd stop coming over to my house and bothering me."
3. "What I want from therapy is to get my son to do better in school. He has no motivation and is almost failing."
4. "Let's see. For me, if therapy was successful, I would have my first girlfriend back. She's the love of my life. The problem is that she's married right now."
5. "My goal for therapy is that some time in the future I'm not depressed."

latter, general goal leaves the client confused since there are too many choices; thus, the client might not know where to begin.

Summary

Questions can be a useful component of the therapeutic interview. They help to bring forth information during the session that both therapist and client can utilize. However, since questions tend to be one of the most overused techniques for therapists, they should be pertinent and useful to what is occurring in the session. These questions should be purposeful; they should work toward the attainment of client goals. Since clients are coming to therapy because of things that are not going well in their lives, therapists can work with them to develop appropriate goals that will move them toward their desired outcomes. This takes skills on the therapist's part to help the client construct goals that will actually be useful and achievable. Thus, goals should be small, measurable, realistic, salient to the client, inclusive of the client's hard work (in the client's control), the start of something (in a positive form), and able to be implemented immediately (in the here-and-now). Once therapist and client have developed good goals, they can prioritize these goals and begin to work toward their completion.

Exercises

1. Perform an experiment in which you take one day and only ask questions. Pay attention to the reaction of other people and how the question asking impacts the exchanges. On another day, do not ask any questions at all. What were the differences in the communication transactions based on only asking questions and not asking any questions?

2. Think about an issue or concern that you are currently having. It does not have to be something for which you would go to therapy, but something that is bothering you. For instance, perhaps your roommate listens to the television too loudly when you are trying to study. Develop a goal that fits all of the criteria for good goals listed in this chapter.

Answers to Exercise 6.3

1. Open
2. Closed
3. Swing
4. Closed
5. Open
6. Swing
7. Closed
8. Swing
9. Closed
10. Open

Answers to Exercise 6.4

1. Negative
2. Long
3. Double-Barreled
4. Leading Push
5. Bias
6. Sharp
7. Guessing Game
8. Specific
9. Double-Barreled
10. Negative

7

Endings in Therapy

Summarizing, Ending Sessions, and Termination

Endings in therapy occur from the very first contact the client makes with the therapist or agency. By making an initial query into the possibility of therapy, clients are potentially ending a relationship with their problems, which have been going on for longer than they would have liked. They are also starting a relationship with someone that they know will only be temporal. Many people have difficulties with endings, regardless of their intensity or the context in which they occur. Therapists should be aware of how gently they engage clients in the various endings that occur in therapy.

There are three main types of endings in therapy. The first is the end of work on a particular issue that has been brought up in the therapeutic interview. The second is the end of a specific therapeutic interview. The third is the end of the whole of therapy and the therapeutic relationship. This chapter explores the issues surrounding each of these different types of endings.

Summarizing Client Stories

Clients sometimes bring many concerns to therapy. Through the use of door openers, minimal encouragers, paraphrases, reflections of feelings, reflections of meaning, and questions (along with any of the other listening and responding skills discussed in the previous chapters), therapeutic interviewers address one particular issue. The last skill in this sequence is summarizing. Sommers-Flanagan and Sommers-Flanagan (2003) explained several of the purposes of summaries: "Summarization demonstrates accurate listening, enhances client and interviewer recall of major themes, helps clients focus on important issues, and extracts or refines the meaning behind client messages" (p. 69).

Young (2005) delineated four different types of summaries: signal, planning, focusing, and thematic. Each of these summaries is used at different places in the therapeutic interview to help the client and the process of therapy move forward.

A *signal summary* occurs when therapeutic interviewer and client have fully addressed one specific client issue. This type of summary allows the client to know that the therapist has been tracking the conversation and understands the whole of the story. A good signal summary begins with the content of the issue, moves on to what the client felt about what happened, and ends with the meaning for the client of how the client felt about the issue. It is neither too short nor too long. It is also neither too specific nor too general. Signal summaries are usually between three to five sentences. Since several client issues can be discussed in any one therapy interview, multiple signal summaries might be utilized in that session. Below is an example of one specific signal summary.

> *Therapist:* I would like to take a second and summarize everything we have been discussing so far today. You talked about a situation that happened at work where your boss yelled at you. You were supposed to follow through on a project and did not do so in a time frame that your boss wanted. You seemed shocked that your boss reacted that way. Further, you were disappointed in yourself for not being as on the ball with this obligation because you think of yourself as a very diligent employee. Is that the gist of it?

A *planning summary* occurs at the end of the therapeutic interview. It is a review of what was discussed in the session so that the client can take that knowledge and move beyond the interview. The planning summary gets clients to take what they have thought about and learned during the session and apply it to their postsession life.

> *Therapist:* We are just about finished for today's session. I was hoping that we could review what we covered. You were discussing how you were feeling lonely and were hoping to feel more connected to other people. During the session, you talked about how one of the things that you wanted to do was to go out more. This might be a good place to start next session discussing what you did during the week to get out of the house more than you have been.

A *focusing summary* occurs in the beginning of the therapeutic interview and helps to give the interview a focus. Young (2005) stated that it "is an intervention that brings the discussion to bear on the major issues and themes, places the spotlight on the client's responsibility for the problem, and reminds the client of the goals" (p. 161). A focusing summary builds from all of the information and activity that occurred in past interviews. It provides the therapist and client with the use of that information as a guide to either go into more depth or to know that they do not have to continue down that path.

> *Therapist:* To begin today's session, I'd like to talk about where we've been. This will help us see where we want to go. In past sessions, you have discussed the idea that for several years you've been quite anxious. This feeling has been increasing in intensity for you lately. You've also talked about feeling lost in terms of what type of career you want for yourself. Perhaps we can begin there today?

A *thematic summary* occurs after many different client issues have been addressed. The therapeutic interviewer is able to connect themes that are running through several client issues. By doing this, new information is usually relayed to the client. Again, thematic summaries cannot be done right away in the therapy process. Several issues have to be addressed to understand how they may fit together in a larger abstraction. However, once connected, they can be quite powerful. Because of this, therapists should have as much information as possible to ensure that they are accurate about the themes they are summarizing.

> *Therapist:* I wanted to take a minute to talk to you about some of the interesting connections that I've been hearing in many of the issues we have been talking about. There seems to be a thread running through our discussions, that of disappointment. You have been disappointed by your parents not respecting you as an adult. You've also been disappointed that your romantic relationships don't seem to materialize in the way that you envisioned them. Lastly, it seems you've been disappointed in yourself that you are not in the place in your life where you were hoping to be. What do you think about this?

The primary type of summary a therapeutic interviewer uses is the signal summary. Clients bring up many different issues during the course of a single interview or the whole of the therapy process. These types of summaries should be integrated with all of the skills previously discussed in this book to assure clients that the therapist understands what the client is talking about.

The following transcript demonstrates how the various listening skills—door openers, minimal encouragers, paraphrases, reflections of feeling, reflections of meaning, and summaries—can be used together to address a single client issue.

> *Therapist:* You look kind of down today, Blake. What's going on for you? (door opener)
>
> *Blake:* I just found out that my girlfriend got into a graduate school in another state.

Therapist: Okay. (minimal encourager)

Blake: That's good for her, because it's a school she wanted to go to. But then she told me that she doesn't want to do the whole long distance thing.

Therapist: Alright. (minimal encourager)

Blake: I asked her why not, and she said that she thought this would be a good time to move to another stage of her life. I guess I'm not included in that new stage.

Therapist: Your girlfriend is moving to another state for graduate school and what you heard from her is that she is going to break up with you. (paraphrase)

Blake: Yeah...(crying) I don't think I've wanted to acknowledge that. We've been together for eight months now, and I fell in love with her.

Therapist: This news must have been shocking for you. (reflection of feeling)

Blake: It came out of the blue. I didn't see it coming at all.

Therapist: Tell me more. (minimal encourager)

Blake: I talked to her about this, asking her to reconsider. Not reconsider moving out there, but in terms of our relationship. I even told her that I'd be willing to move there with her. She said that she thought it would be better if I didn't.

Therapist: I get the sense that that was really like a punch in your stomach that knocked all of the wind out of you. (metaphor/paraphrase)

Blake: Yes. It floored me. I actually thought that I would marry this person. I envisioned what having a family with her would be like.

Therapist: You were extremely disappointed by these dreams being squashed. (reflection of feeling—increasing the intensity level)

Blake: Of course. I really want to be married and start a family. I invested almost the last year with this person because I thought that it could be with her.

Therapist: You feel almost betrayed because you put so much into this relationship—your time, but more importantly your hopes for what your life would be, and now that is taken away from you right now. (reflection of meaning)

Blake: Yes, I know that I'll find someone else. But it really hurts right now.

Therapist: Just to make sure I got everything, your girlfriend recently got accepted to a graduate school in another state and told you that she thinks this would be a good time for the two of you to end your relationship. You were surprised by this news because you were thinking long-term about this relationship. Even more, you are feeling a little lost because you were imagining what your life might be like with her and now those dreams are no longer possible. (summary)

Exercise 7.1   Completing a Full Client Issue

For the following client responses, provide a response based on what is being asked.

Sandy is a twenty-two-year-old female who is coming to the university counseling center because she is doing poorly in her classes.

Start with a door opener:

Sandy: Well, I don't know what's going on. In high school I was always a good student and have been doing okay my first three years. It's just this year, I don't seem to be able to pay as much attention as usual.

Give a minimal encourager:

Sandy: I have four classes and I think I'm failing two. I did break up with my boyfriend this year, and I think that has something to do with this. I also am starting to think about what to do when I graduate and nothing comes to mind.

Give a paraphrase:

Sandy: Yes, this is the first time I've really struggled like this. My boyfriend was my main support system, and now I don't really have anyone I can go to, to talk about things. This is such a new situation for me, being so disoriented, I don't know what to do.

Give a reflection of feeling:

Sandy: That is how I feel. All my life I thought of myself as being a strong person who could handle everything. Now, after my boyfriend broke up with me, I'm feeling lost because school just doesn't seem as important to me.

Give a reflection of meaning (based on everything you've heard so far):

Sandy: Wow, yeah. It's so overwhelming. I want to find out how to cope with all of this.

Give a summary:

Ending a Session

Ending a session can sometimes be one of the most difficult parts of the therapeutic interview. The end of a specific therapeutic interview reminds therapist and client that their meeting is based on a business relationship. It further signals that the relationship the two developed during the interview will end, perhaps until the next time the two meet. It also signals that there will probably be another person for the therapist to work with and engage in a therapeutic relationship. Some clients can get feelings of jealousy knowing that the intimacy they feel with the therapist is shared by other people.

Another reason that ending the session can sometimes be difficult is that some clients tend to bring up some of the most important issues right before the end of the session. When therapists start to let clients know that the session is ending, clients may "drop the bomb." Therapists then have to wrap up the session without trivializing the client's concerns. If therapists agree to focus on what the client has just disclosed at the end of the session (usually with less than five minutes remaining) and go over the specified time allotted for the interview, they might set the precedent for the client to engage in this type of behavior in future interviews.

One thing that can help to provide a frame for the ending of the therapy interview is to let the client know when the session is getting close to the end.

> *Therapist:* Jean, we have about five minutes left. Why don't we spend the last few minutes we have together today talking about what you are taking away from this session and how you might use the time between now and the next session.

Letting the client know how much time is left in the session is a respectful means of orienting her to decide what she wants to do with the remaining time. The client can then decide to bring up new or further information or whether to wait until the next interview. Some Hollywood movies have presented the therapist using an egg timer to gauge how much time is left in sessions. This is hardly ever done by therapists. It adds an air of anxiety into the session because the therapist and client are then focused on time throughout the whole of the interview. Case Scenario 7.1 describes a case in which ending a particular session became quite difficult.

Although the client is ultimately the person who decides what information gets discussed during the session, therapists are generally the ones in charge of structuring the therapeutic interview. They need to keep themselves informed about how much time is left in the session so that they can wrap up the session

CASE SCENARIO 7.1

I was working with a middle-aged female client who was quite verbose. I remember one of our first sessions was coming to an end and I was trying to wrap up the session. I used some of the strategies to close sessions by talking about how we only had a few minutes left, what she might do differently this coming week, and then talking about scheduling the next session. The client continued to sit in her seat and talk about her concerns. I tried to acknowledge the concerns without going into depth and then shifting the conversation to close it. The client continued talking. I then decided that perhaps I could nonverbally prod the client by standing up. Although I was standing (not a normal behavior during the session), the client continued to sit and talk about her problems. I then walked to the door and told the client that the time for our session had ended and that we had gone over the time limit. She still sat and continued talking. I then had to raise my voice and let her know that I had another appointment. In looking back at this session, I think I could have given more verbal prompts earlier on to acknowledge her discourse but also to focus on the ending of the session.

when needed. Ending a session on time has several important benefits. First, it keeps the relationship grounded in that the client does not feel extra special because the therapist went above and beyond normal protocol. Second, it keeps therapists on track so that they are not late with their next session. Third, it keeps the therapist grounded in a business relationship. Therapists do not have to keep the interview going because they are feeling guilty. Therapists are being paid for their time. If the client is going to use more than the agreed on amount of time, a renegotiation of fee might be considered. Fourth, by staying on time, the client is sent a message of keeping focused during the whole of the session and utilizing all the available time.

There are several means of keeping focused on the amount of time in a session without its being an overbearing part of the interview. The therapist can wear a watch and periodically look at it. The therapist can also subtly observe the client's watch. The therapist might have a clock that is strategically placed in the room, perhaps behind the client's chair. Or the therapist can have a timer that makes a subtle noise when there is a certain amount of time left (perhaps five minutes).

Therapists can let clients know in several ways that the session has come to an end. Therapists can discuss future sessions ("We are just about out of time. What would you like to do about the next session?"), summarize the current session ("Just to wrap up what we talked about today, you stated . . ."), transition to another topic ("This seems like a good place to end for today. I saw on the news that the weather is going to be pretty nasty this weekend, so hopefully you stay safe"). Each of these ways transitions from the meat of the interview to the end of the contact.

Besides being overt about ending the session, therapists can use more covert linguistic strategies to signal nearing the end of the session. Tolan (2003) suggested that therapists switch the level of intensity of their replies to clients from high intensity in the beginning of the session to lower intensity at the end of the session. This helps to prevent the client from going into more depth while still allowing the therapist to acknowledge the client's concern.

> *Client:* Well, perhaps we should talk about how my father called this week and cursed me out. This is the first time he's called all year and he disrespects me like that!
>
> *Therapist:* (*at the beginning of the session*) This was pretty devastating for you to have your father treat you in that manner.
>
> *Therapist:* (*at the end of the session*) That must have been tough for you.

The difference between these two responses is one of degrees of intensity. The first one helps open the space for a more in-depth focus of feelings whereas the second one acknowledges the pain, yet doesn't fully encourage more depth of exploration.

Ending the first session with a client can potentially be problematic. This interview sets the stage for all subsequent sessions. If therapists cut clients off or end the session too abruptly, clients may take offense and not return for another session. Part of a good ending is a good beginning. When therapists educate clients on the format and process of the therapeutic interview, the ending is smoother. This entails a discussion of how long the session will be. Case Scenario 7.2 describes a therapist's inadequate job of setting a time frame.

Termination

Termination of the therapeutic relationship is a natural part of the therapy process (Cochran & Cochran, 2006). Termination in therapy can be one of the most difficult parts of the whole process, yet it can also be extremely gratifying. Ending a therapeutic relationship impacts both client and therapist. They have worked together, shared intimacies (although primarily one person's story), and have worked together as a team to reach designated outcomes. Just by engaging in a process where two people come together and accomplish a goal, therapist and client are joined together.

Termination can sometimes be a very awkward but necessary part of the therapy. Each party, for different reasons, has anxiety about not having this relationship anymore. Therapeutic interviewers might be anxious in hopes that the gains made in therapy continue for the client. Clients are anxious as to whether they can continue with the changes they made without the support of the therapist. The anxiety of ending this relationship can be reduced by the therapist working, from the first encounter, toward termination. Given that therapy is about helping the client to gain independence away from the therapist from the very first meeting, termination can be an acknowledgement between therapist and client that the client is on a path of independence away from needing the therapist. In essence, this is the whole goal of therapy; to get the client to, as quickly as possible, not need the services of the therapist.

CASE SCENARIO 7.2

One of my first private practice clients was a couple who was coming to therapy because of infidelity by one of the spouses. The couple came in very eager to talk. I did not set the limits of the counseling session by discussing the length of time we would meet. When the session reached the one-hour mark, the couple was in the middle of a very heated discussion of an issue. I thought that telling them that their time was up would negatively impact them. Further, I did not feel comfortable or confident enough yet to interrupt them and end the session. I had not done a good job of reminding them about how long we had left in the session. Luckily, I did not have another client waiting for me because that first session lasted two hours! I learned from this session that I needed to do a better job of explaining to my clients what the time frame is for the sessions we have together.

As we have been discussing throughout the whole of this book, therapy is a relationship between two people. The ending of this relationship impacts both therapist and client. Sometimes each is looking forward to the ending because they did not appreciate the relationship. Other times, neither party wants the relationship to end. Sometimes one wants the relationship to end more than the other. However the dynamics, termination can bring about feelings of sadness, happiness, fear, anxiety, accomplishment, and loss. Some relationship endings are looked forward to, while others keep getting put off. Whatever the situation, how the therapy ends might be as important as what occurred throughout the duration of it. If therapy is ended too abruptly, clients might lose some sense of competence or feel pushed out and abandoned by the therapist. This could then possibly negate much of the positive change that occurred during the course of therapy. Thus, therapeutic interviewers need to put as much thought into the process of ending the therapy as they did in trying to help clients reach their goals.

Termination can take many forms. It depends on the therapist's situation, the client's situation, whether there was a referring agent, the context in which the relationship is occurring (for instance, an agency or therapy program) and the specific goals that were targeted. There are four main types of termination: client-initiated, therapist-initiated, mutually initiated, and forced terminations.

Client-Initiated Endings

Clients come to therapy with varying expectations of what they will get out of it and how much time and effort they will have to put into it to get their intended outcomes. Clients end therapy for many different reasons. One reason is that they believe they have achieved all of the goals for which they came to therapy. Another reason is that they might not have the time, energy, or finances to continue. Clients might also terminate because they are moving away from the current geographic area. Sometimes clients end therapy with a particular therapist because they do not feel comfortable with the therapist as in Case Scenario 7.3. Clients might also terminate therapy because it is becoming too intense for them.

Clients let therapists know that they want to discontinue therapy in various ways. They might hint for several sessions they might not come back, they might have an open conversation with the therapist, they might say at the end of one session that they won't make another appointment because they want to see how things go, or they might make an appointment but never call or show up again. Tolan (2003) described several client behaviors that might signal clients are ready to terminate including reminiscing about the relationship, reviewing their progress, celebrating their achievements, giving feedback to the therapist, showing appreciation, paying attention to the external world as well as the internal, and looking forward to what else might come in their lives. Therapeutic interviewers should be tuned in to the client's communication so that they are aware of where the client is in the therapy process. They can also be overt and consult with the client about their thoughts on the therapy. One way to do this is not to assume a

CASE SCENARIO 7.3

A student of mine decided to go to therapy at a local community mental health center. She was assigned a male therapist a few years older than herself. She worked with the therapist for several sessions. One day, she came to my faculty office to talk about feeling very uncomfortable in her meetings with the therapist. She found that he was making, what to her, were inappropriate comments. It seemed he was making sexual overtures to her; however, he had never been overt about it or been outright unethical. My student then was in a dilemma because she also felt uncomfortable in telling this therapist that she did not want to meet with him anymore. She did not think that she had reached all of her goals from when she initiated therapy. But she didn't want to continue meeting with this therapist. We then brainstormed various ways that she could switch therapists to ensure that the concerns she had for herself were addressed. This case demonstrated how clients can feel uncomfortable with therapists and want to end the relationship.

next session, but after each time there is a meeting, ask the client about continuing the relationship or not:

> *Therapist:* We are just about finished for today. I just wanted to check in with you to see if this session was helpful and whether you think that we should meet again.

By doing it in this fashion, the therapist is putting the client in the position of strength in the relationship. The client is the one to determine whether there is another meeting or not. However, there are a couple of potential problems in using this approach. First, it might put the client in an uncomfortable position every session. Sometimes clients might not know right then and there if the session was helpful for them. It might take several days (or perhaps weeks) to really digest what occurred (this is assuming that sessions are, or a particular session is, helpful). Some therapists build on this and do not set another appointment with the client, but have the client go home and evaluate their status. Then, if the client thinks that she would like another session, she can call to set up the next meeting with the therapist. A second related pitfall could be the assumption that each and every session will be helpful and that if a session is not helpful, then this might lead to termination. Not every session in therapy helps move clients toward their goals. Sometimes several sessions (or even more) are needed before progress happens (if it happens at all). Therapists, from the start of therapy, should have an expectation that change can happen, but explain to the clients that sometimes change takes time. In this way, clients will not be so quick to end therapy if a single session is not perceived as being helpful.

How therapists respond to a client initiating termination impacts what happens to that client after the ending. Making the client feel bad about her decision can negatively impact the client in the future.

> *Client:* I'm thinking that I really don't need to come back anymore.
>
> *Therapist:* I would have to disagree. Although you have made some gains, I really fear that you'll just go right back into the pattern that brought you here in the first place.

After being made to feel guilty for a personal decision, the client might be hesitant to come back to this therapist or go to any other therapist. Therapists should let the client know their stance on where the client is in terms of progress, yet therapy is always a voluntary choice for the client. Another way of expressing to the client the therapist's views of what should occur might be as follows:

> *Client:* I'm thinking that I really don't need to come back anymore.
>
> *Therapist:* This is ultimately your choice. I think you have made some nice progress in therapy. There is a chance that those gains will maintain and even continue. My concern is that things might slip back as before we started therapy. Let's talk a bit about what is leading you to think this is the right time to end therapy.

Therapist-Initiated Endings

There are times in the course of the therapy process when therapeutic interviewers have to decide to end the therapeutic relationship. Therapists attempt to end therapy with a client when they believe clients have accomplished their goals, have made significant strides and can continue to make progress without the therapist, if they are not skilled enough in that specific area to be of help to the client, if no progress is being made, or if they feel a significant bias toward the client that they have not been able to move past.

Whatever the reason for the therapist wanting to end the therapy, they should not bring it up at the end of a session and have that be the last session. This is too much of a surprise and shock for a client. The client is then not fully able to process what the ending means and how she can best use it for a continuation of progress. Preparation to transition away from the relationship can help maintain the progress made and prevent the client from feeling abandoned. Thus, the therapist might bring up the possible termination several sessions prior to or at least the session before the last session.

If therapists believe that they are not the best suited to work with a client, they should make a referral to someone who is more qualified. This usually occurs when client problems are specific (for example, autism, eating disorder, or substance abuse). Therapists have an ethical obligation to end therapy under certain conditions. If the therapist believes that therapy is not going anywhere, they need to do something different, and if lack of progress continues, they need to terminate the relationship.

One of the most fulfilling points of therapy is when therapists attempt to initiate termination because they believe the client is making enough progress they do not need to come back. When therapists suggest termination because the treatment goals have been reached, they tend to feel satisfaction that they have helped someone grow. This sense of accomplishment can be conveyed to the client to highlight the client's gains in therapy.

> *Therapist:* I'm not sure how much you have thought about this, but I would like to talk about the progress you have made over the course of our meetings. When you first came in, you stated you were not doing very well. We've met seven times, and by your statements, things have really changed for you. Personally, I think you have done a really great job taking control of your life and doing things to get things back in order. I'm really impressed with what you've accomplished. I'm so impressed that I think that this actually is a very good time for us to talk about wrapping things up. I would like you to take this next week to think about all of the progress you have made and when you come back next week, we can talk about your thoughts on whether you need to come back anymore.

Mutually Initiated Endings

Endings when the client and therapist jointly agree are the most common type of ending and can be the most satisfying (Martin, 2000). As in most decision-making processes, when both parties have the same opinion, they tend to feel good about the decision and the relationship. Mutually initiated endings can be enhanced during the course of therapy via the therapeutic interviewer periodically checking in with the client to see how the client views the progress being made. Further, when both therapist and client are on the same page about the treatment goals, it is much clearer as to the direction therapy is taking. If the goals seem not to be met, both parties are aware that termination is still off in the distance. When the client is making incremental progress toward the goals, therapist and client realize that they continue to take steps toward termination. Mutually initiated endings are the more preferred type of endings as both parties will tend to feel good about the process. Even if both therapist and client want to end the relationship because there is a lack of progress, they can do so in a way that validates both individual's views. If one party does not want to end the relationship, lingering aftereffects may impact that person. See Case Scenario 7.4 (p. 172).

CASE SCENARIO 7.4

Nadia worked with her therapist for eleven months. She was dealing with major depression and found the therapy to be extremely helpful for her. She developed an attachment to her therapist and looked forward to the meetings. Her therapist had recommended termination because Nadia had reached her treatment goals, but Nadia was scared that she would revert back to her old self after they stopped meeting. Although they addressed these fears in therapy, once they terminated, Nadia had a difficult time opening up to people for fear that she would lose that relationship. In this case, check-in sessions or some other type of aftercare program might have been useful.

Forced Terminations

Forced terminations occur when one of the members of the therapeutic system is moving away, has been released from a counseling center, or will no longer be serving in a therapist capacity. If, at the point of the forced termination, both parties do not feel that therapy has been successful, each might come away from the termination feeling bad about what occurred. Forced terminations often happen in training facilities or with student therapists. Because many student therapists working in university training programs or during their practicum or internship placements are there in a time-limited manner, they may be leaving the site before the client has finished all of the necessary work in therapy. Therapists can help to ease this transition by being clear from the very beginning of their meetings about the time frame they are working under. Further, therapists can check in with clients periodically during the course of therapy to remind them of when they will be exiting the site. Cochran and Cochran (2006) suggested that when there are these arbitrary endings (based on the number of sessions an agency allows or a therapist leaving a site), the therapist count down the number of sessions with the client to prevent the final session and termination from being abrupt.

Therapists can help ease the transition of termination by foreshadowing. Murphy and Dillon (2003) explained, "It is important that clinicians and clients have as much lead time as possible to discuss ending and allow for the processing and digestion of the transition from this special form of caring and collaboration" (p. 274). Therapists can be doing things from the very beginning of therapy to start to ease the end of the relationship. One way of doing this is by spacing out sessions. If therapist and client are meeting every week, when the therapist tells the client that she should start spacing out the sessions because the client is on a positive path, it sends a message to the client that the client can handle the situation. Clients are then able to work more independently in progressing or maintaining the gains made in therapy. Spacing of sessions can be a very empowering message to the client.

Reflection 7.1

Think about some relationship that you had with someone that ended, where you did not see the person again after the ending. What was it like knowing that you would probably not see that person again? What did you take away from the relationship? How would you have preferred the relationship to end? What things could you have done to make that ending better? How have you handled other endings in your past?

Termination as a Transition Point

Termination has primarily been viewed as a loss, largely for the client, but also for the therapist. Especially for longer-term therapy relationships, the ending of the relationship can be quite awkward. Clients and therapists feel odd knowing that they will probably never see or talk to the other person again. Given the unique ethical frame in which the therapeutic relationship is housed, once therapy ends, the relationship does not shift to being friends; it ends. A final session is fraught with strangeness as the two parties have worked so closely and now will be severing all ties. In order to help ease this transition, therapeutic interviewers should process with clients the clients' perspectives of what the end of therapy means. Clients may understand the ending of the relationship very differently from the way the therapist views it. This is especially true for children and adolescents.

Therapists can use the ending of therapy as a time of reflection in which they and the client look back at what occurred during their meetings. Transposing where the client is now versus where the client was when they first met can bring a sense of pleasure and accomplishment to the client. Certain points can be used as markers, noting where change occurred for the client.

> *Therapist:* I want to remind you about what occurred in our fourth session. At that point, you had said that you didn't think that you would be able to get over your past relationship. Today, it is hard to think that you said that because you have definitely moved ahead in your life in such a positive direction. Congratulations. What do you think about that?

Termination can be seen as a rite of passage (Epston & White, 1995). These authors challenged the metaphor of "termination as loss" and hold that a more useful metaphor is "termination as rite of passage" (p. 341). For them, termination is a ritual where they might have celebrations, prize givings, invite significant members of the client's life to the last session, develop "news releases" of the client's new identity, and consult the clients on cases they may have in the future based on the client's becoming empowered to overcome the problem. Thus, instead of something negative occurring at termination (a loss, which disempowers the client), clients can be respected and empowered.

Many therapists use the last session as a celebration. They might bring in a cake or some other food, as that distinguishes this session as different from all other sessions. Therapists usually do not eat with clients during a therapeutic interview; thus, by engaging in a mutual sharing of food, therapists shift the session from a typical therapeutic interview to a context of commemoration. At most commemorations outside of the therapy context, food is used as a way to celebrate the occasion. For example, most birthday parties have a cake to celebrate another year of life. Food can be used similarly in therapy.

Besides food, there are many other ways to create a context in which the last session is used as a transition point for clients to take all they have learned throughout the course of the therapy and shift that into their nontherapy world. Some therapists tend to think of termination as a graduation and have a celebration around that. With children (and even adolescents and adults), the therapist can print up documents and diplomas that signify the client's attainment of their goals.

Dealing with Dependency

In longer-term therapy relationships, the issue of dependency may become a possibility. Some clients come to therapy because they do not feel a connection with anyone in their social realm. The therapist may then become the person they go to in order to get a sense that someone cares about them. If therapists accept that they are the main person to connect with the client, there is the possibility of their fostering the client's feeling of needing the therapist. Therapists can help decrease the possibility that clients will feel dependent on them by helping clients to connect with people in their social field. From the beginning of therapy, this can be one of the main goals. The more that clients can go to other people besides the therapist for a sense of companionship, the less likely it is they will feel so desperate that no one else would understand them.

Another way of preventing dependency is not allowing the client to give the therapist credit for positive change. When things start to go right for clients, many have the tendency to attribute the positive change to the therapist instead of their own hard work. Therapists can be appreciative of positive client feedback, yet also ensure that the client takes most, if not all, credit for positive movement. This distinction between accepting credit and giving the client credit are depicted in the following scenarios:

Client: Doc, I really want to thank you for all you've done. Without you, I wouldn't have been able to do it.

Therapist: You're welcome. I'm glad I was useful to you.

Client: Yeah, I hope that my luck doesn't change.

Client: Doc, I really want to thank you for all you've done. Without you, I wouldn't have been able to do it.

Therapist: Yes, I've really enjoyed working with you because you were able to really utilize therapy to get what you wanted out of it. Not everyone is able to do that.

Client: You changed my life.

Therapist: I'm not the one who made those changes; you were!

In the first example, the client leaves the therapeutic relationship in a disempowered state. She is not viewing herself as having much personal agency to change her life in the direction she wishes. Change for her has come from a third party and will need to come from a third party to continue (or luck). In the second scenario, the therapist ensures that the client knows that although the therapist might have presented a context of change, it was actually the client who made those changes.

One way of periodically supporting the client's own initiatives toward change throughout the therapeutic process is to use compliments. Each time the client makes a move toward positive change, the therapist can highlight that client action and compliment the client for taking that step. Thus, throughout the course of therapy, the therapist is continually pointing out things that *the client* is doing that are moving in the direction toward her goals.

Relapse Prevention

The notion of relapse has primarily been associated with substance abuse. It is when the person, after stopping taking the substance (problem), returns to the levels of use that brought her to therapy. This is different than a "slip," as a slip is when the person uses once or twice, but not to the level previously used. For clients dealing with serious mental disorders and/or addictions, relapse is the most common outcome (Prochaska & Norcross, 2007). Let me iterate this again. For many problems that clients bring to therapy, the gains seem to be time limited. In the long run, many clients shift back, for some length of time, to earlier patterns of problem behaviors. Thus, it would seem imperative for the therapeutic interviewer to incorporate the notion of relapse into the therapy so that if there are any shifts back to the problem behavior (or to higher levels of the problem behavior), these times could have been accounted for already and utilized as a means to move the client back toward the goal behaviors as quickly as possible.

Therapists can include relapse prevention in their therapy regardless of what the client's presenting complaint is. Relapse prevention does not have to be used only with substance abuse issues. For instance, if a client is coming in because of issues surrounding aggression, the therapist can tell the client that there may be times in the future where she may become aggressive and for the client to view this not as a failure but as an opportunity to learn more about herself.

Therapist: When you first came in to see me, you stated that you were feeling very depressed. We have worked together now for six weeks and each week you've told me that you have been feeling happier and happier. Today, you are saying that you really aren't feeling depressed at all. I think that's great. I hope that continues for you. However, all people, at various points in life feel depressed. There will probably be points in your future when you will feel some of the things that you felt when you first came in. That does not mean that therapy was all a waste and that all of the great changes you have made were for naught. It is just a sign for you that there are things that you can do to get back into a groove where you are happier.

If relapse prevention is not incorporated into the therapy, the client may experience a relapse and think that the whole time spent in therapy was a failure. Therapeutic interviewers can discuss how it is very difficult to maintain the change 100 percent of the time. If the client does experience the problem, it can be reframed as normal in the process of growth as well as being a means of understanding the self to a greater degree.

Some therapists talk about relapse prevention as being an aftercare program. These are things set in place by the client to try to prevent the problem from occurring again and to maintain and continue the positive growth from therapy. The therapist can work with the client so that the client is actively putting into practice activities, rituals, thoughts, and practices to ensure that they maintain the gains made in therapy. For instance, a client who has been dealing with aggression can develop a relaxation program to engage in, even after therapy is over.

Referrals

One important skill for therapists to learn is how to make appropriate referrals. Therapists might not be suited to work with all clients. This realization is sometimes made in the first session, sometimes the second, sometimes the twentieth. An ill fit between therapeutic interviewer and client might be based on many reasons, including a clash of personalities, the client dealing with an issue that is out of the scope of the therapist's expertise, or the client asking for services the therapist is not trained to deliver.

Referring a client to someone else does not mean the therapist or the therapy was a failure. It means the therapist believes there is someone else who is more suited to work with that particular client, dealing with that particular issue, or working in a specific approach the client desires. For instance, if a client is seeking hypnosis for pain management and the therapist is not trained in hypnosis, a referral to a certified hypnotherapist is extremely important. Ethically, therapists have a duty to refer the client to a different therapist when they believe that they are not helping the client progress or the issue is beyond the scope of the therapist's practice.

The introduction of the purpose of the referral is important as the therapist does not want to leave the client with a sense that it is the client's fault (they did something wrong) and that is why the therapist is giving the referral. Some clients might think that the therapist does not like them or does not want to work with them, which would then lower their self-esteem. Case Scenario 7.5 explains how a referral might be what the client is looking for from the therapist.

Therapeutic interviewers should tell the client the purpose of the referral and give the client several referral choices so that they are empowered to shop around

CASE SCENARIO 7.5

I was working with a gay male who was having relationship problems. He had specifically requested a male therapist, but was concerned that I was heterosexual and would not understand some of the issues he was dealing with as a male homosexual. We then discussed my role as a therapist and that my job was to help him understand where he wanted to go in his life. For this client, who had trouble getting over the notion of the difference of sexuality between us this was not enough. After two sessions of his being extremely concerned and thinking that he might not come back to therapy, I offered the possibility of a referral to a therapist who was openly homosexual. The client seemed relieved at this possibility, thanked me for the referral, and apologized that the therapy did not work out.

or make their own choices about their therapy. During the course of treatment, therapeutic interviewers can also check in with the client to see if there seems to be a good fit. For those therapists working in an agency setting who perceive that the client is uncomfortable with them, one possibility is to offer the opportunity to meet with a different therapist within the agency. This is a very tricky situation as many clients do not want to say that they would like a different therapist because they think this might upset their current therapist. Thus, a change of therapists based on gender or age or ethnicity might be easier for clients or therapists to accept. If clients do mention, either on their own or through the therapist's initiative, that they would like to explore the idea of changing therapists, therapists should in no way be punitive toward them. This is information for therapists that something in the relationship is not working as well as it might. This could give the therapist a sense of how he could change to better connect with the client.

Summary

The end of the therapeutic interview or the therapy relationship is as important a part of the therapy process as the beginning or middle. Therapists can use the termination of a specific client issue as a way to let the client know her story was heard and understood. This helps the client to process what was discussed. Therapists can use the end of a single therapeutic interview to plan ahead to the next session or to highlight the issues covered. When appropriate during the course of therapy, therapeutic interviewers should talk to clients about termination and how to end the relationship while also using it as a transition point for clients to continue with all of the progress they made during therapy. The endings that occur in therapy should all be utilized to keep clients moving forward rather than stopping them or causing them to move backwards away from their pursuit of change.

Exercises _____

1. Role-play with a classmate a session in which the client is bringing some new issue to talk about. Use a door opener, minimal encouragers, paraphrases, reflections of feeling, and reflections of meaning, and then end with a signal summary. Get feedback about which skills were helpful, which skills were not helpful, and any suggestions the classmate has for you.

2. Role-play with a classmate a discussion about termination. Practice this conversation in four ways: therapist-initiated termination; client-initiated termination; mutual termination; and forced termination. What differences do you notice during each of the different means of ending?

8

Pitfalls of Therapy
How to Avoid Being Ineffective

Up to this point in the book, we have discussed how therapeutic interviewing can be accomplished by using certain skills and attitudes. Conducting a therapeutic interview is an extremely difficult endeavor. Therapists must come into the conversation having put aside most of the elations, disappointments, sadness, and fears of their own life. Further, therapists have to conduct an improvisation with clients, flowing from what clients are saying and doing, never being able to fully script out the interview. Although therapists might not know exactly what will happen, they will need to have enough skills to be able to be effective. At some point in every therapist's career (probably many more than the person will care to remember), mistakes, errors, failures, blunders, and bad therapy will occur (Kottler & Blau, 1989). "Bad therapy" is a relative term, depending on the theoretical orientation of the observer of the therapeutic interview, the perspective of the client, and the perspective of ethical and legal overseeing bodies. This chapter addresses some of the more common mistakes therapeutic interviewers make. The information presented in this chapter is intended to be used as a guide rather than a be-all and end-all for conducting therapeutic interviews.

Many therapists know when good therapy is occurring. It is when things start to flow between therapist and client. The converse is also true when therapy is not going well. There are times when therapists have a sense that the therapy is not progressing. Just as many clients are hesitant to let the therapist know that therapy is not being productive or useful, therapists tend to experience this same hesitancy. This is another sign for the therapeutic interviewer that things are not going well. Not feeling comfortable talking about progress, or lack of progress, can signify that the therapeutic alliance might need to be strengthened.

This chapter is divided into three sections. The first describes common mistakes in microskills, usually in the wording or overuse of types of responses. The second section covers mistakes that happen internally for the therapeutic interviewer. The final section covers mistakes that happen interpersonally between therapist and client. This introduction to some of the most common mistakes should help therapeutic interviewers to become more aware of them and to decrease the potential for making them. Conscious awareness of common mistakes allows therapists to be cognizant of red flags that might be raised (internally and externally) during the therapeutic interview so that they might avoid a potential pitfall.

Common Mistakes in Microskills

In conducting many therapeutic interviews and supervising and training many therapists-in-training, I have compiled a list of some common microskills mistakes novice therapists tend to make during therapy. These are tactics that almost all novice therapists use at some point. They are also used by more established therapists. Although they are not *always* problematic, the more that therapists can stay away from using them, the better. The following are common mistakes in this area:

- Why questions
- Don't you/do you think questions
- "I understand"
- "Basically"
- "How does that make you feel?"
- "So"
- Using jargon

Why Questions

Why not ask why? There are several reasons for this. Welch (2003) believed that it is disrespectful to ask clients why. The question puts clients in a defensive position since if they knew the answer to why, they might not go to therapy in the first place. Since clients do not know why the problem behavior is happening, the therapist is putting them in a no-win situation. Clients cannot answer why, because if they do, they will be making something up—and if they do not give an answer, they are made to feel stupid.

Why questions are also premised on a notion of cause and effect. Patton (2002) stated, "'Why' questions presuppose that things happen for a reason and that those reasons are knowable" (p. 363). Life is extremely complex and finding a root cause may not be possible. Why questions also infer a causal relationship that occurs in a rational and ordered world. This is not necessarily the case.

Most people respond defensively when asked why questions. These questions have the potential to shift the therapist–client relationship into one that is similar to a parent–child relationship. In the latter scenario, when why questions are used, it is usually because the child did something bad. They implicitly lead the person being asked the why question to justify his or her actions because there was something wrong with those actions. Sommers-Flanagan and Sommers-Flanagan (2003) explained that clients have two typical reactions when asked why questions. The first is with "Because!" Clients will then try to explain themselves, not for the point of elucidation, but to prove their own worth and ideas. The second main type of client reaction is with "Why not?" They might then get into a debate whether what they are doing is good or bad.

Why questions are problematic partly because they may come from the therapist's own curiosity rather than as a thoughtful way to help the client. Welch (2003) argued, "It may well be that counselors and psychotherapists who routinely and typically ask such probing questions (why questions) are acting more out of their own needs—or, more graciously, out of a lack of training—than any concern for client welfare" (p. 206). There is also a third typical client response to a why question: a simple, "I don't know." This is not helpful for the therapist, as it does not add any new information into the interview. It can also be problematic for the client in that it can lead to his feeling disconnected from himself.

Instead of asking why questions, therapists can ask how and what questions. For instance, consider the following why question:

"Why have you chosen this path for yourself?"

A therapist can ask this question instead:

"What has been your decision-making process for going on this path?" or "How have you decided to take this path?"

Don't You/Do You Think Questions

When therapeutic interviewers ask questions that start with "Don't you think" or "Do you think" they tend not to really be asking the client a question. These therapist utterances are designed less to bring forth the client's perceptions than to highlight the therapist's point of view. Take the following therapist statement:

Therapist: Don't you think that you should pay more attention to your wife?

In this situation, the therapist is really saying that *she* thinks the client should pay more attention to his wife. However, in the way that the question is worded, the therapist is not taking ownership of her own thoughts and beliefs. Besides implying that the current way the client is behaving is wrong, the therapist is modeling a way of communicating that doesn't get the person to connect with his own self and ideas. These types of questions should be reworded as either statements or questions exploring the client's worldview. For instance, consider the following two alternatives:

Therapist: Based on my understanding of what is going on for you and your relationship with your wife, it seems to me that taking a more active part in showing attention to your wife might be one step forward for you. What do you think of this?

Therapist: What are your views about your connection to your wife?

"I Understand"

On the surface, "I understand" seems like a very good response from a therapist who is really trying to understand the client's phenomenological world. However, when the therapist tries to be so overt about understanding the client, the client then has to prove to the therapist that the therapist does *not* fully understand. Clients do not want anyone else to fully understand them as that implies that they are simple, not complex human beings. Thus, clients will sense a challenge in that they will then have to demonstrate to the therapist that she does not understand them as much as she thinks she does.

> *Client:* This is so new to me and all these things really confuse me. It's all happening so fast and coming down on me.
> *Therapist:* I understand.
> *Client:* But no, you see, she keeps on calling and I don't know what to do. I'm not sure if it's what I want.
> *Therapist:* I understand, it's very hard for you.
> *Client:* But it's so scary.

The therapist, although following along with the client and trying to relay her connection to the client's situation, is really putting a rift in the therapeutic connection. Instead of using "I understand," therapists can display this by using accurate empathy. By utilizing paraphrases and reflections, therapeutic interviewers never need to utter these words. The client will know the therapist understands because of the accuracy of the reflections.

"Basically"

Clients come to therapy because serious things in their lives are upsetting them. They want to feel acknowledgment that their situation is important. However, if a therapist begins a reflection with "Basically," the therapist is minimizing the client's situation. It takes everything that the client has said that is going wrong (remember, clients come to therapy because life is not good or not good enough) and puts it into one small package. This can feel belittling to the client.

> *Client:* Life is so awful. I have so many things going on right now, and they all seem to be miserable. My love life sucks. My job is about to be downsized. My mother just went into a nursing home. And my diabetes is acting up.
> *Therapist:* Basically, things are overwhelming.

As can be seen, there is no need to use the word "basically" as it only diminishes the seriousness of the client's story.

"How Does That Make You Feel?"

On the surface, this seems like the type of response that every therapist utilizes and is a good question (depending on your theoretical orientation). But that is exactly the problem with this response. It is a stock response. If someone would ask lay people what therapists say, this question would probably be at the top of the list. This is one of the reasons that this response is not a good one; it is extremely trite. When clients hear this from a therapist, they realize the person they are talking to is in "therapist mode." There are other ways to get the information this question is intended to procure:

- "What's going on for you when that happens?"
- "What is that like for you?"
- "How is it for you when that happens?"

"So"

More therapists than not begin their paraphrases and reflections with "So." The problem with this is that it starts to become similar to an inquisition. Too many therapist responses in a row with "so" can get the client to start to become defensive.

> *Therapist:* So, when was it that you realized things were going in this direction?
>
> *Client:* Maybe a few months ago.
>
> *Therapist:* So, what did you do about that?
>
> *Client:* Well, I told her that I thought we could use a break.
>
> *Therapist:* So, for you, you wanted a bit of time.
>
> *Client:* Yes, it seemed the best thing to do.
>
> *Therapist:* So, you're trying to figure out where to go in your life.

In this exchange, the therapist's responses can be taken as more of an interrogation than a conversation. Some therapists might not use the word "so," but will have another catch phrase that they tend to use. Therapists should be aware of their language tendencies to ensure they do not use one word or phrase too often as that might become noticed by the client and thus hinder the communication.

Using Jargon

Although therapists may use technical language when reading or writing academic journals and books, conversing with other professionals, or trying to conceptualize cases, technical language and jargon can put off a client. Most clients do not understand the technical language, thus, the therapist would have to restate the sentence anyway. Second, use of technical language can lead to clients' feeling stupid because they are not comprehending what the therapist is saying. Clients

TABLE 8.1   *Common Microskills Mistakes*

- Why questions
- Don't you/Do you think
- "I understand"
- "Basically"
- "How does that make you feel?"
- "So"
- Using jargon

might also feel degraded, that they are some diagnoses instead of human beings. Turner and Hersen (1987) held that the use of jargon is the sign of an inexperienced therapist. They go on to say even more emphatically, "From our perspective, there is no justification for using technical language with clients at any point in the interview process" (p. 16). The following exchange is an example of this:

> *Client:* So, as I've stated, my life is really bad right now.
>
> *Therapist:* Well, it seems that you have been dealing with an Oedipal dilemma and are fixated in an early stage of development.
>
> *Client:* What?

As discussed in Chapter 4, therapists should utilize language that can be understood by the client. Unless the client is in the psychological health field (that is, a therapist), therapists should not use jargon and should phrase things in a simple and easily understood manner.

Table 8.1 lists the common microskills mistakes.

Common Intrapersonal Mistakes

Novice therapists make several common mistakes in the intrapersonal realm. Even some therapists who have practiced for quite a while make most of these mistakes at some point in their careers. Use of any of these mistakes is not catastrophic, yet therapists' awareness of each of them and attempts to avoid them will help both the interview process and the movement of the client toward success in therapy. To become aware of these mistakes, therapists need to become self-aware. They need to recognize what they are thinking about the client and the therapy process. It is recommended that therapists video or tape record their sessions and then review them with a supervisor so they can address not only the skills that were used but also their own attitudes and belief systems.

Detachment

Therapy is a process of a client's opening up to a therapist in order to get the therapist's expertise to help the client reach certain goals. The therapist needs to be engaged enough to be with the client during the course of the therapeutic interview. Although not every problem is one in which the client will be emoting, even when a client wants to change a problem behavior, the client wants to know that the therapist is "there." Even in nontherapy situations, such as an interaction with the checkout person at the supermarket, there is something distressing about having the other person be disengaged. Therapists can be too connected, but they can also be too detached. Since the brunt of the therapeutic process occurs through the therapeutic relationship and alliance, therapists need to be present enough to develop and maintain this connection. Therapeutic detachment is not the same as therapeutic distance. Therapeutic distance is healthy in that the therapist understands that she is different from the client and has different thoughts, feelings, and behaviors. Therapeutic detachment occurs when the therapist is not present in the therapy and does not have the appropriate amount of caring for the client as a person. When therapists perceive that they are detached in the session, they should spend some time outside the session assessing what it is about the client or the client's situation that is leading to this gap and then try to figure out how they can connect more successfully with the client.

Moralizing

Clients come to therapy already feeling bad about themselves because of the situation that they have not been able to deal effectively with. If the therapist begins to start telling the client how he "should" be feeling, the client will then feel even worse about himself because the therapist is, in essence, saying that what he is doing is wrong. Further, who is to say that what the therapist is saying is wrong is really wrong. When they do this, therapists are demonstrating their own personal biases.

> *Therapist:* Sean, I just wanted to let you know that I don't think how you're acting with your mother is right. She is your mother. She deserves a certain amount of respect, and I don't think you are giving her that.

Before therapists start telling clients how they should act, they should assess where their suggestion is coming from—whether it is based on their own personal beliefs or is housed within a theoretical framework.

Going for Quick Solutions

Most clients have made several, if not many, change attempts before they ever go to see a therapist. If therapists move too fast in trying to solve a client's problems, without getting a good understanding of how the client makes sense of the situation, past solution attempts, and a thorough understanding of the contextual situation, therapists can actually undermine themselves. Consider the following exchange in the middle of a first session:

> *Therapist:* My recommendation would be that you start to keep a log of your eating.
>
> *Client:* I've already been doing that for two months now, and nothing has changed.
>
> *Therapist:* Well then, perhaps you can try to exercise at least thirty minutes a day.
>
> *Client:* I do.

The client in this situation can quickly lose a sense that the therapist can help because everything the therapist is recommending has already been tried. Although therapy is about change (and change *can* happen in only one session), the therapist who pushes the client to change before a more complete understanding of the problem situation is brought forth risks losing the client.

Giving Advice

Clients come to therapy usually after a time—after they have unsuccessfully waited for the problem to get better or asked their friends and relatives to help them. Their friends have probably accommodated this request and given all sorts of advice. Even if the client has taken the advice, he has not felt that it has been effective or as effective as desired. Therapy is not about advice giving. It is about working with clients to explore the situation in ways that are different from those they have tried previously. Advice giving is a very disempowering process whereby the therapist is telling the client how to live. If the client actually takes the advice and things get better, they are then tied to the therapist, needing to get further advice when other problems occur. If the advice does not work, the client can then lose faith that the therapist will be helpful for him. The therapist can then state that the client did not enact the advice in the right way, and thus, the therapist is never responsible for poor advice. Instead of giving advice, therapists are encouraged to help clients come to their own conclusions about the course of their own lives.

Being Overresponsible

Novice therapists have a tendency to think that they know what needs to occur in a case. They then attempt to get the client to do what they think is best. This seems to come from the standard practice of lay persons when someone comes to them with problems, but takes it a step further. The previous issue dealt with giving advice. In being overresponsible, therapists not only give advice, but continue to push clients to do what the therapist thinks is best for them. Sometimes this occurs

CASE SCENARIO 8.1

I supervised a third-year master's mental health counseling student who was working in a community mental health center. She was referred a client in his thirties who was homeless, jobless, dealing with substance abuse, and disconnected from his family. The therapist intern took it upon herself to call around and find her client a temporary shelter bed to sleep in, called up employment agencies that handled temporary work, and tried to track down his family. Although all of these actions are based on a sense of wanting to help, when the therapist took over the whole of each of these endeavors, she actually disempowered the client. Instead of giving the client the opportunity to do them, or at least do them together, she took ownership of action away from him. This did not allow the client to develop some of these skill-building activities.

because the therapist has a need to be wanted and so does most of the work in therapy. Case Scenario 8.1 provides a situation in which a therapist took more ownership of the client's situation than the client did.

Unrealistic Expectations

Both the client and the therapist have expectations about therapy. These expectations are for self, other, and the process. Unrealistic expectations play a role in bad therapy on six levels. The first is when the client expects himself to be perfect and is upset with himself for having problems. The second is when the client expects the therapeutic process to be a cure-all. Third is when the client expects the therapist to be an expert and to be the perfect therapist. Fourth is when the therapist expects herself to be perfect. Fifth is when the therapist expects rapid change and full-fledged motivation from the client. Sixth is when the therapist expects therapy to solve the client's life problems. Each of these unrealistic expectations can lead to problems during the therapeutic process. A combination of these unrealistic expectations can put a dent in the productive flow of therapy.

Therapeutic interviewers can help to prevent all six of these mistakes. First, they can continuously check in with themselves to examine what their own expectations are about their work. Therapy is not a science; there will never be a perfect therapy or a perfect therapist. Therapists can work toward accepting that they do make mistakes. Second, therapists can, when they start to feel frustrated with the client, attempt to understand why the client might not be reaching their expectations for them, and thus, set more realistic expectations for the client. Third, when therapists hear the clients' unrealistic expectations for themselves, the therapy process, or the therapist, they can have a conversation about realistic expectations of self, process, and other.

False Understanding

One of the goals of the therapeutic interviewer is to understand the phenomeno-logical worldview of the client. If the therapist does not quite understand, but falsely states that she does, she runs several risks. First, since she does not really understand the client, the questions, interventions, and other activities used dur-ing the therapeutic interview might not make sense given the client's actual situa-tion. Second, if the client realizes the therapist has been stating she understands when she really doesn't, the client might lose trust in the therapist. It is okay for a therapist not to understand what a client is saying or the client's thought processes. This is when she can use her interviewing skills to help the client bring forth these understandings. Clients actually appreciate that therapists are taking the time and getting to know and understand them rather than quickly classifying them or telling them that they understand when they actually do not.

> *Therapist:* Let me stop you here for a second. I'm not sure I am completely following along with everything you've been saying, and I want to make sure I am with you. Could you explain again what that was like for you when you found out?

Giving Reassurance

Reassurance is based on an assurance that something will happen. This is a guar-antee therapeutic interviewers cannot give. Usually, clients want the reassurance that things are going to change and get better. Although this is the goal of the ther-apist, it is not certain that this will happen. Approximately 60 to 70 percent of clients do find therapy useful. About 20 to 30 percent do not find it that useful and approximately 10 percent of clients actually get worse. There is a difference between reassurance and normalization. In normalization, the therapist explains to the client that the client's behaviors or experiences are things that happen to many, if not most, other people. Reassurance, on the other hand, attempts to pre-dict the future when this is not a possibility for the therapist.

> *Therapist:* Don't worry. All things pass, eventually. Things will get better for you. You just need to keep hanging in there, and it will happen.

Although therapists do want to infuse a sense of hope and expectancy into the therapy, they can do so without making claims that they cannot back. There are other ways of letting clients know that the therapist believes things will get better.

> *Therapist:* During my career as a therapist, I've seen many people change in ways that made their lives more fulfilling. You seem to have a lot of moti-vation and determination to make things better for yourself. I'm very hopeful that you will be able to reach your goals.

Confusing the Diagnosis with the Person

Beginning therapists working in agency settings will often be assigned a client after an intake specialist has met with that client, conducted a biopsychosocial evaluation, and provided a diagnosis. When therapists look at the diagnosis and start to use that as a guiding point for contacting the client, instead of trying to get to know the person who is the client, problems can occur. Kottler and Blau (1989) discussed that when therapists, before ever meeting the client, find out the client has been diagnosed with a "threatening label" (for example, borderline, anorexic, schizoaffective), they might come into the therapeutic encounter with a defensive attitude or prejudice. This prevents them from connecting with the client because they are mainly working with the diagnosis rather than the person. This can be seen in how some therapists talk about their client list (for example, "First I have my manic-depressive and then is my bulimic, and then, unfortunately, I have my borderline"). When this occurs, the personhood seems to be removed from the client. Therapists should continuously focus on who clients are as people rather than the labels that might be associated with them.

Not Accepting Mistakes

Every single person in the world has made mistakes at some point in their lives. Most of us make at least one mistake each and every day (usually a lot more). Thankfully, most of them are extremely minor mistakes. However, the more that we fail to realize we made a mistake, take ownership for it, and learn from it, the more disconnected we are in our own practice and the higher the likelihood we might make similar or other mistakes without even realizing it. When therapists do not acknowledge their own mistakes, they generally make further mistakes. Hopefully therapists do not purposefully make mistakes. Being open to the possibility of making mistakes and then seeing how they can grow from their mistakes is an important skill for therapeutic interviewers.

Negative Reactions to the Client

At the beginning of some business days, therapists look over their appointment books. If there is a client on the list that the therapist is not looking forward to working with, this might signal that some type of problem is involved. Therapeutic interviews are not cut-and-dry. They include the therapist's thoughts and feelings. When therapists have a negative gut reaction, they should take it as an opportunity to explore their own reactions. By picking up on certain cues early, they can attempt to change what is not working.

Therapy is a relationship between two people. Just because someone is a therapist does not guarantee that the two people (therapist and client) will like or get along with each other. When the therapist has a negative reaction to a client, Flemons (2002) recommended using that reaction as a transportation device. Negative reactions are a clue that there is a disconnection between therapist and client.

Therapists can then become curious about what is going on for them that they have this reaction. Further, they can explore what it is that they haven't quite understood yet about the other person. In this way, the negative reaction becomes a tool for better connection with the client instead of something that can separate therapist and client.

Therapist Emotional Distress

Therapy is a process in which one person is available to help another person. The change and movement is all for the client. Some therapists, however, when they have not fully addressed their own current life situations and issues, might find these coming through in the therapy room. The extreme of this is depicted in some sitcoms or movies that have farcically depicted therapists who are emotionally disturbed. The client then comes to therapy, but quickly the therapist is crying and getting therapy from the client. Unfortunately, this situation actually does occur, and therapists need to be on guard against it.

Clients pick up subtle cues from therapists. If a therapist hints at having an issue in the past, clients might go along that path with the therapist. Therapists need to be in tune with themselves to know whether their own personal business is coming through in the therapy. Many therapists, starting with Freud, have suggested that therapists get their own therapy so that their personal issues do not impact the therapy.

Some therapists come into the field because they receive pleasure from knowing that they were needed by someone. Therapy is not about getting clients to rely on therapists to figure out what to do in their lives but for therapists to work with clients to get them to rely on themselves to get their lives moving in the direction they want. One of the things that some therapists have done is to give clients the impression that the client is deficient and needs the therapist to help them get things moving in the right direction. This perception encourages clients to become dependent on the therapist. This is the antithesis of the intention of therapy. A good therapist will try to get the client to stop coming to therapy as soon as possible. If the therapist starts the whole of the therapeutic process with this mind-set, the chances that the client will think that he needs the therapist will be reduced.

Table 8.2 presents the most common intrapersonal mistakes.

Common Interpersonal Mistakes

Mistakes can happen with the words used or with an internal attribute of the therapist. They can also occur in the interpersonal realm between therapist and client. These mistakes usually occur when both parties utilize the therapeutic interview beyond its scope. The therapeutic interview is predicated on designated roles, with rules that define what types of behaviors between the two are acceptable and unacceptable. When these rules are broken, the roles of therapist and client become blurred.

TABLE 8.2   *Common Intrapersonal Mistakes*

- Detachment
- Moralizing
- Going for quick solutions
- Giving advice
- Being overresponsible
- Unrealistic expectations
- False understanding
- Giving reassurance
- Confusing the diagnosis for the person
- Not accepting mistakes
- Negative reactions to the client
- Therapist emotional distress

Friendship Rather Than Therapy

One of the traps that novice therapists find themselves engaging in is a relationship with a client that is more similar to that of friendship than of therapy. It is an easy trap to fall into because many clients come to therapy looking for this type of relationship or feeling such a connection to the therapist that they attempt to gain a friend rather than a therapist.

People in the general public who have not had experience going to therapy may question the intent of going to a professional counselor because they believe that they can get the same outcome by talking their problems over with friends or family members. If they can get what they need from a friend, why pay money to let a stranger into their lives and personal business? They also may not realize that the way they interact with their friend, developing an intimacy and being able to call on one another in a mutual relationship, is not the same experience they will get with a therapist. Many novice therapists have difficulties with the boundaries between the roles of friend and therapist. Therapeutic interviewers work with some clients who, if the two had met outside of the therapy arena, could have been friends. Yet, because their interactions occur within a context of therapy, friendship is not possible.

What occurs between two people in friendship interactions and therapy interviews have some similarities, but are quite different. Hutchins and Vaught (1997) provided several ways in which the helping relationship differs from a typical interpersonal transaction.

1. The client is primarily responsible for content of the interview although the helper determines how the content is addressed.   *Content Client's respons.*
2. The client receives the helper's total attention rather than engaging in a typical two-way discussion. The helper focuses on the client's concerns instead of expressing personal opinions and giving advice.   *total attention*
3. Client concerns are confidential to the extent allowed by law, professional codes, or contractual agreements.

4. The goal of the helping relationships…is to assist the client in taking steps to work through problems or concerns and to achieve realistic goals that resolve problems.
5. The client can try out new ways of behaving in the secure atmosphere of the helping interview.
6. The client becomes more independent. (pp. 15–16).

The therapeutic interview is a type of interpersonal communication in that interviewer and client exchange verbal and nonverbal information simultaneously and mutually influence each other. The purpose of this communication is to manage the therapeutic relationship so that the client gets out of therapy what he signed up for.

Most people have a friend or family member with whom they discuss their everyday problems. Sometimes they find this to be helpful, but friends and family members tend to be quick in trying to move the person from a place of distress to one of comfort. Although this is the eventual goal of therapy, the process is quite different. In therapy, the client is allowed to experience all of the various emotions he is feeling at the moment. Friends tend to try to stop the person from being upset, angry, depressed, and so on. The following example illustrates a typical conversation with a friend who is in distress:

Person A: I can't believe he's leaving me. What am I going to do?

Person B: You don't need him! You have so much going for you.

Person A: Why is this happening to me? I tried so hard to please him.

Person B: Don't cry. He doesn't deserve you. You can do much better.

Person A: No, I can't.

Person B: Yes, you can.

Person A: Do you really think so?

Person B: Of course. A guy would have to be a fool not to want to date you!

Person A: Why would they want to? What do I have to offer?

Although Person B is operating out of a very caring position, their reassurances are not really reassuring for Person A. Friends are very good at trying to support

Reflection 8.1

What sorts of personal issues do you talk about with friends? What issues do you not talk about with them? How come? How much easier do you think it is opening up and talking about painful, embarrassing, anxiety-provoking problems with a stranger rather than with someone you know well? How much do you think that the skills of a therapist help someone address his concerns? How hard is it for you or friends to listen without dispensing advice? How often do you follow advice given to you?

each other; however, they are not very good at allowing the person to explore what it is about the situation that is making them so upset. Further, friends tend to try to restrict all of the person's "negative" emotions. When someone starts crying, their first impulse tends to be to try to get them to stop crying. The therapeutic interviewer's position is very different.

The therapeutic interview is a safe haven for people to express any thought, feeling, or desire they may have. These might be too risky to discuss with friends and family members. Sometimes, people are dealing with issues that they would prefer their friends not know about them (for example, their attraction to children, guilt around having a marital affair, or their sexual orientation). By going to someone who is not in their everyday field of relationships, clients can feel secure opening up. Further, because the therapy relationship is a contractual one where the therapist must hold confidentiality under most conditions, the client's information is pretty secure. With friends, secrets tend to be told to other people in the friendship network.

Therapeutic interviewers sometimes lose perspective as to their role with a specific client. They might feel a connection where they act in ways as they do to their own friends or family. Although being genuine is important in the therapeutic relationship, the dynamics of a friend and a client are extremely different. Therapists should keep alert for signals that the feelings and connection they are having toward a client fall within the range of the normal therapist–client relationship. If they find that their feelings toward a certain client seem to be different than for most of their other clients, they should consult colleagues or their supervisor so that they can ensure they are professionally engaging with the client.

Arguing with Clients

The opposite side of being a friend to the client is getting into a relationship with the client where arguing and trying to prove one's point comes into play. The therapeutic interview is a joint venture between therapist and client. There is no need for the therapist to argue with the client. As with most endeavors in life, more forward movement happens when the two people in the endeavor are working together toward a common goal instead of against each other. Therapists might argue with clients because they believe that they know what the client should do and the client is not engaging in that behavior. They might also argue when the client holds a certain value position that they don't hold. For instance, the client

Reflections 8.2

Think about the last time a friend came to you with a serious problem they were having when they were very emotionally distraught. When they began crying, what was your initial reaction? How did you feel inside? What words did you use with them? Were there a lot of reassurances, attempts to get the person to feel differently and attempts to instill hope?

might be pro-life or anti-gay. Some therapists will take it upon themselves to argue with the client to try to get the client to change his belief system. Therapists should consider what their role is when clients have an opposing position on certain issues. The more therapeutic interviewers argue with their clients, the greater the possibility that clients will take offense to the arguing and stop coming to therapy.

Boundary Violations

As stated in Chapter 1, therapy is a business relationship between two (or more) people. However, it is an extremely unique relationship in that organizations have established ethical codes of conduct for therapeutic practitioners to maintain. These ethical rules establish boundaries between therapist and client. The main type of boundary people think about in this context is in the sexual realm; yet even there, the ethical bodies are not all in agreement as to how long a client is a client. Some hold that therapist and client cannot engage in a sexual relationship for at least two years after terminating therapy. Other ethical codes state that a therapist should never engage in a sexual relationship with an ex-client.

One boundary violation that occurs is dual relationships. Dual relationships are when multiple roles occur between therapist and client. The main role between the two is a therapeutic relationship. Other roles might be friends, family, work partners, professor/student, or other such arrangements. Although things become pretty black and white when it comes to sexual relationships (it does not occur when the person is a client), nonsexual dual relationships with clients and other boundary crossings operate more in the gray area. Therapists should not engage in therapy with friends or family members, but it becomes less clear when someone is a friend of a friend (whom the therapist might bump into at parties because the two are in the same friendship circle) or an occasional business associate. This is especially so for those therapists working in rural areas. For instance, a friend's father, who was a psychologist, lived in an extremely rural area of Kansas. He was the only mental health professional for at least 100 miles in his town. Many of his clients were people whom he had known for many years. He ate at their restaurants and shopped at their stores. He could not avoid engaging in dual relationships.

Lazarus and Zur (2002) distinguished between boundary violations, which have the potential to harm the client, and boundary crossings, which have the potential to aid the client's move toward the client's goals. These boundary crossings are not necessarily unethical. They might include going out to lunch with an anorectic client to work on eating behavior, going to a client's graduation from school (given the striving for schooling was an issue discussed in therapy), or going to watch a client's band if the client was having anxiety issues (stage fright). However, any time therapists do not follow standard protocol (working within the main confines of ethical codes), they are opening themselves up to potential ethical misconduct.

Some *boundary violations* that are considered bad therapy are having sexual relations with the client, exploiting the client, and gaining information from the client about nontherapeutic issues for personal gain. These should be completely avoided; however, more experienced therapists can explore *boundary crossings* to see if, ethically, they can utilize these to assist clients. Novice therapists are recommended to avoid boundary crossings, as they usually occur once a more seasoned understanding of therapy and clients has formed for the therapist. If a therapist does choose to explore boundary crossings, they should consult with their ethical advisory board as they are not standard practice.

Other Interpersonal Mistakes

What has been presented in this chapter is only a smattering of the potential problems and mistakes that can occur during the therapeutic interview. Therapists should be constantly vigilant of the process occurring between themselves and their clients. Dillon (2003) provided several other interpersonal mistakes, including seeming not to care about the client, lack of unconditional positive regard, trying to impress others, and infantilizing clients (treating them like children). Therapists should be on the lookout for potential mistakes in what they say, think, and do during the course of therapy.

Learning from Mistakes

In order to learn from one's mistakes, therapeutic interviewers have to realize they are making mistakes. During a session, they can pay attention to two potential signals of mistakes: client behavior and their own reactions. Dillon (2003) provided the following common client signals of mistakes in progress:

1. The worker says something far afield of where the client is, and the client does not even seem to register it. It's as though the worker's statement is a nonevent.
2. A "huh?" response.
3. The client corrects the worker, expecting him or her to change.
4. The client suddenly shifts emotional contact or focus following a worker offering.
5. The client suddenly questions the worker's competence.
6. The client suddenly becomes more superficial or mechanical in presentation.
7. The client, a faithful attender, suddenly no-shows, cancels, or comes very late.
8. The client suddenly brings someone else to the meeting, and that person's activity or presence affects the work in progress.
9. The client suddenly seems distant or cold toward the worker.
10. The client abruptly discontinues work permanently, permitting no further discussion. (pp. 21–23)

Although the presence of any one or multiple signals does not necessarily mean that the therapist made a mistake, it is a warning sign that there might have

been a potential gaffe during the interview. Dillon also provided common therapist signals of mistakes in progress:

1. The worker has an immediate uneasy or queasy "gut feeling" following
   something she said or did.
2. The worker recognizes from his own developing fund of knowledge that he
   has just blundered.
3. The worker directly observes a clearly upset expression on the client's face,
   and then has matching feelings of distress, but can't tell whether the client's
   expression is due to something the worker did or something else not yet
   identified.
4. The worker can't get an event or a conversation with the client out of his
   mind and is preoccupied for some time with the worry that he hurt or failed
   the client in some major way. He's certain that the client is going to ask the
   agency for a more knowledgeable worker.
5. The worker tries a technique she learned in a recent workshop. It comes out
   awkwardly, and she is more self-conscious and awkward with the client for
   the rest of the meeting, feeling silly and ashamed.
6. The worker detours around a topic about which his supervisor asked him to
   get more information. He simply isn't comfortable exploring the material
   and therefore doesn't do so.
7. For some time, the worker doesn't mention a client in supervision to avoid
   revealing mistakes.
8. The worker forgets a client appointment.
9. The worker constantly asks the client how he feels about the work, and often
   asks him to let her know if something doesn't feel right or needs to be
   changed. (pp. 24–26)

Mistakes impact the therapeutic interview in many ways ranging from minimal
impact to the client stopping treatment and suing the therapist. Therapeutic interviewers' vigilance in trying to prevent mistakes while also being alert to their possible presence can help to alleviate their impact. Perhaps one of the best indicators
of therapy that is not going in a positive direction is when the client keeps coming
but no progress is being made. When any of these situations occur, therapists
should work to get therapy back on track, perhaps through consultation with colleagues or a supervisor.

Making mistakes can actually be beneficial for therapeutic interviewers.
There are positive effects of "failure," mainly when therapists utilize this feedback,
take a more critical look at themselves and then makes constructive changes
(Adleman, Hall, & Porter, 1998; Dillon, 2003; Kottler & Blau, 1989; Kottler & Carlson, 2002).

Again, mistakes do not necessarily have to be bad things. Although therapists try not to intentionally make mistakes, they should be aware of them and
then try to figure out why the mistake happened. This will help to prevent the mistake from happening in the future. Further, when these situations arise, instead of

berating oneself for how poorly they did, therapists can use it as an opportunity to learn. Kottler and Carlson (2002) interviewed master therapists about their worst failures. Each of the master therapists discussed how they had had episodes of "bad therapy." One of the themes that emerged was, after processing the mistake, the master therapists learned something from the occurrence. Further, these therapists tended not to dwell so much on how they might have worked ineffectively, understanding these times as parts of a lifelong process of learning about therapy and becoming a better therapeutic interviewer.

Experiences occur and we make of them what we will. We can take an experience with a client and use that to tell ourselves that we are the worst therapist in the whole world. Without any further disputation or reframing, these therapists are on a path that will probably not be the most productive for their clients, or for themselves. Conversely, therapists can take an experience with a client and use that as a tool for learning. Once you find out what doesn't work, you realize that you then can become creative and search for some other opportunity. Berg (1994) held that when something does not work, the person should not do it again, but should do something different. Therapists can adopt this philosophy to help them figure out what is not productive in their work with clients and find some other way of being, intervening, and interviewing clients that is more productive. Then, they can adopt another principle: Once you find what is working, do more of it (Berg, 1994).

As with most everything in the therapeutic interview, dealing with one's own failure can be viewed as a process. Kottler and Blau (1989) described five stages that therapists' experience when dealing with their own failure. The first stage is that of *illusion*. Here, therapists experience denial of their own ineptitude and mistakes and look for someone else to blame. This person would tend to be the client. The second stage is that of *self-confrontation*. In this stage, the illusion of not being at fault is replaced with anger at oneself. Therapists in this stage tend to accept total responsibility. The third stage, called the *search*, entails the therapist trying to figure out exactly what happened. The therapist examines as many different possibilities as she can. The fourth stage is *resolution*. The therapist, after thoroughly exploring the situation, gains a new perspective about the situation. An acceptance of one's own role in the mistake along with the role the client played, leads to this being a learning experience. The last stage, *application*, is when the therapist puts into place what was learned from the mistake. Further, the therapist develops a positive feeling about self that growth can come from failure. Case Example 8.1 (see page 198) describes how a therapist can go through all five stages.

Summary

Mistakes during the therapeutic interview will happen for all therapists. There are some common pitfalls that most therapists make in various realms, including basic conversation skills, intrapersonally, and interpersonally. Being cognizant of

<hr>

CASE EXAMPLE 8.1

Rebecca had been working with her client, Omar, for five weeks. During the last session, Omar became very defensive and yelled at Rebecca in session. Rebecca then yelled back at Omar and told him he needed to get his act together. After the session, Rebecca was of the opinion that Omar was to blame for the confrontation. She thought that if it wasn't for him getting angry in session, she wouldn't have lashed back at him. After a couple of days of ruminating about the situation, Rebecca started to berate herself and said that it wasn't Omar's fault at all. He's the one coming to therapy, and she should know better. This lasted for a day. Then Rebecca really explored the situation, thinking about what was being discussed before the blowup and thinking back to past sessions and what the alliance was like between the two of them. She also thought about what things might have been going on in Omar's life to lead to him act in the way he did as well as things going on in her life, as she is not the type of person to explode like that. After several days and talking with some colleagues about the episode, Rebecca came to an understanding that both she and Omar contributed to the negative encounter and that both could have done things to change it. She then talked with her colleagues about how she can become more aware of her feelings in therapy so that she does not blow up at a client in future sessions.

these errors is useful in order to avoid making them during sessions. However, when therapists do make mistakes, they should be open to the possibility that they could then use that situation as a chance to learn more about themselves and the therapy process. This will then help them and their clients in future therapeutic interviews. Mistakes should be viewed as growth opportunities so that something productive can come from them.

Exercise

1. Role-play with a fellow classmate a therapy session. For the person who is the therapist, attempt to make as many of the therapy mistakes presented in this chapter as possible. Have other class members guess which mistakes you are making. Then debrief each other and talk about your thoughts of how the mistakes impacted each person and the session as a whole.

9

Strength-Based Interviewing

Interviewing for Client Resources and Solutions

Within the past twenty years, a growing number of therapists have been taking a unique approach in which, aside from focusing on the problems that people are dealing with, they work with clients by highlighting and building on preexisting client strengths (Norman, 2000). Bertolino and O'Hanlon (2002) discussed this as the third wave of therapy. The first wave was intrapsychic theories with a focus on the past. The second wave was interactional theories and a focus on the present. The third wave is a collaborative competency-based approach focused on the future. This position highlights the future and movement toward client goals rather than the past and where clients have been. Having an approach looking for solutions and having a future focus is premised on the notion of expectation of change (Reiter, in press). Working from a strengths perspective leads to possibilities (Saleebey, 2002) as therapy shifts from exploring restrictions to exploring and building on strengths, resources, and capabilities. As Berg and Miller (1992) so nicely described the philosophy behind this approach, "Rather than looking for what is wrong and how to fix it, we tend to look for what is right and how to use it" (p. 3). These strengths and competencies are part of what make up those extra-therapeutic factors that account for 40 percent of the variance of positive outcome for clients. Given this, it would seem imperative for therapists to be conversant in talking with clients about those things they can build on in order to change. This chapter explores and how therapeutic interviewers can incorporate the principles of strength-based interviewing into the therapeutic interview.

The Language of the Strengths Perspective

The DSM-IV-TR is the most common conceptual tool in the field of psychotherapy. Its language may be considered that of pathology, which makes sense for many therapists. The thought behind it is that when we figure out what is wrong, we then know where to target our efforts toward change. However, when working from a strengths perspective, a unique language exists. This language filters into the philosophy of the approach. The two approaches do not have to be mutually exclusive as therapists can utilize an understanding of pathology to know where the client doesn't want to go as well as a strengths perspective to encourage clients toward growth. This section highlights the key terms in the language of the strength-based perspective.

Empowerment

Saleebey (2002) defined empowerment as "the intent to, and the processes of, assisting individuals, groups, families, and communities to discover and expend the resources and tools within and around them" (p. 9). It is developed through helping clients define their own world instead of the therapist imposing it for them (De Jong & Miller, 1995). The more clients realize that other people respect their opinions, the more comfortable they will be and the more likely they will believe in themselves. If therapists do *for* clients instead of working *with* clients so that clients do for themselves, they actually disempower clients. This would lead to clients, without the therapist's intervention, not having as many options as possible. Empowerment is about supporting clients in realizing and then utilizing the skills, knowledge, and strengths available to them.

Membership

Membership is about being connected to other individuals, groups, and community. From a strengths perspective, therapists connect people to internal resources (strengths and competencies) along with external resources (such as friends, local organizations, and support groups). By including outside individuals, the client can take a position against the problem and feel supported by more people than just the therapist.

Besides the theoretical benefits this practice has, it assists in connecting the client to people. Clients come to therapy disconnected from others partly because of the stigma of being a client in therapy, along with whatever problematic behavior is occurring. Getting other people to enter into the therapeutic discourse and support clients in the pursuit of their goals builds a connection between people that they can maintain long after the therapeutic relationship has ended. This also decreases the possibility clients will become dependent on the therapist since there are other people they can go to for support.

Resilience

Although people, groups, and communities might be viewed as having a difficult time overcoming severe obstacles, the norm is for people to rebound from troubles (Saleebey, 2002). Resiliency can be understood as the interaction of risk factors in the presence of protective factors (Norman, 2000). When protective factors are stronger than risk factors, people maintain resiliency. Whereas competence pertains to one's abilities, resiliency is what protects the person from having things stay bad or get worse in their lives.

There is not just one resiliency for people. Wolin and Wolin (1993) provided seven resiliencies: insight, independence, relationships, initiative, creativity, humor, and morality. Each of these resiliencies is present from when people are young through their adolescent years and until the end of their adulthood. The more that people endorse each of these traits, the more likely they are to get over troubled times and move toward growth.

Dialogue and Collaboration

From a strengths perspective, the conversation between therapist and client shifts from expert/patient to one of co-collaborator. This collaborative relationship can be seen through the skills that have been discussed so far in this book. Anderson (1997) explained this process, "Client and therapist were now conversational partners as we combined a client's expertise on his or her self and our expertise on a process, creating new knowledge, understandings, meanings, and possibilities for all" (p. 67). This type of relationship fosters a less hierarchical and more egalitarian dynamic between therapist and client. Thus, dialogue can be seen as two people (or more) engaged in negotiation and consultation rather than one person providing expert answers.

Instead of talking about the person as a patient, the words *client, co-collaborator,* or *consultant* can be used. By including the client's perspective and know-how in solving the current situation, the client is empowered to solve future problems instead of always needing to go back to the therapist, as if the therapist was the expert and had *the answer* for the client.

Suspension of Disbelief

In a strength-based approach, therapists enter into relationships with clients expecting to believe in clients rather than attempting to see how the clients might be deceptive. Since each person has a unique perspective, therapists attempt to understand each client's viewpoint, instead of imposing one on the client. This entails understanding the possibilities of multiple perspectives.

Exercise 9.1

Take part of one day and adopt the perspective that what people are telling you is not true (or at least involves some type of fabrication). How does this attitude impact the way that you relate to people? How do you think your relating to people in this manner impacts their relating to you? Once you have done this, switch your perspective and enter into conversations believing that everything the person is telling you is true. How does this impact the way you are relating to people? How do you think your relating to them in this manner impacts their relating to you?

The language of the strengths perspective does not fully mesh with the primary language of therapy—the clinical language of the Diagnostic and Statistical Manual. The two languages are not mutually exclusive, but if viewed on a continuum, the more that someone talks in one of these languages, the less one will probably talk in the other language. Figure 9.1 provides a visual representation of this distinction between these languages.

FIGURE 9.1 *Continuum of the Two Primary Languages of the Psychotherapy Field*

Diagnostic Perspective ———————————— Strengths Perspective

Client Competence

Every person has strengths, resources, and competence. These strengths, competencies, and resources have probably been helpful to clients in the past and may go unnoticed when a person decides to seek therapy, but can be useful for helping clients change in the present and future (Bertolino & O'Hanlon, 2002). However, clients (or some other significant party) are usually so focused on what is going wrong they have trouble seeing what is going right for them or what they are doing well. Therapeutic interviewers can focus on either of these aspects, or both, depending on what might be most useful for the client. Each lens (problems or competencies) highlights certain possibilities and shades other possibilities. The notion that therapists have to focus on what is going wrong with the client is only one theory of therapeutic process. "We choose to see our clients as competent, while acknowledging that the patterns of behaving and thinking in which they have become caught may have hidden their competence from them" (Durrant & Kowalski, 1993, p. 108).

This assumption creates an extremely different context for the therapeutic interview. The conversation switches from one exploring the past and past mistakes, disabilities, deficiencies, and disorders to delving into strengths, resources, competencies, abilities, positive actions, and the present and future. This distinction is demonstrated in the following two transcripts:

Transcript 1: Pathology-Based Interview

Therapist: What is going on in your life that is bringing you to therapy?

Client: I don't feel happy.

Therapist: How long has this been going on?

Client: For about two years now.

Therapist: When are the times that you feel really low?

Client: Most of the time. Usually when I wake up in the morning and go to bed at night. That's when I feel at my lowest.

Therapist: What things are you not able to do when you are feeling low?

Client: I am not able to get going and go into work. I seem to neglect myself where I don't take a shower, I might not eat, and I really don't interact with my wife or the kids.

Therapist: How often in your past have you felt like this?

Client: It's been on and off for several years now.

Therapist: And how debilitating has that been for you?

Transcript 2: Strength-Based Interview

Therapist: What is it that you were hoping to get out of therapy?

Client: I don't feel happy.

Therapist: So you were hoping to feel happier?

Client: Yes. I've been feeling pretty low for a long time.

Therapist: What about the days where you don't feel as low as other days?

Client: I feel pretty low most of the time, but there are days when I can actually get out of bed.

Therapist: You get out of bed?

Client: Yes.

Therapist: How are you able to do that?

Client: I don't know. I guess I tell myself that it's time for me to get out of bed and stop being a depressed idiot.

Therapist: You must be quite persuasive in that you feel so low, but you're able to tell yourself to get up and you actually do get up.

Client: I guess so. I never thought of it like that.

Therapist: I wonder what other things you haven't thought of yet about this situation.

Exercise 9.2

1. What do you think of the client in Transcript 1?
2. How hopeful are you for this client?
3. On a scale of 0 to 10, how competent would you rate this client?
4. On a scale of 0 to 10, how severe do you think this client's problem is?
5. Would you want to be the therapist in this situation? Why or why not?

Exercise 9.3

1. What do you think of the client in Transcript 2?
2. How hopeful are you for this client?
3. On a scale of 0 to 10, how competent would you rate this client?
4. On a scale of 0 to 10, how severe do you think this client's problem is?
5. Would you want to be the therapist in this situation? Why or why not?

Reflection 9.1

Think of times when you did something that you did not like (perhaps a mistake or a problem behavior). What type of conversation did you have with yourself? Did you focus on what you did wrong and why it happened? If so, was that helpful to you? Did you focus on what you learned from this event? Or did you think about what positive aspects you displayed, even in a situation that was not the most favorable? How did you feel about yourself in looking at yourself either way? Which do you think a client would prefer?

Strength-Based Interviewing

A strength-based approach to client interviewing rests on the assumptions of inherent worth, human dignity, and self-determination (Cummins, Sevel, & Pedrick, 2006). This collaboration of therapist and client produces a result that could not have been achieved without both participants. Instead of trying to find out what is *not* working or what is *wrong* with the client, the strength-based interviewer focuses on what the client has done *well* and validates the client. This tends to give the client a sense of hope, builds self-esteem, and leads to initiative in further movement toward goals (Murphy & Dillon, 2003).

By searching for strengths, the therapist is displaying a certain attitude which then impacts the client's attitude, building a better therapeutic alliance in the search for solutions. Strengths do not have to be physical or intellectual capabilities of the client. They can also be the meaning system of the client, "The strengths perspective asserts that the client's 'meaning' must count for more in the helping process, and scientific labels must count for less" (De Jong & Miller, 1995, p. 729). A corollary analogy can be made between the continuum of the diagnostic language and the strengths language to whose meaning system is being honored. The more that one uses a diagnostic language, the more the therapist's meaning system is honored. The more one uses a strengths language, the more the client's meaning system is honored. This is depicted in Figure 9.2.

Clients appreciate when therapists focus, at least part of the interview, on their strengths and competencies. People feel good when others say good things about them instead of bad things. There is an old adage that it takes five positive statements to equal one negative statement. In a strength-based approach, clients are provided with exploration of many "positives." This can lead them to feel bet-

FIGURE 9.2 *Relationship between Psychotherapy Language and Meaning System*

Diagnostic Language ———————— Strengths Language

Therapist Perspective ———————— Client Perspective

ter not only about themselves, but also about their relationship to the person who is pointing these positives out.

Rapport is enhanced when therapists let clients know they are there to support them in whatever their goals are. This comes from an attitude of believing in clients' ideas and perspectives. Therapists work from the notion that clients know what is good for them, which should be honored, rather than the therapist knowing what the client needs and forcing that on the client. Case Scenario 9.1 describes a situation in which the client's desires were utilized in a nontraditional therapeutic manner.

Now, for the previous case scenarios, provide some of the strengths that you see that each person possesses. After pointing out the strengths, how does this change the way that you view the person?

CASE SCENARIO 9.1

I was working with a twenty-two-year-old client who loved nature and the outdoors. After two sessions working in my office, I asked if he would like to go outside, take a walk, and talk while we appreciated nature. His face lit up with a smile. We walked and talked in the park adjacent to my office. I noticed from that point forward a shift in our relationship. He became more open with me and therapy seemed to progress quickly. Zur (2002) explained that out-of-office experiences with clients can be quite clinically beneficial. However, therapists should take caution in using an approach such as this, as it may be considered a boundary crossing.

Exercise 9.4

For the following case scenarios, provide an explanation of why you think the person is having difficulties and what characteristics you think the person is displaying.

1. Shane is having difficulties with his wife. This is his third marriage. He has certain expectations for his wife that she does not seem to be fulfilling, such as whether she should work outside their home, do the housework, and also take care of the children.
2. Hilary was recently arrested for drunk driving. She had a previous arrest three years ago and had gone through a substance abuse treatment program. She had been sober for two years, but began drinking again several months ago when stressors in her life became overwhelming.
3. Diana has been cutting herself for the past six months. She has received several poor marks in class and feels bad that she is not living up to her big sister's performance as a straight A student. Diana, who is a soccer player, has been missing practices lately.

Strength-Based Practice

Therapists working from a strength-based perspective learn to orient themselves differently in relation to client problems than therapists working from a deficit-based approach. Weick and Chamberlain (2002) held that there are three main strategies for putting problems in their place when working from a strength-based approach. The first is that of context. Client problems do not always occur in all settings and all relationships. The second strategy is to pay more attention to non-problems than to problems. The more that people focus on problems, the larger those problems seem. By focusing on strengths, therapists and clients become motivated at building something strong. The third strategy is using a different type of language to talk about problems. Weick and Chamberlain stated, "Adopting simpler ways of talking about problems is another useful strategy for making human problems less mysterious and unmanageable" (p. 102). By using a language about problems that is simpler, based on everyday language, clients are put in a position of control via the problem and their lives. When something is spoken of in technical language, people have to rely on the professional to explain what is going on and how it needs to be fixed.

Given that each and every person on Earth has strengths, resources, competencies, and resiliencies, therapists can build on what is already present. Therapeutic interviewers can focus on any aspect of clients' lives to see what strengths they have that they might be able to bring to the current situation.

- "Wow. I was really amazed at how you had been dealing with drugs for several years, but had decided on your own to stop. And you did!"
- "I want to go back to something that you had said earlier. You were talking about how you think that this depression is getting the better of you. However, you mentioned that yesterday you decided you were going to have a great day no matter what and you got together with friends and played baseball. How did you do that?"
- "I want to commend you for knowing that you weren't handling this situation in the way that you wanted to and deciding to come into therapy. That is a very courageous decision."

The highlighting of these strengths is known as complimenting.

Compliments

Most people love a compliment. People like to know that other people appreciate something they have said or done, or some trait about them. Simple compliments such as "You look very nice today," "That is a good color for you," or "You really did a good job on that project" not only makes the other person feel good, but also lead to their feeling more connected to the person who gave the compliment.

In a strength-based approach, therapists compliment clients on what the client is doing that is good and should continue to do. Letting clients know that the therapist heard what clients said that is useful, effective, and good for them helps to promote fit between therapist and client (de Shazer, 1988). For clients who come into therapy perseverating on their problems and feeling discouraged, having the therapist let them know that everything is not hopeless can boost their morale and lead to their developing an expectation not of failure, but of success. Further, the use of compliments helps to enhance the therapeutic alliance (Berg & Miller, 1992). The client then knows that the therapist does not look down on them, but holds them in some type of positive regard.

The number of compliments someone receives at one time makes a difference in how they will appreciate and believe those compliments. The use of several compliments can be effective, perhaps one to five in a session. O'Hanlon and Weiner-Davis (1989) believed that four or five compliments per session are the appropriate amount. Thus, compliments used periodically, especially for those things the client is doing that are very resourceful, can be an extremely important component to a good therapeutic interview. However, they need to be honest and sincere. Clients, as with most people, will be turned off if they believe the compliment is fake.

The following interchange exemplifies the use of compliments:

Therapist: Chie, I want to take a moment to let you know what I have been hearing you say.

Chie: Okay.

Therapist: I was very impressed with your heartfelt desire to make things different in your life.

Chie: Yes, it's really been a struggle for me.

Therapist: Right. Although it's been a struggle for you, you've already been doing things to try to make things better. You've stopped hanging around with Naoko, who you used to get into a lot of trouble with.

Chie: Yeah, that wasn't helping me.

Therapist: You've also gone back to community college to try to finish up your associate's degree. And you're now putting money in the bank to save. Wow. That's pretty amazing, given the place that you were in. How did you do that?

After giving the client a compliment that focuses on how the client is taking personal agency toward getting her life in the direction she wants it, therapeutic interviewers can highlight those exceptions and build on them. The question, "How did you do that" lets clients know the therapist realizes they have been doing something right. It also implies that it was *the client* actually doing something, instead of other people or luck, that was leading the client away from problems and toward solutions.

Interviewing for Solutions

Interviewing for solutions is intended to help clients develop an idea of what they want their future to be, as well as the strengths and resources they already have to help them get closer to that future (De Jong & Berg, 1998). This type of interviewing is based on solution-focused therapy, initially developed by Steve de Shazer, Insoo Kim Berg, and colleagues at the Brief Family Therapy Center in Milwaukee, Wisconsin (de Shazer et al., 1986).

This approach utilizes the notion that change is constant and inevitable (Berg, 1994; de Shazer, 1985). This is seen through the language used, where instead of using the word *if*, therapists use the word *when.* For instance, asking a client, "If you weren't depressed any longer, what would your life be like?" leaves an assumption that the client might always be depressed. However, if the therapist instead asks, "When you are no longer depressed, what will your life look like?" the question implies that there will be a time when the client no longer has the current life problem.

Solution-based interviewers utilize three main types of questions: the miracle question, exception questions, and scaling questions.

Miracle Question.   The miracle question is designed to get clients to shift from talking about the problem(s) that brought them to therapy to talking about how life will be once the problem is no longer there. It "is a way to begin constructing a bridge between therapist and client built around the (future) success of the therapy" (Berg, 1994, p. 95). Thus, asking the miracle question joins therapist and client in a language game that shifts the perspective in the therapy room from past or present to future. It also shifts the talk from that of problems and pathology to that of strengths and solutions.

Berg (1994) explained that the miracle question creates a picture of life after the problem, provides a sense of hope that things won't always be as they currently are, and intuits a future that the client wants. Perhaps most importantly, the miracle question gives clients hope and a vision of possibility (Berg & Miller, 1992). These leading figures of solution-focused therapy explained, "When a client can project to the future and imagine a transformation of her painful, hurt, and damaged life into a more coherent, harmonious, and successful life, it is an empowering experience" (p. 78).

The miracle question goes something like this (it can be altered to fit the specifics of what the client has been talking about during the therapeutic interview):

> Suppose tonight, you go home and go to sleep. And during the night, a miracle happens. This miracle is, all the concerns that brought you here to therapy, and that you've been talking about, are gone. When you wake up in the morning, you don't know that a miracle happened because you were sleeping. What will be the first sign for you that something is different, that the miracle has happened?

Clients will then start to answer what they envision their life to be. Further, they will shift from talking about vague goals to more concrete and specific behaviors (de Shazer, 1988). One of the most useful things to do at this point is to expand the miracle as wide as possible. This can be done through the question, "What else?"

> *Therapist:* What will you notice different the day after the miracle?
>
> *Client:* Perhaps that when I wake up, I go for a jog and do some type of exercise.
>
> *Therapist:* Wow. That's good. What else would you notice different?
>
> *Client:* Maybe that I wrote out a "to do" list for the day.
>
> *Therapist:* Okay. What else?

"What else?" might be one of the most powerful questions interviewers can ask. This question implies that there are multiple possibilities for clients.

The miracle question can be utilized with all client types, including children, adults, and those who are mandated to therapy. For clients who might be younger or not into miracles, the miracle question can be adjusted so that it is a magic wand or a genie's lantern.

- Suppose that you go home and go to sleep. And during the night, someone waves a magic wand over you and all the concerns that brought you here to therapy and that you've been talking about are gone. When you wake up in the morning, you don't know that the magic happened because you were sleeping. What will be the first sign for you that something is different, that the magic has happened?
- Suppose that you had a genie's bottle and you rubbed it three times and the genie granted all of your wishes, making your life as you want it. How would your life be different? What would happen tomorrow that would be different from today and would let you know that the wishes were granted?

Depending on the age, culture, and belief system of the client, therapeutic interviewers can change the wording of the miracle question. However, the intent of the question should be the same: having clients explain a future in which they do not have their current problems and are living in a way that they prefer to how they currently are living.

The following transcript demonstrates the use of the miracle question:

> *Therapist:* Mary, suppose tonight you go home and go to sleep, and during the night, a miracle happens. The miracle is that all of the things we've been talking about, you not feeling comfortable at your job, your issues with your weight, your arguments with your boyfriend, they were all gone. When you woke up in the morning, what would be the first thing that would be different that would let you know the miracle happened?
>
> *Mary:* I guess I would look in the mirror and not feel bad about the way I looked.

Therapist: Okay. How would you feel instead?

Mary: I would feel like I'm an attractive enough person.

Therapist: Having that feeling, what would you do tomorrow that you didn't do today?

Mary: Perhaps I would wear a sexy outfit.

Therapist: Okay. What else would be different that would let you know the miracle happened?

Mary: Maybe my boyfriend and I would laugh at breakfast instead of arguing.

Therapist: What would you be doing differently with him to help make that happen?

Mary: I wouldn't go after him about finding a job.

Therapist: Wow. Those sound like they would be quite a change. What would your boyfriend notice different about you, besides not arguing?

Mary: That I was nice to him. Perhaps I gave him a kiss when we woke up in the morning. And that I made him breakfast.

Therapist: Then he would say a miracle really happened, huh?

Mary: Yeah, that would be a miracle!

Therapeutic interviewers can use many different ways to flesh out the miracle. They can ask clients what they would notice different about themselves. They might ask what people in their relational field might notice different. If the client has a pet, the pet could also be used. For instance, "Frank, I was wondering what your dog Jazzy would notice different in you that would let him know the miracle happened for you?" The more differing viewpoints of what might be different in the client's life and behavior, the more possibilities that emerge in the conversation about various sources of strengths and resources.

Once the therapist has worked with the client to describe the miracle in as thorough a means as possible, the therapist can then simplify the miracle (Shilts & Gordon, 1992/1993). Clients are asked to take some time to pick one small achievable piece of their miracle, that *when* it happens, will be a sign that therapy is useful and the client is moving toward her goal.

> *Therapist:* Padma, you have mentioned many things that you would notice that were different for you once the miracle happened. What would be one small piece of that beautiful miracle, that when it happens this week, will let you know that you are on the path toward your miracle?

The therapist can then devise a task that helps the client engage in more of this small piece of the miracle. By breaking down the miracle and getting clients to focus on individual pieces, the therapeutic interviewer adds possibilities to the client's understanding. Instead of an all-or-nothing mentality of "Either I have the whole miracle or nothing is better," simplifying the miracle demonstrates to clients that change comes in all sizes and shapes.

Although the miracle question is usually asked in the middle of the first session, it can be asked at the end of the session for the client to "take home" to think about and come up with the pieces of the miracle for homework (Shilts, Rambo, & Huntley, 2003). Asking the miracle question in this manner slows down the pace of therapy so that clients do not feel forced or rushed. The miracle question has traditionally been used during the first therapeutic interview (de Shazer, 1988), and therefore, therapists should quickly develop a connection and positive working relationship with the client before utilizing it (Nau & Shilts, 2000) so that instead of being rushed, it occurs within the natural flow of the session.

Exception Questions.   Exceptions are those times when the problem could have happened but did not (de Shazer, 1988). They are also when the problem is not as severe as it might have been. Problems do not always happen, every minute of every day. There are times when the problem did not occur or was at a lower intensity than usual.

Exception questions help clients refocus on things in their past or present that they might have forgotten about or not noticed. By highlighting these exception moments, therapists send a message to clients that they have already been doing positive things, and thus, already have competence. Part of therapy is about giving the client hope. When clients realize they have been successful in the past, even if they don't fully realize their own agency in that success, it gives them hope that there can be more success in their life.

Lipchik (1988) noted four times when therapeutic interviewers can begin discussion of exceptions. The first, after the client has discussed the complaint situation, is to ask when the complaint situation does not happen or when the complaint is not as severe. The second strategy is to ask about pre-therapy change. Many times, between when the clients made the initial appointment and the first interview, something has changed for the better. Therapists can build on these client-initiated changes by seeing how they can be enhanced. The third strategy to begin exception sequences is by asking clients if some behavior they are talking about is different from the normal sequence. If so, they can then ask how it is different. For example, a therapist might hear a client who is dealing with depression talk about a fun time she had at some event. This then would be a door opener into that exception. The fourth strategy is to ask clients what will need to happen so they do not have to come back to therapy. Once clients give a response, therapists can ask them about past experiences surrounding the exception and build on them. The following transcript demonstrates how an exception can be focused on.

> *Therapist:* Jimmy, when was the last time you didn't argue with your wife as much?
>
> *Jimmy:* Well, two weeks ago, I actually brought her breakfast in bed.
>
> *Therapist:* For real?

Jimmy: Yeah.

Therapist: What was different about that day?

Jimmy: I wanted to have a good day.

Therapist: And did you?

Jimmy: Yeah, we had a pretty good day.

Therapist: How did you decide, "Today's the day"?

Jimmy: I wanted to feel connected to her.

Therapist: It seems like you know at least one way to have a good day. When were there other times that you decided to have a good day?

Taking note of exceptions is important; however, elaborating on the exception times might be even more so. Once therapeutic interviewers hear the first small piece of an exception, they can begin to stretch it out and find out what the client did to enable the exception to happen. They can then prescribe activities for the client to do more of what worked.

Scaling Questions.   Scaling questions were originally designed because clients were discussing abstract concepts, which made it more difficult for the therapist to be on the same page with the client. When a client says, "I am feeling depressed," the therapist is unsure what the client really means by that. "Depressed" can be experienced very differently by different people. What was needed was a bridge language so therapists would understand what each client meant by the terms they were using. This could be done through the use of numbers. Just as in an emergency room, when a person comes in to be seen by the ER staff, the intake nurse will ask the person on a scale of one to ten, how much pain they are in, scaling questions can be used in therapy to get clients to make abstract concepts more concrete and measurable. Thus, by having a scale where both therapist and client can view whether progress is being made, they can both be clearer about movement in therapy.

Scales can be developed from 0 to 10 or 1 to 10 or any other range that makes sense for therapist and client. Most scales are developed where 0 (or 1) is the height of the problem behavior (the worst that things can get) and 10 is the best that it can be (the client's goal). This way, clients are striving for more of something. However, with an issue such as depression, scales can be developed where zero is the absence of the problem (Reiter & Shilts, 1998).

Therapist: Katya, on a scale of 0 to 10, where 0 is the worst that things can ever be and 10 is the best that you can hope for, where are you now with living the type of life you want?

Any aspect of a client's life can be scaled including their motivation for change, level of anxiety, depression, anger, or how many pieces of their miracle have occurred. Shilts and Gordon (1996) discussed scaling each piece of the client's miracle, which helps therapist and client to periodically gauge the progress the client has been making in multiple areas.

The first time that therapist and client work on a scale, they have developed a baseline for that concept. From then on, they can use this number as a gauge as to whether the client is progressing.

> *Therapist:* Katya, during our first session, you scaled your sense of initiative at a 5. It's been two weeks since we met. Where are you at with that now?
>
> *Katya:* I would say I'm at a 7.
>
> *Therapist:* Wow, a 7. What's the difference between now and then?
>
> *Katya:* Before, I would just sit in my house and tell myself that I would get around to looking for a job.
>
> *Therapist:* And now?
>
> *Katya:* Now, I start to say that, but then tell myself "no." Then I get up and actually start looking in the paper and on the internet for jobs.
>
> *Therapist:* How are you able to do that?

Scaling questions can also be used to help therapist and client develop goals other than those that the miracle question helped to bring to the surface.

> *Therapist:* Katya, you stated that you are at a 5 in terms of initiative.
>
> *Katya:* Yes.
>
> *Therapist:* What would be different in your life if you were at a 6?
>
> *Katya:* I think I wouldn't feel so lazy.
>
> *Therapist:* How would you feel instead?
>
> *Katya:* Energized.
>
> *Therapist:* When you are energized, what sorts of things do you do that you don't do when you feel lazy?
>
> *Katya:* I take a shower the first thing when I wake up. I eat a good breakfast. I actually get dressed in nice clothes.

The things that the client discusses that would be different between the two rating points can then be incorporated into the pieces of the miracle to help add to the goals the client has for change.

The numerical differential the therapist uses in the scale is not as important as the assumption this makes in terms of demonstrating to clients that their problem is not fixed and unchangeable. There are times when the therapist should use caution in using too much of a differential between numeric points on the scale. This is usually with clients coming in stating they are severely depressed. For them, it might be too big a leap for one whole point (10 percent) of change. Thus, therapeutic interviewers can use a very small differential between points to talk about possible change.

Therapist: Harold, you stated that you were at an 8 in terms of depression. What would be different in your life when you are at a 7.9?

Any differences the client can come up with can be incorporated into the therapy and utilized as goals for the client. The .1 difference, although it might seem meaningless, is extremely powerful. Based on giving any type of difference, the client is beginning to acknowledge that the problem situation can change.

Coping Questions.   A fourth type of solution-focused question, although not usually put in the same category as the big three of miracle, exception, and scaling questions, is coping questions. These questions are usually used with clients who are feeling quite hopeless (De Jong & Miller, 1995). Coping questions accept the clients' initial position of hopelessness and ask them how they have been able to deal with that current level of despair. Since things in any person's life can always get worse, therapeutic interviewers can ask clients what they are currently doing to ensure that, although things might be bad, they are not getting worse.

Therapist: Ayesha, you're really in a tough position here. Things have been bad for a long time and it seems to you that they won't be getting better any time soon. Yet, you are still getting up in the morning and going to work every day. How are you doing that?

Ayesha: If I don't work, then I won't have money, and I'll lose my apartment.

Therapist: Right. But even when things seem so bad, you are doing all you can to make sure they don't get worse. What keeps you going?

Ayesha: It can't be this bad for me forever. Something has to get better.

Therapist: Yes, it seems to you that things are awful. Yet you haven't given up. I'm still interested in knowing how you've been able to prevent things from going from pretty darn bad to just awfully dreadful.

By asking the client coping questions, clients realize they are already doing things that are good for them. This helps to reduce the amount of hopelessness the person is feeling and leads to a conversation where the future and hope can play an active role.

What's Better Questions.   Perhaps the opposite of the coping question, which asks the clients how they are ensuring that things do not get worse, is the "What's better" question. Although the "What's better" questions are usually not viewed as a distinct type of question (De Jong & Miller, 1995), they are extremely useful at the beginning of sessions. These questions work from an assumption that change has happened over the duration between sessions. De Jong and Miller provided two reasons for the use of this question at the beginning of sessions. First, using this question will help open the territory for talk about exceptions. Second, it highlights the notion that people, and their problems, are not static. Since people are constantly changing, there is always the possibility that they will change. These changes can then be viewed as exceptions and built on.

Therapist: It's been one week since we last met. I was wondering, in the time from that last meeting, what has been better in your life?

Client: Not that much. It's pretty much the same. I stayed in most days and then on Saturday I went out to the bookstore.

Therapist: You went out to the bookstore. How did that happen?

Client: My niece's birthday is coming up so I thought she might like a book as a present.

Therapist: So that got you motivated enough to get dressed, out of the house, and to the bookstore?

Client: Yeah.

Therapist: All right! That is a big change from last week. Congratulations.

Utilizing the Client's Position

Strength-based interviewers feel strongly that clients come to therapy for different reasons and therefore need to be addressed differently. de Shazer (1988) described three different types of clients who come to therapy. The first are visitors. These are clients who do not think that they have a problem, and thus, do not think they need to make any changes. Berg and Miller (1992) explained, "This relationship exists when, at the end of the session, the therapist and client have not jointly identified a complaint or goal on which to work in treatment" (p. 25). These clients are usually referred to therapy through the courts, employment officials, or a family member. Visitor-type clients tend to be some of the most difficult clients for therapists to work with (De Jong & Berg, 1998) because the therapist expects the client to *want* to change. However, these clients do not fully engage in the therapeutic process because they are at the stage in which personal change does not make sense to them. Visitors would probably be in the precontemplation or perhaps the contemplation stage of the change cycle.

The second type of client is the complainant type. This client has a complaint about a problem that she wants to see different; however, she thinks that someone

---

CASE EXAMPLE 9.1

Harrison, a sixteen year old, was brought to a therapist by his parents. They told the therapist that Harrison has been uncontrollable at home, defiant, curses at them, and is not doing as well as he used to in school. When the therapist asked Harrison what his take was on the situation, Harrison told the therapist that he didn't understand why his parents were getting so upset. He thought that things were going fine at home and in his relationship with his parents. He said that it is not like he does drugs, gets arrested, or anything serious.

else needs to make the changes for things to get better. This type of client tends to view change as needing to come from a romantic partner, spouse, child, parent, or other individual. In this client's mind, if only the other person acted differently, things would be better. Berg and Miller (1992) explained that in a therapeutic interview in a complainant-type relationship, a goal will be identified but not the specific steps to bring the goal about. The complainant-type client tends not to understand how she can play a part in the solution to the problem (De Jong & Berg, 1998). This type of client usually comes to therapy on behalf of someone else. Many parents initially come to therapy as complaint-type relationship clients with concerns about their child. The complainant is probably in the precontemplation or contemplation stage of the problem cycle. Some may even be in the preparation stage once they realize their roles in the change cycle.

The third type of client is the customer type. These clients have a complaint about some problem in their lives, and they want to do something different to make things better. Customers understand that they can and should be part of the solution for the problem. During the therapeutic interview with this type of client, a goal will be developed that is inclusive of the client doing something about it (Berg & Miller, 1992). These types of clients usually come voluntarily to therapy. The customer-type relationship is the one that most therapists prefer to have with their clients, as they perceive the client being the most motivated for change. These clients are usually in the preparation or action stage of the change cycle.

Solution-focused therapists, operating with a notion of utilization, work differently based on the type of client they are in conversation with. For visitors—

CASE EXAMPLE 9.2

Harrison is fed up with his parents always being on his back. He told the therapist that things are chaotic in the house and that he tries not to spend too much time there. In his understanding, if his parents would back off and not nitpick on every little thing, the family would be good. He told the therapist that he thought that he shouldn't be in therapy but that his parents should as they are the ones who are making all the trouble.

CASE EXAMPLE 9.3

Harrison has come to the understanding that, although his parents might overreact at times, he is doing things that warrant concern. He realizes that he has not applied himself as much at school and that he occasionally antagonizes his parents into fights. He thinks that his parents can behave differently toward him; however, he also knows that he needs to behave differently toward them.

Exercise 9.5

For the following case scenarios, determine whether the client is a visitor, complainant, or customer. Answers are provided at the end of the chapter.

1. Maria is coming to therapy after being suspended from school for fighting. The principal stated that unless she completes five sessions of therapy, she will not be allowed back into the school. Maria thinks the principal is overreacting and that she should be let back in school now.
2. Kari is having difficulties with her five-year-old daughter, Naya. Naya is going to the bathroom in her pants instead of the toilet and is smearing her feces when she has a bowel movement. Kari wants Naya to stop doing this.
3. Itzhak has been drinking alcohol for ten years. He has recently been fired from his job and he realizes that he wants his life to be different. His father died in a car accident after a drunk driver hit him, and Itzhak doesn't want to be the cause of something like that himself.
4. Milton finds that when he has conversations with people they tend to end in arguments. When he argues, he gets loud and curses at the other person. His fiancé told him that she would not go through with the wedding until he changes. He doesn't understand why she is making such an ultimatum.
5. Yul hates his job. He feels like his boss picks on him more than any other employee. He thinks that he might actually be happy about his job if his boss would just get off his back.

people who do not think they have a problem and thus do not need to change—they do not ask them to act or do anything different. If they did, it would not make sense for the client and the likelihood that the client would do whatever tasks, intervention, or homework the therapist gave for out-of-session would be minimal. de Shazer (1984) discussed this notion of accepting the client where the client is and utilizing the client's motivation instead of fighting against it as a means of foregoing the notion of client resistance. Therapists might ask clients just to *think* about what is going on, to open the possibility that clients might see some aspect of the situation they would like different. They might also be given no homework assignment. de Shazer (1984) suggested that a therapist accept the client's position and try to utilize her motivation rather than label her "resistant." He has even suggested that when this type of person comes into a therapy office, she is not in a position for therapy to occur. If her position about the complaint and need for change are not openly addressed, therapist and client can waste hours in a roundabout conversation in which the therapist attempts to help the client change while the client does not think she needs to change. For those clients who insist that there is not a problem, therapists can explore a renegotiation with the client to see if they can be of any assistance. If not, they should let the client know that they are available to the client in the future if the client has such need.

> ***Therapist:*** Bill, through our conversation today, it is clear that you disagree with the court's opinion that you need to come here to talk about

aggression. This may be the case. And I was wondering what other things you think might be useful for us to talk about that might help you in your life.

For complainants, those who can discuss a problem but believe someone else should change, therapists might ask them to *notice* what goes on during the problem situation. This opens the door for complainants to realize that they are involved in the problem sequence and might want to do something differently to change the problem complaint. Berg and Miller (1992) explained, "In the complainant-type relationship, the therapist agrees to explore the complaint or goal further with the client and to do so in a way that is intended to facilitate a new perspective that might lead to a solution" (p. 23).

> *Therapist:* Derek, I was quite impressed with the way that you were able to discuss your relationship with Tara. Since you two were married, it seems as if you have put a lot into this relationship and don't feel as if you have been getting back in return. It might be interesting for you this week to notice what happens when Tara is not being with you in the way you want and how you respond to that.

For customers, people who have a complaint and want to do something about it, therapists tend to give them *behavioral tasks* to do something different.

> *Therapist:* Marissa, you have talked about your upset at not being able to meet guys and that you were wanting to change this. I think it might be an interesting experiment for you this weekend to go up to five different guys who you find somewhat attractive and strike up a conversation with them. Not that the conversation has to go anywhere past just a friendly "Hello, how are you." But that you initiate some type of conversation with them.

Thus, each client, based on her unique motivation and understanding about the problem, is treated in a way that is collaborative, instead of pejorative, when the client does not want to change in the way the therapist wants her to.

Summary

In a strength-based approach, therapists believe and know that each and every client they come in contact with has internal and external strengths and resources that can be utilized to help the client reach her goal. Therapists can assess what strengths the client has and then build on these during the course of the interview. One means of focusing on strengths is to interview for solutions. By focusing on those times when problems do not occur, therapists help clients to expand their nonproblem lives. Therapists can also assess the type of client they are working with—in terms of readiness for change—and alter their interviewing and interventions to mesh with the stage the client is in at the present moment.

Exercises

1. Working with a classmate, role-play a first session in which, from the very beginning, the therapist is working from a strength-based perspective. After the session, discuss with one another the differences between working from this model and other types of interviewing.

2. Together with a classmate, develop a role-play depicting a client at one of the types of client positions (visitor, complainant, or customer). Enact this role-play for the class and see if your classmates can guess the client's stage of readiness.

Answers for Exercise 9.5

1. Visitor

2. Complainant

3. Customer

4. Visitor

5. Complainant

10

Therapeutic Assessment Interviewing

Intake Interviewing, Mental Status Exams, and Crisis Counseling

In many clinic and community mental health centers, the first contact therapeutic interviewers have with clients is an intake session, sometimes known as a biopsychosocial evaluation. This chapter breaks down each section of the biopsychosocial and presents how therapists can put these pieces together to have a greater understanding of the client's context and problem(s) in order to provide the most appropriate services possible. Wiger and Huntley (2002) discussed the importance of the assessment interview, "The clinical interview is designed to collect sufficient information to make a diagnosis, determine the level (setting, frequency, intensity, duration) of treatment needed, and develop a treatment plan" (p. 1).

This chapter is distinct in this book because conducting assessment and therapeutic interviews are not the same. Assessment interviewing is most likely a one-session interview, although sometimes two sessions are needed. There are times when the person conducting the assessment interview will not be the person who will continue to work with the client. This may be an uncomfortable situation for some clients because they open up and discuss their personal situation with one person and then have to do the same thing again with the therapist they are assigned. During the assessment interview, not as much time is spent on joining as in the therapy interview, as a lot of information is needed in a short amount of time.

Another reason assessment interviews are different from the therapy interviews that have been previously discussed is that more questions are usually asked in the intake interview than in a therapy interview. Because assessment interviewers have to obtain specific information to complete the assessment, there is not enough time to explore the side stories clients talk about. Assessment interviewers need to keep clients closely focused on the purpose of the interview because assessment interviews usually take a longer time than therapy interviews (sometimes double the amount of time).

A third way that assessment interviews differ is in terms of the goal of the interview. For therapy interviews, the goal is to help move clients closer toward their goals. In assessment interviewing, the goal of the interview is to obtain necessary information. Usually the intent is not to get clients to change during the interview. As a result of the interviewer utilizing empathy and rapport-building strategies, the interview might be somewhat therapeutic for clients. However, it is at a different level from that of a typical therapy interview.

This chapter is designed to give the reader an overview of the issues involved in assessment interviewing. It begins by covering the typical intake interview, focusing on getting a client's history. The chapter then discusses the mental status exam and its place in a diagnostic interview. The chapter concludes with crisis counseling, focusing on suicide assessment and unique interviewing issues when working with clients in crisis.

Intake Interviewing

In many situations, the first interview conducted with a client is an intake interview. This is an assessment of the client's situation to determine what the client is currently dealing with, how severe the client's problems are, and what would be the best type of treatment. Sommers-Flanagan and Sommers-Flanagan (2003) provided three objectives for the intake interview:

1. Identifying, evaluating, and exploring the client's chief complaint and associated therapy goals.
2. Obtaining a sense of the client's interpersonal style, interpersonal skills, and personal history.
3. Evaluating the client's current life situation and functioning. (p. 169)

One of the functions of this type of interview is to establish an atmosphere in which the client feels comfortable opening up to the interviewer so that enough information is obtained to develop a treatment plan. In order to do this, three different sources of information are used: the client's personal history; the client's interpersonal manner; and an evaluation of the client's mental status.

Although the goals of the assessment interview change depending on the situation and the client, all assessment interviews will have the following general goals:

1. To establish a sound engagement of the patient in a therapeutic alliance
2. To collect a valid database
3. To develop an evolving and compassionate understanding of the patient
4. To develop an assessment from which a tentative diagnosis can be made
5. To develop an appropriate disposition and treatment plan
6. To effect some decrease of anxiety in the patient

7. To instill hope and ensure that the client will return for the next appointment. (Shea, 1998, p. 7)

Since the assessment or intake interview is conducted during the first meeting between interviewer and interviewee, a balance is needed between gaining all of the necessary information to work productively with the client while also establishing a positive working relationship. The following sections provide information about each of the sections of the intake assessment.

Identifying Information

The identifying information discusses what might be considered the demographics of the client. This includes the name, date of birth, sex, age, level of education, employment status, and marital status. The identifying information helps to contextualize the client's situation, as certain of the person's presenting problems can be understood differently based on a variation on any of these identifying traits.

Presenting Problem

Clients come to therapy because there is something in their lives that is not going the way they would like. Regardless of whether they have a good sense of what this is or not, interviewers can ask clients about what is bringing them to therapy at the current time. Usually, there is a precipitant that leads clients to feel now is the time for help. For many clients, there are multiple presenting problems. Interviewers should explore the various concerns that bring clients into therapy as multiple problem situations lead to potentially different treatment options.

History

The intake interviewer will spend a lot of time exploring various issues in the history of the client. By exploring the client's history, the interviewer is better able to hypothesize how the client's history has contributed to the formation and continuance of the client's problem. This understanding also gives the interviewer a sense of the client's potential resources, such as individuals in the client's relational field and past challenges and how the person may have overcome those challenges. The three main history areas addressed in the intake interview are the history of the presenting problem, social history, and medical history.

History of the Problem.   Finding out the history of the problem and any historical correlates assists the interviewer in conceptualizing what is going on for the client and developing an appropriate treatment plan (Watson & Gross, 1998). These authors believed that "history taking involves two simple questions: What problems are associated with the complaint? and What problems are differentiated from the complaint?" (p. 58). However, the process of interviewing to get this information is much more complicated. The interviewer must keep the client on target when discussing the past, filtering out information that is not relevant for the interview, but also searching for those areas the client has not spoken about yet that are important. Watson and Gross held that the place to start in history taking is with the primary symptoms of the presenting problem. If there are multiple problems, interviewers will need to explore the process of each of the problems. Things to ask the client about are when the problem began, how severe the problem has been, times when the problem has been at its most severe, times when it hasn't been a problem, and the various ways the problem has impacted the person.

Social History. The social history provides the therapist enough background information about the client to help conceptualize the current difficulties, which will then help to develop a specific treatment plan for the client. Falk (1998) stated that interviewers should attempt to get information about the client's social history in the following areas:

1. Family of origin
2. Extended family
3. Present family constellation
4. Educational level attained—including description of interpersonal aspect of the school experience
5. Occupational training/job history
6. Marital (significant other) history
7. Interpersonal relationship history
8. Recreational preferences
9. Sexual history—including inquiry about abuse
10. Medical history—including significant family medical history and/or current medications
11. Psychiatric/psychotherapy history—including hospitalizations and/or medications
12. Legal history
13. Alcohol and substance use—including recreational and social use
14. Nicotine and caffeine consumption (p. 76)

The social history helps to contextualize some of the stressors and resources the client has had during the course of his life and the life of the presenting problem.

Medical History. The medical history is completed because preexisting or concurrent medical problems may play a role in the psychological functioning of the person. Sometimes there is not a connection between a person's medical issues and his psychological issues. Sometimes there is. Even if the person's medical condition is not specifically related to his psychological problem, it will present more stress for the person, which may make his psychological problem harder to deal with. Both psychological and medical problems cause stress for the client.

Previous Therapy. Therapists will want to talk with the client about previous therapy the client has received. This serves several functions. Therapists are able to understand the therapeutic course of the problem, or other problems. This gives them a sense of the severity of the problem and how that problem changed with the introduction of therapy. They can also talk with the client about what past treatment was helpful and what wasn't. This may help guide them in deciding what the current course of therapy will be. Clients have a sense of what works for them. Especially if there were things they did with a previous therapist, they will be able to let the new therapist know so these things can be tried (or something similar) in the current therapy.

Reason for Coming to Therapy Now

It can be important for therapists to know why it was, at this point, that the client decided to go to therapy. This helps to contextualize the problem and potentially brings forth predisposing factors around the problem. Knowing whether the client came because he wanted to or because he was pressured or forced by someone else allows the interviewer to gauge the client's motivation level. The exploration of any referring body or significant others who are involved with the problem helps with assessing the client's readiness for change.

Major Areas of Stress

Interviewers should talk with clients about their main areas of stress. The presenting problem will probably be one of the main things clients will talk about. However, there will probably be many other stressful situations in their lives. People experience stress in many different ways, including positive and negative stress. Positive stress can include things like preparing for a wedding or getting a job promotion and having to learn new job responsibilities. Negative stress may include an ending of a romantic relationship or being evicted from one's housing.

Academic/Work Functioning

Time should be spent in the session discussing how the client is functioning at school or work. This helps determine the severity of the problem and how it may be impacting multiple contexts for the client. Also, it allows the interviewer to gauge the client's functional abilities and how the client is able to be productive in the academic or work setting. For some diagnoses, such as ADD, the problem behavior needs to occur in multiple locations in order for the clinician to give the client that diagnosis.

Substance Use

Therapists should talk with the client about the client's use of substances, even if the presenting problem is not drug or alcohol related. Just because the client did not state at the beginning of the interview that substances are involved does not mean they have no impact on the client. Many people utilize drugs and alcohol as a means of coping. Substances could include recreational and hard drugs, beer, wine, hard alcohol, as well as caffeine and nicotine. Interviewers should explore which types of drugs the client uses, the severity of their use, how often they are used, and the impact they have on the client.

Social Resources

As discussed in Chapter 9, the social resources a person has available can greatly help in the person's resiliency. The interviewer can assess what relationships the client has toward social resources to see if the person is deficient in this area or whether the person has a good support system. This includes acquaintances, friends, family, and various social groups the client might be associated with.

Initial Impressions

At the end of the interview, the interviewer analyzes all of the information she has accrued during the assessment interview to come up with an initial impression of the client. This focuses on the presenting problem and its severity, along with the strengths of the client, to see if the client might have a psychological condition and, if so, the probable course of therapy.

Treatment Plan

A treatment plan is developed once the therapist has a thorough understanding of the client's situation. It takes into consideration past and present behavior and formulates which approach(es) will best lead to the accomplishment of the therapeutic goals and objectives.

Mental Status Exam

Although the biopsychosocial assessment and the mental status are usually conducted during the same interview, there is a distinct difference between the two. The biopsychosocial assessment is based on information the client provides whereas the mental status exam is based primarily on the interviewer's observations. "The mental status examination (MSE) is an interview screening evaluation of all the important areas of a patient's emotional and cognitive functioning, often augmented with some simple cognitive tests" (Daniel & Crider, 2003, p. 21).

When doing a mental status exam, the interviewer attempts to gain the most accurate information about the client's current psychological functioning. It is a way to document the client's thinking, feeling, and behaving at the current moment. This occurs through asking questions and making observations of the client. Therapists need to be extremely skilled in verbal communication and observational process. Polanski and Hinkle (2000) stated, "Experienced counselors attend to detail and subtlety in behavior, such as the level of affect accompanying the client's thoughts or ideas, the significance of mannerisms and nonverbal behaviors, and the unspoken message associated with conversation" (p. 357). Not only is the MSE used to assess current functioning, but also it can be used to assess progress over the course of the therapy (Golden & Hutchings, 1998). Therapists can periodically conduct MSEs to assess how clients have progressed over the duration of therapy.

The MSE has three domains, with several areas under each domain (Daniel & Crider, 2003). The first domain is *physical* and is determined based on client appearance, behavior, and motor activity. The second domain is *emotional* and is determined by client attitude, mood and affect, thought and perception, and insight/judgment. The third domain is *cognitive* and is based on client orientation, attention/concentration, speech and language, memory, and intelligence/abstraction. Fuller (1982) used the mnemonic of AMSIT as a rough guide to the MSE. *A* is for Appearance, which includes behavior and speech. *M* is for Mood and affect. *S* is for Sensorium (orientation and memory). *I* refers to Intellectual functioning. And the *T* is for Thought. Regardless of method or process of conducting the MSE, they all have roughly a similar format.

A thorough mental status examination includes the following components (Rosenthal & Akiskal, 1985):

- Date and time of interview
- Appearance and behavior
- Attitude toward interviewer
- Psychomotor activity
- Affect and mood
- Speech and thought
- Perceptual disturbances
- Orientation
- Attention, concentration, and memory
- Intelligence
- Reliability, judgment, and insight

Appearance and Behavior

Something to pay attention to during the MSE is the client's dress. If the client is in mismatched clothing or has very dirty and disheveled clothing, this could be signs of more severe distress. Attention should also be paid to the style of dress clients use to express themselves, including modern appurtenances, such as tattoos, jewelry, and piercings. Although a tattoo or nontraditional piercing is not in itself problematic, it can be used in conjunction with all of the other data the interviewer is collecting to develop a richer understanding of the client's present functioning.

Therapists should pay attention to how much eye contact the client is giving and the times that the client does not give eye contact, keeping in mind potential cultural codes of behavior. Therapists should determine how much the client appears his stated age. Some clients who have had very difficult lives tend to look a lot older than their stated age. Pridmore (2000) suggested that a client's appearance could suggest personality traits and mental disorder.

Therapists might also notice the client's weight, height, and any other usual or unusual physical traits. If a client has a deformity or walks in a unique manner (for example, with a limp), the therapist can make mention of it in the MSE report as it helps to understand potential stressors in the client's life.

The client's behavior in relationship to the interviewer is important to pay attention to. The therapist should recognize the client's level of arousal. Some things to look for are if the client is hyperalert, alert, somnolent, or stuporous. The client's level of cooperation is also important to note, as is whether the client is cooperative, guarded, uncooperative, or hostile.

Attitude toward Interviewer

Daniel and Crider (2003) held, "Attitude is how patients feel and what they think about participating in the MSE" (p. 28). It is determined not only by what the client says to the interviewer, but also by nonverbal expressions. Voice tone, eye contact, evasiveness, and volume all contribute to an understanding of client attitude. Wiger and Huntley (2002) stated, "A client's attitude toward the examiner directly influences the validity of the interview and can be indicative of the prognosis of treatment" (p. 170). The interviewer pays attention to how cooperative or not the client is toward her. Some clients might be curt, aggressive, passive, or cooperative with the therapist.

Psychomotor Activity

This section of the MSE refers to the client's movements, including the types and quality. The therapist is looking for movement that is "retarded," that is, the client is extremely slow in his movements. Retarded movement might insinuate that some type of depression is involved. There might also be psychomotor "agitation" in which the client exhibits more movement than is normal. This might demonstrate that the client is in a manic state.

Affect and Mood

There is a difference between affect and mood. Affect is the client's current state whereas mood is a longer-lived emotional tone. The difference can also be viewed as affect being the external state of the client, while mood is the internal state (Daniel & Crider, 2003). Mood can be determined over several days or weeks. When discussing the client's affect, adjectives such as happy, sad, angry, or anxious are appropriate. The intensity of this should be noted as mild, moderate, or severe.

Therapists should pay attention to how the client's affect has, or has not, changed over the course of the interview. Quick changes in affect not related to the content of the conversation give the therapist information about possible serious problems.

In order to assess mood, the client's endorsement is needed (Wiger & Huntley, 2002). Because mood occurs over a length of time longer than the clinical interview, therapists will need to use the client's explanation of how his mood has been or has changed over the last several days and weeks.

Speech and Thought

Speech refers to what clients say and the quality of how they say it (Daniel & Crider, 2003). In observing client speech, several areas should be explored, such as articulation, volume, speed, pressured speech, and pitch (Pridmore, 2000). Therapists look for whether clients are making sense when they are talking, if they are being repetitive in their speech, and if they are talking in a manner that does not seem normal. If the client comprehends what the therapist says and communicates in a normal manner, no further evaluation of speech is necessitated.

Thought refers to clients' internal dialogue (Daniel & Crider, 2003). In the MSE, thought is assessed through process and content. The formulation and organization of thought is known as the process. This refers to whether clients are staying on target or becoming tangential. Therapists assess whether clients are having a flight of ideas, where they shift from one train of thought to another in rapid succession. Content is what the client is thinking about.

Perceptual Disturbances

Perception refers to clients' interpretation of external events. Within this area are hallucinations and delusions. Hallucinations are hearing or seeing things that are not actually there. Delusions are a false belief that the client has even though there is evidence that the belief isn't true. Clients will have to report whether they are experiencing any of these perceptual problems. Interviewers can ask clients, "Have there been times when you have seen things that are not really there? Or heard things when you know there was no noise?"

Orientation

Interviewers assess whether the client is oriented x3 (time, place, and person). Therapists assess this by asking clients what the current day is, where they are, and what their name is. Wiger and Huntley (2002) observed that as clients' orientation diminishes, their orientation to time seems to decrease first, then their orientation to place, and finally to person. When clients become vague or have difficulty answering in these three areas, therapists should investigate further to determine whether something is impacting their cognitive ability.

Attention, Concentration, and Memory

Concentration is being able to maintain one's focus. Therapists can assess the client's level of concentration by observing how often the client shifts from the topic at hand. Some common assessment strategies for concentration are serial tasks and forward and backward tasks. Serial tasks ask clients to count in certain increments. Usually, clients are asked to perform serial threes and serial sevens. Serial threes are usually counting, from 1, in increments of three (that is, 1, 4, 7, 10, 13 … 31). Serial sevens are when the client is asked to count down from one hundred in increments of seven (that is, 100, 93, 86, 79 … 58). Forward tasks include repeating numbers the interviewer presents. These shift in the number of digits presented, increasing one digit each time (i.e., presented three numbers to be repeated, then four, then five). Backward tasks ask the client to take the numbers presented and repeat them backwards.

Memory is the ability to remember. There are three types of memory including sensory memory, short-term memory, and long-term memory. Interviewers usually only assess short-term and long-term memory. Short-term memory is usually thought to be somewhere under two minutes. Therapists can determine clients' long-term memory by how well they remember instances in their past ranging from their childhood, adolescence, adulthood, to recent events such as what they ate the day before the interview.

Intelligence

The assessment of intelligence is not based on a formal intelligence test, but the interviewer's perception of the client based on the client's comprehension of the conversation. If the interviewer asks questions that are common knowledge and the client does not know them, the interviewer might determine that the client is on the moderate to lower end of the intelligence continuum. One of the best means to assess client intelligence is the client's vocabulary (Wiger & Huntley, 2002). As a very rough guide, the simpler the words used, the more likely it is the person's intelligence is within the lower range.

Reliability, Judgment, and Insight

Interviewers also try to assess clients' reliability, judgment, and insight. They do this by giving clients various scenarios and asking what they would do in each situation. Interviewers also pay attention to whether clients can make connections between their own actions and the consequences of those actions.

Not every client will receive the same MSE. The more severe a client's problems, including the impressions of illness, the more in-depth the interviewer should make the exam.

Diagnostic Interviewing

For those therapists who find it useful to obtain a diagnostic impression of the client, the first meeting(s) with the client is (are) spent trying to determine what diagnoses the client is currently exhibiting. Sommers-Flanagan and Sommers-Flanagan (2003) provided several guidelines when conducting a diagnostic interview. First, therapists should not accept the client's self-diagnosis as being accurate. Clients may have read a little bit about psychological disorders and may have self-diagnosed themselves. Further, they might have been given a diagnosis in the past that is no longer valid. Diagnoses are not lifelong, they change in intensity and presence. The second guideline is to keep a diagnostic checklist available. Diagnoses are made based on the client's meeting certain criteria. These criteria come from the Diagnostic and Statistical Manual (DSM-IV-TR). Since there are so many diagnoses and multiple criteria for each diagnosis, memorizing all of them would seem to be an extremely difficult task. Therapists can use a checklist that they can quickly scan to help them determine the appropriate questions to ask the client. The third guideline is to understand that it might take multiple interviews to determine the client's diagnosis. This is assuming that the client even has a diagnosis. Depending on the length of the interview, the severity of the client's problems, the client's style of communicating, the therapist's knowledge of diagnostic criteria, along with other factors involved in interviewing, several sessions may be needed to form an appropriate diagnostic impression.

Diagnostic interviewing is difficult because therapists must use skills in many different domains. They need to be strong in interviewing, diagnostic, and documentation skills (Wiger & Huntley, 2002). These first two skills occur primarily during the interview when the therapist first joins with the client, using rapport-building strategies. During the interview, therapists take in information and use that to help determine what further questions to ask and what avenues to explore. The documentation skills occur during and after the session. Therapists need to know what type of information the agency or third-party requires. When with the client, they need to make sure they ask all necessary information. After the session, using their diagnostic skills, they put together all of the information obtained to develop a diagnosis (or perhaps to decide that there is no diagnosis) and to write all necessary notes, assessments, and reports.

In determining a client's diagnosis, the therapist takes into consideration many different types of data. Therapists use six sources of data (Wiger & Huntley, 2002). The first is the clinical interview. During the interview, therapists obtain all of the verbal data the client discloses in the session. Second, therapists will use their own clinical observations, specifically that information noted in the mental status exam. Another type of data is previous records. When appropriate and available, therapists should have the client sign a release of information to allow them access to records such as past therapy records, inpatient hospital records, or school records. A fourth type of data is testing. Many clients in agency settings will have had some type of intelligence, personality, and/or neurological testing. Therapists can, upon release by the client, gain access to these records and use them to help conceptualize the client's current difficulties. Another type of data is biographical information. This comes from the client, who has discussed his history and some of the unique situations that have occurred for him during his life. The last type of data comes from collateral informants. Therapists might be able to talk to the client's family, friends, past therapists, employer, case worker, or anyone else who has information about the client's problem and functioning.

At the end of the interview, or sometime afterward, clients should be informed about the outcome of the interview. Clients are entitled to the results of the clinical interview. However, as Wiger and Huntley (2002) explained, sharing the results needs to be weighed against how harmful the results might be to the client. Therapists can give the client general information about their conclusions rather than specific diagnostic information. Regardless of what information is shared with the client, it needs to be done in a manner and language the client can readily understand. Too much use of diagnostic criteria, symptoms, and diagnoses can be confusing, and even scary, to the client.

Although it is a standard in clinic- or agency-based programs, therapists should take caution when giving a client a diagnosis, as it becomes part of that client's mental health record, which could potentially negatively impact the client in the future. Therapists need to ensure that the diagnosis is accurate. Since the issuing of a diagnosis to a client is such a significant event, therapists should spend time before putting down a diagnosis for each client, in order to ensure that they ethically feel comfortable making that diagnosis. Case Scenario 10.1 provides an example of how getting a diagnosis can negatively impact a person.

Crisis Counseling

Many beginning therapists find that they are asked to engage in counseling for people in crisis. However, most have not taken any coursework or had any training in crisis intervention (Hillman, 2002). The crisis counseling interview is unique and has a slightly different aim than a typical therapeutic interview. Unfortunately, few graduate training programs include training in crisis intervention (Pitcher & Poland, 1992). Kleespies (1998) proposed a curriculum for a knowledge base in emergency psychological services that includes foundational knowledge about psychological crises, the evaluation and management of life-threatening behavior, risk management in a clinical emergency, emergency-related crises and conditions, medical conditions presenting as psychological crises, and the impact of emergency service on the clinician. The current section serves as a starting point for therapeutic interviewers to become familiar with the issue of crisis counseling.

CASE SCENARIO 10.1

A colleague of mine received his doctorate in counseling. He had gone to therapy several years previously because he was going through a divorce and was upset about it. The clinician he went to had diagnosed him as depressed. When my friend graduated from his doctoral program and became licensed, he opened up a private practice. He applied for malpractice insurance and was *denied* because the insurance company observed that he had a previous psychological diagnosis.

Defining Crises

Okun (1997) defined a crisis as "a state that exists when a person is thrown completely off balance emotionally by an unexpected and potentially harmful event or a difficult developmental transition" (p. 229). Brems (2000) added that a crisis is "any event that outstrips a client's resources or coping skills, thereby creating emotional upheaval, cognitive distortion, and behavioral difficulties" (p. 133). What is a crisis for one person may not be a crisis for another. Each triggering event impacts each person differently, based on that person's coping mechanisms, resources, competencies, past experiences, strengths, and so forth. A crisis has three parts: precipitating events; subjective distress; and ineffective coping methods (Kanel, 2003). The crisis is the interchange between the event, context, and the person (Brems, 2000). Collins and Collins (2005) added that a crisis is time-limited, usually lasting less than two months.

Four situations are considered psychological emergencies (Callahan, 1998). The first is when the client is at risk of killing himself. The second is when the client is at serious risk of harming someone else. The third situation is when the client's judgment is seriously impaired, leading him to be endangered. The final situation is when there is risk to a defenseless victim. These psychological emergencies are distinct from psychological crises, in which there is not the risk of danger and which usually are longer lasting.

Crisis events can be viewed as being situational or developmental (Brems, 2000; Collins & Collins, 2005; Kanel, 2003). A situational crisis occurs because of some unexpected event in the person's life. They tend to have a sudden onset, are unexpected, have an emergency quality, and can have an impact on the community. A developmental crisis is based on the person's normal maturation. People tend to be more prone to problems when they are transitioning from one stage of life to another.

Intervening in Crises

Conducting an interview with a client in crisis can be one of the most important contexts of therapeutic interviewing. The person is at a position where he is feeling overwhelmed because his coping and support measures are very low at that moment. Therapeutic interviewers will need to develop alternative modes of working with the client because of the immediacy and urgency of the situation. Kleespies, Deleppo, Mori, and Niles (1998) explained, "Emergency conditions demand a more immediate, personal, and flexible type of interview and assessment if a tragedy is to be averted" (p. 41).

Crisis counseling yields quick anxiety in the interview. Counselors must be prepared to handle clients who are so anxiety-ridden that they are having a difficult time concentrating, let alone breathing. They need to be able to develop rapport quickly with the person who is in crisis. However, the more upset and in crisis the client is, the more difficult it will be for the therapist to develop rapport with him. Kleespies et al. (1998), along with Meier and Davis (2001), recommended that to aid this situation, therapists should increase the structure of the interview. This allows clients to know that they are in a protected environment. Therapists can also be more overt with clients as to the purpose of the interview and how they will utilize the information gathered from the interview. Thus, assurance of safety becomes a very important part of the crisis interview.

Brems (2000) recommended four procedures when dealing with a client in crisis: (1) The first is relationship-building procedures and communication of safety. This includes connecting with the client so the client can discuss the situation for possible cathartic benefits (talking about the situation relieves some of the tension and anxiety the person has been experiencing). The therapist can thus support the client in the client's sharing of the crisis event. At the same time, the interviewer offers statements and reassurances that the client is safe and will be safe. (2) The second procedure is assessments. The therapist gains enough information about the crisis situation to begin to understand how the client's current functioning is related to the triggering event. The therapist also assesses the client's ability to cope and function, looking for resources the client can use to help move through the crisis. Another aspect of assessment is determining whether the client is a danger to self or others. In almost all crisis situations, clinicians try to determine how much of a suicide threat the client is or whether the client might try to harm someone else. (3) The third type of crisis intervention procedure is an action plan. This is a collaborative process between interviewer and client to develop means for the client to gain support and resources while also gaining important coping strategies. In this phase of intervention, the therapist helps the client put some or all of these action strategies into practice. (4) The last procedure is a follow-up, in which client and therapist evaluate where the client is and whether more intervention is needed or the crisis has passed.

Those therapists conducting crisis interviews need to be cautious in how they handle the session, as the client's life may be at stake. Wainrib and Bloch (1998) provided several pitfalls to avoid when working with clients in crisis. These included telling the client what to do, trying to show off and impress the client, trying to rescue the client, and bringing one's own experience into the interview. A key to remember in all therapy interviews, but even more so in this context, is that the crisis interview is about the client and getting the client stabilized as quickly as possible.

The crisis interviewer, if given the possibility, will have to decide whether to include other people into the crisis interview, such as family and friends. One of the guiding questions as to whether to have other people enter into the interview context is to determine how beneficial or detrimental it would be to have them in the room with the person in crisis (Kleespies et al., 1998). Usually, the therapist will have to make a judgment call about whether the family and friends would be able to calm the person in crisis down and subsequently add significant information to the interview that could lead to helping the client out. If the therapist believes the other people will only inflame the situation, it is better to exclude them.

Once sufficient information has been gathered, the crisis clinician needs to determine the best course of action. Kleespies et al. (1998) proposed that there were three general possibilities to a crisis interview: some type of intervention to alleviate the current crisis; referral for outpatient services; or referral for inpatient services. The decision as to which of these possibilities will be pursued is based on the seriousness of the client's potential harming of self or others. When the client is not at risk of harming himself or others, the crisis can be handled between the crisis counselor and the client. This might be a situation where a child has run away from home and the therapist and client can problem solve to figure out how to find the child. Outpatient therapy might occur when the client is potentially at risk of harming self or others, but is not active in that direction. If the client is potentially going to harm himself or others, and is potentially active in that pursuit, the therapeutic interviewer should help the client get immediate inpatient hospitalization to protect him or others.

Suicide Assessment

Perhaps one of the most harrowing situations for a new therapist is working with a client who is actively suicidal. Given that therapists are supposed to be working to prevent a client from committing suicide, not being able to control a client can lead to a sense of frustration and fear for a therapist. The suicide assessment may be one of the most challenging things therapeutic interviewers must do in the course of their careers. Shea (1998) stated, "If ever there were a moment of critical importance in interviewing, it is the moment when one listens for the harbingers of death" (p. 444).

Assessing risk is not a black-and-white issue. It takes a great deal of skill from the interviewer to engage a person in such a serious conversation. It seems that the public expects the therapeutic interviewer to know (1) whether a person will commit suicide and (2) how to prevent that suicide. Corey, Corey, and Callanan (2007) explained this situation, "Although it is not possible to prevent every suicide, it is possible to recognize the existence of common crises that may precipitate a suicide attempt and reach out to people who are experiencing these crises" (p. 237). Some clinicians believe that every mental health interview should have some type of suicide assessment included in it (Wiger & Huntley, 2002).

In the United States, there are 12.7 suicides per 100,000 persons (Kanel, 2003). Most therapists will work with at least one suicidal client, probably more, during their careers. One of the primary predictors of whether someone will commit suicide is if the person has a plan. Therapists should explore the lethality of the plan, whether the client really intends to follow through with the plan, and whether the client has the means to do so. The following section provides some of the basic definitions involved in the area of suicide assessment.

Definitions.

Suicidal ideation: "Suicidal ideation indicates the extent to which a patient wishes to die or 'be dead'" (Hillman, 2002, p. 119). Having suicidal ideation is not uncommon for many people—those who utilize mental health services and those who do not. Not all suicidal ideation is the same. Some clients engage in active suicidal ideation in which they think, quite often, about being dead and how they would kill themselves. Passive ideation is thinking about suicide but not having an active plan. There is more risk for following through on the suicide with those who are actively suicidal; however, any time a client mentions or suggests suicidal thoughts, therapists should take these comments very seriously and follow up on them.

Suicidal intent: Although many people might have suicidal ideation, not all of these individuals intend to kill themselves. It might be something they have thought about, but would not actually go through with. Intent covers clients' motivation and desire to actually go through with the suicide and kill themselves.

Suicidal threat: A suicidal threat is when the client verbally lets someone know that he is thinking or planning to take his own life. The threat itself is not life-threatening, but is a precursor to the possibility of the person taking some action against his own life.

Suicidal gesture: A suicidal gesture is an act that people commit that would not kill them, but could be seen as a precursor toward suicide (Wiger & Huntley, 2002). This might be an action that gets the person attention, such as cutting one's wrist (but not to such a degree that death results) or driving extremely recklessly.

Suicidal plan: "Suicidal plan represents the extent to which a patient has constructed and prepared a specific plan for suicide" (Hillman, 2002, p. 119). The clearer the plan, the higher the risk that the client is actually going to go through with the plan.

Suicide attempt: Wiger and Huntley (2002) defined suicide attempt as "an action with suicide as the goal" (p. 121). This is the implementation of the suicide plan and shows that there was ideation, intent, and a plan.

Working with Suicidal Clients

When working with suicidal clients, therapists should keep a few guidelines in mind as this context of interviewing is one of the most anxiety-provoking and possibly litigious arenas. Brems (2000) presented several guidelines for the therapeutic interviewer during suicide assessment. The therapist should remain calm as the more the therapist becomes anxious and out of control, the more confused and anxious the client will become. Leon (1982) recommended that, upon knowing a client has attempted suicide or is possibly currently suicidal, it is most productive to acknowledge and address this as early in the interview as possible; otherwise the interview might be strained and unproductive. Therapists need to support the client during this time. Also, therapists should not become preachy and moralistic. Even if a therapist thinks that killing oneself is a sin, this should not be expressed to the client. Therapists should, based on moral and ethical codes, attempt to prevent the client from killing himself; however, they should not use their own religious ideas as justification to clients for not killing themselves. Also, therapists should be straightforward in their language when talking about suicide. Instead of using euphemisms such as "thinking about the end" or "the long walk up to heaven," therapists should talk in terms of "suicide," "killing yourself," and "ending your life." This way, both client and therapist know that they are talking about a very serious situation.

Given the immediacy of a suicidal interview, in that long-term goals lose significance and short-term (perhaps focusing on days, hours, or minutes) goals become primary, a rapid connection between therapist and client is essential. Part of this alliance is the development of a safety plan. Cochran and Cochran (2006) provided several suggestions for developing a safety plan with clients:

- Make it time specific; usually between that day and the next scheduled session.
- Relate the safety plan to avoiding elements within your client's suicide plan or thoughts. For instance, if the client plans on jumping off a tall building, having the client stay away from tall buildings will help.
- Get rid of the means. If the client plans to shoot himself, then he should give away his guns.
- Avoid lowered inhibitions and impulse control. Get the client to avoid drinking or getting into more depressed situations.
- Prevent harm by contacting someone immediately. Just as AA asks the person call someone (his sponsor) when thinking he will drink, the plan can connect people together.

The safety plan can also be used along with a suicide contract. This contract would hold that the client agrees not to harm himself during a certain period of time (perhaps until the next session when another contract can be made, if needed). This contract specifies what each party of the contract should do. The therapist lays out what she will do in case the risk of the suicide rises too high. This usually entails breaking confidentiality to get the client needed resources or hospitalization to ensure that he does not commit suicide. The client may be asked to phone the therapist, family, friends, or a crisis center if things seem to be too overwhelming. However, as Clark (1998) has pointed out, there is no empirical evidence showing that those clients who sign a suicide contract are less likely to commit suicide. This suggests that the crisis interviewer should not use the suicide contract as the sole means of working with and preventing the client from committing suicide.

Therapists can also ask clients who own weapons, especially those weapons they talked about using for this purpose (for example, guns), to have family or friends hold onto the weapons for them so the client does not have access. Therapeutic interviewers might also consider working in conjunction with a medical professional to possibly use anti-psychotic or anti-depressant medications for the duration of the crisis. Suicidal clients usually believe that there is nothing to live for. When therapists can get clients to name things, or at least one thing, that is worth living for, they can engender more hope of living for the client. Thus, therapists can help shift the client's focus from the past to the future. Therapists can also make a distinction between suicidal thoughts and suicidal actions. Clients should know that just because they have the thought, they do not have to follow through with the action. Those therapists working with suicidal clients may want to have the client's contact information handy (even when out of the office) in case they need to contact emergency personnel. Suicidal clients often feel quite alone. Therapists can do well by connecting clients to as many social support systems as possible. When clients begin to express suicidal ideation and/or intent, therapists might consider meeting with the client more often until the crisis passes.

Because of the possibility of legal action against a therapist when a client has committed suicide, ensuring that therapists have performed their job appropriately is of the utmost importance. Brems (2000) recommended that any therapist dealing with a client in significant crisis should get supervision either during or immediately after the crisis. Corey, Corey, and Callanan (2007) highlight that documentation of the steps a therapist has taken is a key when performing suicide assessments. This is to show what the therapist did to assess and prevent the suicide. The following steps should be documented (Wiger & Huntley, 2002):

- Conduct a thorough assessment.
- Obtain a relevant history.
- Obtain previous treatment records.
- Directly evaluate suicidal thoughts.
- Consult with one or more professionals.
- Discuss the limits of confidentiality with the client.
- Implement appropriate suicide interventions.
- Provide resources to the client.
- Contact authorities and family members if a client is at high risk for suicide.

Crisis Intervention over the Phone

Much of crisis counseling occurs via the telephone, through crisis counseling centers or when clients call their therapist between session appointments. When talking on the telephone, therapeutic interviewers do not have the visual nonverbals that help them to understand a client's communication. However, the verbal nonverbals are still present.

Since many paraprofessionals and counselors conduct crisis interviews over the phone, Millman et al. (1998) explained that there are several immediate goals when conducting a telephone interview with a suicidal caller. The interviewer should assess the immediacy of the suicide. Those callers who seem to be in imminent danger should be worked with aggressively. Empathy is a key when working with callers, letting them know that they are being heard. The interviewer should also try to connect the caller with his strengths and resources (internal and external). Interviewer and caller should devise a plan for the caller and then arrange some type of follow-up.

Impact of Conducting Crisis Interviews

Crisis counseling can be extremely stressful for therapeutic interviewers. These clients are usually much more anxious and disoriented than the typical client. Further, therapists have to continually monitor the risk level for clients to determine if clients need a higher level of care to insure they do not harm themselves or someone else. Crisis clinicians tend to be underappreciated, compounding the stress they may feel having to work with sometimes hostile, uncooperative, and challenging clients (Kleespies et al., 1998). Two of the most serious occupational hazards for therapeutic interviewers are patient suicide and burnout (Hillman, 2002). Therapists, especially those who will be regularly working with clients dealing with crisis, and more specifically suicidal clients, should prepare themselves for the potential impact that clients' suicidal threats and possible completion of suicide will have on them. This is particularly important when there is a one in four chance that therapists will have a client commit suicide during treatment (Hillman, 2002).

Summary

One of the contexts of therapeutic interviewing is the assessment interview. This unique type of interviewing requires therapists to alter how they operate the therapy interview. The purpose of the interview needs to be spelled out since the interviewer will be asking the client very pointed and personal questions. Assessment interviews are conducted in order to have a wider contextual understanding of the client's problem, history, and functioning. In conducting the assessment interview, therapists find out about the stressors impacting the client, including any type of crisis that might be occurring and the likelihood of suicide. Ensuring that a proper suicide assessment is conducted is important for the welfare of therapist and client. If there is potential for harm, therapists can then help clients access the needed level of help as quickly as possible.

Exercises

1. Role-play with a colleague an assessment interview. The client should develop a whole client story to give the interviewer as much information as possible.

2. With a fellow student, role-play a crisis interview in which the client is stating that he is suicidal. Make sure that you tape this interview so you can go back and evaluate the impact of your interventions.

11

Cross-Cultural Interviewing
Working with Diverse Clients

In looking at the United States, counseling has traditionally been a field dominated by white male therapists. Within the last thirty years, a growing proportion of female and minority counselors have entered the field. Given the increasing immigration rates (U.S. Census, 2000), leading to the influx of people from a wide range of cultural backgrounds, therapists in the United States will come from and work with clients from extremely diverse worldviews.

The growth in cultural diversity seems to be a continuing process. The U.S. Census Bureau estimates that Hispanics will increase to 15.5 percent of the U.S. population in 2010, 17.8 percent in 2020, 20.1 percent in 2030, 22.3 percent in 2040, and 24.4 percent in 2050. Asians are also expected to increase from 3.8 percent in 2000 to 8 percent in 2050. The Black population is not expected to grow as fast as the Hispanic or Asian population, but will still comprise a significant number of persons in the United States, from 12.7 percent in 2000 to 14.6 percent in 2050.

Therapists working with clients from diverse backgrounds need to understand the issues of cross-cultural counseling in order to prevent harming the client, ensuring client welfare, and honoring the client's autonomy (Howard-Hamilton, Ferguson, & Puleo, 1998). Egan (2006b) stressed the dilemma of working therapeutically with clients from different cultures in that we are always working with someone from a different culture. Everyone has a personal culture that informs how they understand the world. Given that every person is impacted by culture (and usually multiple cultures), therapists need to understand not only their clients' cultural influences, but their own as well.

Multiculturalism can be considered the fourth force in psychology (Pedersen, 1999). Recently, most counseling training programs have updated their curriculum with the inclusion of cross-cultural counseling courses and perspectives. Taking a course in cross-cultural counseling raises students' self-awareness of cultural issues and leads to them being more knowledgeable, sensitive, and aware of clients who are racially and culturally different (Spears, 2004).

Within the last thirty years, issues of working with clients from diverse cultures have become an enormous topic in the field of counseling. Multiculturalism as an ideology developed in the 1970s within the context of the civil rights movement (Axelson, 1999). Today, it is an integral component of graduate training programs as well as various counseling theories.

While most counseling training programs have at least one course on multicultural counseling, others have been highlighting these issues in every course taught in the program. Because the development of a multicultural counselor is a process that takes years, one class, or one chapter in a textbook such as this, is not sufficient. Therapists should be constantly vigilant in exploring their own cultural beliefs and how they diverge and connect with other people's cultures. Parker (1998) explained the various training needs for therapists working with culturally diverse clients, stating that therapists-in-training should do the following:

> (a) examine their own attitudes and feelings toward ethnic minority persons and to change those negative attitudes; (b) gain cultural knowledge about ethnic groups in order to dispel myths and stereotypes and to feel more comfortable with them; (c) become more flexible in their approach in working with ethnic minorities; and (d) become aware of issues, trends, and challenges to be encountered by helping professionals. (p. ix)

These are daily, weekly, monthly, yearly, and lifelong goals. This chapter is one step in the move toward understanding how culture factors into the therapeutic interview.

Orientation to Conducting a Cross-Cultural Therapeutic Interview

Defining Multiculturalism

There is a debate in the counseling field about what constitutes a "multicultural" understanding of people and therapy. Authors such as Sue et al. (1998) have a very general definition, in which multicultural counseling relates to any characteristic where people are treated differently (for example, age, disability, geographic origin, sexual orientation). Corey, Corey, and Callanan (2007) defined it even more broadly as a relationship occurring between two people from diverse groups. Part of the difficulty in deciding on a definition is in understanding what is meant by the notion of culture. Pedersen (2000) explained some of the broad areas that the term *culture* constitutes, such as "within-group demographic variables (e.g., age, sex, and place of residence), status variables (e.g., social, educational, and economic), and affiliations (formal and informal), as well as ethnographic variables such as nationality, ethnicity, language, and religion" (p. 36). Others believe multiculturalism only occurs between people of a different race or nationality. Although therapists have primarily understood *multicultural* to mean a difference in racial category, it is starting to be used more broadly.

Reflection 11.1

What culture would you say you come from? How does coming from that culture inform the way that you understand the world? How does it inform the choices that you make in your life? How aware are you of your cultural heritage and how it impacts you in the present?

Whatever the definition of multiculturalism used, most authors and therapists agree that therapeutic interviewers will be working with clients from many different types of demographic characteristics. Therapists need to have awareness and comfort in working with people from diverse backgrounds. Given that people come to know themselves based on their gender, race, culture, socioeconomic status, sexuality, and other types of influencing factors, therapists should pay attention to these to better contextualize clients' problems. Sciarra (1999) explained that multiculturalism does not have to emphasize sameness or diversity, but could best be understood by thinking of each and every person as the result of cultural variables. He stated, "Culture, when more broadly defined and understood, should help to remove the 'exotic' nature of multiculturalism by appearing not as an obstacle but as a universal construct that helps to gain more accurate understanding of oneself and the client" (p. 11).

Determining someone's unique cultural influences is extremely hard. This is because people operate based on a variety of levels of culture (Axelson, 1999). Most people can understand the objective culture, which is made up of the more obvious features of a group of people. This might be the material elements such as food, clothing, language, and rituals that other people know about (for example, some Jewish people sit Shiva after someone passes away, some women in India are painted with Henna when they are about to marry, and many Japanese people bow to one another for greetings and departures). However, there is much more to each culture than what can be seen on the surface. This is known as the subjective culture. Axelson (1999) explained these features as "the deep inner layers of personal attitudes, beliefs, feelings, values and norms of behaviors, and roles that are widely shared among group members and that guide specific ways of being and behaving" (p. 3). These norms are more difficult to understand, yet therapists, if giving conscious effort to understanding another culture, can begin to distinguish them.

Egan (2006b) defined a group's culture as when "the shared beliefs and assumptions of a group interact with the group's shared values to produce group norms" (p. 2). These norms help to lead people from that culture to engage or not engage in a certain set or type of behaviors. Not every person from that cultural group will exhibit the attitudes, ideas, and behaviors that are the norm for the group. Norms may be the standard, but they are not the mandate. Not only should therapists have a good understanding of various cultures, but also they should understand how clients may be similar to and different from the norms for their culture. This gives therapists a sense of how the cultural norms, and the client's adherence to or lack of them, may be impacting the client.

The term *cross-cultural counseling* can be understood in two different ways (Atkinson, 2004). First, it may refer to a counseling relationship where therapist and client have ethnic differences. Second, it can be used when therapist and client are culturally different. This second definition would then apply to therapist and client from the same ethnic group (for example, Hispanic, African American, or Asian) but with differences within that group (for instance, one being highly acculturated, while the other is not). Thus, therapists should keep in mind that although a client may be from their same ethnic group, the two may not necessarily share the same culture.

Cultural Difference between Therapist and Client

Beginning around the mid-1980s, the field of counseling developed a significant interest in intergroup versus intragroup differences (Sciarra, 1999). The issue of difference between therapist and client can seem problematic to define, as two people from the same cultural group can be quite diverse. Corey, Corey, and Callanan (2002) defined diversity as "individual differences such as age, gender, sexual orientation, religion, and physical ability or disability" (p. 111). Any of these differences could make it difficult for the therapist to understand the client's perspective and means of communication. The difference might also lead the client to be hesitant to trust the therapist, which would inhibit building a strong therapeutic alliance. Although two people might be from the United States, there are so many subcultures that they may be more different than two people who come from different countries. The idea of multiculturalism allows people to view how they are both similar to and different from others (Pedersen, 2000). Therapeutic interviewers can learn how to connect with their clients based on the similarities they have with them, but also through the differences. Connection and rapport is not only about having similarity, but also about having differences. The connection comes through an openness to talk about each of these. This then leads to the notion of cultural pluralism in which the richness of different cultural values and beliefs is appreciated (Corey, Corey, & Callanan, 2007).

Given that most theories of counseling and psychotherapy were developed in Western nations, they may sometimes be at odds with clients from non-Western cultures (Sue, Ivey, & Pedersen, 1996). Further, the differences of client and therapist may impact the way that words, thoughts, and behaviors are expressed, interpreted, and understood. Sciarra (1999) explained this situation, "Often clients from diverse cultures will attach meanings to events and experiences that are quite different than the counselor's own meanings and interpretations for the very same event" (p. 7). Whatever the difference between therapist and client, it is not the difference itself that is important, but the ability to use that difference to foster unity (Smith et al., 2004). Thus, therapists and clients engage in a process of mutual enrichment.

As a start, therapists should attempt to gain a sense of the historical and contemporary relationship between their own culture/race and that of the client (Lago & Thompson, 2002). Although cultural differences are usually viewed through the lens of the therapist coming from the dominant culture and the client from a minority, unique circumstances arise when the therapist is of color (Rastogi & Wieling, 2005). In this situation, there is both a cross-cultural situation occurring between therapist and client and also potential barriers because the therapist, who is usually from the majority culture of that locale, is not from the culture.

There is debate in the field about the importance of ethnic matching between therapist and client (Alladin, 2002; Ward & Banks, 2002). Some people think that therapist and client should come from the same cultural background as that would aid them in understanding each other better. Others think that therapists should be color-blind and that they should treat every client the same, regardless of racial or cultural background. Perhaps Alladin best supplied the answer to the question of how important ethnic matching is in counseling when he stated, "It depends" (p. 175).

Skills for Conducting a Cross-Cultural Therapeutic Interview

Objectives of Multicultural Competence

The field of psychotherapy is based on a notion of core competencies that therapists should espouse. Various regulatory bodies have a listing of competencies a therapist should have in order to practice in that area. Sue et al. (1998) listed four objectives of multicultural competence. The first is that psychotherapists "become culturally aware of their own values, biases, and assumptions about human behavior" (p. 17). This is to enable them to realize the ways that their own preconceptions, worldviews, biases, prejudices, stereotypes, and values impact them and thus the way they understand, structure, and engage in the therapeutic process. The second objective of multicultural competence is "having mental health professionals acquire knowledge and understanding of the worldview of minority or culturally different groups and clients" (p. 17). Not only is it important for a therapist to understand his own culturally relevant issues, but also he should understand the client's values, perceptions, worldviews, biases, preconceptions, and anything else that impacts how the client acts inside and outside of the therapy room. The more that therapeutic interviewers understand various cultures, the more they can act in ways to connect with clients and design appropriate intervention styles for working with diverse people. The third objective is "having mental health professionals begin the process of developing appropriate and effective intervention strategies in working with culturally different clients" (p. 17). Once therapists understand their own and their clients' perceptions, they can better implement techniques and utilize their skills to best work with that particular client. The fourth multicultural competence objective Sue et al. described is "having mental health professionals understand how organizational and institutional forces may either enhance or negate the development of multicultural competence" (p. 17). Culture is embedded in the social structures of groups and organizations. Becoming aware of these potential biases helps therapists navigate the organizational system effectively.

By understanding that culture impacts an individual, the therapeutic interviewer appreciates the power of context. People's behaviors are housed within specific contexts, which open certain doors and close others. The therapeutic interview occurs in multiple contexts based on involvement of culture, the legal system, the medical system, and familial systems, among others. The context in which therapeutic interviewers provide therapy, from private practice to schools to home-based to agency settings provides ideas as to how people should be with one another.

Multicultural Competencies (MCC)

In the field of counseling, a major focus on the issue of multicultural competencies occurred around 1992 (Arredondo, 2003). This transpired with Sue, Arredondo, and McDavis's (1992a, 1992b) article, "Multicultural Counseling Competencies and Standards: A Call to the Profession." This article was so important that it was simultaneously published in two separate journals. The competencies discussed in this article set the stage for how the field of counseling understood cross-cultural therapy. Therapeutic interviewers are encouraged to review the competencies and standards these authors put forth.

The Association of Multicultural Counseling and Development devised the Multicultural Counseling Competencies, which was built around a 3 × 3 model (general factors model by counseling dimensions model) (Sue, Arredondo, & McDavis, 1992a, 1992b). General factors include attitudes and beliefs, knowledge, and skills while the counseling dimensions model includes counselor awareness of own cultural values and biases, counselor awareness of client's worldview, and culturally appropriate intervention strategies. The following section describes each of these areas in more depth.

Counselor Awareness of Own Assumptions, Values, and Biases. Therapists need to be aware of their own background, perceptions, values, and biases when working with clients. Pedersen (2000) stated, "The first level of developing multiculturally skilled counselors requires developing an awareness of the culturally learned starting points in the counselor's thinking" (p. 19). There are four main ways a therapist can accomplish this task (Roysircar, 2003). First, therapists need to make an assessment of their own self-awareness. Most people do not fully reflect on where their ideas, rituals, behaviors, and worldviews came from and how they have been impacted by them. This assessment entails understanding one's own biases, how one's societal viewpoints are reflected in one's theoretical orientation and an immersion in one's culture-of-origin. A second task is counselors' examination of their own defensiveness. This includes how comfortable, or uncomfortable,

they are in dealing with issues of race and homosexuality. Counselors need to honestly assess how racist or homophobic they are. Part of working in this area is developing an openness to individuality and understanding that multiculturalism is an ongoing process. A third task of developing awareness of one's own assumptions, values, and biases is through counselor self-disclosure. Roysircar explained that "the role and person of the counselor is critical, with the use of 'self as a tool' at the core of MCC" (p. 25). Besides the typical issues surrounding self-disclosure, therapists should understand how their own self-disclosure (both the content of it and the desire to do it) is predicated, at least partly, on their cultural background. Therapeutic interviewers must realize how the self-disclosure will impact the client, especially if there is a difference in cultural background between the two. The last task is an understanding of a multicultural counseling relationship. This occurs through "ethnotherapeutic empathy" wherein the therapist understands not only what the client is saying, but also how it is housed in the client's subjective culture.

Therapists have many ways of understanding their own culture. Hays (2001) provided an acronym to help organize the cultural influences that impact people—ADDRESSING:

- **Age** and generational influences
- Developmental and acquired **Disabilities**
- **Religion** and spiritual orientation
- **Ethnicity**
- **Socioeconomic** status
- **Sexual** orientation
- **Indigenous** heritage
- **National** origin
- **Gender**

This entails a twofold process in which the therapist looks into himself for greater understanding while also looking outside himself to understand other people's cultures. Therapists can conduct a cultural self-assessment to become more aware of their own cultural influences and how these might be impacting their perception of the client and their behavior during the therapeutic interview.

Counselor Awareness of Client's Worldview. The first step for therapists working with clients from diverse cultures is to have a better sense of their own cultural background and how that informs their understanding of self and others. Next, therapists become aware of the client's worldview. Having information about various cultures allows therapists to understand "normal" behavior for certain groups of people. One of the best ways to gain an awareness of other cultures is to go outside the classroom or therapy room and interact with racial and ethnic minority people at various festivals and restaurants, or to travel. Roysircar et al. (2003) have their students meet with someone from a different racial and ethnic group for ten meetings, interviewing them for about fifty minutes each time. The therapy trainee interacts with the person, exchanging stories of their lives that focus on race, ethnicity, culture, and class. This activity is not designed to be therapeutic, but to inform each individual's awareness of the other person's cultural background. There is the possibility that therapists will try to understand the client based on the group the client is associated with rather than how that client might exhibit those cultural traits. Thus, therapists might start with a general view and then move quickly to gain a specific understanding of the client.

Culturally Appropriate Intervention Strategies.   Therapists should be aware of how their own interventions are based on certain cultural understandings and that their normal interventions might not be appropriate for all clients. Counselors should attempt to gauge what types of interventions will fit within the client's cultural background. For instance, a therapist from an individualistic culture suggesting that an adult client from a collectivistic culture not listen to what her parents have to say to her about her occupational and marital future would be problematic. Part of a therapist's intervention strategies is accurately and appropriately utilizing the client's verbal and nonverbal messages. In the verbal realm, if a therapist cannot speak the client's language, he should either use an interpreter or refer the client to someone who is more competent conversing in that language. However, caution should be taken when using an interpreter as many therapists find that there is a difficulty and disconnect when interpreters are used (Rea, 2004). The interpreter may become part of the therapy process, the client and therapist may tend to start talking to (and giving eye contact to the interpreter rather than to each other), and direct translation of words may not occur; thus, the person's full meaning may not come through. Case Scenario 11.1 demonstrates what happens when therapist and client cannot fully understand each other's language.

CASE SCENARIO 11.1

I was supervising a team of therapists in live supervision, and we began work with a Bangladeshi family who had recently moved to the United States. The father refused to come to therapy because he did not think it important. The thirteen-year-old son was developmentally delayed and engaging in harmful behavior at home and at school. Since the family spoke very little English, they brought either an uncle or a cousin with them to translate. Sometimes the eleven-year-old son had to translate in the sessions. The team had to tread somewhat lightly in interventions as the father was the primary authority figure in the house, yet would not attend sessions. We had a difficult time getting the thirteen year old to make a connection with us since he was mainly talking to his family members because he did not know any English.

Characteristics of Effective Multicultural Counselors

Chapter 3 discussed characteristics for effective therapeutic interviewers. Those are the same traits for therapists interviewing someone from a different cultural background. However, there are more specific characteristics for those working with cross-cultural clients. Sodowsky, Kuo-Jackson, and Loya (1997) provided several counselor variables that are important when engaging in a multicultural counseling relationship. First, therapists should feel comfortable exploring their own racial, cultural, and ethnic backgrounds. The more they are comfortable with themselves and exploring these types of issues in themselves, the more they can understand where some of their beliefs and values come from. Next, counselors should have a certain comfort in dealing with others' obvious differences. When the therapist is not able to deal with someone else's difference, the other person will be less likely to feel comfortable exploring cultural and racial issues with the therapist. Third, counselors should be flexible. Because people can be quite different, one set method of working with people will probably not always work with everyone. Therapists need to be able to change and adapt based on the unique circumstances of various clients. Lastly, therapists should develop an ability to deal with the ambiguities of cultural mysteries. No amount of education will allow therapists to know everything about all cultures. However, therapists can attempt to learn as much as they can, especially with cultural groups that they are likely to come into contact with.

Baruth and Manning (1999) described several ways that therapists can develop respect for their own and their clients' cultural identities:

- Developing an understanding and respect for clients' different worlds and how their worlds differ
- Considering perspectives that vary from the counselor's identity perspective
- Recognizing, respecting, counseling, and preserving clients' identities that are culturally different from the counselor's
- Holding on to one's cultural identity, values, and ways of knowing, yet being open to others
- Knowing that clients' symbols, meanings, and messages of their cultures contribute to achieving cross-cultural identity
- Listening carefully, asking sensitive questions, and reading and studying about clients' cultural, racial, and ethnic backgrounds
- Recognizing clients as experts in their realms of experience and transposing oneself into those unique worlds
- Developing a firm sense of self in clients (p. 51)

One key for the effective multicultural counselor is that of awareness. This awareness is intended for an understanding of self, other, and context. Hays (2001) found that the most common response that people gave for the most important characteristic for someone doing cross-cultural work was that the person needs to be humble. When people are humble, they can critically think about their own assumptions, values, and behaviors and are open to changing them if they are not working.

Culture-Based Interviewing Skills

This chapter has thus far presented a contextualization for why culture plays an integral role in the therapeutic interview. Describing specific cross-cultural skills is both difficult and beyond the scope of this book. Hays (2001) suggested that "although MCT [Multicultural Therapy] certainly involves a paradigm shift in that it calls into question the usefulness of all preceding theories, the diversity and complexity of clients' identities rule out the possibility of easy prescriptions" (p. 155). There are, however, some general guidelines for cross-cultural interviewing.

Therapists can structure and organize the therapeutic interview to help create a positive cross-cultural context (Pederson & Ivey, 1993). Pederson and Ivey provided a generic five-stage sequence for a culture-centered counseling interview. The first stage is the initiation in which the therapist orients the client to the purpose of therapy. The interviewer, using mainly open-ended questions, gets the client to open up and talk about what is going on. Based on the cultural background of the client, along with the client's unique personality, the therapeutic interviewer may need to take a leadership position, showing some experience in being able to engage in this type of conversation. The second stage is listening, where the therapist uses the skills of active listening to let the client know he is following along with the story and gaining the deeper level of meanings of the client's communication. The third stage is focusing, where the therapist focuses on specific lines of client discourse to get further clarification about them. The fourth stage is probing, when the therapeutic interviewer gets the client to talk about certain information that seems to have been missing from the main story. The last stage is use, where therapist and client take the information from the interview to help reach the goals of the interview. This is a very basic template wherein therapeutic interviewers will need to use additional therapeutic skills to ensure that they are working with the client in ways that fit that client's cultural worldview.

During the first therapeutic interview with culturally different clients, therapists might need to spend more time explaining the process of therapy (Wohl, 2000). Since many minority clients may not have utilized therapeutic services in the past, or might come with a negative view toward it, the process should be explained and their perceptions garnered so those issues are brought forth and addressed. Lago and Thompson (2002) agreed that therapeutic interviewers should be clear and concise about what they are offering the client. They also suggested avoiding talking in jargon or colloquialisms. Since the culturally different client may not fully understand the therapist, therapeutic interviewers should periodically check in with clients to ensure they understand what is being said. This might entail lengthening the time allotted for the interview.

To conclude this section on skills, therapists need to be able to work on many levels during the therapeutic interview. There is the content of what the client is saying, the context of the client's culture and how that impacts the problem, and the context of the connection between therapist and client. Hays (2001) provided twelve culturally responsive interventions therapists can implement when working with clients from diverse backgrounds:

1. Develop knowledge of culturally related therapies and strategies.
2. Consider religion as a potential source of strength and support.
3. Adapt mainstream approaches (e.g., psychodynamic, humanistic/existential, behavioral, cognitive-behavioral, family systems therapist) to the cultural context of the client.
4. Become familiar with nonverbal expressive therapies, and obtain additional training when appropriate.
5. Use family systems interventions whenever possible.
6. Conceptualize "family" broadly to include gay and lesbian parents, single parents, elders, relatives, and non-kin family members.
7. Be willing to see individual members or subsystems of the family on an as-needed basis.
8. Recognize power differentials related to each of the ADDRESSING domains.
9. Use group therapy to create a multicultural environment in which clients can learn from others, practice behaviors, and obtain support.
10. Intervene at sociocultural, institutional, and political levels when appropriate and possible.
11. Set goals, develop treatment plans, and choose interventions in collaboration with clients.
12. When medications are prescribed, be aware of ethnic and age-related differences in metabolism and cultural expectations regarding medications. (pp. 174–175)

Thus, the skills that culturally sensitive therapists espouse are found in three main areas: awareness, knowledge, and application (Yan & Wong, 2005).

Special Issues When Conducting a Cross-Cultural Therapeutic Interview

Barriers to Effective Multicultural Counseling

Since therapy and interviewing are based on communication, both people need to send and receive messages in ways the other person can understand. Therapist and client need to be encoding and decoding based on the same meaning system. Even between individuals from the same culture, people misinterpret the verbal and nonverbal signals each gives off. This potential breakdown in communication is heightened when people from different cultures interact with one another. Not being fully able to understand each other, based on cultural variations, can potentially lead to a loss of trust and rapport in the therapeutic relationship (Sue & Sue, 2003). It can also lead to frustration for the therapist who has been used to communicating with those of his own culture.

Baruth and Manning (1999) described several barriers to effective multicultural counseling including differing class and cultural values, differing languages between counselor and client, stereotyping clients, counselor encapsulation, counselors understanding their own culture, client resistance and reluctance, differing worldviews and lack of cultural relativity, differing languages between counselor and client, labeling women, multicultural populations, and the poor, and expecting all clients to conform to counselors' standards and expectations. Each of these will be briefly explained.

Differing Class and Cultural Values.   People's socioeconomic background may impact how they behave and perceive the world. Some social classes may place varying importance to things such as time orientation, use of slang, and material goods. Clients from a different culture than the therapist might have expectations the therapist never expected.

Clients from different cultures, especially those born in countries outside the United States, may not have the same proficiency with the English language as the therapist. This then becomes a possible barrier to effective communication. Colloquial phrases and jokes become incidents for misunderstandings between therapist and client. For some clients, an interpreter is needed, which then diminishes the impact of the therapist's carefully chosen words.

Stereotyping Clients.   All individuals use the perceptual process of stereotyping to help categorize things and people into manageable cognitive items. Therapists need to consider how they stereotype different cultural groups so that they become more conscious of this process. Once they realize how they might be stereotyping someone, they can more actively engage in attempts to prevent doing this in the future. The opposite of this is to assume nothing about one's clients. This is a problematic assumption because people cannot *not* have preconceptions about others. Since having preconceptions about groups is pervasive, therapists thinking that they do not have these preconceptions run the risk of having them affect the therapy without even realizing it. Parker (1998) recommended that therapists become aware of specific stereotypes in order to be able to help other people without bias and to better understand their clients' needs.

Counselor Encapsulation.   When therapists believe their stereotypes of clients instead of realizing that clients are unique and more than the limited understand-

Reflection 11.2

Think about how you have been stereotyped by other people in your life. What was the context in which another person had preconceived notions of you based on a group you were associated with? How did you feel when you realized the person was using stereotypes when making attributions about you? What were your reactions? How did you interact with the person after this occurrence?

ing of the therapist, they can be described as being encapsulated in their own cultural borders. These individuals tend to be ethnocentric, believing that the way that their cultural group views and operates in the world is the correct way of living life.

Counselors' Understanding of Their Own Cultures. Therapeutic interviewers need to have an understanding of their own cultural heritage and background from which to work to understand other people's cultures. During training programs, novice therapists should take time to get in touch with their own culture so that they can have a better sense of where their thought processes, worldviews, and behaviors come from.

Client Reluctance and Resistance. Some clients come to therapy ready to self-disclose and talk about their problems. Others are extremely hesitant. Therapists should pay attention to how much of a client's reluctance to open up to a helping professional is based on the newness of the situation, the relationship (or lack thereof) between therapist and client, or the client's cultural view of what going for help means. Some cultural groups may feel that counselors who are not from their culture would be nonresponsive and not understand their particular problems and needs. Culturally diverse clients may be hesitant opening up to a therapist until the therapist opens up and self-discloses first to them (Sue & Sue, 2003).

Differing Worldviews and Lack of Cultural Relativity. Although no two people have exactly the same worldview, many people from the same cultural group share similar worldviews. However, people from different cultural groups will probably have differences, sometimes huge differences, in how they perceive the world around them. For some, certain issues might not be problematic (such as the use of alcohol), whereas for other cultures the same issues might be extremely problematic. Axelson (1999) discussed the view of cultural relativism, explaining the various features of this position:

- All cultures are equal.
- All cultures have intrinsic value.
- One culture's values cannot be imposed on another culture.
- All cultures are equally entitled to respect.
- No culture is better or worse than any other culture.
- All cultures are appreciated for their differences.
- Cultural differences should be understood without applying critical standards or evaluations; no transcultural standards can be applied. (p. 16)

Labeling Women, Multicultural Populations, and the Poor. People from other cultural groups, women, and the poor have been viewed as being more mentally ill when they have strayed from the normal patterns of behavior than the majority group (Baruth & Manning, 1999). Therapists need to keep attuned to how they might perceive the client based on any type of demographic characteristic as having a stereotype shifts and biases one's perspective of another person.

Expecting All Clients to Conform to Counselors' Standards and Expectations.   Therapists who grew up in Western societies, especially those who grew up in the United States and have not done much traveling, might develop a perception that clients should conform to Western standards. This expectation, probably without the therapists' realization, can impact the way in which they feel about and act toward clients. One problem therapists may face is that they tend to develop assumptions and preconceptions of clients. Hays (2001) provided several questions therapists can ask themselves to try to prevent this from happening:

- How did I come to this understanding? How do I know that this is true?
- Are there alternative explanations or opinions that might be equally valid in this situation?
- How might my view of the client's situation be influenced by my own context, for example, my age or generational experiences, my ethnic background, my socioeconomic status?
- Might there be some information that lends validity to the view with which I disagree?
- Might there be a positive, culturally related purpose for the behavior, belief, or feeling that I judge to be dysfunctional or unhealthy? (p. 27)

This fits in with the notion of therapists continually being aware of their own beliefs and how they are impacting therapy along with the client's unique belief system. Therapists should be conscious that their perceptions are just hypotheses, which always need adjusting based on new information.

As can be seen, therapeutic interviewers must explore not only how their own cultural biases might come into play during the session, but also the cultural make-up of the client. Keats (2000) suggested interview scenarios that might be potentially problematic based on the culture of the client:

- To send a woman to interview a man.
- To send a man to interview a woman.
- To interview a married woman alone.
- To interview a married woman without her husband being present.
- To send a person of one religion to interview a person of a different religion when factions from each are in conflict.
- To mention the names of recently deceased persons.
- To refer directly to matters which are taboo.
- To ask questions as the means of obtaining information.
- To make direct rather than circuitous replies.
- To look directly into a person's face when speaking.
- To respond in a manner which will cause the questioner to lose face. (pp. 83–84)

Therapeutic interviewers can be alert to potential problems and to times when clients seem uncomfortable. They might ask the clients if there are any cultural rules that might play into the therapy or they can read up on the client's cultural rules before or during the course of therapy. One of the most important characteristics for effective cross-cultural work is having an openness to difference and

CASE SCENARIO 11.2

I was working with a woman whose two children were taken away from her by the state child welfare agency. The program I was working with was designed as a crisis stabilization program for the purposes of reunification of children and parents. When I went to the client's house, she was extremely hesitant to talk with me. She was a Black female whose children were taken away by White authority figures, and I was a White male coming into her home. She did not trust me. I spent the first several sessions attempting to do two things. First, I wanted to distinguish myself from the child welfare agency. Second, I discussed with her how the difference in our cultural background might impact the way we worked together. The client discussed her concerns about this with me. Although I tried to be open about our racial differences and what race meant for her, I think that the wound of having her children taken away from her was too great and we did not build a strong therapeutic alliance. My sense was that she did not move past my race and thus, never trusted me enough to open up. However, alternative hypotheses about the therapeutic alliance could also be made.

diversity. Case Scenario 11.2 provides an example of what can happen when there are racial and hierarchical differences between therapist and client.

A Theory of Multicultural Counseling and Therapy

Culture can be incorporated into therapy in many different fashions. The therapist needs to understand the client in context. This can be viewed in four different levels, each one more specific than the next (Axelson, 1999). The broadest context is that of common human experience. Human beings are more similar than different. Cross-cultural studies have shown that people across the globe engage in the same types of behaviors and processes. The particulars of how they do this might be different, but in essence, we are all one and the same. The next context is specific cultural experiences. The client's culture impacts them in ways similar to and different from other cultures. The third context is individual experiences. Axelson explained this context in terms of the therapist needing to "gain an understanding of how the individual relates to important objects of motivation, *what* his or her personal constructs are and *how* they are constructed to form his or her worldview" (p. 28). In the center is the context of the client as a unique human being. The three other contexts combine to lead clients to experience the world in their own unique way.

Sue, Ivey, and Pedersen (1996), three of the leading figures in the field of multicultural counseling, developed six propositions that are the foundational assumptions of a theory of multicultural counseling and therapy (MCT). Proposition one holds that MCT is a theory that can be a framework for all other theories. It does not distinguish between Western or non-Western counseling and healing approaches, but recognizes all theories. Proposition two states that both therapist and client identities develop based on unique experiences and contexts. Therapy revolves around the interrelationships of these experiences and contexts. Proposition three holds that therapists are influenced by the level of cultural/racial identity they are currently experiencing. This identity will then influence how clients and therapists come to understand what is occurring during the therapy process. Proposition four of MCT states that therapists should utilize therapeutic techniques, skills, orientations, and goals that match the client's value system. Thus, no one approach should be used with all people of all cultures. Proposition five explains that the role of the therapist is neither fully defined nor limited. It is based on the cultural context the therapist is working in and may influence how many people to work with, which people to work with, and what social units the therapist interacts with. The final proposition, proposition six, holds that consciousness arousal and awareness is one of the basic goals of MCT. This expansion of awareness should occur on an individual, family, group, and organizational level.

The multicultural counseling and therapy theory is a meta-theory that can be used in conjunction with existing theories of counseling. It can be considered as a "cultural quilt" (Pope-Davis & Constantine, 1996, p. 113). MCT theory aids the therapist in the type of perspective taken when viewing clients, shifting from a dichotomous one (right and wrong) to a view of client behaviors on a continuum that is based in the context of culture.

Summary

Conducting therapeutic interviews with clients from different cultures brings an added dimension for therapeutic interviewers. An awareness of one's own cultural background and influence, knowledge of the client's cultural context, and utilization of the appropriate multicultural skills all play a factor in determining the effectiveness of the therapeutic interview. There is not a specific counseling theory of cross-cultural counseling; therapists can use the principles of multiculturalism to apply to whatever theory makes the most sense to them. The future of cross-cultural counseling may include more input from the client about the therapeutic interviewer's cross-cultural competencies and more process and outcome indexes of counseling regarding cross-cultural competencies (Fuertes, Bartolomeo, & Nichols, 2001).

Exercises

1. In class, write down the values, rituals, and customs of your primary culture. Then discuss with classmates from different cultures the similarities and differences among you. Debate how these differences might play out during the therapeutic interview and how you, as a potential therapist, would deal with that.

2. Discuss in class the various stereotypes that you have about different cultural groups. Talk about how having these stereotypes might impact your work with clients. Talk with each other about various ways you might have of trying to reduce these stereotypes.

12

Therapeutic Interviewing with Children

The skills presented so far in this book have primarily been talked about in terms of adult clients. All of the skills that have been previously discussed apply equally to adults and children. However, therapeutic interviewing with children requires some other unique skills or adaptations (although some of these adaptations are applicable in working with adults). Children are developmentally different from adults: physically, emotionally, cognitively, and psychologically. Therapeutic interviewers working with children need to be able to connect and be therapeutic with someone much younger than themselves. They also need to keep track of what is developmentally appropriate for the child client they are working with as that will help to determine how best to conduct the interview.

Although most skills and concepts are similar for therapeutic interviews with adults and children, children's unique worldviews and perspectives mean that interviews with them need to be conducted differently from those with adults. There are some potential challenges when working with children (Barker, 1990). First, most children have fewer cognitive and language skills than adults. This leads to the potential of talking over the child's head. Second, children are usually brought to therapy not because they want to come, but because someone else wants them to come. Children may be unaware of why they are there or might even oppose and be offended by the implications made when they are sent to therapy. Third, the reason for children being brought to therapy is usually some type of misdeed. This might lead them to view the therapist as a detective of wrongdoing instead of as an accomplice for positive change. Fourth, children usually do not understand the purpose of the interview or might have been given false information, such as that the therapist will teach them how to behave properly. Fifth, many children have negative perceptions of therapists and counselors. They may think that they are being seen by a therapist because they are crazy. Lastly, some childhood disorders consist of some difficulties with language. Children do not have the language facility of adults, and when a child is dealing with a communication difficulty, conducting a productive therapeutic interview becomes even more difficult. This chapter explores these and other challenges and issues of conducting a therapeutic interview with a child.

Orientation to Conducting a Therapeutic Interview with a Child

The Relationship

The relationship between child client and adult therapeutic interviewer is very unique. In this relationship, two processes underlie the relationship developed in the clinical interview (Ginsburg, 1997). The first is that the two people learn to talk to one another. This includes figuring out the rules of communication in *this* particular context with *that* specific person. The child needs to learn who the therapist is, how the therapist operates, what can and cannot be said, and the effect talking has on all aspects of life, including interpersonal interactions and one's own cognitions and psychological functioning.

The second process is that the child and adult develop a relationship of trust and respect. The child trusts that the therapist will not punish him for what he says or does. This also pertains to the therapist not viewing the client as "the problem," especially when the parents bring the child in because they are overwhelmed by the child's negative behaviors. Minuchin explained, "Few children are truly unmanageable, and most respond to a genuine interest in the part of their lives that doesn't carry a label of trouble" (Minuchin, Nichols, & Lee, 2007, p. 38). The therapist respects the child client as a unique person, worthy of the devoting of time, energy, and attention. By gaining the respect of the therapist, children are more likely to engage in therapy. As with adult clients, it is the therapist's respecting the child client that leads the child to feel respect for the therapist and security in the therapy room (Axline, 1969).

One of the difficulties that can occur in developing the relationship with a child client is how well that child individuates from his parent(s). As with going to school, some children have an easier time leaving the parent for an extended period of time. Other children may become extremely anxious. Therapists help establish a positive relationship by having an initial meeting with both child and parent so the child can get acclimated to the therapist, in the presence of his parents, before being alone with this new person, who is relatively a stranger to the child. The attachment problem between child and parent can also be problematic in the other direction. Some parents may become upset or threatened when the therapist develops a close bond with the child. When this happens, therapists can include the parent in treatment as much as possible. This helps ensure the parent's participation and cooperation in therapy.

Sometimes, when working with child clients, the role of the therapist is not that clear. Even with adults, some clients might misconstrue the therapist's "caring" as that of being a potential friend. Children, more than adults, view the therapist less as a professional change agent and more as a buddy. Child clients will ask the therapist if the therapist is their friend. The answer to this question is tricky, because a "yes" would not quite be accurate. For children, friends go to each other's homes, celebrate birthdays together, and play together. A "no" answer might upset the child who does not understand why he is going to see the therapist. Therapists working with children should consider potential answers to this question—answers that let the child know his importance to the therapist but also include the therapist's role for change.

Language

Because children's language is not as developed as adults', therapists must be careful in using language the child does not understand. Although children have the ability to understand adult speech structures by four years of age (Zwiers & Morrissette, 1999), they might not give the same meaning to words as adults do (Hughes & Baker, 1990; Lukas, 1993). Children also think differently than adults do (House, 2002).

When children do not understand a word(s) the therapist used, they tend to respond through either silence or letting the interviewer know he does not understand (Aldridge & Wood, 1998). Therapeutic interviewers should use a more simplified language with children than they do with most adults; yet, therapists do not want to talk on a level below the client, as this would be disrespectful. Interviewers should use clear and plain language without talking down to the child. When working with teenaged clients, therapists should be cautious in trying to use the slang and lingo current in that age group. There is the possibility that, although it is intended to join with the youth, it can make the therapist seem as a fake. For instance, when talking with a fifteen year old, a forty-year-old therapist might come across the wrong way in saying, "What posse do you run with on the weekends?"

Making one's language simple and clear is important when working with children. The following provide several examples of appropriate and inappropriate language with children:

Inappropriate Language: What types of extracurricular activities do you engage in?
Appropriate Language: What types of things do you do after school?

Reflection 12.1

What is your feeling about interacting with children? How well do you get along with them? What are the main ways you connect with children? How might you put them off? Evaluate yourself honestly on how much you enjoy being in the company of children of various ages? What are the differences based on age and gender?

Inappropriate Language: Have you ever urinated during the night?
Appropriate Language: Have you ever wet your bed?

Inappropriate Language: What disciplinary style do your parents have?
Appropriate Language: How do your parents punish you?

Therapists should consider trying to shorten their use of sentences, especially questions. The longer a question is worded, the more likely it is the child will not comprehend the question and will become confused.

Children also have a harder time than adults in talking about and with abstractions. Children tend to be concrete when they communicate, necessitating the therapist to be more concrete in the use of her language. Thus, children may be quite literal in their understanding of words (Wilson & Powell, 2001).

Children's Knowledge of the Therapist

Children have a tendency not to let the other person they are in conversation with know that they are not following along with them. One possible reason for this is that children do not want to let the other person know they do not know the meaning of certain words, which they think might make them look dumb in the other person's eyes. Therapists can periodically check in with child clients to ensure they understand what the therapist is saying. Brief check-ins with clients can be very useful to gauge the level of comprehension. They might do this by saying something like, "Sammy, I just want to make sure you understand what I'm saying. If you don't, please let me know. Don't feel bad if you don't. Sometimes, even I don't understand what I'm saying!"

Therapists can also alter their use of language and questioning to try to work on the child's level. Through the use of simple questions rather than complex ones, therapists can converse with the child in a means the child more easily understands. Not only should questions be simple, but also they should be short. The longer a question, the more chance there is that the client will become confused.

> *Poor Question:* Sammy, I wanted to know how things were going at school, because when you first came in, your mother was really concerned that you were getting bad grades and were getting into some fights. She said that you weren't really bringing your homework home, but that she has seen a bit of improvement. What do you think?

In this example, the child has to keep in mind the original question of how things are going at school while also taking into consideration his mother's viewpoint of his situation. This double-barreled question might confuse the child.

> *Good Question:* How is school going for you now that you've begun to make some changes?

This question omits the mother's influence, which might get the child to try to appease the mother or answer in ways that confirm what she wants.

Another way of trying to help the child understand is to pay attention to the temporal aspect in questions. Children's sense of time (past, current, and future) is not as developed as adults. The more that therapists keep discussion of time focused on the very recent past, present, or very near future, the more likely the child will understand.

> *Poor Question:* Billy, how are you different now from five months ago when you first came in?
>
> *Good Question:* Billy, how are you doing now with not fighting?

Usually when asking about before-and-now questions (for example, how have you changed?), it is done for the purpose of recounting the positive changes the client has made. Adult clients are able to work back and forth from the distant past to the present. Children are not as able to do this. Therapeutic interviewers, by staying primarily in the present, can avoid any confusion of the time frame the therapist is talking about and then can provide the changes that they have noticed as positive reinforcement for the child.

Skills for Conducting a Therapeutic Interview with a Child

Explaining the Interview

Children are taken to therapy usually because they are engaging in certain behaviors their parents (or other adult authority figures) find distressing. They are usually not traditional voluntary clients (Lukas, 1993), as many adult clients are. Sometimes what the parents find distressing is that the child's teacher is having concerns about the child. Since most adults do not have an accurate portrayal of therapy, it is not clear what children have been told by their parents about therapy. Some parents, in an attempt not to have their child mad at them, or to at least be willing to go for one session, lie to their child about therapy. Case Scenario 12.1 highlights how child clients are sometimes provided erroneous information about beginning therapy.

As with adults, children come to therapy for a variety of reasons. Thompson and Rudolph (1992) classified children's problems into five categories: interpersonal conflict; intrapersonal conflict; lack of information about self; lack of information about the environment; and lack of skill. Based on age, children might not be able to articulate exactly what is going on for them. This is why it might be important, especially for the first session, but also throughout the whole of the therapy process, to have parents and children in the room at the same time when explaining important components of the therapy. Usually, first sessions are planned so there is some time with parent(s) and child present, when the parent

CASE SCENARIO 12.1

I had a first session with a nine-year-old boy. When he first came in, I asked him why he thought he was there. He told me that his mother had told him that they were going to see the doctor. I then asked him why he thought his mom wanted him to go see a doctor. He told me that she told him that it was just a normal check-up. I then had to work with the child and bring in his mother to have a more straightforward and open agreement about my usefulness to the boy and the family. It would have been difficult for me to be therapeutic when the child was thinking that I was going to operate in ways that his pediatrician would. After this session, I began to talk to the parents on the phone before the first session about ways that they could introduce therapy to their children that would be helpful in preparing them for the first session.

explains what the troubling behavior(s) is that the child is exhibiting. Therapists should interact with parent and child during this portion. This puts children in a more respected position. Therapists can use the first session to explain to the child, with the parent(s) present, the purpose, processes, and relationships that occur in therapy. When explained in the presence of the adult(s), the adult, in and out of session, can reinforce the therapist's position and intent. Further, potential misconceptions that might have been present before the first session can be cleared up.

> *Therapist:* Lamar, how come you are here today?
>
> *Lamar:* I don't know.
>
> *Therapist:* What did your parents tell you about what would happen here?
>
> *Lamar:* Something about you would make me behave better.
>
> *Therapist:* Let me tell you about what I do. I work with a lot of children where things aren't going as they want in their home, school, or with their friends. We talk, and sometimes play, and try to figure out how we can make your life happier. What questions do you have for me?

Discussing Confidentiality and Informed Consent/Assent

Because children's facilitation with and understanding of language are not fully developed, therapeutic interviewers must take extra care when explaining issues of the therapeutic process, such as confidentiality and informed consent/assent. A child can assent to treatment (they agree to be a part of it), but the parent(s) of that child needs to consent to allow the child to have the therapy. Children are used to telling secrets with their friends. When you tell someone a secret, there is an expectation that the other person will not tell anyone else. In therapy, there is an obligation on the therapist to disclose the secret, given certain conditions (for instance, child abuse, self-harm). Therapeutic interviewers should explain to child clients each of the areas the therapist would have to disclose. However, just saying, "I would have to tell someone if I hear about child abuse" might not be sufficient, as the child might not understand what child abuse is. The therapist might need to be more concrete in the explanation:

> *Therapist:* Sammy, you know I told you that what you tell me I won't tell someone else.
>
> *Sammy:* Yes.
>
> *Therapist:* But there are certain times when I do have to tell someone. Such as if I know that someone is hurting you or your brother. Or if someone, really an adult, hits, punches, or kicks you.

Although therapeutic interviewers cannot discuss every possible scenario for when they might have to disclose what was discussed in the session, the more therapists try to talk so the child understands, the more the child has ownership of what is said and the process of the session.

Talking with Parents

Another topic that needs to be discussed with the child is what and how much of what is discussed in the session will be disclosed to the parents. Legally, parents have a right to know how the therapy is progressing with their child as well as access to the child's medical records. Fortunately, many parents understand that their child, especially adolescent children, have a need to talk with someone in privacy. Many therapists who work with children individually attempt to negotiate with the parents about what will and will not be disclosed.

> *Therapist:* I just wanted to take a second to go over how I work. I will be meeting alone with Sammy. In order to maintain a trust with him, I would like to keep what he and I talk about between just him and me. However, if he does disclose anything that is very serious and potentially dangerous, I will disclose that to you.

In this way, parents are assured that they will become active agents in therapy if something serious is occurring, but the integrity of the therapeutic relationship is still maintained.

Parents have a legal right to information about their child. Therapists have an ethical responsibility to maintain confidentiality with their client while also providing legal guardians information about a minor child. These obligations may sometimes come in conflict with one another. By being upfront with the client and his parents, therapists set a stage where client and parents are protected.

Beginning the Session

Adult clients might be able to jump right into therapy and begin talking about the problem situation. They were most likely the person to make the appointment with the therapist. They have even probably rehearsed in their head the speech they want to make to the therapist describing their concerns. Yet, with adult clients, most first sessions begin with a joining period. This might be even more important when working with child clients. Children usually need some time to ease into the therapeutic process. Therapists should start by trying to make a genuine connection with the child. This might come from seeing an article of clothing they are wearing (i.e., a sports team shirt or hat or some type of jewelry) or asking them about hobbies, school, or television. Case Scenario 12.2 describes how a therapist quickly connected with a young client.

Hughes and Baker (1990) discouraged therapists from starting a session focusing on what the problem is that brought the child to therapy. They also suggested that therapists ensure the child can answer the first question asked of them. Some type of joining question, such as what grade the child is in school, favorite subjects, hobbies, or what the child does for fun are good opening gambits.

Lukas (1993) took a bit of a different path by asking children early on why they thought their mother or father (or guardian) brought them to therapy. Although most children will not have an adult-like explanation for why they are being brought to therapy, this tactic can help the therapist understand children's frame of understanding about why they are there.

Some therapists working with children meet with the parent(s) before ever meeting with the child to get the parent's view of the presenting situation. Sometimes there is background information that parents do not want the child to hear (perhaps the child is adopted and does not yet know it, there is a marital affair, or some other adult issue). At other times, the parents might be so angry at the child that having them berate the child in session might negatively impact the child.

CASE SCENARIO 12.2

I had a first session with a mother and her eleven-year-old son. The son had been getting into trouble at school and his mother brought him in to see if I could work with him so that he didn't keep getting after-school detentions. When he first came in, he was a little nervous. Knowing from the intake that they were coming in with the primary complaint of school problems, I began the interview by asking him what he liked to do outside school. He said that he loved to go to Monster Truck shows. I asked if his favorite was "Graveddigger." His face lit up when he realized that I knew something about Monster Trucks. We talked about what it was like for him to be at the truck shows and then eased into talking about the problems he was encountering. Throughout the course of therapy, I would check in with him about the latest truck show he had been to, which continued to further establish the rapport we had developed.

Interview Length

Since children's sense of time, along with their attention span, is quite different from adults', it would seem that the length of time spent with children should be different from that spent with adult clients. For most adult clients, therapists work with an hour session (usually between forty-five to sixty minutes). For many children, especially younger children, forty-five minutes might be too long to work together. Therapists might consider shortening the length of time they spend in the interview with children, perhaps working with them somewhere between thirty and forty-five minutes.

Once an amount of time is established, it should be maintained (Axline, 1969). For instance, if it was agreed that sessions would last fifty minutes and the client comes to therapy twenty minutes late, only thirty minutes should be allowed for the session. Therapeutic interviewers should be alert to nonverbal behavior of the child that might signal that the child is tired of the interview, such as distraction, wriggling around, or lethargy. Keats (2000) suggested that when therapists sense the child is losing focus in the interview, a change of activity might be helpful to reengage him.

Closing the Session

Children are not as aware as adults of time. Because of this, therapists should help ease the child into the flow and ending of the session. Therapists can let the client know that the end of the session is quickly approaching. However, young children might not understand the notion of time as much as they would with something more concrete. For instance, instead of saying that there are five minutes left, the therapist might say something about having enough time left for two more rounds of the game they are playing. Semrud-Clikeman (1995) recommended that therapists be firm but gentle with children who are having a difficult time ending the session. Setting the stage for a smooth transition from therapy to the end of therapy and the resumption of the child's day is important as therapists want to ensure not only that a strong alliance is maintained with the child, but with the parent as well. If parents have to deal with children who are upset at the end of therapy sessions, they will be less likely to bring the child back to that therapist. Case Scenario 12.3 presents a harrowing case in which a new first session with a therapist and not following a standard routine became overwhelming for a child client.

Goal Setting

Most therapists agree that client and therapist should jointly agree on the goals of therapy so that they are working collaboratively on the same outcome. For children, the outcome of therapy might be unclear. Since they were probably brought to therapy because someone else had some type of complaint against them, children's sense of what they want different for themselves might not be clear. Thus, they sometimes have difficulty in formulating goals.

CASE SCENARIO 12.3

I was working in a child outpatient clinic and was transferred a case of a very intelligent and precocious six-year-old boy. For the first session, I met with him and his mother. There was paperwork that needed to be signed by the mother. This took about thirty minutes of our sixty-minute session. When mom left the room at this halfway point, the client stated he wanted to go to a play therapy room. By the time we found one that was open, there were about twenty minutes left. I counted down the time starting at ten minutes. When our time ran out and I told him we would have to end the session and leave the room, he became very upset. He told me that a kid needs one hour to play (he obviously had a good sense of time and had, with his previous therapist, been able to utilize the full hour for play). He ran out of the room and into the center of the clinic screaming that I was abusing him. There were many things I could have done differently to try to prevent his sense of disorientation, including having a separate meeting with the mother to handle the paperwork and being clearer about the amount of time that was left.

Therapeutic interviewers can help children by giving an appropriate explanation of the intention of the interview and the therapy process. Further, goal development can be a twofold process, in which it is engaged in by therapist, client, and parents as well as by therapist and client separately. Although the parents may have certain outcomes of therapy they want for the child, the child/adolescent might have his own or additional goals. When trying to obtain the goals of the child, therapists can ask the child in ways somewhat different from those they would use with adults. Therapists might alter a therapeutic tool, such as the miracle question, to ask it in a way that children might better understand:

> *Therapist:* Sammy, I have a pretty interesting question for you. Let's say I had a magic wand and I tapped you on the head with it. And the magic wand made all of the things in your life and your family as you hoped and wanted them to be. What would happen? What would be different for you?

Sommers-Flanagan and Sommers-Flanagan (2003) proposed a similar approach for goal attainment with children. They introduced the notion of a wish. The following question is one example of this:

> Let me put the question another way. If you had three wishes, or if you had a magic lamp, like in the movie *Aladdin,* and you could wish to change something about yourself, your parents, or your school, what would you wish for? (p. 318)

Sometimes children can understand the concept of wishes or magic more than they can miracles or using the word *goals.* Thus, asking children how they would want things in their life, family, school, or other social settings helps them to begin discussing goals.

Special Issues When Conducting a Therapeutic Interview with a Child

Who Is the Client?

As stated previously, children, especially younger children, are usually taken to therapy at the behest of their parents, school personnel, doctors, or other people in contact with them. It is not until adolescence that children might be the initiators of therapy. This poses a problem for therapeutic interviewers because the person in the therapy room might not necessarily be the person who has a complaint.

Therapeutic interviewers can meet with the referring person, along with the child, to talk about what the problem situation seems to be and what the referring person is hoping to gain from therapy. It is important to keep the referring person in mind because the therapist might work with the child on goals developed between the two that might not be what the referring agent had in mind; that person might have a desire for other services for the child. By incorporating the views of the referring person and the child (and anyone else concerned about the problem situation), therapeutic interviewers can best address all of the concerns that people have about the situation.

From a systems perspective, many of the problems children exhibit can find etiology in the family system. This issue will be discussed in the next chapter. Therapeutic interviewers can talk to the parents to see if they might be customers of change instead of complainants. The therapist does not have to work therapeutically with the parents, but can make a recommendation to the parents that they might consider seeing a therapist of their own. This is a tricky discussion, as parents might think they are being accused by the therapist.

Depending on the interviewer's therapeutic orientation, working with just the child client may or may not make sense. Therapists should have a clear sense of how they can and cannot be helpful to younger clients. If the therapeutic interviewer does not think she would be effective with just the child, then she should either attempt to work with the parents and/or whole family or should refer the case to someone who works with children.

Many parents tend to come in and expect the therapist to work strictly with the child, since from their perception, it is the child who is exhibiting the problematic behavior. They do not want to think that what they are doing is contributing to the problem behavior and do not want to be blamed. Parents can be included in the therapy by helping to maintain the gains from the therapy interview into the child's day-to-day life. Given that the parents spend a lot more time with the child than the therapeutic interviewer does, their help in the therapy process is integral.

> *Therapist:* Mrs. Blake, I was hoping that you could come into the sessions each week, probably for the last five to ten minutes. Hope and I are doing some very good work and she is progressing, but I only meet with her for one hour each week. You are with her every day. I was hoping you could come in, and we could discuss what could happen during the week to

reinforce the positive changes that Hope is making. Would that be okay with you?

When framed as the parent aiding the therapist, parents will tend to work *with* rather than *against* the therapist.

Touch

The use of touch with children is quite different than with adults. Children, especially those between five and ten years old, tend to want to hug the person they are close to. In therapy with adults, the default setting is not to hug the client, unless it seems appropriate and therapeutic. For children, there is more room for the possibility of a hug or other physical touch, given that the touch is client-initiated. Case Scenario 12.4 presents a case where the use of touch was extremely powerful for the client.

Many children, on their way from the waiting room to the therapy office, or from the therapy office to the bathroom, will want to hold the therapist's hand. Unless there is a rationale of why not, this would seem to be not only acceptable, but also beneficial in maintaining a connection and relationship. The client is able to feel, literally and figuratively, a connection between self and therapist. The therapist sends a message that she cares about the client. The caution here is that the hug or touching (for example, hand-holding) should be *client-initiated* instead of therapist-initiated. If the therapist initiates the touching, the child is put in an awkward position of not being fully able to articulate his desires or dislikes. Case Scenario 12.5 focuses on how therapists might overuse touch.

Caring for Children

Therapists working with children tend to feel affection for them. Although this is a very good thing, sometimes therapists might care too much about their clients, especially when the client is a child. Perhaps this is because they believe the child

CASE SCENARIO 12.4

I was working with a sixteen-year-old female. Six sessions into therapy, she talked to me about being gang-raped. It was a very emotional session, and she cried a lot during it. At the end of the session I walked her out to the waiting room. She turned to me and said, "I wish I could give you a hug." I answered, "Why can't you?" and hugged her back when she came to hug me. She seemed to relax after that. I believe this helped her to feel like she wasn't "damaged goods." Some may argue in this case that an older male should not hug a younger female, especially one who was just raped repeatedly by several men. However, I believed that it showed her that men and women can engage in positive touch. It also let her know that I did not think she was dirtied by the experience. If I did not hug her, she might have perceived that I thought there was something wrong with her.

================ CASE SCENARIO 12.5

I was supervising a master's intern in a child outpatient program. I observed several of her cases and at the end of each of them, she knelt down and said to the child client, "Come here and give me a hug," while opening her arms for a hug. The children did go over and give her a hug; however, in supervision, we discussed the precarious position this puts children in. It is difficult for them to say "no" to adults. So they might feel scared not to give the hug but uncomfortable in giving it. Although the attempt of the therapist of a hug was based on caring, the power differential between adult and child makes this demonstration of caring potentially problematic. Thus, therapists should wait until the child initiates the touching.

is innocent and defenseless, but when therapists begin to care too much, they respond from a place of reactiveness rather than thoughtfulness.

Therapists who find themselves having serious caring feelings (feelings of wanting to rescue the child) should discuss these issues in supervision. Sommers-Flanagan and Sommers-Flanagan (2003) explained the seriousness of this situation, "Overinvolvers need to achieve some understanding of themselves in this area and find other ways to meet their needs to rescue and provide extensive nurturing before working therapeutically with children" (p. 308).

Self-Disclosure

Children can be put off by someone telling them that their questions and inquiries about the person are none of their business. They want to know that the person they are talking to and engaged with is a human being. Children will oftentimes ask the therapist if she has had a similar experience to what the client is going through. The child might also ask personal questions as to whether the therapist has a brother or sister, how they get along with their siblings, where they went on vacation if there was a break in the therapy, or any of a number of questions. Therapists can help aid the process of rapport by self-disclosing topics with the child, as long as the topic is appropriate (things such as sexuality, religion, and drug use might be problematic to talk about with a child).

The therapist can also utilize the self-disclosure as a means of having the client go into more depth about his own situation. Consider the following situation of a therapist working with a child client who is having sibling rivalry issues:

> *Client:* Do you have a brother or sister?
>
> *Therapist:* Yes, I have one brother.
>
> *Client:* Is he older or younger?
>
> *Therapist:* He is two years older.
>
> *Client:* Do you two fight?
>
> *Therapist:* We used to, when we were younger. Then we learned how to be brothers without fighting. What's it like with your brother?

In this situation, the therapist has connected with the child by acknowledging that she has had similar situations. Further, by answering the client, the therapist has validated him as a person. This is especially important when it is coming from an adult to a child. One possible disadvantage of this is if the child thinks that he can handle the situation the same way the therapist did. The therapist might try to avoid this by saying something like the following:

> *Therapist:* My brother and I figured out *our* way to be together without fighting real bad. It will be interesting to see how you and your brother figure things out in *your* way.

Thompson and Rudolph (1992) suggested that for some children, asking the therapist personal questions is a way to deflect the session off themselves. Therapists can, depending on their own comfort level, answer some of the personal questions while folding the answer back into how the client is experiencing his own problems. For example, take the following exchange:

> *Therapist:* It seems that not feeling loved by your parents is really troubling for you.
>
> *Client:* What do you like to do for fun?
>
> *Therapist:* I have lots of things I like to do for fun like taking nature walks, reading, and spending time with friends. What sorts of things do you do with your parents that you find are fun?

Here, the therapist has answered the client's question but has returned the conversation back to the client and the situation they were discussing. Further, since the therapist surmised that the client was having some anxiety about the previous statement, she still focused on the client's relationship with his parents, but in a safer way by exploring what they do for fun. This will allow them to explore the relationship topic in greater depth.

Interviewing for Abuse and Neglect

Therapists have a legal duty to report suspected abuse or neglect of children. They do not have to prove the abuse happened, as that is the responsibility of the child welfare worker, yet the therapists' responsibility is to present all of the evidence they have. Sometimes, abuse and neglect issues are very apparent. At other times, therapists might get only a hint that there might be something askance. For instance, if a child comes into therapy with a bruise, this does not mean that abuse happened. Children get bruises from all sorts of reasons. They might have fallen down while running, another child in school might have punched them, or they might have been hit by an adult. Therapists have to make a determination, based on all of the information they have received from the child and other informants, whether to pursue a line of inquiry about the bruise.

Three main areas are associated with child abuse: physical symptoms, behavioral signs, and caretaker characteristics (Lukas, 1993). The more physical signs, such as cuts and bruises, dirty appearance, and abnormal weight (i.e., being extremely thin), might be warning signs of abuse. Behavioral signs of abuse include children engaging in behaviors such as doing poorly at school, stealing food, fighting, exhibiting age inappropriate behavior, running away from home, or being very compliant. As for the person who is the guardian of the child, the care-taker characteristics to look for are attempting to get the child to caretake for the adult, the child being isolated from others, the caretaker engaging in some type of substance abuse, the caretaker having difficulties psychologically, or the like. These can be associated with abuse. Although these behaviors might be warning signs, they do not necessarily mean that abuse is occurring. Therapists need to explore in greater depth whether abuse is occurring.

Therapists, without any signs, might take it upon themselves to go fishing for whether abuse is occurring. This happens usually when they are interviewing the child alone, asking whether the child has ever been punished or disciplined by the parents, and if so, how. It is recommended that, unless therapists begin to sense that there is something serious going on in the house, they refrain from fishing for abuse.

Therapists might wonder when they should or should not talk with children about what their own role is when dealing with these issues. Being up front with the child is extremely important, as many children who disclose abuse expect that the information will be held confidential by the therapist. Therapists should fre-quently discuss with the child the limits of confidentiality. When the child begins a discussion by stating, "I have a secret and you can't tell anybody," therapists need to take the time to explain again, in the language that the child can understand, what constitutes abuse and the ethical and legal responsibility they have when they know, or even suspect, child abuse. If therapists do not remind clients of this limit, the child may feel blindsided by the break in confidentiality.

Reporting abuse impacts the therapeutic relationship and possible outcomes of therapy. Therapists do not have to report in secrecy. Many therapists discuss their ethical obligation with both child and parent(s) and then call up the child welfare agency while the clients are in the room so that the process is out in the open. Therapists may refrain from informing the parents about the abuse report if they fear the parents might beat the child for reporting the abuse.

Many clients who have had the therapist call protective services on their behalf feel betrayed by the therapist. Even though the therapist might have dis-cussed the implications of suspecting abuse in the first interview, when discussing confidentiality, clients might feel that the therapist betrayed their trust. This then becomes something to work on in therapy and adds to the therapeutic process. Case Scenario 12.6 demonstrates how reporting abuse can impact the therapeutic process.

Leading the Child

Perhaps the group of clients where there is the greatest potential of leading, in terms of getting them to answer in ways the therapist is expecting, is children. Because children's verbal repertoire is not as advanced as that of adults, and they

CASE SCENARIO 12.6

A doctoral therapist I was supervising had worked with a child for several months. In one of the therapeutic interviews, the child made comments about being beaten by the father. The therapist interviewed the child and got all of the details. She then called up the child protective services. The caseworker went to the family's house, interviewed everyone, and concluded that there was an event, but it was not severe enough to remove the child from the home. The father called up the agency to complain about the therapist and stated that he wanted his child to work with a new therapist because he didn't trust the current therapist not to do this again. We brought the father, mother, child, therapist, and myself together to process what had occurred and see if we could reestablish the therapeutic alliance. When we explained that the therapist had no choice, ethically, but to report, the father was somewhat appeased, but it still impacted his role in therapy for the duration of therapy. One thing that the therapist could have done differently was to bring the father and mother into the session before she reported the abuse. Even if the parents contradicted the child's story, the child's disclosure still led to a suspicion of abuse and thus the reporting should have occurred.

tend to be less verbally communicative, people who interview children tend to push them in expected directions. Wilson and Powell (2001) explained this phenomenon, "Leading questions are those questions that suggest a certain answer is desired or assume the existence of facts that have not yet been proved or have not already been mentioned by the child" (p. 58).

There are several reasons why adults think that children might need to be pushed to help them talk about the past. Given that children's memory framework is not as developed as adults', along with their not having a metamemory system, children are not able to recognize their memories as well as adults (Hughes & Baker, 1990). Children might also want to please the adult interviewers by giving them the answer they are looking for. This leads to a potential problem of accepting what children say because there is already a social view that children's responses aren't trustworthy. The following is an example of how a therapist might begin to lead a child:

> *Interviewer:* Paco, did he touch you? It's okay if you tell me. You can tell me where he touched you. It's all right.

In this example, the interviewer already has an assumption that the child was touched in some way. She is now pushing the child to substantiate her assumption.

Although some professionals think it is necessary to use direct questions, there is too much risk that the therapist's questions will contaminate the client's story (Wilson & Powell, 2001; Zwiers & Morrissette, 1999). Wilson and Powell argued that "of all the questions put by an interviewer, leading and suggestive questions are the most likely to result in errors in the child's account (particularly in young children, that is, those below six years of age)" (p. 59). Hughes and Baker (1990) recommended using a combination of open-ended questions, specific questions that avoid leading the person, and a lot of minimal encouragers to help the child client to open up in session. Relying on the basic conversational skills and reflecting skills presented in Part Two of this book is usually a safe bet when dealing with these issues.

One mistake that a lot of people who interview children make is using the forced-choice question. These types of questions, like closed-ended questions, usually have a one-word answer outcome.

> *Interviewer:* Do you like to go to school?
>
> *Client:* Sometimes.
>
> *Interviewer:* What do you like more about school, learning the material or being with friends?
>
> *Client:* Being with friends.
>
> *Interviewer:* Are your friends in school the same friends you have outside of school?
>
> *Client:* Yes.

As can be seen, if this type of interviewing persists, the child can feel like they are being interrogated. Therapeutic interviewers should try to give the child more freedom of responses during the conversation.

> *Interviewer:* What is school like?
>
> *Client:* I don't know. It's all right. I learn a lot. I have to go every day during the week, except weekends.
>
> *Interviewer:* What sorts of things do you learn?
>
> *Client:* Math. And spelling and writing. And art.
>
> *Interviewer:* Tell me a bit more.
>
> *Client:* I have five classes a day. And then recess.
>
> *Interviewer:* What sorts of things do you do during recess?

Although questions are being used, they allow the child more room to express himself in his own way.

Handling Termination

Termination has already been discussed in Chapter 7; however, the ending of the therapeutic relationship with children leads to some unique situations. Children do not have a full grasp of what the therapeutic relationship is and its purposes. Many children come to think of the therapist not as a helper, but as a friend. This might be especially so for those therapeutic relationships in which play is an integral part of the therapy. Just as with adults, therapists should discuss termination several sessions before the last session. With children, this becomes even more important. Not only should therapists discuss how many sessions are left, they should explain, to a greater extent, why termination is happening.

When termination is initially brought up, some children, after developing a relationship with the therapist, will think that they did something wrong and thus the therapist is not going to have a relationship with them anymore. It goes a little contradictory in their thinking, that as they progress and reach the goals of therapy, they lose someone who has become a significant figure in their lives. Children, once they realize that their improvement in behavior is leading toward losing the therapist, might reengage in some of the problematic behavior. Therapists can understand this more as an issue with termination rather than as a problem with the child.

Some therapists decide to make the final session a celebration. Semrud-Clikeman (1995) explained how she handles termination when working with children, "With children I suggest the ending as a type of 'graduation,' thus making the point that termination indicates success not just loss" (p. 144). Some therapists might invite the child's parents, siblings, and friends as a marker of the child's progress and change. Other therapists make this a one-on-one session, so that the two can discuss what termination means for the client. However therapists conduct the last session with children, it should be almost completely about termination issues (Barker, 1990).

Therapists might also discuss the possibility of the client coming back in the future if the need ever arises. Some children (as well as adults) feel better when they know that there is a possibility to continue the relationship if need be. Some therapists do a "follow-up" with the client, calling approximately three months after the last session. The therapist might phrase this as, "One of the things that I find useful as a therapist is to know how the people I have been working with are doing months after we stop meeting. If it's all right, I would like to give you a call in about three months, just to check in and see how things are going. Would that be all right?"

Play Therapy

Many therapeutic interviews with children include some sort of play. The process of play therapy is too vast to be talked about fully in this book, yet the therapeutic interviewer working with children should understand its importance as it often has a key role in the therapeutic process. Hughes and Baker (1990) stated, "Because play is a natural medium of communication for young children, they reveal thoughts, fears, and perceptions of recurring or significant events as well as reasoning ability in their play" (p. 27). All play, but especially children's play, can be thought of as language (Lukas, 1993). Therapeutic interviewers working with young children will need to begin to understand and be able to communicate in this language. When they do, they can enhance their connection to the client and possible gains for the child. Reid (2001) explained, "Playing a game can help strengthen the therapeutic alliance and provide a metaphorical stage for the expression and resolution of conflict" (p. 12).

Play might be used during the first session as an ice breaker. Because some children and adolescents might have a difficult time connecting with someone on a strictly verbal level, play allows the two to connect on a different level, a more anxiety-free type of session.

The role of the therapeutic interviewer changes when engaging the child in play rather than doing a traditional verbal interview. Instead of taking a more directive approach by asking the client questions, therapists develop a more nondirective posture in which they follow the lead of the client. Because the child may unconsciously be put off by a therapist who is too directive in play, therapists are encouraged to be a lot more lenient in accepting the various ways that the client wants to utilize play. Case Scenario 12.7 demonstrates a therapist being too directive in the play of a child.

Although play is a very integral part of working therapeutically with children, most therapists do not get formal training in it. Corey, Corey, and Callanan (2007) recommended that therapists get special training in working with children, especially regarding the laws relating to minors and specific nonverbal treatment approaches, such as play therapy, art therapy, music therapy, and recreational therapy.

In designing the therapy room, therapists should consider not having their room too sparse of objects and not too cluttered. If there are too many stimulating objects in the room, the child might be so focused on them that they cannot focus on the therapeutic interviewer. If there are few or no play objects in the room, the child might feel uncomfortable and put on the spot. There is not an exact science to this, so therapeutic interviewers should experiment with the amount of toys, games, stuffed animals, and other play objects in their office and see how children react.

CASE SCENARIO 12.7

I was supervising a master's intern who was working in a child outpatient program. In viewing one of her sessions with a five-year-old boy, I noticed that the therapist kept on trying to correct the child when the child was not playing with items or games in the "normal" way. This occurred on several occasions throughout the course of that session. I noticed the child becoming frustrated in the session. In supervision, we talked about her issues of trying to control the session and of her needing to learn to hold back so the child became the leader and she the follower. When she started to allow the child to play in his own way, the child began making quicker progress in therapy.

Reflection 12.2

How playful a person are you? When you interact with children, how much are you able to not force the play and to just follow the child's lead? How much do you think about what children are trying to say through their play?

Documents and Awards

Children sometimes need more tangible objects in order to transfer what occurred during the therapeutic interview to their life outside therapy. Physical objects such as charts, lists, awards, and certificates can serve an important function when working with children.

Narrative therapists have worked extensively with what they call counter documents (White & Epston, 1990). These documents go counter to traditional psychotherapy documents such as psychiatric reports, mental status exams, and assessment tests and evaluations. These therapists tend to give clients, especially young clients, awards when they have achieved their goals or made significant movement toward it. Receiving a physical document, such as an award, becomes a "ritual of inclusion" (White & Epston, 1990). White and Epston explained, "Such awards often signal the person's arrival at a new status in the community, one that brings with it new responsibilities and privileges" (1990, p. 191). These documents, awards, and certificates can be shared with those in the child's field of relationships to help substantiate and continue the positive progress made in therapy. These documents, especially charts and lists, can then be shared with other children who are dealing with similar situations (White, 1999). Case Scenario 12.8 describes how a certificate was used with a client to demarcate his positive changes in therapy.

CASE SCENARIO 12.8

I was working with a mother and her eleven-year-old son. The boy had been getting into fights almost every day at school, many of these fights were with a same-aged cousin. In therapy we discussed how "fighting" was getting the best of him and utilized his skills of knowing how to fight to use them against fighting. After three months, he had not had a fight with anyone. I printed up an award, the "Fight Fighting Award." His mother, he, and I all signed this award in recognition of his accomplishment. We then discussed that he had learned how to fight fighting, but that fighting might try to sneak into his life again. If so, he could always look at this award and know that he had beaten fighting in the past and could do it again if need be.

Summary

Therapeutic interviews with children are a unique context of therapy. Children come to therapy, usually at the behest of a third party, with an understanding of the process that may be very different from that of an adult. Therapists need to learn how to connect and join with children so they can build a strong therapeutic alliance. During the therapeutic interview, issues such as language, cognitive ability, and other developmental factors play a role in the therapist's actions and the client's responses. Therapists will need to simplify their interviewing approach without being demeaning to the client. They can then integrate some alternative types of skills such as play therapy and more visual cues for the client. However, therapists will need to be on guard to prevent leading child clients or being too directive with them. They can do this by utilizing more open-ended questions and basic conversational and reflecting skills. In ending relationships with children, therapists can engage in some type of ritual, such as a celebration or a document, to highlight the children's successful completion of reaching their goals.

Exercises

1. Observe a child in normal interaction with other children and with adults. Notice the type of language the child uses, the amount of eye contact, the use of nonverbal behaviors. Observe children at different age ranges where one is from two to six years old, seven to eleven years old, and twelve to fifteen years old. Observe both male and female children from each age range to see if you notice any differences based on age or gender.

2. Role-play with a fellow student a therapeutic interview with a child. Tape record the session and then go back through the interview to assess how well you used language that was appropriate for someone of the age your colleague was role-playing.

13

Therapeutic Interviewing with Couples and Families

Couples and family interviewing is a special form of therapeutic interviewing requiring additional skill sets and perceptual lenses. Although the whole unit may be the "client," it is composed of individuals who may have their own ideas of the problem, the goals of therapy, and the paths to reach those goals. This chapter addresses how therapeutic interviewers can effectively work with couples and families. The term *family interview* will be used to discuss the therapeutic interview with couples or families.

As can be seen in the previous chapters, conducting a therapeutic interview with just one person is extremely complex. The level of complexity in the interview increases as each additional person enters the room. There are more personalities, more worldviews, more differing ways of talking, and greater dynamics of interactions between the people in the room. In an individual therapeutic interview, the only interpersonal process occurs between the therapist and client. In a couple therapeutic interview, there are four interpersonal processes occurring: one between the two members of the couple, one between the therapist and one member of the couple, one between the therapist and the other member of the couple, and the last, which includes all three people. During the family therapeutic interview, as each additional family member enters into the session, an increasing number of connections and relationships come into play. Family interviewers must keep track of not only what every single person in the therapy room is talking about, but also how they are talking about it and how it is being perceived by every other person. If not handled properly, the family interview can easily become chaotic with people talking over each other, verbally attacking one another, or sometimes physically attacking one another, and with some members getting lost in the dissonance of multiple voices. Therapists who conduct family interviews may feel like the conductor of an orchestra—encouraging some to raise their voices, suggesting others soften their tones, and even having a crescendo of all voices reach a harmonic whole.

Family interviewers must be competent in a variety of activities in providing therapeutic services to clients. The American Association of Marriage and Family Therapy (AAMFT), perhaps the primary professional organization for family therapists in the United States, developed a list of the core competencies a family therapist needs in order to practice. Table 13.1 provides several of the AAMFT core competencies that a therapist should be familiar with to conduct family interviews.

This chapter presents an overview for conducting a therapeutic interview with a couple or family. Further, it incorporates many of the principles of the AAMFT core competencies, aiding the family interviewer to become proficient in the basic skills of couple and family interviewing.

TABLE 13.1   *American Association of Marriage and Family Therapy's Core Competencies*

Number	Competency
1.3.2	Determine who should attend therapy and in what configuration (e.g., individual, couple, family, extrafamilial resources).
1.3.3	Facilitate therapeutic involvement of all necessary participants in treatment.
1.3.4	Explain practice setting rules, fees, rights, and responsibilities of each party, including privacy, confidentiality policies, and duty to care to client or legal guardian.
1.3.5	Obtain consent to treatment from all responsible persons.
1.3.6	Establish and maintain appropriate and productive therapeutic alliances with the clients.
2.2.1	Assess each client's engagement in the change process.
2.3.9	Elucidate presenting problem from the perspective of each member of the therapeutic system.
3.3.1	Develop, with client input, measurable outcomes, treatment goals, treatment plans, and after-care plans with clients utilizing a systemic perspective.
3.3.7	Work collaboratively with other stakeholders, including family members, other significant persons, and professionals not present.
4.2.2	Distinguish differences between content and process issues, their role in therapy, and their potential impact on therapeutic outcomes.
4.3.4	Generate relational questions and reflexive comments in the therapy room.
4.3.5	Engage each family member in the treatment process as appropriate.
4.5.3	Articulate rationales for interventions related to treatment goals and plan, assessment information, and systemic understanding of clients' context and dynamics.
5.3.3	Inform clients and legal guardian of limitations to confidentiality and parameters of mandatory reporting.

Source: Adapted from the American Association of Marriage and Family Therapy. (2004). Marriage and Family Therapy Core Competencies.

Orientation to Conducting a Therapeutic Family Interview

Individual versus Family Therapy

Most therapists are primarily trained in individual counseling and become comfortable with the skills of reflecting and empathy in a one-to-one relationship. This does not fully prepare them for the seeming cacophony of a family interview. Suddenly the novice therapist is paying attention to the thoughts, feelings, meanings, and nonverbal behaviors of as many family members as are in the room. It is no surprise then that new therapists feel overwhelmed when multiple clients are in the room.

Staying attuned to what is occurring within an individual family member, between family members, and between family members and therapist is a complex skill. Minuchin (1974) defined this skill as tracking, "The therapist follows the content of the family's communications and behavior and encourages them to continue" (p. 127). In tracking, the therapist consciously attends to who says what, to whom, how, and what predicated each person's behavior. Once attained, this skill lets therapists work with individuals, couples, and families with comfort and confidence in their ability to help. This confidence affects family members; it tells them that they are safe to explore what is going on in their family.

Neutrality

Neutrality is a fundamental stance for the family interviewer. Operating from the position that each person in the therapy room (and family members who are not there) has a valid viewpoint, the therapist supports each person and the family as a whole, sending an implicit message that people are allowed to have their own view while still being connected to the other people in the family. When done successfully, each person believes that the therapist heard and acknowledged what they had to say without having to ignore or squelch someone else's voice.

When therapists slip from a neutral position, certain members will not feel heard or connected during the interview. For instance, if a husband complains that his wife is not affectionate enough with him, the therapist can acknowledge this by saying, "You want a greater connection with your wife." But, if the therapist then turns to the wife and states, "How come you are not more affectionate with your husband," the husband's position has been honored at the expense of the wife's position. It could be that she thinks that she is affectionate enough with her husband. A neutral therapeutic response to the wife might be, "Your husband thinks that you aren't affectionate enough with him. What is your perspective on that?" Now, the wife has the right to agree or disagree in her own words. Neutrality permits differences to enter the room.

When therapists take a stance of neutrality, they move away from making moral judgments of what is happening and take a more systemic view of what is going on in the family. Neutral family interviewers will be able to hear every member of the family. They are focused on bringing forth the individual perspectives in the family, to understand how these perspectives fit together in order to make a complete whole.

Neutrality should not be mistaken for a distanced and cold position. Cecchin (1987) talked about neutrality as curiosity, "Curiosity leads to an exploration and invention of alternative views and moves, and different moves and views breed curiosity" (p. 406). Curiosity from a therapist is often the spark that encourages family members to move away from a hard-and-fast perspective of what *is* to a position of possibilities.

The family interviewer does not know what is correct, but knows that there are different ways of viewing what is occurring. Take the following interchange during a family interview:

Therapist: Who would like to talk about what is going on in the family?

Father: I'm pretty much fed up. My daughter doesn't listen. She goes out late at night and has been having sex with a bunch of different guys. It's awful.

Daughter: I do not have sex with a bunch of different people. I have one boyfriend.

Mother: That's one boyfriend too many!

Therapist: [To mother and father] It seems that you are very concerned about your daughter and what's happening when she goes out at night.

Father: Of course. She's my daughter. I don't want her pregnant now. Or sleeping around.

Therapist: That must be tough to try to protect her from these things.

Father: It is. But that's my job.

Therapist: [To daughter] And it seems that you see it differently. That instead of Dad being protective of you, he is a bit overbearing.

Daughter: He's out of control. He thinks I'm sleeping with everyone. I'm not like that. I'm not a slut!

Therapist: It doesn't seem like you want your parents to have that type of view of you. Especially when you don't think they have that much to be concerned about.

Daughter: No, they don't have to worry about me like they do. I'm sixteen. I know about sex and getting pregnant. I don't want a baby now, and I wouldn't do that to myself.

Therapist: How much do they know that about you, that you don't want that for yourself?

Daughter: I don't know. They usually won't talk about these things with me.

Therapist: [To father] What is that like for you to hear that?

Father: I hope it's true.

In this interchange, the family interviewer has respected both positions. With the father, the therapist accepted his concerns about his daughter. With the daughter, the therapist accepted her need for respect and trust. Further, by accepting both positions, the family interviewer was able to open up space for the opportunity of a new type of conversation to occur.

Although it is recommended that therapists maintain a neutral position, several family therapy theories attempt to have the therapist strategically take sides during a session. Structural family therapists utilize a technique called *unbalancing* in which the therapist takes sides with various family members. Minuchin and Fishman (1981) described this ploy, "The therapist joins and supports one individual or one subsystem at the expense of the others. She affiliates with a family member low in the hierarchy, empowering him instead of undercutting him" (p. 161). Therapists who utilize this technique tend to engage in this type of side taking with various individuals throughout the course of the interview/therapy, thus, they do not favor one person over any other for the whole of the therapy.

Who Is the Client?

When interviewing a couple or family, the client is the family system. This entails taking a relational perspective in which behavior is housed within the network of connections between family members. Families usually come to therapy with the notion that there is one primary problematic person. Therapists refer to this person as the identified patient (IP). Too much focus on what this person is doing wrong will move the family interview from a relational conversation exploring family dynamics to a complaint fest against the IP. The therapist needs to help the family members understand how their complaints—even if all directed at the IP—are interrelated and interdependent on the family's overall distress and well-being.

One difficulty of the family interview comes when therapy sessions are being reimbursed through a managed care company. If so, therapy will need to be billed through one family member's insurance (including giving that person a diagnosis). Ethically, therapists should only put down a diagnosis if they believe the client fits the criteria. Even if they do believe that, diagnosing one member helps solidify that person as the problem in the family. Through the use of relational questions, the therapist can start to counteract this and join all family members together in a desire to reach certain goals. A hypothetical explanation of how a therapist can reduce the chance that the diagnosis will be used against the IP is given here:

> *Therapist:* For insurance purposes, I will be setting up a file under Steve's name. However, I want to make it clear that any difficulty any one member is experiencing is housed within the family as a whole. I believe that no one member is solely problematic. So, during our sessions, we will explore how all members are involved in what is going on in the family.

Content versus Process

In the individual interview, therapists work between content, feeling, and meaning. Moving from the surface level of content to the emotional impact of feelings and then to the deepest level of meaning allows clients to move away from talking about something to understanding how that something is impacting them. The same is true in family interviews. In conducting a family interview, it is important to work at two levels of complexity: the content and process levels. Content, in this context, refers to the more concrete issues of *what* the family is talking about. Process refers to *how* they talk about these issues. Consider the following interchange:

> *Mother:* I just can't get Ahmed to listen to me. He won't clean his room or take out the garbage.
>
> *Father:* I tell him every day that he needs to keep better care of the house.
>
> *Ahmed:* I do. But you want everything cleaned to perfection.
>
> *Mother:* We just want you to be more conscientious.

The content of this example is that mother and father are complaining that Ahmed does not do as he is asked and does not do his chores around the house. Ahmed states that he does, but not to his parents' standards. The process of this is that mother and father unite to try to get Ahmed to do as they ask, and Ahmed is able to argue with his parents.

Process can be noted through the rules of interaction of the family. The rules of the previous family allowed the son to enter into a debate with the parents. Although families continuously operate at both levels, they are mainly aware of the content level, not the process level. They know what they are arguing about. However, they are usually not as clear as to the rules of how they argue. This is where the therapeutic interviewer can assist the family by being attentive to family process and vocalizing it so that it is more overt. This is an important skill for the family interviewer to be able to get beneath the *what* of family discourse to the *how*; it is a shift from the details of behavior to sequences and patterns of relationship dynamics. Being able to work at both levels helps connect the interviewer to the family and then helps them move toward their goals.

As a family interviewer, it is usually important to start at the content level in the very beginning so the family knows that you understand what they are talking about. Yet, change for the family seems to happen more when time is spent in the process area of the conversation. This is similar to starting with paraphrases (reflection of content), then moving to reflection of feelings, and then to reflection of meaning.

Taibbi (1996) presented the following questions therapists can ask themselves, which can distinguish between content and process:

Content Information

What is the presenting problem? Who has the problem? Who is most concerned about the problem?

What is the family's theory, or theories, about the problem?

What has the family tried so far to solve the problem?

What are the family's expectations of therapy?

What is the larger context and history of the problem? Who else may be involved? What themes seem to constantly reappear?

Process Information

How well do the family members communicate with each other (don't talk, have trouble expressing how they feel, interrupt and don't listen, and so on)?
What are the family members' reactions to you as the therapist (intimidated, highly sensitive, seductive, skeptical, dependent, passive, angry, aggressive)?
How anxious are the various family members? How resistant?
What is the emotional range of the various family members? What emotion is each person most comfortable expressing?
What's missing?
What patterns do you see? (p. 44)

This distinction between content and process helps the interviewer and the family move from the story of what occurred to how family members interact around that story. By tracking and highlighting the family's process, more focus is placed on the themes, meanings, and covert rules of interaction of the family.

Being comfortable in the process level of interaction is one of the most important skills for the family interviewer. Strict focus on the content of a family bogs down the session. Family members will talk about the things they do not like about the other members of the family. However, they usually do not talk much about the mutuality involved in interactions and the rules that have been established in the family, which lead to the family's current level of homeostasis. Homeostasis is the steady state of the family's functioning. It occurs based on the patterned relationships in the family, where these patterns are based on the rules of the system. These rules and patterns are what are known as the family's process. Those families coming in to therapy are usually not happy at their current level of functioning (homeostasis). Each family has a different functioning level, and thus, family interviewers cannot expect that all families will be the same.

By first exploring the content of the family's communication and then moving to the process of their interactions, family interviewers establish an assumption that members are intertwined in each others' lives. This helps to prevent the scapegoating and blaming that might otherwise occur in family sessions.

Therapist's Impact on the Family

Therapeutic interviewers not only listen to and respond to clients, but also impact and are impacted by clients. Second order cybernetics is an idea that postulates that an observer of any system is also a part of that system. As a result, objectivity is impossible. In working with families, then, the interviewer is not some outside observer of the family. Being in the room with the family, the therapist becomes part of a therapeutic system composed of the family's system and the therapist's theoretical system. As such, the therapist is influencing the family at the same time the therapist is being influenced.

More importantly, the family in therapy is not the same as the family at home. Certainly, there are overlaps in how individual members and the whole of the family act between therapy and home, but there are also differences. The child might be more vocal at home than during the family interview. The father might yell more at home than during therapy. The mother might be more domineering at home than in session.

Family interviewers can use this understanding in their questioning of the family:

Therapist: How similar are you all at home to how you are in here?

By understanding that their very presence in the therapy room has potential impact on how the system is currently functioning, interviewers can then discuss the differences between family process in the therapy room and at home. Although many of the processes occurring in the family will be similar across contexts, family interviewers should be cautious in thinking that they have the "whole" or "true" picture.

Circular Epistemology

Most family therapists prefer the systemic perspective that relationships are circular instead of linear. From a linear perspective, some A causes a B. For instance, a client might state that he avoids coming home because other household members are negative. From a linear perspective, this person becomes a passive recipient of other people's actions. Such causality diminishes the impact that this person has on his environment. From the vantage of circular causality, one sees a different arrangement, understanding that A and B (and C and D, and so on) mutually influence one another. Therefore, family members may be acting negatively toward the individual, but that person also contributes to the negativity, intentionally or not, and influences whether other family members continue to be negative toward him.

No one person operates in isolation. And, in a family, there are continuous interpersonal influences. Each family member uniquely punctuates these influences. The husband might exclaim that his wife and son are too close and keep him out. The son might question whether the father is jealous because of his connection with mother. And the mother might comment on the problem of having to find a connection with her son because her husband is distant.

Each person in the family has his or her own view of reality. Applying a circular causality epistemology allows therapists to appreciate multiple perspectives. Good family interviewers will move from one person's reality to another's and accept each reality equally. In action, therapists acknowledge each family member's viewpoint without diminishing another member's perspective. An example of how this can be achieved follows:

> *Daughter:* I don't think this family is very close. We don't do much together.
>
> *Mother:* Jamie, yes, we do. We have dinner together most nights.
>
> *Daughter:* But we don't have much fun at dinner. We don't do things for fun.
>
> *Father:* We are a very close family. It's just that you want to be by yourself.
>
> *Therapist:* It's interesting. In this family, some people feel very connected while others feel quite disconnected. How does that happen?

In this example, the therapist makes room for people in the family to have differing views, yet feel comfortable about such differences.

Furthermore, embracing a circular causality epistemology allows therapists to put family members' complaints into perspective. Many people see problems from a linear perspective; however, family interviewers accept a client's perspective as a current understanding of that person at a particular time, rather than as an absolute truth of the family. When they begin to link each person's perspective in the family, a wider web of understanding for all members of the therapeutic system develops.

Circularity may also be viewed as complementarity. One member's behavior complements and is mutually impacted by another person's behavior. This is what makes the family a system in that each family member comes together to function as a whole. Family interviewers can utilize complementarity by asking family members how their own behavior is impacted by and impacts other members. The following scenario provides an example of how this theory can be put into practice.

> *Father:* When I come home at night, no one listens to me.
>
> *Therapist:* What things do you notice your wife doing that make you think she isn't listening?
>
> *Father:* Well, she doesn't ask me how my day was. She continues focusing on the children.
>
> *Therapist:* And when she continues doing that, what do you do?

The therapist's questions connect husband and wife in a mutual process of interaction. The therapist can then question the father about what he sees his children doing that gets him to view the situation as he is, along with how he reacts to their behavior.

Circular Questioning

Based on a circular epistemology, therapeutic interviewers can utilize a process of questioning called circular questioning. Circular questioning involves asking one member of the family to comment on the relationship between two or more other

Reflection 13.1

Think about your view of why people have problems. What do you think the roles of all members in the family are during the family interview? Are they there to give you information about the identified patient? How much do you think that problems in a family are wrought in a series of relationships among people? What difference do you think it makes to take a linear versus a circular viewpoint when interviewing a family?

people in the family (Selvini Palazzoli et al., 1980). By having one member communicate about the connection between two other people in the family, the possibility of difference, or new information, enters the therapy room. Circular questions can also be conceived as asking one member about one or more members. The use of circular questions also guarantees a more equitable division of the amount of time each family member talks. Rather than asking questions to one person—which is what individual therapy accustoms us to do—the therapist tries to pose questions about family members to other family members.

Circular questions are relational questions that join the multiple opinions and observations of each family member around the problem facing the family. Nelson et al. (1986) discussed four types of circular questions: problem definition; sequence of interaction; comparison/classification; and intervention. (See Table 13.2.)

Circular questioning helps to connect family members into a relational system around the problem. New information is allowed to come forth since the therapist is questioning about difference. It also provides a flow in the dialogue between the therapist and all members of the family, an approach that reduces the problem of long speeches by one person. Family interviewers can use circular questioning to connect with each family member, understand the relationships (behavioral and meaning systems), and clarify a person's response by asking another family member about the first person. If the father says he has trouble expressing feelings, the interviewer might then ask the mother, "How does he express his feelings?" By asking another member of the family to clarify what someone else said or did, family members become connected in a web of relationships that form together to showcase the family system.

Interactional Sequences

One aspect of circular questioning is that it helps to bring forth the interactional sequences between family members. Family interviewers can track how interactions occur between various family members without asking circular questions, but by exploring with the whole family how things occur in the family. Utilizing the notion of circular causality, family interviewers continuously ask questions and probe into the family dynamics in terms of how any one person's thoughts, actions, and feelings are intertwined in a relational field that impacts others and then impacts the original person.

TABLE 13.2   *Four Types of Circular Questions*

Problem definition questions focus on how the different members of the family view the problem. Such questions might be:

- What is the current complaint in the family?
- Who most thinks that this is a problem?
- How is this problem different now than in the past?
- What would the family be like if things stayed the same?

Sequence of interaction questions ask each family member about issues surrounding the problem, such as who, what, where, and when. Such questions might be:

- When your husband and son are in a verbal fight, what do you do?
- What happens after the two of you agree not to talk to each other?
- Who agrees with you that your mother is overinvolved in your marriage?
- What do you think your son would do if you and your husband did not fight?

Comparison/classification questions ask a family member about other family members. The main types of questions in this category are those that ask one member to discuss the relationship between two or more other family members. These types of questions are also known as triadic questions. Such questions might be:

- Who is most upset about the current situation?
- Who gets along better, you and your daughter or your wife and your daughter?
- Before Jackson started getting into fights at school, who was he closest to?
- Who do you think would be most relieved if the problem was resolved?

Intervention questions are designed to be change producing. Such questions might be:
- What things have you all done as a family that went well?
- Who do you think in your family will be the first to change?
- What do you think Dad needs to do to reconnect with Mom?

Source: Adapted from Nelson et al. (1986).

Circular questions are not the only means of getting at the family's interactional sequences. Interviewers can ask family members what it is that they do and how other people react to those actions. Minuchin explained the benefit of focusing on interactional sequences rather than suggesting how the family should be different, "Pointing out what people are doing and its consequences helps them to see themselves more clearly and allows them to consider making changes. Telling them what to do puts their backs up" (Minuchin, Nichols, & Lee, 2007, p. 33).

Families operate based on a sequence of behaviors occurring between members. Much of what family interviewers do is to bring forth these interactional sequences. Consider the following exchange that might occur in a family interview:

Father: We did not have a good week this week.

Therapist: What happened?

Father: Yimali and I got into a big fight. She refused to clean her room and I went off on her.

Therapist: What did she do when you went off on her?

Father: She screamed at me saying that I was too controlling of her.

Therapist: Then what did you do?

Father: I yelled back at her that until she shows maturity, I'll be supervising her.

Therapist: How did she take that?

Father: Not well. There was crying and yelling for a while.

Therapist: After all of the yelling, what happened next?

As can be seen, it was not as important to focus on *what* the family was arguing about, but the *process of how* they argued. A good family interviewer will be constantly looking for patterns of interactions. Too much focus on the what (content) can get the therapy bogged down in details. Focusing on the how (process) of interactions leads to awareness that cuts across many content issues.

Skills for Conducting a Therapeutic Family Interview

Preliminary Information

Some family interviewers prefer to have preliminary information to help them determine whether it is appropriate to work with one, all, or a subset of members of the family. This is usually done during the initial telephone call from the family (usually from the chief complainant). Who calls and what that person says is information interviewers can use to begin to form an initial understanding of what is going on in the current situation. Patterson et al. (1998) provided several questions that can help family interviewers in their initial contact with a family:

1. What is the problem and how does the client present it? Is this a crisis, a severe or moderate problem, a discrete situation, a chronic difficulty?
2. How has the family responded to the situation? How have they managed so far?
3. Has there been previous therapy?
4. Why is the family seeking treatment now?
5. What additional factors are influencing the situation (e.g., nature and frequency of various stressors—whether they are vocational, personal, physical, or otherwise)? (p. 15)

Reflection 13.2

Think about what would happen if everyone in your family attempted to label you as the problematic individual in the family. How open to connection would you feel? How much would you find the therapy session to be a supportive environment? What do you think you would be like in therapy?

Family interviewers should be cautious if this information is taken during an intake phone conversation. If so, the communication is usually with the person who is either the customer or the complainant. Their explanation of what is occurring should not be taken as truth, but as one viewpoint of potentially many; not every family member may agree. This is where the family interviewer can begin the initial family session by explaining what was discussed during the intake interview (if there was one) and inquiring from *all* family members what they think about what was discussed.

During the initial phone call, therapists want to get a preliminary sense of the presenting problem and who is in the family so that they can determine who should come to the first interview (Nichols & Schwarz, 2007). When talking to the family member, the family interviewer will need to balance the person's desires with how the therapist operates. For instance, if a client is calling because her adolescent son is out of control and she wants the therapist to work individually with the son, the therapist can risk the mother not bringing the son in if he requests that every member of the family attend. The therapist can then begin to expand the scope of the caller's complaint from the individual to how that person's behaviors are impacting other family members. If the therapist does not explain how he operates (conducting family interviews), he may be misguiding the client and leading to potential problems once he attempts to get the whole family in after meeting individually with the identified patient. Nichols and Schwarz (2007) recommended, "If you expect to meet with the whole family, a matter-of-fact statement that that's how you work, at least for the initial assessment, will get most families to agree to a consultation" (p. 35).

Confidentiality

During the initial session, every family member should sign an informed consent form to conduct the therapy. Everyone eighteen years and older in the family must sign that form. However, it is useful to have everyone sign the form, regardless of age. When everyone in the family engages in this process, even a six year old, therapists are sending the implicit message that everyone has a stake about being there.

In explaining the informed consent form, family therapists should use language so that they are understood by even the youngest verbal person in the room. If therapists use technical terms and adult language, there is the possibility of excluding the children from understanding what the informed consent form explains. It also sends a message that they are not as important as are the adults in the session. By discussing the form at a level that the children can understand, the adults should be able to understand also. From the beginning then, the family interviewer is setting the stage that this is going to be an interview that involves participation from every member of the family. The following therapist explanation provides an example of how this process can be discussed with the family:

> **Therapist:** I wanted to explain the informed consent form. This is our contract of how we are going to work together. First, there is confidentiality.

That is, whatever anyone says in here I will keep to myself and not tell anyone else. You can tell who you want, but I can't. Only in special circumstances. If you tell me that you really want to hurt yourself or someone else, I would have to tell someone. If someone talks about child abuse, then I'd have to let the state social service know. Also, sometimes a judge might ask me to talk about what is going on. Other than that, everything we talk about is private. Does anyone have any questions?

By taking time in the beginning of the session to answer any questions, the therapist helps to set the stage for a collaborative relationship.

Joining

One of the most important parts of a first interview is developing an alliance with the family (Nichols & Schwartz, 2007). This alliance is procured through the process of joining. Minuchin and Fishman (1981) stated, "Joining is letting the family know that the therapist understands them and is working with and for them" (pp. 31–32). Joining occurs from the first contact with a family until the very last communication.

Joining with a family is not one discrete experience; there are various types of joining. Therapists can join the family in the beginning of the first session by greeting each person and getting a response from each member to establish a connection and set the stage that in this interview, each person will contribute. Haley (1987) discussed this in terms of the social stage of therapy. At this point, therapists can move from person to person getting each person's name and possibly something about each person, such as grade in school or occupation. Usually, at this point in the session, therapists should refrain from talking about the problem, so that an initial connection can be made with each person. Lipchik and de Shazer (1986) held that therapists should start with these types of connecting questions. They stated, "These questions [informal greetings] are asked in the most non-confrontative, non-judgmental, and non-demanding way possible to convey an interested and neutral stance on the part of the therapist" (p. 92).

The opening moments of the therapeutic interview set the stage for what is to come during the course of the therapy. By laying the groundwork for what will occur during the sessions, therapists provide a starting point for productive work. Whitaker and Bumberry (1988) explained this:

> This is a time for establishing some personal connection, not for remaining "professional" and aloof. One of the initial tasks is to let them know something of how I operate and what I expect from them. I need to establish the parameters of my involvement with them and to clarify my conditions for the relationship. (p. 6)

By joining in this manner, the therapist brings himself into the room by being a human being instead of a cold and distant figure. Further, the family is oriented to the style of the therapist so they are prepared to engage him as a distinct member of the therapeutic system.

Therapists can also join the family on the level of the family's operations. Minuchin (1974) called this "accommodation" whereby the therapist makes adjustments to himself so that he connects better with the family. One of the techniques of accommodation is mimesis. This is when the therapist changes his communications based on those of the family. The therapist attempts to match the tempo, affective range, tone, style, and other aspects of communication that the family is delivering. If the family members talk slowly, then the therapist should slow his speech. This should not be an exaggerated effort; rather, the therapist tries to get "in tune" with the family gradually and naturally. If the therapist's attempts at mimesis seem insincere, then he may lose the family's trust, instead of encouraging collaboration.

Explaining the Purpose of the Family Interview

Because families tend to believe that one person is the problem, it is important to explain the importance of meeting with most, if not all, of the family members. Family members might come in as a favor to another family member or to provide information about how the identified patient is having difficulties. Further, family members might be unaware of how a family interview is conducted and how participatory they should be in session. Family interviewers can explain that by all parties being together at the same time during the interview, new and more effective means of communication and interacting can occur. Boyer and Jeffrey (1984) provided some potential explanations family interviewers can offer. They suggested letting the family know that meeting all together they can do the following:

1. Express and share feelings in order to gain a greater understanding of each other's perceptions.
2. Mutually discuss problems and ideas as part of a search for workable, satisfying solutions for the problems the family may be experiencing.
3. Try new ways of dealing with their problems both in the session and outside of the session under the therapist's guidance. (p. 59)

The following is one potential way of introducing the purpose of the family interview:

> *Therapist:* I'm not quite sure how things are in your house. Here, I really prefer to meet with all family members together because each one of you is a very significant part of this family. When everyone is here together, we have more people working toward the same goal: getting this family to function in a way that all of you want so that everyone is happier.

Virginia Satir (1967) eloquently explained the purpose of having all family members in the interview, "No one person can see the whole picture because he is limited to his own perspective. By having everyone together we can get the whole picture more clearly. Every person has a unique contribution to make which cannot be duplicated by anyone else" (p. 109). This phrasing allows for the uniqueness of each person, intuiting that no one person's viewpoint is more right (or wrong) than any other member's perspective.

Who to Start with in the Family Interview

Family interviewers have many opening gambits to start the interview. They can throw out a generic opening statement for anyone to answer: "Who would like to begin about what brings you in?" They can also start with the person who made the referral, who in many cases is the mother. "Mary, you initially called the clinic wanting therapy for your family. What led to you making that call?" This allows everyone else in the family interview an opportunity to hear what was discussed during the initial phone call. Therapists might also start with the husband, to offset the notion that men are more distant in family therapy and to involve him from the very beginning. "Frank, what is your perspective on the family being here today?" Therapists might start with the person blamed for most of the family problems, the IP (scapegoat). "Malcolm, what are your thoughts about being here today?"

How and with whom therapists start is an important decision in the family interview. In some families, culture might play a role. In patriarchal families, it might be important to start with the father. Having the head of the household provide entrance into the family system can give therapists more credibility and freedom of exploration in the family system. In some cultures and families, it would be disrespectful for children to speak first or to voice their opinions. Family interviewers should be aware of how culture might impact the family dynamics and interactions in the therapy room. Therapists could ask the family how culture informs how they are as a family. This would then give the family interviewer some clues as to how to best approach working with this specific family. Case Scenario 13.1 explains how a therapist utilized a basic understanding of a family's culture to connect with the family system.

CASE SCENARIO 13.1

I was the supervisor for a live supervision family therapy team. One of the supervisees had originally worked with a seventeen-year-old Hispanic male. The family then requested family therapy. The therapist was an American Caucasian female, which hampered full connection with the father of the family. I decided to join the therapist in co-therapy. The family was composed of the father, mother, and three children. The oldest child was the identified client. The middle child was a son, fourteen years old. The youngest was a daughter, nine years old. The parents were both born in Colombia and had moved to South Florida before the children were born. When I first entered the room, I introduced myself to everyone and then asked the father what he saw going on in the family. Knowing the dynamics in this family, as in many Hispanic families, I had to validate the father's place as the head of the household. Further, by asking him about what was happening in *the family*, instead of one specific member, I was able to keep the therapy focused on the system rather than an individual.

Reflection 13.3

Think about your own family. Who is the most vocal person in the family? Next vocal? Least? Where do you fit in? When the whole family is together, whose voice gets heard more than any other person's? How validated and open to expression are those on the lower end of verbal expression? If your family was in therapy, how would each member want the therapist to help the flow of the conversation?

The First Family Interview

The first family interview sets the stage for subsequent work with that client family. Therapists have two main goals for the first session: developing rapport with the family and developing a hypothesis of what is occurring in the family (Nichols & Schwartz, 2007). There are many different ways of doing this, primarily based on the therapist's theoretical orientation and the therapist's personality. The first session is used by both therapist and family to gauge whether the relationship seems to be a productive one, whether change has been made, and what change is possible.

Nichols and Schwartz (2007) provided a first session checklist to ensure that family interviewers start off the family therapy process on the right note. First, therapists should connect with each and every person in the family. This allows each family member a chance to be heard, which would then further motivate them to take part in the family interviews. Second, family interviewers should gauge how much they have been the leader in the session, helping to control the structure and pacing of the session. Third, and perhaps most important, therapists should have developed a good working alliance with the family. Fourth, family interviewers should be able to observe and point out the strengths and positives of each individual member and the family as a whole. The next item is respecting the family's process while developing an empathic understanding of the members of the family. Sixth, therapists should understand what the specific problems are that the family is struggling with and how they have attempted to deal with these problems. Seventh, family interviewers should have begun to conceptualize why the family is experiencing their problems. Eighth, therapists should attempt to understand how people who are connected to the family, but not present in the interview, impact the problem situation. Ninth, therapist and family should mutually enter into a treatment contract in which they are working on the goals that the family finds important. Lastly, family interviewers should be open to questions from all family members about the process or the content of the interviews.

Establishing Mutual Goals

One key to an effective family interview is to find a common cause for all members. In attempting to identify what each family member wants from therapy, the therapist gains an understanding of each family member's expectations about family therapy and, in uniting them around a common cause, encourages them to buy into the therapy process. Haley (1987) stated, "It is important to obtain from the family a reasonably clear statement of what changes everyone, including the problem child, wants from the therapy" (p. 38). By getting the whole family to agree on a goal, each member is more likely to work together to accomplish that goal.

Therapists should ask each individual member of the family what he or she is hoping to get out of therapy. This will give information as to the hierarchy, interactional patterns, and level of open expression in the family. If a child is hesitant to express himself or states that he "doesn't know" why he is there, this then becomes information for the family interviewer.

If one or a subset of family members are allowed to choose the goals, the other family members will be less likely to work toward those goals. However, if one or more goals can be developed where each and every family member has a share in that outcome, the family will be more likely to work together toward those goals.

> *Therapist:* What are you hoping to get out of therapy?
>
> *Father:* I was hoping that Stacey would do more of what she is asked to do.
>
> *Therapist:* And you, Mom?
>
> *Mother:* I want our family to be able to eat dinner together without getting into a fight.
>
> *Therapist:* What about you, Johnnie?
>
> *Son:* I want my sister to stop picking on me.
>
> *Therapist:* And Stacey?
>
> *Daughter:* I want my parents to get off my case.
>
> *Therapist:* Wow. It seems that there is something that each person wants that would help this family to work better together. What does everyone think is something that each of you agree on that would be important for all of you?

In this manner, the therapist attempts to connect all of the family members together to work toward a common goal. When people are united toward a goal instead of each person in isolation, cohesion can occur.

Handling Emotionality

Having family members express emotionality is potentially useful in the family interview. However, too much emotionality might lead to an unproductive session. Even worse, it could potentially lead to violence. In family therapy, more than in individual therapy, there is the potential for verbal and/or physical aggression to occur in session. Because there are multiple people in the room who are sometimes very frustrated with one another, there is a higher chance that members will insult and attack each other. If the client becomes verbally aggressive in individual therapy, the main outlet for that emotional intensity is the therapist. During a family interview, clients will more likely discharge their emotionality on other family members.

One way to decrease emotionality in a session is to have family members talk to the therapist instead of each other. The more that members converse with one another, the greater the likelihood anxiety will increase and tempers flare. Therefore, if anxiety and emotionality of certain family members in the room is reaching an unhelpful point, the family interviewer can direct members to stop talking to each other and talk to him. Conversely, if family members avoid each other by talking to the family interviewer, they can be directed to speak with each other.

Father: You never do anything right. I'm embarrassed to have you as a son.

Son: It doesn't matter what I do, it's never good enough.

Mother: You don't try as hard as you should.

Son: (voice quivering) I do too.

Father: Well, I don't see it.

As can be seen, if left unabated, this interchange may escalate into greater negative feelings and unproductive actions. The therapist can intervene in this situation to help reduce the emotionality.

Therapist: Malcolm, it seems as if it is tough for you to be believed in this family.

Malcolm: Yes, I really do try. But I don't think my parents will ever believe me.

Therapist: What would you wish they would know about your intentions that you think they don't know?

Malcolm: I know I make mistakes. But I really do want things to be good between us. Yet, it's hard when you know that they won't believe you or support you.

Therapist: Dad, what's it like for you to hear that from your son?

Father: If I truly believed him, I would feel good. But I just don't see the effort.

Therapist: What do you think about Malcolm's statement that there is already a preconception that he won't do things right?

Father: He has to prove himself first before we believe in him.

Therapist: Mom, where do you come in in all this?

Mom: I don't like how things are going. I think my husband and I have given Malcolm so many chances. And he keeps messing up.

Therapist: Wow, if I didn't know any better, I would think that there is nothing right with your son.

Mom: It's not like that. He's a good kid, but we're just frustrated.

By getting the members to stop escalating their verbal altercation and talking through the therapist, the family members are better able to sit back and listen to each other.

A second way to decrease emotionality that is leading to arguing and fighting in a session by family members is to take an active stance in the therapy room. Family interviewers can do this by stating:

> *Therapist:* All right everyone. I would like for you to stop arguing. It is quite clear how everyone argues. Jim, you and Sally seem to be the main combatants, while April, you seem to sit back until Sally becomes frustrated. Then you come into the argument on her side against Jim. This seems to be a very frustrating pattern for everyone.

At this point, the family interviewer has intervened in a problematic transaction in the session, provided some family process feedback on how the family argues, and has opened space for a discussion of how change might occur.

Some further possibilities when things are getting too charged in the family interview is to switch the topic, move from the present to the past, or move from the realm of feelings to connect them to facts (Satir, 1967). Family interviewers can segue from the heated topic to one that might be less charged through wording such as, "Money seems to be an especially difficult topic to discuss right now, perhaps we might be best suited if we talk about the rules around chores that you had brought up last week." This gives family members the opportunity to calm down so they are better able to be productive during the interview.

Therapists can also decrease emotionality by moving from a place of confrontation to one of inquiry. Minuchin has shifted from a stance of challenging and confronting clients to showing interest in what was said. He explained his stance, "Surprise raises questions but invites the family to join in deciphering a puzzle, rather than defending themselves against a perceived attack" (Minuchin, Nichols, & Lee, 2007).

If there is too little emotionality in the room, therapists can get family members to begin talking to one another. In this case, family interviewers can ask family members to turn and face one another and look each other in the eye when expressing what they are thinking and feeling. Emotionality is neither good nor bad; the way in which it is utilized by the family is what can be explored. The main thing is for family interviewers to be aware of when too little or too much emotionality is not being productive and help the family change its patterns to lead to new and more productive interactions.

Special Issues When Conducting a Therapeutic Interview with Couples/Families

Triangulation

Therapeutic interviewers working with individuals have to deal with the issue of triangulation, but triangulation becomes more prominent in couples and family interviews because the person who they are trying to triangulate with the therapist is actually in the therapy room. Triangulation occurs when one person attempts to bring a third person into the middle of a conflict they are having with a second party.

Therapeutic interviewers get triangulated into family processes all of the time. It is usually very apparent when two people have a disagreement that they are having difficulty getting beyond. Each will then try to get the therapist on his or her side and against the other person. Case Scenario 13.2 presents a situation in which a couple attempted to triangulate the therapist into taking sides about who was "right" in regard to an affair.

When family members are trying to triangulate the therapist, he should become a nonreactive part of that triangle. In this way, he is not taking either person's side, but is still staying actively engaged in the interchange and thus modeling for the clients how they can stay connected to one another even when they are in disagreement.

Overtalkative Family Members

When one family member monopolizes the interview, the opportunity for differences to emerge becomes lost. Instead of a polyphony of voices, the interview becomes a monologue. Usually, the most talkative person in the room has an organized complaint about someone else, and if he is allowed to continue to vent uninterrupted, the other family members may feel they are a captive audience rather than participants in a dialogue. The challenge facing therapists is to validate

CASE SCENARIO 13.2

I met for a first session with a husband and wife. They were coming to therapy because the wife had been having an affair with another man for the last year. The husband had recently found out about the affair. She had ended the affair and wanted to move forward in her relationship with the husband. He wanted her to come clean with everything that happened during the affair, including where they went, what presents she had given him, the sexual positions they engaged in, and all other details. In that pursuit, he tried to get me to make his wife tell everything. She tried to get me to have him get over the affair and not ask any questions about it. I maintained my neutrality and discussed what each of them wanted without taking any one person's side. This wasn't what either one of them wanted, and they did not come back for a second session. Each had wanted me to join them and explain to the other person how wrong the other person was. This was a position I was not willing to take. I had attempted not to get sucked into either person's triangulation attempt. Husband and wife both wanted me, the therapist, to take their side against the other.

a dominating person's perspective while also making room for others to speak their minds. Here is an interchange that demonstrates this skill:

> *Father:* And I just want him to learn that he needs to grow up at this point. He's thirteen. He's not a little kid anymore. I tell my wife, but she still treats him like a child.
>
> *Mother:* But . . . [trying to interject]
>
> *Father:* [continuing without stopping] I had to work from the time I was twelve. I'm not even asking that of him. I just want him to know that he can't just play around all the time and he has to get more serious. He . . .
>
> *Therapist:* That's an interesting idea; that your son needs to get more serious. Mom, how do you understand what your husband is saying?

In this example, the father's ideas are acknowledged and then expanded to include the mother through a question that follows up what he said. This allows the family interviewer to see how other family members think about the issue.

During a family interview, when one person is doing a majority of the speaking, the interviewer tends to continue engaging that person through questioning. Skilled family interviewers ask questions of everyone present in the room to produce an interview with as many perspectives as possible. Sometimes, as in the transcript just presented, an extremely overtalkive member might be interrupted by the therapist so that additional voices can be included in the multilogue necessary for positive change.

Absent Family Members

Sometimes one or more family members cannot or will not come to the session. Surprisingly, this does not prevent their involvement. Even though the person is physically absent, their impression on the family can be made known by asking those present what the person in absentia might think about the discussion at hand. This helps maintain the understanding that a family system operates at all times, even when members are not present, and that change is always possible. Another solution can involve sending written reports of the session home with the family to be given to or read with the missing member.

> *Mother:* We're more-or-less a happy family. We do have a problem with violence every now and then.
>
> *Father:* Well, some people in the family need to get hit when they do stupid things.
>
> *Son:* When things are calm, it's okay. But anything out of line, and we know that Dad is going to blow up.
>
> *Therapist:* Mom, what do you think your daughter, Kayleigh [not present in the session], would say if I asked her how things are in the family?

> *Mother:* I think she'd say the same thing as Petey.
>
> *Therapist:* Dad, what do you think?
>
> *Father:* She also doesn't like to get punished, but she keeps getting into trouble.

Through this one question, the therapist is able to expand the concern of the problem in this family to all members, even those who are not there.

There are many other ways to get nonattending family members into therapy. Family therapists might develop a standard letter that explains the purpose of the family interview and how it can be aided by all members attending. The more open the family interviewer is to all members' opinions, the better the likelihood that the family members attending the sessions will help recruit the nonattending member.

Some family therapists, such as Carl Whitaker, will not meet with the family unless all of the individuals that they want in the therapy room are present. Whitaker (1976) would sometimes request that three or four generations of the family attend the family session. Taking the stance of not conducting the session if not every family member across all of the generations comes can be a risky proposition as families may not come in for therapy after not being able to get the nonattending person into therapy. Whitaker was working from the proposition that the family's normal way of operating was going to have to change. Making a demand of refusal of service unless everyone is in attendance should be used when the therapist has articulated an extremely clear theoretical orientation and that this stance makes sense to help the client family achieve its goal. Further, in the thirty years since Whitaker expressed this idea, the demography of families has changed. No longer do family members continue to reside in the same locale as their parents, grandparents, and great grandparents. The dispersion of family members from a local neighborhood presents a challenge for family interviewers who want as many people in the family as possible to attend the session.

Inappropriate Topics for a Family Interview

Having all members of the family together in the interview helps those members understand each other. However, there are topics that might not be suitable for everyone present. For instance, discussing the parents' lack of sexual intimacy and how that tension enters into why they fight with the children might be better left to a private meeting with the husband and wife rather than in front of the children. Other areas that may require a separate meeting with the parents include infidelity, finances, medical problems, or issues the parents are afraid to broach before their children. Once therapists have allotted parents a private session, they can then decide whether they think such information may be suitable for the whole family to know. What is surprising is that in families there are seldom secrets. Even if the children don't know how frequently their parents are sexually intimate, they know instinctively that intimacy is a problem for their parents.

Reflection 13.4

Think about those things that you would be comfortable discussing in front of a therapist. Which topics would you also be comfortable talking about with your significant other? Children? Parents? Which topics would you not be comfortable talking about? How do you think you can ease clients in feeling comfortable talking about delicate issues during a family interview?

Meeting Individually with Family Members

Family interviewers must make a choice about how to conduct the session. Some family interviewers prefer to meet with all members of the family together, without ever seeing any members individually. Other interviewers prefer to meet with the whole family, and then each person alone, so that they can allow a time for a more personal connection. Further, in case a family member has something that he or she wants to discuss but does not feel comfortable doing so in front of the other family members, meeting alone with the family therapist provides a safe session in which to discuss these issues.

A potential pitfall of meeting with all members individually is that if one party tells the family interviewer something that is a secret to the other family members, the therapist will then have to censor himself while meeting with the whole family. This can be a difficult task in that he will have to consider what information he received with the whole family present (information that can be freely discussed) or what was told to him in confidence during an individual meeting (information that cannot be freely discussed). Further, by meeting individually with each family member, this could help perpetuate the notion that there are secrets in the family. Conducting a family interview with everyone present might help set the stage that there should not be secrets in the family. If the family therapist does decide to meet individually with family members, there should be an agreement beforehand of whether information brought up in these solo sessions will be discussed when everyone gets together or whether they will be kept confidential.

Seating Arrangements

Various family therapy theories stress the importance of where family members sit during session. Usually, family interviewers allow family members to sit where they wish, because seating positions can be information about how the family is operating. For example, if a family enters the therapy room and mother and daughter sit on one couch and father and son sit on the other, one hypothesis can be that there is a significant gender subsystem in the family. Another hypothesis is that mother and father are not fully united as parents. Once therapists gauge the potential meaning of seating position, they may adjust the seating pattern, in order to distinguish certain subsystems. If therapists think it could help get members to be more participative and help the family toward its goals, they can request that members change seats during the course of the session. Asking politely, "Mother, could you please switch seats with your son?" can get the family moving toward change as it sends a message of connection and disconnection in the family.

Discipline in Session

Many times families come for family therapy because they have what they consider to be disobedient children. In session, the children might act up. This is an excellent opportunity to observe how parents discipline their children and how the children respond. Many times, parents are reluctant to discipline their children during an interview, unsure whether they or the therapist should. A welcoming comment is to tell the parents, "I notice you seem displeased with your children's behavior. Please feel free to discipline them as you would at home." From this opening comment, the therapist has the opportunity to observe the parenting styles and also to ask other questions. For example, the therapist may inquire, "Do you attempt different types of discipline at home?" As an illustration, a mother, father, and six-year-old son have come to therapy. The son is running all over the office, opening up drawers, banging items on the therapist's desk, and yelling. The parents say to the therapist, "See, he's uncontrollable." The therapist can then ask the parents, "When he is like this at home, how do the two of you react?" This then switches the occurrence in the therapy room from problem to potential avenue into better understanding of family process.

In general, therapists are in a better position to help the family if they avoid the role of disciplinarian. The child already has parents. By switching roles from therapist to parent, therapists may unwittingly compromise the parents, enter into a hopeless power struggle with the child or simply insult the family with a silent message that they are incompetent. This may impair the therapist's position with the family. There are times when the therapist can help the parents with parenting by offering them suggestions and coaching them during the session to try new approaches with their children. Sometimes, therapists are better off doing nothing and letting the family lose control in session, so that they can understand the steps that take place in the family when attempting to discipline. However, if therapists sense any potential violence, they should intervene. One caution in letting the parents discipline in session is if therapists think that parents might engage in discipline styles that could be considered abusive. Therapists should remind parents about what constitutes abuse so that they do not engage in these types of behaviors.

Should the Whole Family Always Come?

Family therapists differ in their views on whether every single member of the family needs to come or if certain subsystems of the family should come during various sessions. Family therapists such as Whitaker preferred to see all members of the family for each session. Therapists such as Minuchin would request that different subsystems attend various sessions based on his treatment plan. Other family therapists, such as Murray Bowen, might only see one member of the family. Whatever the configuration, family interviews are based on the notion that each part comes together to function as a whole and that one change in one part or person of the system leads to systemwide change.

A caution should be taken when not having all of the members come to a session. Those members who are asked not to come to the next session may take offense at not being invited back for the next session. Conversely, those not invited may take this as evidence that they are not part of the problem and that those people invited back need to go because they are the problem. Therapists should explain the rationale for asking certain members to come and others not to so that those not initially invited back can more easily be reincorporated into the therapy.

There are some advantages of meeting the family as a whole:

1. The family interviewer is able to observe each family member's interaction with each other. This gives the family interviewer a more complete view of the family system.
2. Family members are able to hear the perceptions of other family members. This allows them to get a better sense of where each member is coming from and can potentially rectify false perceptions.
3. The family interviewer has a stronger position meeting all members together because family members will have a harder time making claims that may compromise the therapist. When the family interviewer meets members individually, some members might use that to antagonize others and put the therapist in the middle. For instance, mother could say to son, "Well, when I met with the therapist, he stated that he thought that you were out of control and needed better discipline." The therapist then becomes triangulated.
4. By having everyone present when difficult issues are discussed, the family interviewer can set the stage for more open communication. Further, the notion of secrets is reduced because everything is out in the open between all family members.

Many family therapists start off with as many family members as they can get in the initial family interview and then request various subsets of the family, based on the progress the family is making and the types of issues that are to be addressed at that point in the therapy process. It is important to explain up front with the family why certain members will be invited to some sessions while others will not. This preserves the notion that all family members are intertwined in the process of moving toward the family's goals. However family therapy starts, members can always come and go based on schedules and the purpose of individual therapeutic interviews. Therapists should not get tied down to only meeting with specific family members but should be open to having whoever thinks that they can contribute to what is occurring in therapy.

Private Meetings with an Individual Family Member

There are some times when meeting with family members individually can be conducive to positive outcome in therapy. Some family members might be hesitant to open up and disclose in front of other family members. In private meetings with the family interviewer, the family member might feel more comfortable talking individually rather than in front of the rest of the family. This may be especially the case with couples, where one party might be having an affair or thinking about leaving the marriage. That person might be hesitant to openly discuss the situation with the spouse present, but would be willing to discuss it with the therapist privately.

Whether family interviewers meet with family members individually, they should have an agreement with the family members about secrets. In order to prevent being accused of being unfair, therapists should be open with family members about how they will handle secrets. Allowing clients to tell the therapist a secret puts the therapist in an unenviable position of possibly colluding with one or more family members. Therapists who meet individually with family members should be alert to the increased possibility of being triangulated into the family dynamics.

If family therapists do decide to meet with members individually, they should negotiate the parameters of these meetings. They might also set up an agreement that what gets talked about in the individual meetings will be integrated into the interviews with the full family.

Summary

Conducting a couple or family interview is a unique context in which to work therapeutically. By having multiple members of the family in the room at the same time, there are more possibilities for openings into what is going on in the family system. More relational types of issues occur during a couple or family meeting, requiring therapists to keep track of multiple levels of dynamics. Therapists need to hone their skills of being able to connect family members into a mutual understanding of what the purpose of therapy is so that all members will work toward the family goals. Family members are linked to each other through behavioral sequences and meaning systems that the family therapist can make overt to help the flow of the therapy session and get the family closer to its goals.

Exercises _____

1. Watch a television show or movie where the main action occurs between family members. On a notepad or computer, keep track of instances of circular causality and mutuality. How does each person's actions impact other family members? How are each person's actions impacted by the other family members? What is the content and the process of what is occurring?

2. Go to your university or public library and check out any psychotherapy/counseling video that deals with families. Pay specific attention to how the family therapist starts the interview, includes (or does not include) all of the family members, works on both the content and process levels, and handles increased or decreased emotionality. Try to ensure that you watch several videos with therapists from varying theoretical orientations.

3. With several members of your class, devise a list of qualities that a family therapist should have in order to conduct therapeutic interviews with families. Discuss what makes this list different from doing individual interviewing.

4. Ask several members of your class to role-play a family. Conduct a therapeutic interview in which you practice the skills of neutrality and circular questioning. After the interview, debrief your classmates, asking them which skills you used well and which you can improve.

14

Therapeutic Interviewing with Groups

Many therapeutic interviewers, especially in the beginning of their training, conduct some form of group therapy. There are various types of groups including education, discussion, task, growth and experiential, support, self-help, and therapy groups. The majority of what will be presented in this chapter deals with therapy groups, while also being applicable to most of the other groups (self-help groups would probably be the main exception as they tend not to have a professional therapist leading the group).

Conducting a group therapy interview, rather than working with that person individually, occurs for several reasons. Group interviews are beneficial since people, in their relationships with other people, engage in problematic behaviors. By addressing these difficulties in relating through the process of relating to others, people change based on their work with other people they encounter during the group process. They gain a sense of how other people perceive them and can, in the moment, work at developing better relating skills. They are then able to take this interpersonal learning and apply it to their life outside of the therapy room.

Group therapy is also advantageous for the therapeutic interviewer. In the span of sixty minutes, the interviewer can work with, and potentially positively impact, more people. It becomes an affordable means of gaining needed counseling for the clients while being financially sound for the therapist. In an individual session, even if a client cancelled within an accepted amount of time before the session (usually twenty-four hours), it is very hard for therapists to fill that slot with another client. Thus, they will have an open hour in which they will not be working with a client. In a group counseling interview, if several clients do not show up, the session can still occur.

Orientation to Conducting a Therapeutic Group Interview

Therapeutic Factors

Irvin Yalom (2005), perhaps the most influential person in the realm of group therapy, proposed eleven primary factors in group therapy: instillation of hope, universality, imparting information, altruism, the corrective recapitulation of the primary family group, development of socializing techniques, imitative behavior, interpersonal learning, group cohesiveness, catharsis, and existential factors. This section briefly describes each of these factors.

Instillation of Hope. Because clients are coming into therapy feeling down about themselves, the instillation of hope is key to getting them believing that change is possible. In the group setting, clients gain hope by seeing other people change for the positive. Group interviewers, from the beginning of the first interview, can discuss with the group what positive changes they may be able to expect from therapy. During the course of the group, they can highlight the positive changes members are making and explain that each and every member of the group can make positive changes. All counseling, regardless of the types and issues presented, should try to instill hope for the client. Group therapy allows the therapist to engage in this process with multiple clients simultaneously.

Universality. Many times, people come into counseling thinking that there is something seriously wrong with them. They may not have told too many people about the difficulties they are struggling with, perhaps because they are embarrassed. They might think that what they are dealing with is so unique that no one else has had this type of experience. Group interviewers can help members understand that the issues they are dealing with are felt by many other people. Members get to see that other people in the world (and even closer than that) are having experiences very similar to their experiences. The notion of universality—that a person is not a solitary being disconnected from the rest of humanity—can be a very powerful realization for clients.

Imparting Information. Many novice therapists run psychoeducational groups. Although these might not be fully considered "therapeutic," there is something therapeutic about receiving information. Therapists can overtly inform clients about the specific problem they are dealing with or might run a skills training group. They also inform clients about how they might get along with others more effectively. Because clients have come to therapy not quite knowing what is going on within themselves in terms of the problem, they become very relieved when they realize that the problem is something other people have experienced and that the therapist and other professionals have information that they can then receive and put into practice. This information might be suggestions of changing dietary, exercise, or psychological activities that they can put into practice to control, reduce, or eliminate the problem they are experiencing.

Altruism. One of the benefits of being a group member is that the client is a change recipient and change giver at the same time. Clients feel a sense of altruism when they realize that their contributions to the group can help someone else. They share information with other members, give supportive responses, and show that they care about the other person. People like to know that they are useful to someone else. By being an active member in the group, members realize that they are not only working toward their own positive change, but also that they are helping multiple members of the group.

The Corrective Recapitulation of the Primary Family Group. Since there are several other individuals in the group, there are enough other people so that a variety of relationships can occur. Many people entering groups have had an unsatisfactory family life (Yalom, 2005). The group can be seen as the corrective recapitulation of the primary family group. The group leader(s) would be seen as the parent(s) so the group member may relive earlier family patterns. By engaging with therapist and other group members, the individual is able to experience a more positive way of relating that did not occur in the client's family. The group interviewer would then be able to address these patterns.

Development of Socializing Techniques. People learn from one another through a process of socializing. It is the way that we learn rules of communication, proper decorum, and how we might be interacting in positive and negative ways. Group members are able to learn social skills from one another while the session is occurring. Since they are primarily interacting with each other for the duration of the group interview, they learn how they are coming across to other people and can then alter their own behavior so that they have more fulfilling interactions. Not only does the group leader give the client feedback as to how that client is coming across and interacting in the group, the other group members give this feedback. Clients are then able to see how a variety of people perceive and experience how they are coming across. They can then use this feedback to change the way they relate to others so that they can make better connections to others—within the group as well as with individuals in their nontherapy life.

Imitative Behavior. Besides gaining the benefit of feedback from others to help develop better socializing techniques, members are able to view how other people in the group behave. They may then imitate those behaviors they think are useful and productive. If a client sees how another member reacts calmly and considerately in a disagreement with another member, the client might then try to imitate that behavior. Psychologists discuss this in terms of social learning theory, where we learn how to behave by watching the actions of others around us. Perhaps the person whom group members are likeliest to imitate is the group leader (Yalom, 2005). This imitation may be most important in the early stages of the group development as it not only allows the new group member to learn how he or she might behave in the group, but also gives a guide to positive behavior.

Interpersonal Learning. One of the most important factors in group therapy is the interpersonal learning that occurs for everyone involved. The group can be seen as a social microcosm in which what is learned in the group can be transferred to interpersonal relationships outside the group. Since people live their lives in connection with others, learning how people get along with one another (and don't get along with one another) is important. In the group, clients will demonstrate the problematic interpersonal behaviors they have shown throughout their lives. They are then able to learn, via feedback from the therapist and other group members, what they are doing that is coming across to enhance or hinder their connections with others. Based on this interpersonal learning, they can then attempt changes to connect better with people inside and outside the group.

Group Cohesiveness. The group is a system in which each member comes together with others so as to function as a whole with the joint purpose of enabling positive change for each of the members. In this process, group members join together, along with the therapist, and develop a sense of "we-ness." Yalom (2005) related group cohesiveness to the relationship between therapist and client in individual therapy. It is the medium in which change happens. For a group to run effectively, the members need to trust not only the therapist, but also each other. Cohesive groups do not always have to be nice to one another, as a good group will have effective confrontations involved in the process. Yet, the group members feel a connection to one another and a sense of we-ness. By being involved with the group, members gain a sense of connection to other people. This connection is therapeutic. People have a need for belonging, which being a part of the therapy group helps to satiate.

Catharsis. The therapeutic factor of catharsis refers to an individual's being able to emote and experience it as therapeutic. The thought is that letting something out that has been building up will prevent it from getting worse. In group therapy interviews, the emoting of members allows the group to be vibrant and active. Catharsis comes about when clients trust the therapist and other members of the group so that they can open up and be themselves in the session. They will be revealing parts of themselves so that they are vulnerable. This vulnerability is usually not a part of their relationships outside of therapy. The group provides the context for individuals to be able to express themselves honestly and strongly. Yalom (1985) described the connection between catharsis and group cohesiveness, "Strong expression of emotion enhances the development of cohesiveness: members who express strong feelings toward one another and work honestly with these feelings will develop close mutual bonds" (p. 85). However, just emoting is not sufficient. People have to have some type of cognitive learning to go along with this expression.

Existential Factors. The final therapeutic factor, existential factors, concerns issues of morality and responsibility. Each person is responsible for his own behaviors. In the group interview, members are made aware that each and every action (behavioral, psychological, and emotional) is their own responsibility. They cannot pawn their own actions off on someone else. Although they can discuss their feelings toward someone else, they will need to take ownership of their feelings. In groups, individuals are confronted with their own actions (words and behaviors) and how they are making their own choices. They are not able to ask others what they should do, as the other members will not take on this ownership. Thus, people are confronted in the group with the fact that they are inevitably responsible for their own path. Further, they realize that they cannot run away from the pain of their lives and must learn how to confront and live with their pain.

Equality among Members

Group therapy is a unique context of interviewing in that it is composed of people who come to the group with varying levels of comfort in what they communicate, how they communicate, and how often they communicate. In any group, some members will be more vocal than other members. Some people may intimidate others. Some may annoy others. And others will get along with some members more than others. In group counseling, it can be problematic when one or two members of the group attempt to monopolize the time during the interview. Although the norm for group leaders is to spend more time trying to get group members to talk, there will be times when they will need to get members to talk less (Posthuma, 2003). A group member who is allowed to go through a whole session without talking is neither being helped as much as possible nor helping the other group members. Conversely, a group member who talks the whole session is not being helped with his interpersonal skills, as he is continuing to engage in problematic behavior. Effective group interviewers must help group members to change their relating patterns, toning down those who are overly talkative and bringing forth the voices of those who might be shy. This is not an easy endeavor as too much pushing for a member to talk or restraining another member from talking may upset either person and leave that person hesitant to participate in future sessions.

The group interviewer does not need to ensure that each member speaks for the same amount of time, but will inherently have a sense of who has been contributing to the group and who hasn't. It is the group interviewer's role to encourage participation from all members. An overtalkative member can be acknowledged for his contribution and then have that topic redistributed to a less talkative member. For instance,

> *Therapist:* Harold, you have been bringing up some very interesting points today. Joseph, you haven't said much today. I was wondering what your

Exercise 14.1

Pay attention to various groups you may encounter. They do not have to be therapy groups. They might be work groups, a group of friends, a sports team, or any other unit. Keep track of how much various members of the group talk or do not talk. What impact do you think each person's contributions have to the group? How do the members respond to each other when someone talks more or talks less?

reactions were to Harold's statement about him not thinking that there is enough confrontation happening in the group.

Process Instead of Content

One key to being an effective group therapist is to be able to discern between content and process. Jacobs, Masson, and Harvill (1998) defined group process as "the interaction and energy exchange between members and leaders—how the leader reacts to the members, and how the members talk to each other and the leader" (p. 33). Looking at group process is similar to looking at couple or family process, with one component that becomes more visible. Although good couples/family therapists will pay attention to what is going on between the people they are working with, they will also be focused on how they are part of the therapeutic system. However, this is usually not a primary frame for the therapy. In group therapy, this is even more central as therapists usually play a more inclusive role in the process. Group therapy tends to focus not only on how each of the group members interacts with one another, but also how each interacts with the group therapist and how the group members as a whole interact with the therapist. These interactions then become a more focal point of the therapy as opposed to what occurs in individual or couples/family therapy.

For group interviewers, being able to navigate the *how* of people's problems is probably more important than the *why*. Group therapists should pay attention to who in the group talks, who doesn't, who talks to whom, who avoids whom, and how often each person speaks to someone else. These observations lead to understanding interactional patterns that give group interviewers a better sense of how the group is functioning and thus how to work with the group to help each and every member of the group grow from the experience. One way to note process is to observe nonverbal behavior. The actions may give clues to certain themes that are pertinent for individual members, as well as dyads, triads, or other configurations of group members.

When clients in a group counseling interview begin talking content, they tend to start talking about the past. Group interviewers can then shift clients to focus on the process, which leads them to work more in the here-and-now. Group therapists help keep the group members focused on how what is happening in the group, at that moment, is impacting them instead of talking about past transgressions or problems.

Skills for Conducting a Therapeutic Group Interview

Core Competencies of Group Work

In 2000, the Association for Specialists in Group Work (ASGW) developed professional standards for the training of group workers. The clinical skills described are as follows:

Implementation of Group Interventions
1. *Knowledge Objectives.* Identify and describe:
   a. principles of group formation including recruiting, screening, and selecting group members
   b. principles for effective performance of group leadership functions
   c. therapeutic factors within group work and when group work approaches are indicated and contraindicated
   d. principles of group dynamics including group process components, developmental stage theories, group member roles, group member behaviors
2. *Skill Objectives.* Demonstrate skill in:
   a. encouraging participation of group members
   b. attending to, describing, acknowledging, confronting, understanding, and responding empathically to group member behavior
   c. attending to, acknowledging, clarifying, summarizing, confronting, and responding empathically to group member statements
   d. attending to, acknowledging, clarifying, summarizing, confronting, and responding empathically to group themes
   e. eliciting information from and imparting information to group members
   f. providing appropriate self-disclosure
   g. maintaining group focus; keeping a group on task
   h. giving and receiving feedback in a group setting

Conyne, Wilson, and Ward (1997) organized the ASGW's Training Standards into five clusters: defining group work, pregroup preparation, therapeutic dynamics and leader skills, research and evaluation, and ethics. Therapeutic interviewers who will be working with groups are encouraged to read over these standards and work with a supervisor who has expertise in group work.

An effective group leader will not only have a persona that works in conjunction with the group members, but also specific group leadership skills. Many of these skills are the same as the ones discussed in Part Two of this book, such as active listening, restating, clarifying, summarizing, questioning, confronting, reflecting feelings, supporting, empathizing, setting goals, giving feedback, disclosing oneself, and terminating. Some of the skills that are more particular for the group counseling context include interpreting, facilitating, initiating, suggesting, modeling, linking, and blocking. Skills such as protecting, linking, and blocking are also more commonly used in couples and family interviews than they are in individual interviews. The following section describes each of these skills further:

Interpreting. Group therapists tend to engage in a lot of interpretation of members' behaviors. This relates to the therapeutic factor of recapitulation of the primary family group. Therapists must be able to take what is occurring in the therapy room and make sense of it via the client's history. Some of this interpretation also occurs when the therapist is trying to understand the transference that might be occurring in the therapy room. Many group therapists find the notion of transference, wherein the client is relating (consciously or unconsciously) to the therapist or other group members based on a relationship with someone in their past relational field. This person is usually someone from the family-of-origin, such as the client's mother, father, or sibling. Therapists will then have to interpret the transference situation and bring it out into the open of the conversation of the interview so that the client can understand the patterns he is engaging in.

Facilitating. Group therapists must facilitate a conversation in which all members of the group feel comfortable enough to utilize the group to help them reach their goals. This comes in the form of utilizing the active listening skills presented in Part Two of this book and also demonstrating a therapeutic caring for the members. Therapists facilitate clients to be open in the group and to engage in the group process. If a member seems to be hesitant to disclose in the group, or to challenge and confront another member, the group therapist will facilitate that member's more active engagement in the group so that the group experience will be more useful for him.

Initiating. Group therapists will need to be able to initiate the group process and some of the activities occurring within the group. This skill is especially important in the beginning of the group process when group members, especially those who are first time group clients, are unsure of what to do or how to proceed. Therapists might give more directions in the beginning of the group, perhaps even calling on various people to engage in the group process. Once the group has started, members tend to take on more leadership roles, allowing the therapist to not have to initiate as much as she did in the beginning of the group.

Protecting. Given that part of the group process is an open forum in which members interact and sometimes challenge one another, there is the potential for harm to happen to a member's self-esteem. Group members are not trained interviewers or therapists. They are in the group probably because they are having some type of interpersonal difficulty. Sometimes when group members challenge other members, their remarks can come across more as an attack than as supportive confrontation. Group interviewers need to be cognizant of when a member's confrontation crosses the line and become an assault on another member. They will then need to protect that member if the member is not protecting himself.

Modeling.   As described by Yalom, one of the key therapeutic factors for groups is imitative learning. Since the main person group members will focus on to observe is the group leader, group therapists should learn how to be conscious of and actively behave in ways that can be used as a guide for the members of the group. Although people observe others all of the time and take from others what they idealize, therapists can proactively behave in the group interview in ways that they want clients to emulate.

Linking.   Group therapists should be aware of how the experiences of various group members overlap. Since most groups have people who are dealing with similar issues, therapists can help to connect people's struggles, resources, and pathways to solution to other group members' experiences. Thus, if one member of the group is discussing how he is having a difficult time opening up in the group, the therapist can relate that to how a second member is or was having difficulties opening up. This skill helps build on the group therapeutic factor of universality, wherein group members become connected to one another, each having similar experiences.

Blocking.   Because there are multiple individuals in the group interview, and each person has a unique personality, therapists must be able to allow certain client behavior to happen and prevent other behavior. Domineering group members hamper the group process as too much energy is taken to focus on them rather than all members of the group. The group then becomes more individually focused, on that client, rather than on all members. Therapists must know when and how to block members from being too overbearing in the group interview.

Effective Group Therapists

Just as learning how to become an effective individual, child, couple, or family therapist takes time, the same is true of the group therapist. It takes a combination of learning the specific skills and contexts of the group format with the personality of the therapist. Jacobs, Masson, and Harvill (1998) summarized some of the traits of an effective group leader, including "caring, openness, flexibility, warmth, objectivity, trustworthiness, honesty, strength, patience, and sensitivity" along with "comfort with oneself and others; a liking of people; comfort in a position of authority; confidence in one's ability to lead; and the ability to tune in to others' feelings, reactions, moods, and words" (p. 26). They further stated that effective leaders should have experience with individuals, experience with groups, good planning and organizational skills, knowledge of the topic, a good understanding of basic human conflicts and dilemmas, and a good understanding of counseling theory. However, therapists need to be able to understand how their own characteristics, traits, and styles are impacting the various members of the group.

One of the key therapist traits that is even more significant in the group interview than in the individual interview is the ability to be a leader. Since the group interview includes multiple people (usually somewhere between five and ten, but sometimes less or more than this), there is more chance for the interview to stray from its intent. Group members might become engaged in tangential or irrelevant conversations during the interview. For instance, if there is an upcoming political vote or sporting event (such as the World Series or Super Bowl), people can get engrossed in that conversation rather than the issues bringing them to therapy. The group therapist must be able to muster the group members into a unified whole, all working together toward a common goal: change.

Corey (2004) provided various personal characteristics needed for an effective group therapist: presence, personal power, courage, willingness to confront oneself, sincerity and authenticity, sense of identity, belief in the group process and enthusiasm, and inventiveness and creativity. The group interview is focused and channeled through the group interviewer, and thus the therapist's self plays a vital role in how the group functions. These traits do not magically appear; they take years of work.

One means of becoming an effective group leader is for the therapist to be a group participant in her own group therapy so that she can both see what it is like to be a group member and to gain the benefits of group therapy (Fehr, 2003; Yalom, 2005). By being a member in a group counseling process, the future group interviewer can get feedback from other people about how she comes across to others. This is an extremely important factor since therapy is based on the interpersonal realm where the person of the therapist and the person of the client come into contact with one another. The group therapist does not have to be perfect, but should be in a continual process of self-exploration and self-reflection (Corey, 2004). She should continually try to improve herself.

After a significant amount of time, group interviewers develop the necessary skills to move beyond the basics of group interviewing. Kottler (1994) provided some characteristics that make someone an advanced group leader. These include being more knowledgeable, faster, and more proficient. Because people who have been conducting group interviews have a vast amount of experience and have presumably learned what has worked and what has not worked, they are better able to handle both the common and rare occurrences in group interactions. Kottler also stated that advanced group therapists can think more abstractly, which helps to bring creativity to how they deal with new situations. Because they have conducted enough group sessions, they have developed a repertoire of helping skills they can use as their foundational base while they implement more advanced skills.

However, just because someone gains more experience does not mean that that person will become a better therapist. Becoming better entails learning from one's actions. It is an ideal that not only clients take what has occurred and build on it, but that therapists also do so. Thus, therapists are living what they are espousing. Sometimes, those therapists who have become very experienced may start to engage in practices that can be detrimental to the group therapy. Pitfalls, mistakes, and failures happen to all therapists in all contexts with all types of clientele. Therapists will hopefully take these occurrences as points of inquiry of how to grow rather than how to fail. In the group context, therapists will have plenty of opportunities to make mistakes and then to see how those mistakes can make them more effective therapists. Conyne (1999) wrote a whole book exploring how group interviewers can learn from their mistakes in group work. Kottler (1994) provided some potential areas of error for group interviewers:

- Verbal abuse and subsequent casualties are more likely to occur in groups than in individual treatment.
- The therapist has less control over proceedings and client behavior. Potentially more things can go wrong before the leader can intervene.
- The therapist has more control in influencing capabilities, a power that can be used for better or for worse.
- Confidentiality can neither be guaranteed nor enforced because other group members don't necessarily live by the same moral code that we do.
- Many group leaders practice without benefit of training, education, or supervision. There are no standardized criteria for acceptable qualifications. In the same city, a psychiatrist, psychologist, astrologer, palm reader, and prostitute can all label their professional activities as "group therapy."
- Because groups are such intense environments, the risks for each member are greater. Change and damage are accelerated.
- The screening of clients is frequently haphazard. Clients are often required to participate in the experience involuntarily.
- Dependency effects are more pronounced in groups.
- There is no licensure, certification, or regulation that can effectively enforce the practice of responsible group leadership. (p. 300)

Group therapists must use all of their skills and personal characteristics to navigate the abundance of various roles they have to fulfill. Group therapists function as emotional support, provide objective perspective, are gatekeepers for people potentially entering the group, serve as role models, are administrators, and help move the group along in its purpose by building morale, facilitating group interaction, and providing meaning to the group (Spitz & Spitz, 1999).

Group Leadership Styles

Just as there are many ways and styles to conduct a therapeutic interview with a child, adult, couple, or family, there are many different types of group leadership styles. There is a debate in the field of group counseling as to how active, directive, and structured the group therapist should be (Jacobs, Masson, & Harvill, 1998). Those group counselors working with short-term groups will probably find that they will need to be more directive and active because of the time restrictions (Corey, 2004). Jacobs, Masson, and Harvill (1998) expressed that, for the most part, group leaders should have an active style of leadership. This entails honing and utilizing the skills of initiating, blocking, protecting, facilitating, and linking. It is usually safer to be a bit more active with a group than passive, as a passive leadership style might allow the group to lose focus and become chaotic. The active leader can begin the group by employing more structure at the start, and then loosening the structure and how active and directive they are throughout the process of therapy. It is more difficult to move from more passive to more active.

Each group therapy interviewer will find her own personal style. It will probably take many group sessions and much training to find a style that one is comfortable with. Because one's group leadership style is based on one's theoretical orientation and how that meshes with one's personality, educational training and self-growth explorations are needed to be able to analyze what is occurring in and out of the session and whether that seems to be effective, not only for the clients but for self. Corey (2004) explained about developing a group leadership style, "What is most important is that you know yourself and develop a style that fits your personality" (p. 51).

Beginning Group Therapy Interviews

Getting off to a good start in the group counseling interview is extremely important. The beginning of the group therapy interview sets the tone for how that session, as well as subsequent sessions, will go. Clients feel out the therapist, along

Exercise 14.2 Leadership Style

Answer the following questions based on how you perceive yourself.

1 = Not at all   2 = Usually not   3 = Sometimes   4 = Usually   5 = Almost always

1. I like to be the leader in the various groups I'm a part of.
2. I like to sit back and be quiet in groups and let someone else take a leadership role.
3. I tend to tell people what to do when I am a group/task leader.
4. I get excited when I am the group/team leader.
5. When people in a group look to me for answers, I get very nervous.

Reverse score questions 2 and 5 (i.e., if you chose 4, then the reverse score would be a 2). Add up the score for all five statements (the range is from 5 to 25). Lower scores (10 or less) reflect a more nondirective attitude. Higher scores (20 to 25) reflect a more active and directive approach.

Reflection 14.1

In looking at Exercise 14.2, how much do you agree with your score? How flexible are you that you could move back and forth between a directive and nondirective approach? What strategies might you put in place for yourself to feel more comfortable with using various types of styles?

with other members, and judge how safe it is for them to open up in this multiple-person format.

Corey (2004) provided several suggestions for the group leader in beginning a session. The interviewer might ask each member of the group what they wanted to get out of the interview. If this is not a first session, therapists can ask about the previous session and see if people had comments or questions about it. They might also be asked about what type of progress they have made from the previous session(s). Instead of starting out focusing on the clients, group interviewers might begin the session by self-disclosing what they have been thinking about since the previous session. In this way, they model open communication.

All therapy groups should have a contract that establishes the rules and guidelines for everyone to follow (Fehr, 2003). First, punctuality is important. All members need to be on time since the beginning of many groups is a time for announcements. Anyone who cannot make a session should contact the group leader before the start of the group. The group leader should then inform the rest of the group. A second guideline is that all members hold confidential anything that is said in the group. Although the group leader cannot guarantee members will follow this guideline, she can highlight that discussing group issues to others outside of group can diminish the potential benefits of the group. Third, the group is a safe place to express oneself—whatever one is feeling. The group is not a place to constrict feelings and thoughts. Members need to come to group prepared to open themselves to express their thoughts and feelings as well as to be open to the honest thoughts and feelings of other people. This is one of the therapeutic keys to a group; it is interactive. Clients are forced to think about their own situations as well as take into consideration other people's. A fourth guideline is that group members should not socialize outside of the group environment. Group leaders can request that if a meeting between group members does occur outside of the therapy interview, the members then discuss that meeting during the group session. As an offshoot of this, the fifth rule is for group members not to engage in a sexual relationship with one another. If there is an attraction between members, it is better to use this as discussion material during the session rather than acting on it outside of session. The final rule regards payment. Although there is not a hard-and-fast rule of when payment occurs, group members should pay for the session on the day of the session, either before or after the interview. If they do not cancel within twenty-four hours, they should be charged for the session.

Group rules and group norms are not the same thing (Earley, 2000). Group rules refer to those specifications of behavior that are explicit and are meant not to be broken. Group norms are more socially created guidelines of behavior. Earley explained that there are two types of group norms. The first is prohibitions, which determine what members cannot do. The other type is positive norms, which determine the behaviors group members want others to engage in. Group rules are generally developed by the group leader, whereas group norms can originate from the group leader, the group, or negotiation between group and group leader. For example, a group rule can be that members who meet outside of session must discuss in session what occurred in their outside meeting. A group norm may be that members don't interrupt one another.

Conducting Group Therapy Interviews

Group therapy interviews usually last longer than individual therapeutic interviews. Whereas the average length of an individual interview is fifty to sixty minutes, group interviews last from one to two hours. Ninety minutes is probably the average for the group interview.

Group therapy interviewers should check in with clients around the midpoint of the interview to determine how the group clients are experiencing the session and to see if it is fulfilling their expectations (Corey, 2004). If the group members are displeased by how the session is progressing, the group leader can find ways to alter the session so that it can be more beneficial to everyone.

Rutan and Alonso (1999) provided several guidelines for group therapists in the conduct of the session including building hypotheses, taking time, noting the beginning, thinking in analogies, observing one's own affective states, keeping the presenting problem and family history in mind at all times, and formulating a summary. Each of these guidelines will be explained. Group therapists are able to develop hypotheses about each individual client as well as the group as a whole. They can then test these hypotheses out during the group and develop further hypotheses based on what occurs during the session. Therapists can also take their time during the beginning of the session so that group members can take a more active role instead of the therapist taking over and potentially stifling group process. Rutan and Alonso pointed out that group therapists should be extra alert during the very first moments of the session, "This is predicated on the notion that the very first group behavior often forecasts the group theme that will follow" (p. 75). Group therapists need to pay attention to analogies, meaning realizing that the importance of what happens in the group session occurs on multiple levels, the content and the process. By observing one's own affective state, the group therapist understands that she is a person who is being impacted by what is happening in the group. Group therapists should gain a sense of not only the presenting problem, but also the family history of each client in case it becomes significant in the group process. Lastly, these authors recommend that from the very beginning of the group session, therapists should be formulating their summary. This is because it allows the therapist to keep track of the themes occurring during the session.

As can be seen, group therapists have to think and understand what is going on at many different levels before making an intervention. A group therapist's interventions can be viewed on three levels (Spitz & Spitz, 1999). The first is the individual/intrapsychic. This refers to what is going on for each group member, separate from any other person in the group. The second level is the interpersonal/group. Group leaders pay attention to how group members are relating to one another (including the therapist) during sessions. The third level is the group-as-a-whole. Here, group therapists pay attention to the group identity and how that is impacted by what is occurring in the group process. Thus, group therapists are moving back and forth between each of these levels and keeping them all in mind before, during, and after the group interview.

Ending Group Therapy Interviews

Just as the opening moments of a group counseling interview are important for how that session functions, the ending of the interview is very important. Group leaders should not abruptly end a session but should allow enough time for the processing of what occurred during the session. This will bring the session, and the themes discussed in it, to some type of conclusion.

Corey (2004) provided several guidelines for a group therapist when ending a group interview. Group therapists do not have to wrap up an issue when they wrap up a session. There can be therapeutic benefit by having closed the session while clients are still thinking about a particular topic. This gives them something to ponder during the time between sessions. The following therapist response demonstrates how clients can be primed to think about an unresolved discussion:

> *Therapist:* As we can see, our time for today is just about over. It seems like we were in the middle of a very important discussion about putting oneself out there and being vulnerable. This would seem like a very good thing for us all to think about this week, and we can pick up next week focusing on this topic.

Group leaders should also summarize what occurred during the session, including the process of the session and the themes discussed. When closing a session, group interviewers might want to have each member talk about what they got out of the session and provide comments and feedback to anyone, including the therapist. Group leaders might also end the session by giving their reactions to what happened during the interview. For group leaders, when they provide feedback, they should remember to give members positive feedback. Leaders should be cautious though that one person does not receive more feedback than another person, as members may become upset or jealous. Group interviewers can also end the session by asking various members what they would like to talk about for the next session. Another strategy that can be used is for leaders to discuss with each member how he or she can take what was discussed and learned in the session into action during the week.

Termination in group therapy interviews can be more problematic than in other types of therapy interviews. Each group member has not only developed a rapport with the group leader(s), but also with most other members of the group. The loss involved in the termination process is increased because there are multiple people from whom to disengage. Further, there is a loss of the group as a whole, which has been a place of safety and learning. Since the group has provided clients with a place of safety, they may feel scared that they will not have this forum in their nontherapy world. Therapeutic interviewers can use the last session(s) with group members to process the growth that they've made throughout the course of therapy and help them to develop ways to continue in their self-growth and exploration once the group has ended.

Special Issues When Conducting a Therapeutic Group Interview

Co-therapy

Therapeutic interviewers in agencies, private practice, or residential settings work with a variety of clients and a variety of other therapists. Sometimes they will work together with therapists as consultants on each other's cases. They may also work together at the same time with the same client(s) to conduct the therapeutic interview. This is referred to as co-therapy. Roller and Nelson (1991) provided the following definition of co-therapy, "A special practice of psychotherapy in which two therapists treat a patient or patients in any mode of treatment at the same time and in the same place" (p. 2). More than any other type of therapeutic interviewing, therapists who work with groups tend to engage in co-therapy. Although it has not been demonstrated that co-therapy is more effective in groups than a single therapist (Kline, 2003), there are distinct benefits. When therapeutic interviewers engage in co-therapy, unique issues come to the forefront. This section addresses some of the benefits as well as potential pitfalls of co-therapy.

Advantages of Co-therapy. Roller and Nelson (1991) explained that there seems to be a lack of information on how therapists relate to one another. Many books, such as this one, discuss how the therapist can enter into a relationship with a client, but little literature has addressed how two therapists can relate to one another for the purpose of being therapeutic for other people. This relationship becomes essential for what occurs during the interview.

Co-therapy brings with it some unique possibilities not present in individual therapeutic interviews. Corey (2004) provided some of the advantages of conducting group therapy interviews with a co-therapist:

- Two people can give the clients the benefit of their life experiences and insight.
- Co-therapists are able to complement one another. Shapiro (1999) explained that co-therapists may be able to supplement one another, where they can provide those skills the other therapist may not excel in.
- Co-therapists can act as role models for clients in how two people can relate to one another.
- Co-therapists, when one is male and one is female, may re-create some of the dynamics of the client's parental situation.
- Co-therapists can serve as a way of providing feedback for each other.

- Co-therapists can learn from each other, just as group members can learn from each other.
- Co-therapists can work together to be able to view more of the processes going on in session. While one therapist is talking to group members, the other therapist can be viewing the group process.
- Because there are two people leading the group, if one person has to miss the session, the group can still operate because there is at least one therapist present.
- Group clients are able to get feedback from more than one therapy professional.

When alone, therapists might have a hard time handling a client's emotionality or processing what occurred during the therapy session. Co-therapists may have an easier time dealing with the hostility that sometimes arises in groups (Shapiro, 1999). By having more than one person working with the group, more potential ideas, strategies, and hunches are developed (Yalom, 2005).

Co-therapy is also an excellent means of training. Many beginning therapists, while in their training programs, begin to provide therapy through means of co-therapy. When a novice therapist is paired up with a more experienced therapist, the novice therapist is able to ease into therapy. This is especially important because most training programs are not geared for teaching group therapy. Students may have one course on group therapy, but have primarily been trained to work with individuals. Thus, they can observe a more experienced therapist while also having the freedom to begin to be a group leader. Case Scenario 14.1 presents how co-therapy can be an anxiety-reducing process for the therapist.

Many co-therapists work together extremely well and are quite effective with most of the clients they work with. What are the factors that lead to a co-therapy team being effective? Roller and Nelson (1991) found the following six factors to

CASE SCENARIO 14.1

For the first group therapy session I ever conducted, I was paired with an older and more experienced therapist. I was twenty-two years old and was fairly new in my master's training program. The thought of running a group on my own was pretty overwhelming. When I found out through my practicum site that I would be working with a co-therapist, I was relieved, as the full burden of the session was taken off of my shoulders. Although I knew that I wasn't going to sit back in the group session and not say anything, I could rely on my co-therapist to be the primary therapist of the group. Before the first session, she and I met and discussed what we wanted from the first session for the clients who were going to be in the group as well as ourselves. I talked to her about my nervousness, and we discussed what we expected from one another. We then checked in with each other before and after each session to ensure that we were on the same page as well as processing what we thought was occurring in the group.

be important: complementary balance of therapist skills, compatibility of thera-pists' theoretical viewpoints, openness in communication, equality of participa-tion, liking each other as people, and respect. What was interesting were two factors that were not important in the success of the co-therapists: the professional discipline of each person and their ages. Co-therapists do not need to be in the same counseling area (i.e., clinical psychology, marriage and family therapy, or mental health counseling) and they do not need to be around the same age as the other therapist. Sometimes, having a wide age disparity between the therapists is beneficial as they will be more aware of generational issues that might be occur-ring inside the group.

Co-therapists tend to work together in such a way that they take complemen-tary roles (Yalom, 2005). For instance, one may be the more provocative one while the other is more conciliatory. Or one might be more directive while the other does more observing. Shapiro (1999) explained that a benefit of co-therapy is that it "may allow blind spots in one therapist to be counteracted by the other's insight and perceptions" (p. 54). One way to aid in making the co-therapy productive is for the therapists to engage in dialogue once the session has ended. By doing this, they can exchange ideas of what occurred in the session and discuss any potential pitfalls that arose or might arise and then work them out between themselves or develop a strategy to use with the group.

Disadvantages of Co-therapy. Having a co-therapist is not always advanta-geous. Clients may attempt to pit one therapist against the other. Although this could be used as discussion material in the group about how that client might be conducting himself in the same manner with his own family, it puts extra pressure on the therapists to function properly. There is a distinction between co-therapists that make mistakes and then learn from them and dysfunctional co-therapy teams, who are usually unaware of their mistakes or may not acknowledge that they are being problematic (Roller & Nelson, 1991).

Co-therapists might also not be on the same page when it comes to what they want to do with the group. When therapists begin to challenge one another, they open up the possibility for disagreement between them, which can then be seen by the clients. If the co-therapists have such a differing leadership style that their incompatibility begins to infuse itself into the session, the group may become divided between the two group leaders (Corey, 2004). As stated previously, co-therapists have the advantage of modeling effective interpersonal relating to one another. However, if they do not get along with one another, they might inadver-tently model negative interactional patterns.

Roller and Nelson (1991) explained that many of the co-therapy dilemmas can be viewed through the five Cs: competition, countertransference (a therapist reacting, unconsciously, to a client based on the therapist's past relational experi-ence), confusion and lack of communication, lack of congruence between co-therapists, and codependency between co-therapists. As we have discussed repeatedly throughout this book, therapeutic interviewers are human beings and have all of the marvelous attributes that make people unique while also having their fallibilities. One of these is that they may desire to be appreciated and respected. When conducting co-therapy, some of the fanfare and idolization is lost because someone shares the limelight of being the therapist. Some therapists will have difficulty, knowing that one or more clients favor the other therapist. Even before this point, they may struggle with each other to be the better therapist. Group therapists have the possibilities of experiencing countertransference not only with the clients in the group, but with each other. Although some counter-transferences are useful in the group situation and some are not (Fehr, 2003), group therapists may have a tougher time distinguishing when the countertransference is being obstructive because they have to consider their reactions to not only one client, but to many people (including their co-therapist). Co-therapists should be able to help each other work through this dilemma, but problems come when they are either unaware of it or do not act on it and keep silent. Confusion comes into play when co-therapists are not clear in their communication with each other about what they see going on in the group and the direction that they want to take it. This confusion between therapists then filters into the group and leaves the clients as confused as the therapists. This confusion can be due to a lack of congru-ence between the co-therapists. Each therapist may think that she is able to work collaboratively with someone else and be flexible. However, teamwork is a very difficult thing to do, especially in a setting such as a group interview in which each therapist wants to use her skills and knowledge base. Sometimes, the theoretical orientations the duo is working from do not mesh together. Therapists may believe that they can overcome this chasm, but sometimes this only leads to further diffi-culties. Lastly, therapists may develop a co-dependency in which they rely, more than is normal, on each other. This leads to the potential for stagnation and lack of growth. A positive co-therapy situation is one in which each therapist challenges the other in a supportive framework to grow as both a person and a therapist.

One way to help prevent the possible negative situations that can occur in co-therapy is for the two leaders to get together between sessions so that they can process any of their differences along with coming up with a plan of action for the next session. Roller and Nelson (1991) explained that after co-therapists become aware of the difficulties happening between them, along with how the difficulties are impacting them, the clients, and the therapy process, therapists can either problem solve between themselves or use an external consultant to help break the impasse. If there continues to be an impasse for the co-therapists, it might be best if they agree not to conduct therapy together.

Confronting the Leader

Therapeutic interviewers know that the skill of confrontation is an extremely ben-eficial tool when used in an appropriate and time-sensitive manner. In group ther-apy, challenging is a key skill therapists and group members use to push other group members to deal with current individual or group issues. However, group members may be more likely to challenge and confront the group therapist than would occur in other interviewing settings. Thus, therapists should be aware of this potential and the reasons group members may do so.

One potential reason for a group member to confront the leader, especially in the first meeting or two of the group, is because of resistance or fear (Spitz & Spitz, 1999). Clients may challenge the leader on the leadership style she is using (e.g., how active or passive she is), preferring certain group members over others, not caring enough, or a variety of other issues. Effective group leaders will understand the confrontation not as an attack on themselves, but as a message about the other person's interpersonal state. Instead of becoming defensive, the group therapist can highlight the group member's doubts.

> *Harold:* Why are you focusing mainly on Joseph and not me, or the rest of the members?
>
> *Therapist:* Harold, my job is to focus on everyone in the group, as every member of this group is important. It seems that you are very concerned about whether this is the right group for you. That is a normal reaction in a first session of a group.

Confrontation of the group leader by the members is also common during the early phases of groups. After the initial uneasiness of group members in the very beginning of the group, they then begin a reactive phase in which they begin to be more active and start taking risks in the group (Fehr, 2003). These risks may be directed at the group leader. This might come via testing limits and trying to take control of the group. Fehr recommended that group leaders be patient as the group members' actions of uniting against the therapist will pass, forming a greater bond between group members, which then allows them to move forward in the group process.

Ethics and Group Counseling

Most of the ethical issues affecting therapeutic interviewers who are conducting individual, couple, or family interviews are the same when conducting group counseling interviews. However, there are some unique ethical issues that the group counselor will have to deal with. Whereas in individual sessions, the issue of confidentiality occurs between the two people, in group counseling there are other people who are privy to a client's self-disclosures. Therapists are still obligated to break confidentiality when certain conditions arise (i.e., the client is potentially harmful to self or others, they discuss child abuse, and so forth). In the group, members have to trust each other not to self-disclose to people not in the group what was said and who said it. Although therapists cannot control what group members do, they can try to reduce the possibility of group members talking about other members outside the group. There is a common saying in group counseling, "What occurs in the group stays in the group." Corey (2004) recommended that the group leader periodically throughout the course of the group remind individuals about not telling other people about specific group members. They can do this in a variety of ways. Here is one possibility:

> *Therapist:* I just want to remind everyone that everything that we talk about in this group is confidential. I am governed by ethical rules that prevent me from telling other people what we talked about. As you know, there are a few instances where I do have to break this confidentiality; when someone talks about having committed child abuse, or seriously going to harm oneself or someone else. However, you are not held to those same standards. But one of the important things about groups is trust. Each of you should trust that no one else is going outside the group and talking about what you said. You should also do the same. Thus, all of us will keep everything that happens in this room in this room. What questions are there about this policy?

Summary

Conducting effective group therapy interviews requires therapists to build on their skills of working with individuals so that they can work on many different levels. They do this by encouraging the use of various therapeutic factors that occur in groups. Group therapists need to understand the content of the conversation, but more importantly the process of the interactions. This then needs to occur for each member in the room. Too much focus on content bogs down the session. Group therapists must also understand multiple process experiences; those for each member, those between group members, and those between the group and the therapist. By having a co-therapist, group leaders are better able to work with group members in their pursuit of positive change.

Exercises

1. Watch either a live or videotaped session of group therapy. Pay attention to the group therapist(s). What characteristics do they employ that you find effective? Ineffective? Discuss with classmates how these various characteristics play a role in the effective functioning of the group.

2. Role-play a group therapy interview with your classmates. Take turns being the group leader and attempting to keep the focus on group process rather than content. Audiotape this and make sure you get a lot of feedback from your instructor about how you utilized your therapy skills in the group context.

Office-Based Therapy

Interviewing in the Therapist's Domain

Most therapeutic interviewers conduct their sessions in an office, where they work on a permanent or semi-permanent basis (perhaps they share it with a few other people if working in a group practice). Novice therapists in practicum or internship placements may have to use any of the available offices at the agency they are working in; however, they are still conducting therapy in a place where the office is considered to be the primary domain of the therapist and the client is coming into it as a guest.

This chapter discusses many of the issues surrounding office-based interviewing. These include the setting of the office and waiting room, seating arrangements, dealing with telephone calls between sessions, and issues of safety. Given that much of office-based interviewing occurs through those therapists in private practice, the chapter ends with a discussion for those therapeutic interviewers working in this context. This includes a discussion of how managed-care impacts the therapeutic interview. This chapter is designed as a basic guide for beginning therapists to help them become aware of some of the basic issues involved in providing therapy in an office setting.

Orientation to Conducting a Therapeutic Interview in the Office

Office-based therapeutic interviewing offers a unique context for providing therapeutic services. From the point when clients first enter the office, the ambience for the therapeutic interview is being developed. Therapists must consider not only what and how they behave during the interview, but also the physical setting and the rules around the session. Each aspect of the interview from the neighborhood, to the building, to the waiting room, to the specific office, and to the specific therapist may impact clients in various ways. This section briefly describes how therapists can structure the office setting for optimal effectiveness.

Waiting Room

The first thing clients notice when they come for a session, besides the neighborhood and the building, is the waiting room. The waiting room cannot just be put together on the fly. Clients will be spending time, before the session, in this space; thus, it can aid in preparing them for the interview, or conversely, it can negatively affect them.

The waiting room should be designed so that clients can comfortably sit without being viewed by people outside the office. This is to help protect their privacy. Given the stigma against those who go to therapy, therapists should do what they can to not put clients in an awkward position.

The décor of the room should be appropriate for the profession. There should not be provocative pictures or art on the wall. Imagery that feels serene is a safe bet. Music, if played, should offer relaxation, not excitement or tension. Therapists might want to have an assortment of magazines (*Time, Architectural Digest, Better Living, Sports Illustrated*, and *Consumer Reports*, to name a few) that appeal to a wide range of interests available for their clients. The chairs and/or couches in the waiting room should be purchased for comfort and then style.

The Office

For office-based practice, the physical setting can help to enhance the experience for clients. Therapists want the office to feel comfortable for clients without being overly stuffy or too sparse. Clients are coming in with serious concerns and how the office is decorated can impact them. Therapists might have nice but neutral artwork for the wall. Furniture should be comfortable. The type of furniture the therapist chooses depends on where the office is located. In an agency setting, the furniture will probably be functional, but not overly fancy. If the office is in a private practice in a higher socioeconomic neighborhood, therapists should decorate with more expensive furniture.

Fehr (2003) recommended that therapists who work in an office should not use fluorescent lighting as it can feel cold and potentially lead to negative effects on the clients. The office should be clean and comfortable. Clients may be put off by a therapist whose office is in disarray. A messy office leads to the potential notion that the therapist does not have his own life in order and thus may not be that helpful to someone else. As in the waiting room, artwork should be calming, such as nature scenes. Therapists might have a mild room deodorizer to ensure that the room smells nice. Caution should be taken however. Deodorizer that is too powerful can negatively impact some clients, especially those who have allergies.

Therapists should consider not having personal pictures of their family out in the open. This is common practice in many other professions, but in therapy it opens the door to more focus on the therapist's life. However, as with most every-

I was working in a child outpatient program. We had designated play therapy offices that had various games and toys. My office, since I was doing a lot of family therapy, didn't have these items for the children. However, on my desk I did have a picture of my cat. I purposely had this picture there, not only for my enjoyment, but also as a means to connect with the children and adults. I found that many children would go over to look at the picture of my cat and ask me about her. I would answer their questions and then ask them whether they had a pet. If they did, this was an avenue for joining. If they didn't, I would ask them about what they thought of animals, which was their favorite, and other lines of inquiry in order to connect with them. The picture gave the clients a sense that I was a real person and gave me a topic to connect with the clients. I didn't worry if they weren't "cat people" as this would then be something we could talk about and use to discuss how people are different and that we can accept people when they have likes and dislikes that are different from our own.

thing, there are exceptions to this. Case Scenario 15.1 explains how small personal items in a therapy room can be used to join with clients.

Seating Arrangements

The question of where people will sit in the therapist's office is an interesting one. Many therapists allow clients to enter the office first and take a seat where they feel most comfortable. They might then use this information of where the client sits as information about that person, their interpersonal relating style, and how it might be related to the presenting problem. Other therapists may gesture toward a certain seat for clients to sit in, while others may have a chair that is clearly for the therapist. Whatever the arrangement of the room, therapeutic interviewers should consider their own placement so that they are closest to the door for easy access in case of an emergency (DeSole, 2006).

Therapists should have enough chairs in the room to work with the configuration of clients they will be serving. To have only one couch and a chair for the therapist while working with a family of four is nonfunctional. Having too many seats in a room might also be problematic. The individual client coming into an office where group therapy occurs can leave that person feeling distant, losing the sense of security and intimacy.

Although the therapist may have a desk in the office, it is recommended that he not sit behind it with the client seated on the other side. This may be appropriate for a business interview, but hampers the therapeutic interview. The desk puts distance between therapist and client. This distance may lead to a reduction in the connection between the two parties. It sets up a hierarchy in which the therapist is an untouchable professional, which dampens their ability to make connections with one another.

Interruptions

Therapeutic interviews are usually thought of as sacred time. Once the process gets started, it should not be interrupted lest the interruption damage the alliance and the process of what has been occurring in session. This notion will be challenged in the next chapter when therapeutic interviewers are in the client's home; however, for office-based therapists, interruptions should be held to a minimum.

For those therapists working in an agency or group practice, there should be some type of sign that distinguishes when a session is in progress and when a room is free. Case Scenario 15.2 highlights what happens when interruptions occur.

Another type of interruption is the telephone call. Today, many people have cell phones, which tend to ring at inopportune moments. Just as in a movie theater where, before the movie starts, there is a public service ad for people to shut off their cell phones, therapeutic interviewers can ask clients to shut off their phone. Some clients might protest, if they have it in case of an emergency. However, most clients will agree to shut it off. Therapists will also have to ensure that they turn off their own phone. If the therapist took a call during the session, besides disrupting the flow of the session, clients could take this to mean that they are not important. The therapeutic interview is a context in which the expectation from all parties is that the time designated for the interview is held only for the interview and that the parties stay engaged in it, without interruption, for the duration of the interview.

When therapists work in an agency, they may have a phone with a button that prevents calls from coming through and goes straight to voice mail. This is the best thing to do so that a ringing phone does not interrupt the session. In private practice or agency settings, there might be a receptionist who will take all incoming calls. There will probably be an arrangement whereby the therapist is not inter-

---

CASE SCENARIO 15.2

I was working in a community mental health center that had approximately twenty therapy rooms. One day I was having a therapeutic interview with a client, and we were approximately halfway through the interview. The client was beginning to talk about some serious material, potentially thinking about leaving her husband. Without a knock or any warning, a student-therapist opened the door and entered the room with a client. The student-therapist stated that she had reserved the room. I excused myself from my client, walked the student-therapist outside, explained that I was in the middle of a session and had reserved the room already, pointing to the "Session in Progress" sign that was on the door. I then went back to my session. I apologized to the client for the interruption. It took several minutes for us to get back to the place in the interview that we had reached before the interruption. After the session, I talked with the student-therapist who had interrupted us. She apologized, stating that she had signed up for a different room and mixed up the room numbers.

rupted in session unless it is a life-or-death emergency. If there is no receptionist, therapists should have calls forwarded to a voice mail or a service so that they can devote their full uninterrupted attention to the client during the session.

Telephone Calls between Sessions

Office-based therapists, who are getting paid only when they have a session with a client, will need to determine how they will handle the phone call from a client who is having an emergency (or what may seem like an emergency to the client at the time). These phone calls, although they may only last five minutes, sometimes fifteen, sometimes thirty, require the therapist to take time away from other activities. Therapists will need to have some type of procedure in place for clients who are having a serious emergency (i.e., someone's life is in jeopardy). However, many clients call the therapist with "emergencies" that are not really emergencies, when the client is very upset about a situation that has occurred.

If the therapist does talk with the client over the phone and the client finds this useful, and the client does not have to pay for that "mini-session," the client may then be reinforced to engage in this type of behavior in the future. Clients may then begin to call more often and at times and days inconvenient for therapists (such as evenings or weekends). Therapists can then potentially become resentful of the client's behaviors.

These types of interactions can lead to what is known as dependency phone calls (Bender & Messner, 2003). This is when the therapist has talked for extended periods of time to the client on the phone and then, either consciously or unconsciously, encouraged the client to continue to use the phone contacts. This then further increases the possibility the client will become dependent on the therapist and begin to call more often, usually at the first sign of any discomfort or anxiety. This becomes problematic because clients do not learn how to trust themselves and develop appropriate coping mechanisms to handle life's difficulties. They then are even further connected in needing the therapist rather than learning how to be more autonomous.

Most clinicians agree that there should be a set time for the interview and that unless a serious emergency exists, therapists should not encourage phone calls outside of session. Some therapists inform their clients upfront that they will charge for any therapy that is conducted over the phone (this would exclude phone calls about cancellations or other such issues). By working upfront, therapeutic interviewers set some parameters around the relationship. However, some therapists believe that when a client pays for therapy, they are not necessarily paying for an individual session but for the therapist's participation in that therapy, regardless of when and how often it occurs.

Therapists probably do not want to completely eliminate the option of clients' calling them between sessions. This is for the purpose of ensuring that if the client is in a serious emergency in which the client's life, or someone else's, is in jeopardy, the client does receive services. Therapists in private practice should have some type of emergency crisis line associated with their practice. Some therapists may have a cell phone clients can call. Therapists can explain to clients during the first session what would constitute a crisis. Other therapists have answering machines that state that if it is an emergency, the client should hang up and call 911.

No-Shows, Late Arrivals, and Late Departures

In working in private practice and agency-based work, the issue of a client not coming to the session (no-show) is quite problematic. Clients will no-show on the therapist for approximately 25 to 40 percent of sessions. This percentage is much lower in home-based therapy, where excuses such as the car breaking down or someone being sick do not have the same justification.

In private practice, if a client does not show, the therapist is left with one hour of time he had set aside for that person. It is a very different situation in a medical office where there may be one to five other patients scheduled at the same time. This is why it is very important for the therapist to be up-front with clients about the consequences of missing an appointment. Most therapists have a 24-hour cancellation policy. If the client does not cancel within 24 hours of the appointment, she is charged for that appointment. For some reason, people do not seem to hold ensuring that they attend the therapy session as high in regard as they do appointments for medical doctors, dentists, or other medical practitioners. In order to prevent clients from not showing up for appointments, therapists can engage in a variety of behaviors to increase the client's participation in therapy. Just as medical doctors call clients a day or two before the appointment as a reminder, therapists (or staff members working for them) can call ahead as a reminder. One caveat to this practice is that therapists still need to maintain confidentiality. Thus, they should not be overt in who they are when leaving phone messages or talking to third parties. Kelley (2006) provided some alternative strategies for increasing client attendance including giving them an appointment card at the end of each session for the next session. The appointment card can even have the therapist's no-show policy on it. Therapists can also give homework or some other type of assignment at the end of sessions—projects that are to be read or completed for the next session. Therapists might also periodically give the client a satisfaction questionnaire to assess how useful the therapy is for them. If the therapist finds that the client is dissatisfied somehow, this can become a topic of conversation between the two to figure out how to change this and increase the therapeutic alliance.

Besides completely missing a session, some clients will come late to the session. Therapists have to decide how to handle these situations. Some therapists will not see the client, in order to help the client learn about the importance of being prompt. This may depend on the types of issues the client is working on. For instance, those clients who are dealing with issues of procrastination or control may be prime candidates for this type of action, as it can be used in a therapeutic manner. Other therapists will tell the client they have the rest of the hour to do whatever work they can in that short time frame. And then there are other therapists, depending on whether they have another client booked after that appointment, who will still give the client the full hour.

The first time the client is late, it is recommended that therapists work with them for the rest of the allotted time for the session. During that time, they should have a conversation with the client about what will occur the next time the client is late. Meeting with clients for the full hour, when the client is very late, potentially sends a negative message to the client and reinforces problematic behavior. The client may begin to come late to sessions and expect the full time from the therapist.

Skills for Conducting a Therapeutic Interview in the Office

As with providing therapeutic interviewing in any context, the primary skills of active listening and accurate empathic responding are the same. All of the skills presented in Part Two of this book are applicable in the office-based interview. This section discusses two main issues of how those skills will be used perhaps a bit differently in this setting: hierarchy and termination.

Hierarchy

When clients enter the therapist's office, they are putting themselves on another person's turf. Although therapists may try to develop a collaborative relationship, there is still a distinction in hierarchy between the two parties. The therapist (or agency) is paying for the rent, electricity, water, air conditioning, and other expenses of the office. The client is the guest of the therapist. As such, the dynamics are different from what they would be if the therapist were to conduct the interview at the client's home (see Chapter 16).

Therapists are encouraged to engage in practices that attempt to decrease the inherent hierarchy in the relationship so that it is more collaborative. This will aid in the development of a positive therapeutic alliance. Perhaps the first way to do this is to ensure that the therapist joins with the client. As discussed in Chapter 4, a balance must be struck between setting the parameters of the session and making a connection with the client.

Therapists are ultimately in charge of the session. Although they ask for input from the client, they cannot get around being perceived as being in a higher position than the client. This is more prominent when the therapist has a private practice, since the client will be coming to the therapist and then paying the therapist for the services.

Therapeutic interviewers can attempt to decrease the hierarchy clients may feel by giving clients as much input into the therapy process as possible. The client can have a say in what day or time the interviews are, how far apart the interviews are spaced, what topics are discussed, and who should come to the sessions. By keeping in mind that therapy is about and for the client, therapists send a message to the client that they are there *for* the client, thus decreasing, to some degree, the disparity in hierarchy.

Termination

For office-based therapists, termination means the end of meeting with a client and the beginning of finding new clients to work into the schedule. Therapists should consider all of the issues of termination presented in Chapter 7 when working in any setting of therapy. However, termination does not have to be only about endings. Therapists should also use termination as a way to maintain clients or gain new clients.

Given that the therapist's job is to have the client, as quickly as possible, not need the therapist's services, the private practice therapist is in an odd position. It is difficult to gain new clients into one's practice. Although therapists do not want to keep clients coming back for therapy when clients don't need it, therapists do want an active client base. When terminating with a client, therapists can do two things to help both the client and themselves. First, they should make sure the termination is a positive experience (Grodzki, 2000). When clients leave the therapy process having had a good experience, they feel good about the changes they have made and will more likely continue with those changes in the future. They will also be more likely to reenter therapy in the future. If they had a positive experience with a specific therapist, they will tend to go back to that therapist if they ever want therapy again. Thus, therapeutic interviewers can maintain clients over long periods of time, even if there are large gaps of time between interviews. Second, when the clients have a positive experience upon termination, they are more likely to refer the therapist to people they know. Word-of-mouth is a very powerful means of gaining new clients. Satisfied clients may tell friends, family, or other professionals who might refer clients for therapy (for instance, lawyers or doctors) about their positive experience, helping the therapist to develop a positive reputation in the community.

Special Issues When Conducting a Therapeutic Interview in the Office

Safety

Therapist safety is of paramount importance during the therapeutic interview. Many times, therapists are alone in the interview room with clients and are vulnerable to being harmed by the people they work with. Approximately 40 percent of all psychiatrists have been physically attacked by patients (Tardiff, 1995). The rate for other types of mental health professionals is probably somewhat lower, as many of the clients who attack clinicians are dealing with a severe mental health issue, such as schizophrenia or some type of personality disorder. However, this does not take into account the higher percentage of therapists who are verbally intimidated by their clients.

Safety can be viewed on multiple levels including material, physical, and psychological. Material safety concerns the therapist's possessions that might be damaged or stolen by clients. For instance, a colleague of mine who was working in a group home for troubled adolescents had the keyhole to her car door damaged by one of her clients who was angry after a specific therapeutic interview. Therapists should put any personal items such as wallets, purses, and other valuables in a locked desk drawer. Other items such as client files should never be left out for clients to have access to.

Physical safety deals with bodily harm. Clients can become agitated during the therapeutic interview. For those that might want to discharge their anger immediately, the therapeutic interviewer is the most visible person available. Therapists should have some type of safety plan in case a client becomes potentially dangerous during the session. This includes ensuring that they are sitting closest to the door, having a quick dial button on their phone that goes to the front office, security personnel, or the police, and an agreement with other therapists and staff in the office to be conscious of potential problems.

Psychological safety focuses on the mental harm some clients attempt to cause the therapist. This usually happens through intimidation strategies. Clients may say or behave in ways to try to show the therapist that they could, if they wanted to, hurt the therapist. This behavior usually occurs in residential settings or with court-ordered clients.

Safety is always a concern for therapeutic interviewers, regardless of the context the interview occurs in. Psychiatric hospitals seem to be the location with the highest rates of patient violence (Turns & Blumenreich, 1993). In residential and agency settings, clients might be there because of more severe behavior; however, there are other people around who can help. In home-based work, therapists are on their own (unless conducting co-therapy) and will need to take necessary precautions. For online counseling, the issue of safety has more to do with protecting client information than with personal safety. In office-based counseling, safety is an issue because therapists are usually alone in a room with the client. Therapists should arrange their practice so they are not alone in the office (not including the specific therapy room) with clients, especially at night or on weekends. This can sometimes be difficult if the therapist is in a sole practice instead of a group practice. Case Scenario 15.3 explains how a therapist was put in a very uncomfortable position with a client because she was alone in a private practice setting.

Given the possibility of violence occurring during the therapeutic interview, therapists should be observant of possible warning signals of client violence, as well as having a strategy for handling an outburst. Some client predictors of violence include "a history of violence, intoxication, active threats, access to weapons, social isolation, and suicidal ideation" (Eichelman, 1995). In psychiatric hospitals, therapists might be trained on how to use physical restraint on the client or work with someone who can administer pharmacological restraint (such as tranquilizers). Therapists should have a behavioral intervention plan that consists of a

========================== **CASE SCENARIO 15.3**

> A colleague was working at a group private practice, renting space from the group. The practice was located in a strip mall. She was working with a male client who was bigger than she was and who, during the course of therapy, had hinted about being attracted to her. One night, after the interview ended, she walked the client to the front door. She was also leaving the practice and when she opened the front door she noticed that the light was out in the walkway of the building. Further, there were high hedges so that people in the parking lot could not see the front door of the practice. The client walked her to her car and did not try anything sexual or violent. She felt so uncomfortable, however, that she did not work with clients there again at night or when no one else was there.

strategy of what to do in case of patient violence, such as contacting colleagues or having a staff member contact the police (Eichelman, 1995). Therapists are encouraged to talk with supervisors or colleagues at the first hint of discomfort based on a client's demeanor or verbal and physical threats.

The Business of Private Practice

Almost all of the therapists-in-training that I encounter, when asked what they want to do once they complete their graduate training, state they want to go into private practice. They say this before they have learned what is entailed working in or developing one's own private practice. The private practice context is not the most appropriate place for all therapists, particularly those who come from a more research-oriented graduate program (Forman & Silverman, 1998). These authors described the characteristics it takes to succeed in private practice:

> To succeed as a private practitioner you must be entrepreneurial, ready to take financial risks, able to work without supervision, survive in isolation, have a high tolerance for ambiguity, have a support system, have sufficient savings to cover living costs for six months or longer, be confident in your clinical skills, have a referral network, possess a standing in the community as a competent professional, have the ability to handle lack of structure, be comfortable without a regular paycheck, be a self-starter, be organized about records and finances, and be knowledgeable about the local market. (p. 3)

Thus, private practice is not as simple as many people believe. It is a business like all other businesses and takes time, energy, patience, and money to run.

Private practice allows therapeutic interviewers a sense of autonomy they will not have in an agency or residential setting. In in-patient facilities, most staff members have set times and days they must come to work. They have a limited number of vacation days, sick days, and other such amenities. Private practice therapists have independence in that they can set their own hours, days, and vacations. However, they do not have the fixed income and must fend for themselves when it comes to having medical insurance, malpractice insurance, and other benefits that a company provides.

Therapists conducting agency-based or home-based therapy usually do so through a community program where they do not have to negotiate the cost of sessions, how the client will pay, and what happens if the client cannot pay for a session. For office-based therapeutic interviewers, especially those who are in private practice, the issue of setting fees and billings becomes integral. Avoiding money matters is the biggest stumbling block for therapists when they are developing a private practice (Haber, Rodino, & Lipner, 2001). Most novice therapists have difficulty in talking with clients about how much a session costs. What can be even more harrowing is when clients begin to haggle with the therapist about the fee to see if it can be negotiated. Some therapists operate on a strict scale where each and every session for every client will be a set fee. Other therapists work on a sliding fee scale so that those clients who have the finances pay the full fee while those clients who are not as financially well off have reduced fees. Therapists should decide how they will work financially with clients and become comfortable in talking about fees and whether or not those fees are negotiable.

New therapists who are still trying to gain experience may not consider that their services are worth the going rate of counseling sessions in the area. Thus, they may be hesitant to ask clients for a certain fee. Other therapists may think they deserve an extravagant fee; especially if they have student loans they are paying off. The development of what the therapist's fee will be and whether they will negotiate with clients based on financial need is multi-factored. It depends on the therapist's financial situation, the therapist's training level and experience, the costs of the location where the practice is, and what the standards of fees are in the area.

The desire for making money is healthy and appropriate. Therapists should not feel bad about accepting payment for their services. Therapeutic interviewing is a skill and expertise that takes many years to develop. People who work hard to get the education and training they need to perform professional services deserve to get remunerated for their services.

Therapeutic interviewers should have open conversations with their clients before the first session ever begins. These conversations ought to include the parameters of the therapy including fees, orientation, and typical time frames in which the therapist works. This would then be covered again in the informed consent form. One of the things therapists do not want to do is blind-side clients.

Reflection 15.1

In thinking about what you would charge for a session, what do you think one hour of your therapeutic services is worth? Why did you choose that amount? How do you think you would feel if a client told you that your rates were too high?

Clients could be potentially damaged if they work with a therapist in a first interview, develop rapport, feel a connection, begin working on goals, and then get hit with a bill that is so out of their price range that going to therapy would be a significant financial hardship. This puts clients in a tough position of not coming back to therapy, paying for therapy when it is beyond their means, or getting into a negotiation (and potential battle) with the therapist about the fees. For instance, the therapist can state, "My fee is _____ for a one hour session." He can then gauge the client's reaction. If the client seems to be put off by the amount, the therapist, if working from a sliding fee scale, can introduce that possibility: "That is my regular fee. For clients who are not financially able to afford that fee, we can negotiate a fee that would be in your price range." If therapists do not work on a sliding fee scale and the client states that the fees are too high, therapists can either do pro bono work or refer the client to someone else who has fees in the client's range.

Once the fees are decided on, therapists are then put in the very awkward position of billing. Collecting payments from clients is another area in which most therapists are not trained. In graduate schools, therapists learn about listening skills, theoretical orientations, various types of therapy configurations (for instance, couple, family, group), and the ethical and cultural issues associated with the field. However, very few learn the business side of therapy. When placed in the situation of running their own practice, many therapists find it to be not only uncomfortable but also overwhelming. Grodzki (2000) provided private practice therapists with six criteria for the development of fees: therapist's vision of the practice; adhering to one's business goals; market forces; perceived value; the therapist's time line; and professional courtesy. Grodzki also listed several criteria therapeutic interviewers should *not* use when setting fees: anxiety, guilt, zero-sum game mentality, love, anger, and identity questions. Each of these does not fit within a business plan mentality. It will probably take therapists time to adjust from a helping mentality to a business mentality in that the business of therapy is helping others.

Given the context of the therapy relationship in which one person is self-disclosing very personal, upsetting, and highly emotional issues, people can forget that it is, at its core, a business relationship. Having clients in the office crying about the dilemmas of their life and then asking them for money for having talked with them about their problems can seem to be a very awkward practice. By asking for payment at the end of the session, clients may feel cutoff as if their pouring out of emotions and the therapist's empathizing and listening to them was just an act for the money.

In order to get around this potential pitfall, therapists might ask clients to pay upfront or bill them some time during the week or perhaps at the end of the month so the end of the session is not hampered by having to deal with an exchange of money. Some therapists, if the client is having a difficult time with payments, will shorten session length. For instance, if the normal fee is $100, and the client can only pay $50, therapists might explain to the client that they will work with them and provide 30-minute sessions, where each session will cost $50.

This is an opportunity for clients to obtain the desired services while also working within their financial situations.

One of the biggest difficulties in billing comes when clients do not pay the bill. This may be because clients forget to bring their checkbook or let the therapist know they are having a financially difficult time. Therapists are then put in a position that, if this continues, they are providing services and not getting payment for them. Therapists then have the potential for developing animosity toward that client.

For those office-based therapists who are working in their own private practice, developing a clientele so that enough clients are coming in to offset the costs of having the office (that is, rent and electricity) is a difficult endeavor. Many therapists haven't learned how to network, get onto insurance panels, or where and how to market oneself. Grodzki (2003) explained that one of the most important things for developing a private practice is for the therapist to develop a business plan. This business plan has three parts; preparation, building blocks, and finishing touches (Grodzki, 2000). Preparation occurs when an assessment of support is made, a business vision is created, and an entrepreneurial mind-set is developed. Next, a building blocks stage occurs where the therapist implements strategies and actions. The finishing touches stage helps position the therapist's practice in the community so that others are aware of the services and the quality provided to clients.

Developing a private practice puts a lot of stress on therapists. It is to therapists' benefit to market themselves as well as possible to bring in referrals and clients. Private practice therapists need to network and connect with colleagues, as they are the most frequent means of generating new clients (Haber, Rodino, & Lipner, 2001). One of the primary traits this entails is confidence (Beigel & Earle, 1990). Private practice therapists have to have confidence in themselves as both therapist and entrepreneur. They become the face of their practice, necessitating their being able to relate to individuals and organizations while providing a positive persona to prospective referral sources. Those therapeutic interviewers planning on going into private practice are encouraged to take classes, read books, and consult with other private practice therapists and business consultants on how to develop an effective private practice.

In office-based therapy, as in all contexts of therapy, the connection with clients is perhaps the most important factor leading to effective treatment outcomes. Grodzki (2000) provided four client connection strategies: developing client loyalty; developing client advocacy; developing client enthusiasm; and developing a value-added aspect to the practice. These value-added aspects refer primarily to the outcomes that clients have gotten from that particular therapist.

One risk that many private practice therapists have is becoming burned out. Not only do therapists have to deal with the emotional turmoil discussed by clients in session, but also they have to deal with their own struggles of making a business work (as well as any of their own personal problems). Because many clients have difficulty coming to sessions during normal business hours/days since they are working themselves, therapists may have very early morning, evening, or possibly weekend sessions. The more therapists work during nonregular business times, the more likely they are to become disconnected to their friends and family. These are the people who serve as their support systems. Further, therapists tend to try to fill every hour of their working days with clients. Therapy is the type of job where breaks in the day are extremely beneficial. Thus, besides a lunch (or dinner) break, therapists working in office-based settings are encouraged to schedule 15-, 30-, or 60-minute breaks throughout the day. During this time they can get caught up on necessary paperwork, meditate, take a walk, listen to music, or engage in some other activity that helps them recharge their batteries, not only for their next clients but also for themselves. If they are not able to recharge between sessions and between work days, therapists will probably not function at their optimal level of performance.

Managed Care

The field of psychotherapy seems to have changed in the past ten to twenty years. Chambliss (2000) explained, "In addition to adapting to the new demands for measurable outcomes, flexible service delivery, and efficiency derived from the influence of MCOs (Managed Care Organizations), therapists must sort out a wide variety of discrepant etiological models and conflicting treatment theories and methods" (p. 7). Many therapists in office-based private practices have been working more and more with clients who carry insurance. Clients who come to therapy through managed care are becoming the primary type of client (as opposed to cash pay clients). When working with managed care clients, therapists have a lot more issues they need to focus on than with clients who are strictly cash pay.

One issue when working with insurance companies and managed care is that of confidentiality. In a private practice setting, with a cash pay client, therapeutic interviewers need only to break confidentiality when the rules of confidentiality need to be broken (for example, potential for self-harm, child abuse, court order). When working with an insurance company, therapists need to provide the company with certain client information, such as a diagnosis and treatment plan. Therapists will need to have the client sign certain forms (release of information) in the first session, giving them permission to share client information with the insurance company.

Therapists are also constricted by how many sessions they can have with an insured client. The number of sessions an insurance company allows varies from company to company. Some state that a person can have only three sessions while others allow over twenty. Once the client has exhausted the allotted amount of sessions, therapists have to petition the insurance company for extra sessions, explaining the necessity of the extra sessions. Some managed care companies prefer having the sessions spaced out longer than once per week. Others do not suggest the time frame between sessions, just an overall maximum number of sessions. Therapeutic interviewers working with managed care have to decide the frequency of the sessions, based on what will be most efficacious for the client.

One of the main problems that occur because of the limited number of sessions some managed care companies allow is that the number of sessions will run out before the therapist and client have attained the treatment goals. Therapists cannot just abandon a client who is in need because of payment issues. They will have to determine the best course of action for the client. The therapist can continue seeing the client or work with the client until an appropriate referral is made.

Given the time-limited nature of sessions allowed by most managed care companies, brief therapy models work well in the treatment of clients coming through this source. Therapists who are going to be working through managed care should gain extra training in several of the brief therapy approaches to see how they can integrate the principles into their practice to help their clients as well as they possibly can and still satisfy the guidelines of the insurance company.

Since most managed care companies operate from the medical model (Davis & Meier, 2001), therapists need to be very familiar with the latest edition of the DSM. Therapists should discuss the process of diagnosing with the client, and when they have formulated a diagnosis, they should discuss what this means to the client. Since the diagnosis will be on file with the insurance company and in the permanent record of the client, clients have the right to know what that diagnosis is.

During the first session, therapists should talk with clients about how therapy is impacted by the managed care company. This does not need to be a negative conversation, but one that clearly stipulates what the parameters are. These are things such as billing, co-payments, confidentiality, session limits, and treatment planning. For therapeutic interviewers working with managed care, the first interview or two may be spent collecting all of the necessary information to develop a treatment plan for the managed care company's utilization review (Davis & Meier, 2001), including the following information: symptom description; risk; drugs and alcohol; psychosocial and mental health history; medications; mental status exam; and diagnosis. This is the type of material that was presented in Chapter 10.

Once an understanding of the client's situation is developed, along with a sense of the client as a person, the therapeutic interviewer can tailor the treatment for the client. Chambliss (2000) explained, "'Tailoring' refers to specific ways of customizing treatment approaches to 'fit' the unique needs, cognitive and emotional styles, and treatment expectations of the patient" (p. 185).

Therapists working with managed care must focus on outcomes. They do not have the luxury of a cash-pay therapist of not having to justify to an outside body what type of treatment they are delivering, why they are using that treatment, how long the treatment is taking, and the outcomes of that treatment. These are things therapists working with managed care have to consider. One of the recent pushes in the field, and especially for those working with managed care, is empirically supported treatment (Chambliss, 2000). These are treatment approaches that have been shown to be effective, through research studies, with specific populations or treatment issues. Empirically supported treatment has become one of the fastest growing areas in the field of therapy, and thus, therapeutic interviewers should consider whether it is relevant and useful to their practice.

Summary

Office-based therapeutic interviewing entails an understanding of the process of a client's experience inside and outside the therapy room. Therapists need not only to consider their therapy skills, but also to plan for designing the physical setting and the procedural operations of the office practice so clients are provided the most beneficial experience possible. Office-based practitioners usually find themselves walking the line between therapist and businessperson. Having a thorough understanding of the business aspect of therapy helps the private practice therapist in maintaining a functional office. This helps prevent potential anxiety about a business that is not running smoothly. Therapists working through managed care must understand the managed care organization's stipulations for treatment and be conscientious about following through on all paperwork and treatment guidelines.

Exercises

1. Interview several therapists who are in private practice. Ask them how they got started in private practice, what they charge as fees, what types of clients they see, and what tips they have for someone just starting out.

2. Working in student groups, brainstorm a design for a private practice office. Develop a rationale for the type of furniture, placement, wall colors, art work, and so forth. Present your design to the rest of the class. Discuss with one another the differences in the designs and strategies.

16

Home-Based Therapy
Interviewing in the Client's Domain

Home-based interviewing has been a part of the field of helping in the United States for over one hundred years. In the very early years of social work, before the field was even known as social work, helpers were called "friendly visitors." These individuals would go into the homes of people in need and bring necessities such as food and clothing. During the early and middle parts of the twentieth century, therapists went into the home for a one-time evaluation of a client's family. Late in the twentieth century, when a professional entered someone's home, it was usually to determine whether abuse or neglect had occurred and whether a child should be removed from the home. Today, home-based therapy is becoming more popular as it allows many individuals who might not otherwise receive services an opportunity to work with a mental health professional. This chapter addresses therapeutic interviewing in the client's home and details some of the practical skills and challenges of working in this context.

Orientation to Conducting a Therapeutic Interview in the Home

The Clientele

Most home-based work happens via family treatment as opposed to individual or group treatment. For some clients, it makes more sense to work with them in their homes rather than at an agency or private office. Boyd-Franklin and Bry (2000) stated, "Home-based family treatment offers a rare opportunity to observe family interactions in vivo, and it provides significant advantages over office-based family treatment" (p. 37).

Home-based work also tends to happen with those individuals and families about whom there was a complaint or allegation that children in the family have been harmed in some manner (that is, abused, neglected, or witness to violence). This might lead one to believe that since home-based therapy usually happens with court-ordered cases or severe problems, that it would not be as amenable to success. This is not the case. Yorgason, McWey, and Felts (2005) found that home-based family therapy made significant improvements for families. It can be a very effective means of working with special populations dealing with serious issues impacting the whole family.

Home-based therapy tends to occur with individuals and families who are in the lower realm of the socioeconomic ladder. This is something important to keep in mind in terms of attire, level of language, and hospitality. Home-based therapists tend to dress more casually than office-based therapists. Having someone come into their home with a tie or formal dress can be off-putting for clients. However, having someone come into their home with flip-flops, shorts, and a t-shirt doesn't give the sense of professionalism. Thus, home-based therapists should wear something comfortable yet casually formal. For male therapists, khakis and a polo shirt seem to be appropriate.

The Programs

Therapists in private practice tend not to conduct home-based therapy sessions. Practically, it is not feasible for them since they would be losing out on potential earnings because of time constraints and the amount they could charge for sessions. It usually takes about thirty minutes to get to a client's home and then thirty minutes to return. This is all dependent on location, time of day, and traffic. Therapists in private practice doing home-based work would only be able to have half the client load (or perhaps even less) as their office-based colleagues. Further, most clients receiving home-based therapy are toward the lower range of income. Thus, most home-based work occurs through agency settings that are grant or federally funded so clients can receive services for free or very reduced prices.

With the passage in 1980 of Public Law 96-272, the Adoption Assistance and Child Welfare Act, the federal government made a push for keeping families intact. Various family preservation programs were developed to work with families who were at risk of having one or more children removed from the home or who were in some type of crisis situation. Programs such as Homebuilders and Intensive Family Preservation Services started to emerge in rapid succession in the 1980s and 1990s. These programs tend to be staffed by entry-level therapists, since they are federally funded and cannot pay much to their employees. Therapists working in the programs tend to have a low caseload, perhaps between five and ten families. This allows them to spend extra time with the families and meet with them several times per week.

Families are seen for short durations, usually from one to six weeks. Most home-based sessions last between one to two hours. The length of each session and the frequency of sessions are designed to be able to work quickly with the families to stabilize the crisis situation. Many times, therapists will work with home-based clients one to three times per week.

Advantages of Home-Based Therapeutic Interviewing

Developing programs in which therapy is provided in the home makes sense on many levels. Since the issues these families are dealing with are severe, families usually need multiple weekly sessions, perhaps for extended periods of time. Home-based therapists must adjust their normal expectation for what a session is when they are working with clients in their homes.

Home-based therapy allows some clients who would not be able to access office-based sessions the therapeutic interventions they need. Those without cars, alternative transportation, or other practical issues such as not having the extra hour or two needed for traveling to a therapist's office will not have to worry about how to get to the session. They will also be more comfortable since they are on their own turf. This is important since the families are usually referred to treatment by some agency that is concerned about the family's functioning.

By taking the time to go to the client's home to conduct the therapeutic interview, the therapist is sending a message to the client that he is important (we have this idealized image of the family physician making house calls). Not many professionals take the time to go to clients' homes. The therapist's entrance into the family's home marks the interview as important. It also shifts the roles of therapist and client so that the client is now the host and the therapist, the guest.

For home-based therapists, entering into clients' homes leads to the possibilities of accruing additional information, besides the content and process of what might happen during the therapy interview. The family's home is ripe for observations, beginning from the neighborhood where the family lives, the decorations, the cleanliness, all the way to living arrangements. Case Scenario 16.1 describes how observing the client's home can give the therapist information about how the client functions that the therapist might not have in an office-based session.

CASE SCENARIO 16.1

I was working with a family consisting of mother, eighteen-year-old daughter, and sixteen-year-old brother. The family was referred to the agency because the brother had been getting into serious trouble at school and in the neighborhood. Upon entering their house for the first time, they showed me around. They lived in a one-bedroom apartment where the mother and daughter slept in the same bed and the brother slept in another bed in the same room. This allowed me to conceptualize the notion of space and privacy (or lack of it) this family was living with. By being in the house and actually seeing the living arrangements, I was better able to conceptualize how the family members were not able to have a sense of individuality and privacy. This was then something that we discussed in sessions; how could each member, given the conditions they had, be able to find their own alone time and allow the others to have theirs. This was further understood in terms of developmental stages, in which this late adolescent male had to share close living quarters with his mother and sister.

Being in the client's actual environment allows important people in the family's life opportunities to participate in sessions. Individuals in the client's social circle (for example, grandparents, cousins, and close friends) who might not have attended an office-based session might be at the house where they can aid in the therapy. There are also times when friends, neighbors, or other family members will pass by the house. Given the problem situation and the client's relationship to these other individuals, they might be utilized to partake in the therapeutic conversation (given the client's desire and agreement to have them involved).

The home environment is also more palatable for some individuals who might feel stigmatized by seeking services in a professional's office. They will not have to walk into an office that has some type of information demarcating it as a therapist's office. They will also not have to sit in a waiting room where other people might notice them. When the therapist goes to their house, there is no sign on the therapist's car stating what service they are providing; thus, there is greater anonymity.

Challenges of Home-Based Therapy

Although therapeutic interviewing as a whole is difficult work, home-based therapy may be even more so. Boyd-Franklin and Bry (2000) explored several challenges in conducting home-based work including "resistance," angry clients, family conflict, and "multiproblem" families. Given that home-based clients are referred to therapists usually because of some type of abuse, neglect, or violence, they tend to be forced into therapy rather than willing individuals who solicited the therapy. As a whole, the families may be in the precontemplation, contemplation, or preparation stages. Further, individuals in the family may differ in terms of what stage of readiness for change they have reached. Therapists will need to be able to understand each member's level of motivation for change and work with all of them to help the family move forward. Since many home-based interviewers have little training specific to this context (Cortes, 2004; Sprengle, 2000) and are isolated from colleagues, they may not fully know what to do when various situations arise.

One of the primary issues that occurs in the home-based context but not in the office is that of distractions. These might come in the form of telephones ringing, clients doing their laundry or cooking dinner during the session, or neighbors knocking on the door. Nichols and Schwartz (2007) explained that it is only after the home-based interviewer makes a connection with the client(s) and develops rapport that the interviewer can request that the client diminish some of the distractions in the home (for example, loud music from the radio, ringing phones, or a dishwasher). Christensen (1995) found that several of the therapists she interviewed had trouble dealing with all of the distractions occurring in the home and went so far as to request that the families meet in the office so they could get a rest from the distractions. This situation is more difficult for the therapist than for the client. Therapists need to learn how to conduct therapy sessions under less than

=========   **CASE SCENARIO 16.2**

I worked with a woman and her ten-year-old son, conducting the sessions in their home. They lived in an apartment complex in a very poor neighborhood. Their home was a one bedroom apartment with the kitchen and living room combined. The couches were very old, stained, and full of holes. Upon my arrival in the home, the mother asked me to sit down on the couch. I did so and a cockroach crawled out from between the cushions. During the course of the interview, several other cockroaches could be seen crawling around the home. For me, this experience highlighted the notion that I needed to learn how to adapt to a family's environment so that the client/family would become comfortable with me.

ideal conditions. Case Scenario 16.2 provides a picture of how these conditions might be uncomfortable to work in.

Being in their own home allows clients to be more spontaneous and genuine in their behavior during the interview. Family interactions can be quite pronounced, and the family may attempt to draw the therapist into its problematic process. Therapists can attempt to avoid this induction by working with a co-therapist while conducting home-based therapy (Nichols & Schwartz, 2007). A potential problem occurs when clients feel as if the therapist is not a guest but is an imposition to them. Although clients may feel more comfortable in their home, they can also feel more of a sense that an authority figure is coming into their private world and imposing sanctions on them.

Adams and Maynard (2000) interviewed therapists and supervisors who engaged in home-based therapy. They found that some of the main issues these individuals faced in providing home-based services were crisis/safety issues; multiproblem families; sexual abuse; single-parent families; drug and alcohol abuse; severe mental illness; adolescent development; and therapist demoralization. The therapists stated some apprehension when it came to how to handle a crisis situation in the home and how to deal with severe mental illness. They were sometimes overwhelmed by the severity of the problems.

Skills for Conducting a Therapeutic Interview in the Home

Characteristics of Effective Home-Based Therapists

Home-based therapeutic interviewers need all of the characteristics of effective interviewers presented in Chapter 3. However, being in the home context leads to their needing certain additional skills to be effective. It is a setting the therapist has probably not been trained to work in. It takes someone who is adaptable, as she will need to transfer the skills she learned from her training in office-based practice to the home.

Home-based interviewers should be mature (Wasik & Bryant, 2001). This is an interesting situation since they will probably be at the start of their careers. However, emotional maturity is built more on the personality rather than age. Home-based therapists will be interacting with individuals and families, usually who are in crisis, in a place where some of the normal boundaries of therapy are blurred. They will need to be able to walk the line of casualness and formality, which can be thought of as "professional friendliness" (Reiter, 1999). In this approach, they need to be friendly enough to quickly develop a positive therapeutic alliance, yet not so informal that the client doesn't view them as a serious professional.

Lindblad-Goldberg, Dore, and Stern (1998) listed the following core clinical competencies for home-based therapists:

1. Maintaining a systemic perspective
2. Maintaining professional boundaries within a collaborative relationship
3. Being effective on someone else's turf
4. Making the most of crises
5. Encouraging positive change and competence
6. Assessing with complexity yet focusing treatment with simplicity (p. 132)

For many home-based therapists, they have to learn "on the job." Those practicing in this context should be able to handle ambiguity and be accepting of chaos. The home-based interview is not as structured as the office-based session, requiring the home-based therapist to be able to handle the wider variety of situations that might occur.

Home-based therapists usually have training as office-based therapists, and thus, office-based and home-based therapists should not have different personality characteristics. McCain and Day (1999) found no differences in the personal or interpersonal characteristics of those people providing office-based versus home-based therapy. Unfortunately, home-based therapists tend to be looked down upon by office-based/private practice therapists (Woodford, 1999). Hopefully, given the importance of home-based therapists, who work with some of the most severe cases, the field will begin to fully appreciate these therapists. This might be difficult in a capitalist society in which prestige is based in large part on the amount of income that someone makes. Home-based therapists are probably on the lower end of the salary scale.

Becoming a Home-Based Therapist

Since most home-based therapists were originally trained in office-based models, a transition is needed when they begin to work in the home. A model of the transition from clinic-based to home-based therapist has been developed (Snyder & McCollum, 1999; Thomas, McCollum, & Snyder, 1999) that explains the progression of therapists learning to do in-home therapy. The first process is familiarity whereby home-based therapists gain greater information about and social intimacy with the clients. Therapists then develop a challenged view of therapy. Their learned views of therapy, based on an office-based model, do not fit their experience of working in the home. They mainly feel that their boundaries with clients are challenged, including issues of hierarchy, confidentiality, and the timing and pacing of therapy. These differences then raise therapists' anxiety. Once the initial anxiety wears off, novice home-based therapists begin to reformulate their views by redefining some of the main concepts of therapy, developing strategies for dealing with their anxiety and disorientation, and accepting their role in the home where they cannot change everything. When these therapists reformulate their view of therapy, they experience lowered anxiety. Further, they find that their clinic-based therapy also changes, as they become more personal with their office-based clients.

What to Do in the Home

Although how each therapist operates in a home is greatly informed by that person's theoretical orientation, there are some general guidelines all therapists can use, regardless of model. Berg (1994) provided several pointers for the therapist conducting a home visit:

1. Therapists should be casual and act as if they are accepted in the home, as the family will take cues from the therapist.
2. Therapists should use everyday language in a conversational manner, trying to use positive instead of negative words.
3. Therapists should use their own judgment and intuition. This entails being respectful toward the client(s).
4. Therapists should use themselves as a tool during the therapeutic interview.
5. Therapists should maintain a positive view of their client, from before the first interview begins until the last interview.
6. Therapists should pay attention to each and every member of the family, from children to parents.
7. Therapists should find ways to compliment the parents about their parenting.

All of these pointers are designed to assist in the development of a positive working relationship with each member of the household. The better the relationship, the more the family members will commit themselves to the therapy process.

In terms of the practical skills home-based therapists might use, Berg (1994) suggested the following:

1. Therapists should make an appointment to go over to the house instead of showing up unannounced. Because many home-based therapists operate through an agency that has been asked to look after the family, an inherent power differential exists. Therapists should do whatever they can to help empower the clients. Letting clients know that the therapist understands that they are in charge of their house is one way to do this.
2. Upon entering the client's home, the therapist can find something in the house to compliment the client about. This might be artwork, floral designs, or some type of collection the family has.

3. Given that many families have family pictures displayed around their house, therapists can ask questions about the various pictures. These are good sources of information, including who is in the family, vacations the family may have taken, and people who are important to the family who might not live in the house.

4. By being in the family's home, therapists gain access to information that would not normally be readily available in an office-based visit. Therapists can find something in the home in which the client is the expert. By asking questions to the client about something the client is very familiar with, such as something the client made or a hobby, the therapist is expressing to the client that the client has resources and is productive.

5. Therapists may want to consider establishing a set time and day of the week for having the therapeutic interviews with the clients. This allows for the therapy to become a fixed point in what might otherwise be a very hectic and chaotic life.

6. Safety is one of the most important concerns for home-based therapists. If the therapist does not feel safe, the interview should not occur. The therapist can discuss with the client the safety concerns to try to figure out ways to alleviate them. More will be discussed later in the chapter about safety issues in the home context.

7. Because this is not the office setting, the therapist does not have as much control to prevent possible distractions, such as people knocking on the door, the telephone ringing, or tasks of the house needing to be accomplished. Therapists can use these distractions, however, as a way to better understand and connect with the clients.

Home-based therapists can help the therapy process along when they adhere to all of these guidelines. Therapists who feel a need to control everything and be able to thoroughly plan a session may find that they have a difficult time conducting home-based interviews.

Utilizing the Home Environment

Being in the home leads the therapeutic interviewer to not only have a different relationship with clients (clients are in more of a position of authority than they would be in an office-based session), but also allows the therapist to use aspects of the client's home or occurrences in the home as opportunities to both join and conduct therapy. As in other contexts of therapeutic interviewing, joining is one of the most important skills, as it leads to the development of a productive therapeutic alliance. In home-based therapy this is perhaps even more important, since most client families receiving home-based therapy have abuse/neglect issues, are court-ordered, and/or have severe issues they are dealing with. Johnson, Wright, and Ketring (2002) agreed that the therapeutic alliance was very important in home-based therapy. Interestingly, in their study, it was most salient for fathers (55 percent), then adolescents (39 percent), and then mothers (19 percent).

Since the process of joining is so important in the home-based context, therapists should be constantly vigilant for possible joining opportunities. Reiter (2000a) described three areas home-based therapists might use to join with clients: the physical environment; interactive games; and food and drinks.

The Physical Environment.   A person's home is both a safe haven and a display for other people. The pictures, furniture, and objects in the home are for the enjoyment of the people living in the home as well as their visitors. Each object, the arrangement, and the décor are all information therapists can use to get a better sense of the client and to then join with the client.

When therapeutic interviewers enter a client's home, a multitude of possibilities in the home can be used to make a connection with the client. However, therapists are cautioned not to force themselves through the home. If the client offers to give a tour of the house, the therapist can accept, but therapists should not request this. If they do, they put themselves at risk of being considered a member of a social service agency rather than a therapist.

Therapists can ask clients about various pieces of furniture or artwork since many people display their collectibles. This can then become an excellent opening for discussion. Case Scenario 16.3 explains how this can happen.

Interactive Games.   Most home-based therapy cases involve either a child or the whole family, including one or more children. When in the home, children have at their disposal the full range of toys and activities they own. Therapists can join in with clients as they play their various games as a way of not only connecting, but also perhaps even being therapeutic.

Play therapy can occur in an office or in the client's home. When working with a child in the child's own home, therapists can see more clearly what typical play is like for the child. Further, the interaction between the parent and the child becomes an important point of observation, as therapists can understand the family dynamics better.

Most games that children have are designed for two or more players. Therapists can work with the child by playing these games and talking about the current concerns at the same time. Case Scenario 16.4 describes how a therapist can use a game to first join and then as a therapeutic change technique.

CASE SCENARIO 16.3

I was working with a family of father, mother, and twelve-year-old son. Upon entering the house, I noticed that the theme throughout was cows. There were cow-print pillows, cow clocks, cow porcelain figures, cow dishtowels, and cow paintings. I asked the family who the cow lover in the family was. Father and son both stated it was mother. I was then able to connect with her by asking her how she got into cow collecting. I was also able to connect to the father and the son by asking them about their thoughts regarding having so many cows in the house.

CASE SCENARIO 16.4

I worked with a family consisting of a mother, five-year-old son, James, and six-month-old son. The five-year-old son was the identified patient; mother claiming that he was too anxious and did not handle rules well. When I arrived at the house on the first interview visit, James asked me if I wanted to play Uno. Uno is a card game where the object is to get rid of your cards first by placing them down on a pile based on the number of the card or the color of the card. I agreed to play a game of Uno with him as this was a nice ice breaker for him to get to know me and for me to get to know him, while also engaging in an activity that he found enjoyable. While playing, we were able to talk with one another and get to know each other a little. After two rounds, I noticed that James would change the rules of the game so that he would not lose, which he called "house rules." As a therapeutic ploy, I stated that we would work based on the list of rules that came with the game. James became very agitated and upset. I was then able to reflect back to him his frustration and his desire to be able to have things the way he would like. Thus, playing the game was a way not only to connect, but to begin to make therapeutic interventions.

Food and Drinks.   When therapists enter a client's home, they become the guests of that client. Most people are good hosts and will try to make the therapist comfortable in their home. They may make tea or coffee or ask the therapist what they can get her to drink. They may even put out snacks or invite the therapist to partake in a meal with them.

Most home-based sessions happen during the late afternoon or early evening. At this time many family members are preparing meals or getting ready to sit down to eat. Home-based therapists conduct sessions in kitchens, dining rooms, and living rooms. Therapists must weigh a decision of asking clients to stop what they are doing in preparation or consumption of the food with having their undivided attention on the therapy session.

The acceptance or denial of an offer of food and drink can be critical on how the therapist is or is not accepted into the family context. For many people, having someone share in food or drink is a very connecting ritual. For thousands of years, food and drink have been used as a way to bring people together in a cordial atmosphere. There are romantic dates, which usually include some type of food/drink (a coffee or dinner date), business meetings over lunch, and weddings or birthday parties with food and drink (and cake). By accepting a soda, water, lemonade, or other such drink, the therapist lets the clients know that she appreciates their hospitality.

Collaborative Hierarchy

When therapeutic interviewers conduct the session in a client's home, some of the rules of therapy change. In office-based sessions, clients are on the therapist's turf. In home-based therapy, the therapist is on the client's turf. Therapists should defer to the client for the main rules of where to sit, how long to stay, and so forth, but should maintain the primary rules concerning the process of the interview.

Because there entails a more informal setting in the home, clients and therapists may find the lines of formal therapy get blurred. Knapp and Slattery (2004) described three areas in which professional boundaries might be challenged while conducting therapeutic interviews in a client's home. Given that there are more opportunities for clients to open up to therapists in ways other than the personal verbal disclosures they make in an office, the home setting is ripe for offers of food, tours of a house (and bedrooms), and a greater intimate look into clients' lives. Second, there are more opportunities for clients to challenge boundaries. Since the interview is being conducted on the client's turf, the client may take the opportunity to enforce various rules or to ignore potential stressors on the therapist, such as a dog that is making the therapist feel uncomfortable. Third, trainees and supervisees might not be adequately trained to handle these potential boundary issues.

Therapists and clients develop appropriate roles while conducting home-based therapy (Nichols & Schwartz, 2007). This process of clarifying the roles that each person will play in the interview is important so that everyone is clear as to the nature and purpose of the interview. The defining of roles leads to a setting of ground rules for the interview, which allows people to then work together collaboratively.

As discussed previously, while in the home, many therapists take on the persona of "professional friendliness" in which they are more casual than they would be in the office setting but still maintain a professional role as the therapist (Reiter, 1999). Christensen (1995) found that home-based therapists were less likely to confront clients than they would be in the office environment. Part of this was due to feeling that they were a guest in the client's home and shouldn't push too hard on certain issues.

Home-based therapists need to develop a therapeutic flexibility whereby they are able to change and adapt the skills they have learned that might have worked in an office-based setting but might not be fully appropriate in a home-based session. Because there are more potential distractions and interruptions in the home, home-based interviewers need to be flexible not only with the skills and theories they operate from, but also with the clients they are working with.

Special Issues When Conducting a Therapeutic Family Interview

Phases of Home-Based Sessions

All therapy, regardless of theory or context, involves phases or stages. Home-based interviewing is not an exception. Reiter (2000b) explained that home-based therapy could be understood as consisting of four phases: the beginning, transition, middle, and end.

The beginning phase home-based therapy deals with the entry of the therapist into the home. It can be more complicated than the beginning phase of office-based therapy. Not only does the therapist have to join with the client(s) to develop an effective working alliance, but also she has to do so in a way that she does not overpower the client in the client's own home. Because the situations these clients are dealing with tend to be severe, with some type of third party request for the services, therapists can be placed in a position where they are seen as the authoritative body. In the beginning phase of therapy, they will need to distinguish themselves from the referring party while also opening up the possibility of providing services.

The transition stage occurs when therapists transition from a nontherapy moment back to a therapy moment. This usually happens after there has been some distraction in the home. Part of this transition occurs when therapists engage with clients in nontherapy talk. In a qualitative research study about home-based therapists' experiences conducting therapy in the home, one of the things therapists noticed was that they spent more time talking about nontherapy issues with clients when they were conducting the interview in the home rather than in an office setting (Reiter, 1999). An example of this transition is as follows:

> *Client:* Those were my neighbors. They're good neighbors.
>
> *Therapist:* It's always nice to get along with your neighbors. If I was to have asked them what they thought was going on in your family, what do you think they would have said?

In this way, the therapist has transitioned from an interruption of neighbors coming over to talking about a different perspective of what might be happening in the family.

The middle phase can also be viewed as the working phase. This is the part of the interview where, using the therapist's theoretical orientation, she works with the clients in an attempt to reach the treatment goals. This phase is enhanced in home-based therapy because the therapist has the advantages of viewing the social and physical factors impacting the family. This aids in understanding person-environment interactions (Tracy & McDonell, 1991). The middle phase of home-based therapy is improved when therapeutic interviewers utilize the transition stage as more than just a go-between from therapy talk to nontherapy talk back to therapy talk. They can do this by weaving back into the conversation the difficulties that families might have in being able to focus and work together because of the various issues and distractions that might arise.

> *Therapist:* Wow, when you first told me that things in the family were chaotic, I didn't quite get a good sense of that. But seeing all of the phone calls, knocks at the door, and everything that goes on in the house, it is clear that things in this family are difficult. Let's talk about ways that you have been able to manage this.

The final stage is the end phase, which can also be considered the departure phase. Each session has a departure stage and the therapy process as a whole has an ending phase. In a specific interview, the therapist and family will end a particular session. Although there are many of the same issues in ending a session in home-based therapy and in office-based, there are distinct processes that occur in the home. Because the therapist is in the family's environment, she cannot be as structured and directive as in the office. There is not another client waiting in the waiting room for her. When people (nontherapists) visit someone's home, there is not a sense of a time-line of when the people have to leave the house. In office-based therapy, the therapist and client agree that the client will come in at a certain time and leave at a certain time. In home-based therapy, therapist and client will agree on the therapist coming at a certain time, but there is an openness about when she will leave. As for termination with a family, it becomes more difficult because home-based therapists are more readily accepted as a part of the family system. They have done what most other professionals haven't; they have been in the client's home, the sacred place for the family. Termination means that a piece of the family system is leaving.

Handling Crises

Since most of the families home-based therapists work with are dealing with crises, therapists will need to put into place several measures to help reduce the immediacy of the crisis. One way of doing this is to meet with the clients more frequently and for longer periods of time. Most clients, when in crises, benefit from multiple sessions per week (sometimes twice a week, sometimes every other day) as well as having those sessions last longer (perhaps one-and-a-half to two hours). Therapists can also help the family change the environment (Kinney, Haapala, & Booth, 1991)—for instance, having other family members stay at the house to help calm the situation. Kinney, Haapala, and Booth recommended helping the family develop a daily routine, assigning homework, contracting with the family members, and developing crisis cards. When family members have a routine they are following, they can stay more focused on engaging in behaviors that are productive instead of destructive. Each family member can do the necessary recommendations from the therapist so that the family can get out of the problem sequence. Homework can also help them do this. The homework would be about developing and maintaining positive relationship patterns rather than the problematic ones they have been engaging in. Home-based therapists might also contract with clients. Having a written description of what someone has agreed to may lead to that person's being more likely to follow through on it. For instance, an adolescent might sign a contract stating he will not hit his brother anymore. Crisis cards can also be developed. When clients start to experience increasingly volatile feelings, they can review the crisis card, which walks them step-by-step through a process of controlling the situation, with both individual things they can do (i.e., leave the room, engage in an enjoyable activity) or how to bring in outside resources (i.e., call a friend or the therapist).

Almost all home-based therapists have some way for clients to get hold of them between sessions. This is usually through a cell phone specifically designated for the home-based program. Given that these families have come to the attention of the therapist because of some type of crisis, the likelihood that another one will occur during treatment is heightened. Many home-based therapists are on call twenty-four hours a day, or rotate crisis calls with colleagues in the program. Clients should also be given the phone number for a mobile crisis unit. Also, the therapist can discuss with clients that if they are faced with an immediate emergency that could be life-threatening, they should contact 911.

Safety Issues

In office-based sessions, therapists usually have other therapists, staff, or security personnel present. The same does not hold true for home-based therapy. It is usually the interviewer, by herself, working with the members of the family. In the client's home, family members have access to potential weapons, such as knives, guns, and chemicals. In her interview with therapists who provided therapy in the home, Christensen (1995) found that safety was a major theme. Therapists in her study were concerned about their own and their client's safety and adjusted how they worked with clients, perhaps arranging sessions early in the day so that they would not be in certain neighborhoods toward evening hours. Case Scenario 16.5 demonstrates the immediacy of safety issues for both therapist and client when working in clients' homes.

CASE SCENARIO 16.5

A colleague of mine was working with a family who had been referred by the local child protection agency for issues of violence in the house. He had met with them several times and had established a fairly good working alliance with the mother, father, and the seven-year-old son. On his fifth visit to the house, as he pulled up to the driveway, the father was sitting out on the front lawn with a shotgun. The wife had upset him, and he was so mad that he got the shotgun and sat out front so she would not come home and try to go inside. My colleague, even though there was a shotgun that was presumably loaded, went over and began talking with the father. During their conversation, he agreed with the father to go inside and to put the shotgun away. In this situation, perhaps the safer thing for the therapist to do was to leave the scene and call the police and let them defuse the situation. My colleague believed that he could calm the father down, maintain the connection they made, and then use the situation therapeutically. Novice therapists are encouraged to leave the house if there are weapons present. Case Scenario 16.6 describes another situation where being in the home provided a quicker avenue for potential violence for clients.

CASE SCENARIO 16.6

I was working with a stepfamily consisting of the stepfather, mother, and her two sons, ages twelve and ten. The parents' complaint was that the children were out of control and misbehaving. The boys' complaint was that the parents were overcontrolling, especially the stepfather, with whom they had had numerous arguments. During one of the home-based sessions, the mother and I were sitting in the living room, the stepfather was in another part of the house, and the two boys were in the kitchen. One boy said something derogatory to the other, and they began a verbal confrontation. Suddenly, one of the boys reached onto the counter, grabbed a steak knife and placed it at the other boy's throat. Within a few seconds, the stepfather came around the corner and saw what was going on. He grabbed the older boy, who was holding the knife to his brother's throat, and threw the boy down to the ground. Immediately, the younger boy, who just had a knife held to his throat by his brother, ran to the kitchen table and grabbed a chair. He lifted it over his head to strike the stepfather. I ran over and took the chair from the boy. The stepfather, after yelling at the older boy, let him go. The boy ran out of the house and ten minutes later the police were at the door wanting to know what happened. In an office setting not as many potential weapons are readily available. Further, as in all contexts, therapists cannot control everything. There will always be the possibility of violence by one or more members. Therapists should be prepared to think on their feet to deal with whatever might happen during a session.

Boyd-Franklin and Bry (2000) provided several safety guidelines for therapists working in clients' homes. They recommended that therapists conduct their sessions during the day. This has to do with being able to navigate the local area and working within the confines of the standard workday. However, this might not always be possible. Many family members work and might not be home until five or six o'clock at night. If therapists will be meeting with the family, it is recommended that they, during daylight hours, do a dry run of how to get to the home. On the day of or preceding the scheduled meeting, therapists can call up the family to remind them that they will be coming so that they do not show up at the door unexpected. Home-based therapists should have a cell phone with them so they can call the family if they get lost or call for emergency aid if they need it while driving to the client's house or during the interview if they feel threatened. Therapeutic interviewers might also bring a co-worker with them to the session. They can either do co-therapy or have the person along for the first visit. When arriving at the client's residence, therapists should park as close to the home as possible, in a well-lighted area that is not isolated. When leaving the client's residence, if the therapist feels uncomfortable in the neighborhood, she can ask one or more family members to walk her to her car. Case Scenario 16.7 highlights how clients can be aware of safety issues for the therapist.

CASE SCENARIO 16.7

I was working with a mother who had been referred by the local child protection service because of possible issues of neglect. She was very pleasant to me and welcomed me into her home each time that I came for a session. After the third meeting, I realized something interesting. At the end of every interview, she would walk me all the way to my car. I thought this a little strange since I had not had this experience with any of the other people that I did home-based work with. They would walk me to the door of the house and go no farther. When I was driving away after that third session and thinking about it, I was looking around the neighborhood. I realized that I was the only Caucasian in the area. The neighborhood was a predominantly African American area. Then I realized why she was walking me to my car. She was protecting me and making sure that no one would bother me. If she had come to my office, this dynamic would not have happened. This demonstrated to me the shift in hierarchy that happens while doing home-based work.

Summary

Home-based therapy is an ever-increasing context for therapeutic interviewing that requires therapists to use all of their skills while also being able to be flexible and adaptable. It is a context that those who operate within it find more enjoyable and productive than the office-based setting. Conducting therapeutic interviews in the home provides opportunities for connecting with, observing, and working with clients that might not happen in other settings. Home-based interviewers should develop certain skills to be effective with these clients including learning how to utilize whatever occurs in the home as a way to connect and intervene in families, dealing with family systems issues, and handling crises.

Exercises

1. Role-play with several classmates a therapeutic interview occurring in the client's home. For the people playing the family, engage in various activities that might happen in the home during a session, such as phone ringing, needing to go to the bathroom, or having to wash the dishes. For the therapist, attempt to utilize each of these situations to get to know how the family functions. If possible, conduct this role-play in someone's home to make it more realistic.

2. Interview a home-based therapist, asking that person what she sees as the advantages and disadvantages to working in the client's home. Ask her about the differences between office-based and home-based interviewing and how she has been able to adjust.

17

Therapeutic Interviewing in Alternative Settings

Schools, Residential and Inpatient Facilities, and Online Counseling

Therapeutic interviewers find themselves providing services in many different contexts. The previous two chapters covered issues and strategies for therapeutic interviewers working with clients in office-based and home-based settings. This chapter covers some of the other main contexts in which therapists operate, including schools, residential or inpatient settings, and the newest arena for therapists, online counseling. A brief overview of each of these contexts and some of the therapeutic skills that are prominently utilized in these contexts is presented. These are not the only alternative settings wherein therapeutic interviews occur. Therapists should be prepared to understand the unique issues that occur in every setting in which they provide therapy.

School-Based Interviewing

Many beginning therapists engage in therapeutic interviewing with children and adolescents through school-based practicum placements. Non-novice therapists, such as school guidance counselors and school psychologists, work with children and adolescents during school hours on school property. Being in the school setting provides a unique context for engaging in therapeutic interviews where there are several important points to keep in mind.

School-based intervention is extremely important, especially since children spend almost half of their waking time (between September and June) in school or preparing for or conducting school-based activities (Miller, 2002). Miller explained that school-based counselors are in an excellent position to bridge the world of home and family with that of school since they understand developmental and psychological issues as well as having a thorough understanding of the school system. Thus, school-based interviewers can be there for the child and also be the link between the child, the teachers, the school, the parents, and the community.

Boyd-Franklin and Bry (2000) provided two main reasons for integrating schools into the work of therapy. First, by working with teachers and school personnel, therapists can get more objective evidence of the child's performance and behavior. Second, by having the teacher(s) on board in working with the child, more people can work as a team to try to implement change. Therapy is enhanced when multiple people are collaboratively working toward change.

Therapeutic interviewers generally work in the school in two ways. First, they may actually conduct the therapeutic interview with the child in the school during regular school hours or immediately after school. Second, therapists may work with teachers and school guidance counselors as informants or collaborators in their work with the child and the family. Those individuals who become school counselors may conduct individual, group, family or parent, and teacher counseling. This happens in the school, in the therapist's office, either during regular school hours or immediately after in hopes that family members can join the session.

Since most schools are self-sufficient systems that have their own therapists (usually psychologists and/or school guidance counselors), they may not be the most amenable to having outside therapists come onto their property. There are several ways therapeutic interviewers can enhance the probability of gaining access to a school (Boyd-Franklin & Bry, 2000):

1. Therapists should introduce themselves or be introduced to the school administrator. This might be done through someone who the school administrator trusts. Having the top person at the school advocating for the therapist gives the therapist more clout at that school.
2. Therapists can discuss with the school administrator how they can assist in servicing the needs of the students at that school. This entails highlighting the current services and exploring where some children's needs are not currently being met.
3. Therapists can discuss with school personnel how their participation with the children at the school will enhance the school personnel's work with the children. School personnel are usually already overburdened and want to ensure that they will not have to do more work because of the school-based therapist's presence.

Since there is already a social stigma about going to therapy, school-based interviewers need to take extra precaution to help avoid stigmatizing the youth they are working with. Given that children tend to tease one another, along with having an immature sense of what therapy is and who utilizes the services, therapists do not want to make overt that the child is getting services. Children tend to think that "crazy" people go for therapy, and if one of their peers went for counseling, they might then act differently toward that child as if that child were crazy in some manner.

Schools do not usually have rooms that were specifically designed for therapeutic interviewing when the school was built. For therapists who are employed full-time in a school, they will usually have an office; however, it might not be soundproofed. For those schools where there is not a designed therapy room, therapeutic interviewers will have to make do with what the school has to offer. Many times, this brings issues such as privacy and confidentiality to the forefront. Therapists should do their best to work with the school administration to gain access to rooms that are as soundproof and closed-off as possible.

School-Based Interviewer as Consultant

The school-based interviewer at times becomes a consultant for various individuals or groups, such as teachers, students, parents, or other agencies (Schmidt, 1999, 1991; Thompson, 2002). For situational consulting, the school-based interviewer forms a triangular relationship between the counselor, the consultee (student, parent, or teacher), and the situation (concern) (Schmidt, 1991). Many school counselors have some familiarity with consultation theory and learn how to incorporate various systems into the therapy of a student. School-based counselors may meet with the student, teacher, parent, sibling or other family member, probation officer, school administrator, community resource people, or anyone else involved in the life of the student. Schmidt (1999) encouraged school-based therapists to utilize additional resources as needed, such as school and community programs.

Perhaps most important to work with, besides the actual student, are the parents or guardians of the student (Schmidt, 1999). Working with the family may be the most challenging because they tend to be very difficult to gain access to and get to attend meetings that occur in the school, usually during school hours or immediately afterward. Montgomery (1999) presented many strategies for the school-based interviewer to get the parents of clients involved in the counseling process, including the following: appreciating and accepting everyone's concerns (student, each parent, and school personnel—if applicable); developing goals that everyone agrees on; putting parents in a respected position regarding decision making; staying committed in the process; modeling good teamwork; arranging for meeting times that enable parents to attend; and being respectful. Once one or more of the family members attends the session, therapists should utilize the conceptualization and skills presented in Chapter 13.

Teachers are another important auxiliary resource for the school-based therapist. Teachers are referral and information sources, and can help implement change programs for students. Developing a working alliance with teachers is imperative for the school-based interviewer. Sessions occur during class time, and teachers will be losing that student for that period of time. They want to know that the student is gaining something just as valuable as the information they are missing in class.

One of the main benefits of being in the school is that therapeutic interviewers are actually able to observe the child in the school setting. Therapists can occasionally sit in on classes, lunch time, or recess to observe their clients and how they are behaving in these assorted contexts. This can give them information to help the child function better.

Dealing with Difficult Students

School-based therapeutic interviewers will have, as clients, children and adolescents. Many of these students will actively engage in the therapy process. However, school-based therapists will definitely come across difficult students. Kottler (1997) grouped difficult students into those who violate rules, those who have given up, those who are manipulative, those who withhold communication, those who are severely impaired, those who are "at risk," and those who push the therapist's buttons. Many of these types of students are in the precontemplation, contemplation, or perhaps the preparation stage of readiness for change. Therapists should be conscious of their willingness and desire for therapy.

School-based therapists will probably have to include, at least in theory, those people the difficult student comes in contact with, such as teachers, school administration, and family members as these individuals may already have given up or are close to giving up on this person. Kottler recommended that therapists working with difficult students, especially those who do not fight fair, protect themselves from the self-destructive ploys of the student. This entails taking a stance of neutral detachment. School-based counselors want students to know they are there for the student, if the student wants to utilize their services. However, they should not get enmeshed in the emotional turmoil that can come from these cases.

The challenge of difficult students can lead to elation (when the student makes significant positive changes) or frustration (when they do not change or become even more problematic). There will be many times during portions of the therapy when there is an impasse with this group of clients. Kottler (1997) recommended the school-based counselor ask himself the following questions:

- What personal issues of yours are being triggered by this encounter?
- What expectations are you demanding of this student?
- What are you doing to create or exacerbate the problems?
- Who does this challenging child remind you of?
- Which of your needs are not being met? (p. 32)

These questions can aid therapeutic interviewers in determining what is happening for them (and the case) and then develop a plan for changing the situation.

Ethics in School-Based Interviewing

School-based interviewers are held to all of the ethical standards of the regulatory bodies of which they are members. One of the most significant issues when working in a school is that of who is the client and what types of confidentiality that person can be afforded. The student is the primary person for the therapist to consider, but in some states, the parents have the right to waive privileged communication (Schmidt, 1999). Student clients, especially adolescents, will want to know that the therapist will not disclose their personal information to the teacher or parent. Therapists can ensure that they will not disclose material to teachers, but they cannot always make the same guarantee about disclosing information to the client's parents.

While working in the schools, therapeutic interviewers are accountable to many different individuals. Schmidt (1999) discussed that the school-based therapist is ethically responsible to students, parents, colleagues and professional associates, the school and community, the self, and the profession. Thus, therapeutic interviewers working in the school system must understand not only the dynamics of therapy, but also of the context. They should be flexible and respectful, so that they engage the various individuals at the site as well as the client's parents or guardians so that as many people are on board for helping the client as possible.

Residential and Inpatient Interviewing

Many novice therapists, either in their practicum and internship placements or when they are working toward licensure, find themselves working in a residential or inpatient facility. These might be substance abuse hospitals, psychiatric hospitals, correctional facilities, or adolescent treatment facilities. A variety of mental health care professionals work in these contexts, including psychiatrists, psychologists, social workers, mental health counselors, family therapists, and a variety of mental health technicians. Given that the clients are forced to stay on-site throughout the day, or even throughout the week or month, unique treatment issues arise. Although the length of stay in residential placements has been decreasing due to a lack of financial support, what was once many months in treatment is still weeks or a month (Brunstetter, 1998). For crisis inpatient hospitalizations, clients might be there about one day to one week.

One of the major differences between inpatient/residential interviewing and all other contexts of therapeutic interviewing is that the clients are at the site for twenty-four hours a day. In the other contexts, clients may be in the therapy office (or engaged in therapy in their house or online) for perhaps one to five hours per week. In residential programs, the notion of therapy is not confined just to the therapy room. It happens in what is known as a therapeutic milieu, where treatment occurs not only for the one hour in the therapist's office, but also for the other twenty-three hours (Trieschman, Whittaker, & Bredntro, 1969).

For residential settings, therapeutic interviewers do not work alone. They are one piece of a much larger whole. This milieu is designed so the client is provided with countless growth opportunities throughout the day instead of only during the time the client is meeting with the therapist. One of the primary goals for therapists, as well as all other staff members of the residential setting, is developing a place of physical and psychological safety (Lyman & Campbell, 1996).

Who Is the Client?

Therapeutic interviewers working in residential treatment facilities will most likely be working with children and adolescents. Edwards (1994) explained that many children are put into residential facilities for psychiatric reasons, but some are placed there because their families are confused about what to do with them. Edwards found, after surveying 144 residential treatment facilities, that conduct disorder undifferentiated type (312.90) seemed to be the most common diagnosis for children. Attention deficit hyperactivity disorder, oppositional defiant disorder, and depressive disorder NOS were the next most frequently used diagnostic categories.

Many of the individuals in residential or inpatient settings are not there of their own volition. They may have been signed into the facility by their parents, significant others, law enforcement personnel, or the legal system. This puts added pressure on therapeutic interviewers to make a good connection and develop a positive working alliance with clients. Many of the clients in these settings, especially when they first arrive, are in the pre-contemplation or contemplation stage of change. Further, they view the therapist as part of the establishment that is keeping them locked in the facility and taking away their freedom. Therapists will need to attempt to disengage themselves from being the arbiter of whether the client is in or out of the facility, but can work with the person while she is in there. If the person's goal is not to be in the facility, therapists help her toward that goal.

For many residential treatment programs, step wise growth is designed for clients so they start off with few privileges and by working with the program and following the rules, gradually earn more and more privileges (such as free time or time away from the treatment facility). Therapeutic interviewers in residential placements are put in an awkward position because they, at times, will have to report activities their client is doing that will get the client to lose points, privileges, or other possibilities in the setting. This puts the therapist in a hierarchical position to the client. Therapists are encouraged to let their clients know that they will follow the guidelines and policies of the treatment program and will not "look the other way" if an event happens. By being up-front, and being consistent across clients, therapists attempt to not be the arbiter of what the penalty is or who is right or wrong in a dispute but just a conduit of information to the administration. If a client knows that the therapist did not report another resident but did report her, she will then lose trust and respect for the therapist. However, if she knows that the therapist cares about her, but consistently follows the guidelines, she can engage in a relationship with the therapist in which she will not feel betrayed if the therapist reports a misdeed. Durrant (1993) recommended that residential-based interviewers use these times as a chance to create a therapeutic opportunity instead of just being a consequence, disciplinary action, or punishment. Therapists may focus on what the client can learn from the negative event so that it becomes useful for them instead of something that will impede their progress. Lyman and Campbell (1996) concurred, stating, "The treatment environment should be positive, nurturing, and upbeat rather than punitive or repressive in tone" (p. 48).

Since most residential treatment programs have a behavior contingency management system in place for the residents, therapeutic interviewers working in these settings should be familiar with the principles behind behavior therapy. Given that psychotherapy in residential treatment facilities is viewed by some as an extension of the behavior management system of the program (Lyman & Campbell, 1996), therapists may want to consider integrating their treatment with that of the program's guidelines so that the therapeutic milieu and the specific therapy interviews work conjointly with one another. This can be a difficult process since therapeutic interviewers need to develop trust with their clients. Since many of the clients in residential placements have histories of past abuse, trauma, and problematic family relationships, they are likely to have attachment issues (Lyman & Campbell, 1996). Further, having been placed in the residential center, the child may be feeling separation and loss (Swanson & Schaefer, 1988) or possibly anger at family members. This leads to either a lack of connection from the client or an overattachment. Therapists should be cognizant of both possibilities and do their best to develop a quick alliance without becoming too connected or detached.

Therapeutic interviewers will also want to help clients experience as normal an environment as possible (Lyman & Campbell, 1996). Although the residential/inpatient setting is not a normal environment, therapists can aid clients in being able to take their progress in the residential placement and continue to apply it once they get out of the treatment facility. Although normalization is a key objective, it becomes difficult when clients with severe behavioral and psychological problems are living with one another, separated from family and friends. Therapeutic interviewers who work in a residential setting must have a thorough knowledge of crisis intervention techniques (Brunsetter, 1988; Katz, 1988; Lyman & Campbell, 1996; Stein, 1995) as crises are a frequent occurrence in residential treatment programs. They should also be quite adept at being able to lead group therapy sessions (Stein, 1995). Other primary issues residential therapists must deal with include sexually acting out (Crenshaw, 1988), peer influence (Gwynn, Meyer, & Schaefer, 1988), violence (Brunsetter, 1988), and family issues (Brunsetter, 1988; Durrant, 1993; Van Hagen, 1988).

Being that clients are at the residential or inpatient facility full-time, the setting becomes a second home for clients, however temporary it may be. This shifts the role of the therapeutic interviewer from being strictly a therapist to sometimes being an administrator, pseudo-parent, or friend. Therapists are around the client more than just the session. They gain information about the client based on casually observing the client walking around the facility and interacting with other residents and staff members. The residential facility is also different from all other contexts of therapy in that special events, such as holidays and birthdays, occur when the clients are in the residence rather than at home. Cormack (1988) suggested that therapists and the therapy programs use these events as ways to enhance the treatment process. Although therapists do not have to give gifts to clients on birthdays or holidays, they can give vocal gifts (i.e., "Happy Birthday, John" or "Merry Christmas, Susie").

Online Counseling

One of the fastest growing areas in therapeutic interviewing is that of e-therapy (also known as online counseling). Although the roots of e-therapy are founded before the invention of the internet (Grohol, 2004), most people think of it as having begun in the 1990s. The early history of psychotherapy via computers was usually on bulletin boards or other online forums. These tended to be therapists who provided resources for individuals regarding what therapy is and how to connect with others. They tended to provide these resources for free. Once the internet became open for public consumption in the early 1990s, therapists began using it as a fee-for-service medium. Although this is quickly growing as a context of therapeutic interviewing, very few graduate programs discuss online counseling in their curriculum. Finn (2002) explained that it is very likely that, because of the rise of e-therapy, graduate programs will begin to integrate it into their curriculum.

Online counseling provides many advantages that office-based counseling cannot. In the comfort of their own home, office, or anywhere they have access to a computer, clients can get the benefits of therapy. Thus, if a client is going on vacation for extended periods of time, she can still engage in the therapy process without having to take any time off. The same holds true for therapeutic interviewers; they do not have to be in an office during a fixed time. They can work from home, while they are on vacation, or anywhere else there is computer access. E-therapy is fast, convenient, and efficient (Riemer-Reiss, 2000).

Because most insurance companies will not pay for clients engaging in e-therapy, online counseling is usually a cash pay endeavor (Grohol, 2004). This can be done through having the client mail checks to the therapist or having an online payment system such as automatic bank/credit card transfer or a system such as Paypal. Although e-therapy is not currently readily reimbursable, Grohol believes that insurance companies will realize that e-therapy can be a cost effective means of providing needed services to individuals.

Online counseling does not have to be the sole means of conducting therapy with a specific client. Kraus (2004) suggested that therapists meet face-to-face occasionally with clients during the course of therapy. This might be for intake or evaluation purposes or at certain times during the therapy, perhaps when the client is experiencing some type of crisis. Kraus goes so far as to say that the responsible therapeutic interviewer who is engaging in online interviewing should not accept a client unless the client and therapist are close enough geographically that a potential face-to-face interview is feasible and therapist and client agree on a plan of action for a contingency referral if in-office care is necessitated and the therapist cannot provide those services. This is usually for situations that are deemed crises.

Modes of Online Counseling

There are several different ways therapeutic interviewers can provide e-therapy. The most basic is through email. More and more people are becoming familiar with email and are able to use this technology to communicate with other people. Email has the advantage of allowing people to talk with one another with only minimal technology (computer and internet connection). However, this type of communication is asynchronous, meaning that both people are not communicating with one another at the same time. Thus, it is not clear how long the time will be between when one person sends an email, the other person receives and reads it, and then posts a reply (and vice-versa to continue the cycle of emails back-and-forth).

Another means of online counseling is through a chat program. There are many different chat programs available for downloading and each has advantages and disadvantages over the other. A chat allows therapist and client to communicate in real-time. Instead of waiting hours or possibly days for a response from a query, during a chat, each person is immediately reading what the other person is writing. However, since everything is text based, the subtle nuances of nonverbal communication can be lost. One way to get around this is to use emoticons, text-based symbols that describe emotions (for example, :) means "happy").

Therapists and clients who have higher levels of technology available to them might use a videoconferencing program or a webcam. Videoconferencing programs send videostreams across computers and can give better resolution. However, they are more difficult to use because they require that both end parties be connected to specific software (Zack, 2004). People can buy webcams that connect to their computer. These can display visual and auditory information to people connected online. This allows people, in real-time, to see and hear each other. Thus, subtle nuances of voice inflection or body language become part of the therapy interview. One of the problems with webcams is that, depending on the program and the speed of the internet connection, there may be slight delays in the video and audio. Similarly, the quality of the picture and the sound may be inferior.

As can be seen, online therapy comes in many different forms. Therapists can provide information to clients (usually through FAQs—Frequently Asked Questions—on their website), give advice, or provide individual therapy. E-therapy can also be used to provide group treatment (Bellafiore, Colon, & Rosenberg, 2004) and psychological testing and assessment (Barak & Buchanan, 2004).

Is Online for Everyone?

Is e-therapy right for everyone? Obviously, no one approach is right for every person. There are clients who want to have that face-to-face contact with another person. There are therapists who would feel detached and not as effective working through a keyboard rather than in the immediacy of a therapy room. And there are clients who find that what they can receive through online counseling is all they need to help them accomplish their goals. Some therapists find emotional satisfaction and financial benefits in being online therapists, while others do not.

Therapeutic interviewers and clients who engage in online counseling should feel comfortable with technology, computers, and the internet. This allows them to engage in the process of the counseling without worrying about how to work the technology. Therapists should not try to push clients to use a technology level more advanced than they are comfortable with, as clients might feel overwhelmed or pushed away (Elleven & Allen, 2004). For instance, if a client is only comfortable with emails and unsure of doing live chats, the therapist should accept this and, without pushing, open the possibility of other types of engagement.

Leibert et al. (2006) surveyed clients who engaged in online therapy. They found that the majority were women who had good familiarity with the internet. Overall, the levels of satisfaction with the therapy and the working alliance were not as high as clients who had face-to-face therapy. However, the researchers found that one of the main advantages of e-therapy was the anonymity it afforded the clients especially with potentially embarrassing self-disclosures in the beginning of therapy. Derrig-Palumbo and Zeine (2005) concurred, explaining that clients may feel more comfortable and safer opening up in an online environment. This leads more quickly to self-disclosing to the therapist. The disadvantage Leibert et al. found was that clients believed therapy was not as good online because they did not have access to the nonverbal behaviors of the therapist.

There are times when online counseling is not indicated. Kraus (2004) held that online consults are not recommended when a client is potentially suicidal or homicidal, there is a life-threatening situation, there is recent suicidal, violent, or abusive behavior, the client is delusional or has hallucinations, or the client is actively abusing drugs or alcohol. Given that many clients with these issues may need some type of hospitalization or perhaps medication, having a therapist who is present only over the internet is probably not a sound decision.

The online environment helps take away some of the misperceptions of people that others make, usually those that are visual. Counseling on the internet may help to brush away some of the potential cultural biases people have (Skinner & Latchford, 2004). Since people do not see skin color or hear someone's accent, they may be able to focus more clearly on the therapy issues. An additional benefit of online counseling is that people may be better able to find a therapist of the same culture since their therapist can be from any geographic region instead of only a few miles from home.

Specific Online Counseling Skills

Although the goals of therapy are the same regardless of format, how therapist and client reach those goals changes depending on the who, where, and when of therapeutic interviewing. In the online counseling arena, the skills needed are mainly the same as those for ordinary counseling, but change slightly because of the context of the online environment. Novice therapists are not encouraged to start off providing online counseling in lieu of face-to-face counseling. This is because it takes a while to develop the skills of therapy with all of the available communication channels. In the online environment, the nonverbal cues are removed. Further, therapists should have good facility with the computer and typing skills, along with good grammar and spelling.

Stofle and Chechele (2004) examined five broad categories of therapist skills when counseling online: engagement, sessional contracting, teaching/training/modeling, supportive confrontation, and sessional summary.

1. *Engagement skills* are similar to the joining and reflecting skills discussed in Part Two of this book. Since the therapeutic alliance is key for productive therapeutic work, regardless of format, online therapists must join and connect with their clients. How they do so is somewhat different from face-to-face interviews. Because they do not have their physical and verbal behaviors to demonstrate their desire for a therapeutic alliance (that is, voice tone, smiling, open body position), they must demonstrate their caring for the client through text (Derrig-Palumbo & Zeine, 2005). There are certain strategies therapists can use to help this process along in the online environment. For instance, in e-therapy where sessions are occurring via email, therapists can use the subject line as a way to ensure that clients open the email and also to frame what has been talked about so far in therapy (Stofle & Chechele, 2004). They could put a theme that is important for the client, such as "Maintaining connections" or "Doubting oneself."

2. *Sessional contracting skills* are things therapists do to help organize the online communications. In chat sessions, this can be accomplished by starting off the chat by developing a plan of action for what will occur in the chat (Stofle & Chechele, 2004). In email correspondence, therapeutic interviewers can use the first paragraph to set the stage for the rest of the message, perhaps summarizing what has been talked about in previous correspondence or what will come. Online therapists may have to be more active in the early stages of the online therapeutic encounter through the use of prompting and appropriate questions to get the client to begin to discuss the pertinent issues (Derrig-Palumbo & Zeine, 2005). Therapists cannot sit back and not be active in the interchange since the client may question whether the therapist is on the other end of the chat program. Therapists should consider using shorter responses and making them tentative so clients can agree or disagree with them (Derrig-Palumbo & Zeine, 2005).

3. *Teaching/training/modeling skills* are more theory specific. They are at the heart of therapy and are the skills used to help the client attain the desired change. Stofle and Chechele (2004) held that those face-to-face therapies utilizing the written word, such as cognitive-behavioral therapy homework assignments or narrative therapy's use of therapeutic letters, work well in the online environment. This includes the use of stories, journaling, and bibliotherapy. Cognitive-based theories seem to fit well within an online medium, especially those that are of a brief nature (Derrig-Palumbo & Zeine, 2005). Within cognitive-based theories are rational-emotive behavioral therapy, Beck's cognitive therapy, and solution-focused therapy, as well as narrative therapy. The specific use of the skills of the theory would not change regardless of being face-to-face or online; however, therapists would need to be more aware of the possible ways their communication was perceived by the client and how the client might express the impact of the therapist's messages. In email correspondence, therapists need to pay attention to how their previous email was taken and understood by the client, areas the client omitted, areas the client misperceived, and those areas the client is hinting at but not fully saying.

4. *Supportive confrontation skills* consist of understanding the core beliefs of the client and confronting, in a positive and supportive way, those beliefs that do not seem to be useful or productive for the client. Just as therapists need to have developed a good working alliance before challenging a client when conducting face-to-face therapeutic interviews, online therapists need to ensure that clients are connected to them. In online therapy, this may occur earlier than in face-to-face therapy. Derrig-Palumbo and Zeine (2005) explained, "The act of writing allows clients to process material directly and bypass tendencies toward circular thinking" (p. 68). This then leads to their being able to address issues sooner than they might in an office setting.

5. *Sessional summary skills* are those skills discussed in Chapter 7 about how to end specific sessions. The summary skills of therapy are the same regardless of format, but usually are done for keeping the client focused on the therapy, acknowledging and encouraging the client's progress, explaining what the next steps of therapy are, and putting what was learned into a smaller package for the client to grasp easily (Stofle & Chechele, 2004).

Derrig-Palumbo and Zeine (2005) provided several ideas about therapeutic skills to emphasize and also to avoid when conducting online sessions. Therapeutic interviewers should emphasize joining with clients and developing a strong therapeutic alliance. Therapists and clients should be able to utilize and feel comfortable working in the online medium agreed on. Therapists should also collaborate with the client and get the client's agreement on the process of working. For instance, these authors suggested therapists ask clients if it is okay to use emoticons. Therapeutic interviewers should also emphasize those techniques that are more conducive to online therapy (for example, using journaling instead of an empty chair technique). These authors recommended that online therapists not try to be different from the way they are as face-to-face therapists, but perhaps use techniques more appropriate for online therapy. Therapists should also be cautious in thinking that they fully understand a client's communication. Checking in with clients to gauge the accuracy of perceptions is important. Therapists should also use full words instead of abbreviations (for example, "In my opinion" instead of "IMO"). Along these lines, therapists should not change the typographical manner of the text, such as moving back and forth between capitals and lowercase. This goes along with putting too many exclamation points or question marks after sentences, as therapists cannot be sure how clients will perceive this.

Online Crises

Regardless of context or format, clients experience crises at various times during their treatment. This is the same for online clients. Although face-to-face meetings might be more appropriate when working with clients in severe or immediate crisis, some clients will not seek that sort of help and will want to work with someone in e-therapy (Zelvin & Speyer, 2004). Online therapists should try to get a phone contact number for clients in case there is a crisis situation. Therapists should also get a home address in case they need to call law enforcement personnel. When an online client is in crisis, therapists should increase the frequency of their correspondence and attempt to get the client to agree to a no-harm contract.

Availability

Online therapists should negotiate with their clients when and how often they will be available. If therapists will not check email for an extended period of time (perhaps several days or weeks), they should inform their clients so the client is not expecting a response sooner than it will come. Therapists can talk with clients about how often per week they will respond to emails so clients are not feeling abandoned if the therapist isn't replying as quickly as they would like.

Security Issues in Online Counseling

Because private and confidential information is being discussed during the therapeutic interview, there is concern in the online environment that this information may be procured by people who should not have access. Given the amount of identity theft and other online theft (such as credit cards), clients and clinicians should be concerned about how to ensure that all information is secure. Although this may seem to be the case, online counseling may actually be more secure than face-to-face counseling (Zack, 2004). In office settings, most therapists may not have soundproof rooms, may leave client charts around the office, and do not always keep their charts in locked filing cabinets (although they should). Zack provided several measures to help protect the security of the client's information. First, therapists can have password protection on their computer. This prevents anyone besides the therapist (or a qualified staff person) from gaining access to the material on the computer. Therapists might also have a feature on their computer so that, after a certain amount of time of non-use, a password is needed to reen-

Reflection 17.1

Think about how available you think would be most optimal in online therapy. Develop an explanation to clients as to how often and when you will check your email and how often you will respond to them.

gage the computer. Because client information may be needed if something happens to the therapist (vacation or serious illness), the password should be available to a colleague or professional who understands the importance of confidentiality in the mental health field.

Therapists can also use encryption software to help protect client information. There are two basic encryption strategies, symmetric encryption and public key encryption (Zack, 2004). Zack recommended that symmetric encryption be used for storing documents on a personal computer. A public key encryption has two different keys (public and private) and allows computers to connect securely to one another. Therapists should also use firewalls to help prevent hackers from gaining access to their computers via the internet. Firewalls prevent certain information from coming into or exiting the computer. Thus, the therapist can ensure that client files do not leave the computer and find themselves somewhere on the internet.

When deleting information from a computer, it is not sufficient to just delete it. Zack (2004) suggested that therapists use a wiping program. This program writes a random series of ones and zeros on the data that is to be deleted so that no one can later access the computer and restore what was deleted.

Ethical Issues in Online Counseling

Online therapeutic interviewers are held to all of the same ethical standards as their counterparts who hold face-to-face sessions. Ethical bodies, such as the American Counseling Association and the National Board for Certified Counselors, have developed specific ethical standards that deal with internet online counseling. Kanani and Regehr (2003) addressed four of the major ethical issues when working in an online environment: the duty to obtain informed consent, the duty to maintain confidentiality, the duty to warn third parties of harm, and the duty to maintain professional boundaries.

Informed consent is a necessity in the therapeutic relationship. In face-to-face meetings, therapists have clients read the informed consent and then discuss it with them. Once the client has had any questions answered, she signs the form. Therapists can gauge how well the client has understood the form. In online therapy, it is not as clear as to the mind-set of the client, how well she understands the parameters of the informed consent, and if it is actually that person who is agreeing to treatment. Therapists might consider having a telephone conversation with the client so that they can gauge the client's understanding of the informed consent. The signed consent form can then be emailed or faxed to the therapist.

Regarding confidentiality, online therapeutic interviewers have a twofold obligation. They must ensure they do what they can to protect the client's information in their computer while also protecting it during transmission from their computer to the client's. They can do this with security programs, as previously discussed, such as passwords, encryption, and firewalls.

Therapists have a duty to warn third parties if their client is at risk of harming that person. In e-therapy, this becomes tricky. First, clients have a lot more freedom to be anonymous in the online arena. Even if therapists knew about potential harm, they may not know where the client lives or how to contact them outside the online environment. Second, because the therapist does not have the nonverbal channels at their disposal to be able to evaluate the seriousness of the client's communication, they must be more overt in asking the client about this potential harm.

Although on first glance it might seem that maintaining professional boundaries in online counseling would be easier than in face-to-face counseling, there are possibilities that clients can lose the distinction between therapist and idealized image (Kanani & Regehr, 2003). Since the client in most cases (unless using videoconferencing or webcams) cannot see the therapist, she may impose her own perceptions of who the therapist is. Further, because e-therapy may occur during nontraditional times (if the therapist answers emails late at night or on the weekends), the client may develop a connection to the therapist that is beyond the scope of the relationship. Many times, people will feel more open to disclose when they are talking to people through email or chat rather than face-to-face. This openness can also occur in the online therapy interview.

Therapeutic interviewers working in the online environment may find that they are more likely to get queries from clients asking for advice or opinions before a therapeutic contract is ever developed. Kraus (2004) explained that there is a difference between therapy and an educational consult. Those therapists who have a website with information may not have the same responsibilities as an office-based therapist who is meeting face-to-face with a client. However, the e-therapist should quickly decide what type of relationship he will have with clients, whether to refer them to information sources or another mental health professional or to establish a therapeutic relationship.

Summary

Therapeutic interviewers find themselves providing therapy services in many different treatment contexts. Each has its unique issues to be addressed. Those therapists working in these alternate contexts can build on the foundation they developed for conducting therapeutic interviews and learn how they can adapt their skills and theories to better work with their clients based on the context in which the interview occurs. Although many of the skills discussed in the previous chapters of this book are the primary skills used in these alternative settings, there are unique treatment issues therapists should keep in mind when working in an alternative context. However, each setting is unique and within that setting there are differences based on geographical location, organization structure, and a variety of other issues. This then necessitates that therapeutic interviewers take time to understand the unique idiosyncrasies of that context/setting of therapy.

Exercises _____

1. With a group of classmates, develop guidelines for a residential treatment program. Primarily focus your plan on what types of interactions you want to have occurring between therapeutic interviewers and clients. Provide a rationale for the number and length of therapy sessions.

2. Surf the web and find websites for online psychotherapists. Based on the person's (agency's) website, what questions do you still have? What similarities and differences do you notice about the various therapy websites?

References

Adams, J. F., & Maynard, P. E. (2000). Evaluating training needs for home-based family therapy: A focus group approach. *The American Journal of Family Therapy, 28*, 41–52.

Adleman, J., Hall, M., & Porter, N. (1998). Meanings and implications of failure in therapy. In M. Hill & E. D. Rothblum (Eds.), *Learning from our mistakes: Difficulties and failures in feminist therapy* (pp. 69–100). New York: Haworth Press.

Aldridge, M., & Wood, J. (1998). *Interviewing children.* New York: John Wiley & Sons.

Alladin, W. J. (2002). Ethnic matching in counseling. In S. Palmer (Ed.), *Multicultural counseling* (pp. 175–180). Thousand Oaks, CA: Sage.

Anderson, H. (1997). *Conversation, language, and possibilities.* New York: Basic Books.

Arredondo, P. (2003). Evolution of the multicultural counseling competencies: Background and context. In G. Roysircar, P. Arredondo, J. B. Fuertes, J. G. Ponterotto, & R. L. Toporek, *Multicultural counseling competencies 2003: Association for multicultural counseling and development* (pp. 1–16). Alexandria, VA: American Counseling Association.

Association for Specialists in Group Work. http://www. asgw. org/ training_standards .htm. Retrieved March 12, 2006.

Atkinson, D. R. (2004). *Counseling American minorities* (6th ed.). Boston: McGraw Hill.

Axelson, J. A. (1999). *Counseling and development in a multicultural society* (3rd ed.). Pacific Grove, CA: Brooks/Cole.

Axline, V. M. (1969). *Play therapy.* New York: Ballantine Books.

Bamond-Hanson, R. (2002). *The reflexive effects of marital and family therapy training on trainees' spousal relationships: A qualitative inquiry.* Unpublished Doctoral Dissertation. Nova Southeastern University, Fort Lauderdale-Davie.

Barak, A., & Buchanan, T. (2004). Internet-based psychological testing and assessment. In R. Kraus, J. Zack, & G. Stricker (Eds.), *Online counseling* (pp. 217–239). Boston: Elsevier Academic Press.

Barker, P. (1990). *Clinical interviews with children and adolescents.* New York: W. W. Norton.

Barnlund, D. C. (1990). Therapeutic communication. In G. Gumpert & S. L. Fish (Eds.), *Talking to strangers: Mediated therapeutic communication* (pp. 10–28). Norwood, NJ: Ablex.

Barone, D. F., Hutchings, P. S., Kimmel, H. J., & Traub, H. L. (2005). Increasing empathic accuracy through practice and feedback in a clinical interviewing course. *Journal of Social and Clinical Psychology, 24*, 156–172.

Barone, J. T., & Switzer, J. Y. (1995). *Interviewing: Art and skill.* Boston: Allyn & Bacon.

Barry, M. M., Doherty, A., Hope, A., Sixsmith, J., & Kelleher, C. C. (2000). A community needs assessment for rural mental health promotion. *Health Education Research, 15*, 293–304.

Baruth, L. G., & Manning, M. L. (1999). *Multicultural counseling and psychotherapy: A lifespan perspective.* Upper Saddle River, NJ: Prentice Hall.

Beebe, S. A., Beebe, S. J., & Redmond, M. V. (2005). *Interpersonal communication: Relating to others* (3rd ed.). Boston: Allyn & Bacon.

Beigel, J. K., & Earle, R. H. (1990). *Successful private practice in the 1990s.* New York: Brunner/Mazel.

Bellafiore, D. R., Colon, Y., & Rosenberg, P. (2004). Online counseling groups. In R. Kraus, J. Zack, & G. Stricker (Eds.), *Online counseling* (pp. 197–216). Boston: Elsevier Academic Press.

Bender, S., & Messner, E. (2003). *Becoming a therapist.* New York: Guilford.

Berg, B. L. (2004). *Qualitative research methods for the social sciences* (5th ed.). Boston: Allyn & Bacon.

Berg, I. K. (1994). *Family-based services: A solution-focused approach.* New York: W. W. Norton.

Berg, I. K., & Miller, S. D. (1992). *Working with the problem drinker.* New York: W. W. Norton.

Bertolino, B., & O'Hanlon, B. (2002). *Collaborative, competency-based counseling and therapy.* Boston: Allyn & Bacon.

Borcherdt, B. (2002). Humor and its contribution to mental health. *Journal of Rational-Emotive & Cognitive-Behavioral Therapy, 20,* 247–257.

Boyd-Franklin, N., & Bry, B. H. (2000). *Reaching out in family therapy: Home-based, school, and community interventions.* New York: Guilford.

Boyer, P. A., & Jeffrey, R. J. (1984). *A guide for the family therapist.* New York: Jason Aronson.

Boyle, G. J., & Joss-Reid, J. M. (2004). Relationship of humour to health: A psychometric investigation. *British Journal of Health Psychology, 9,* 51–67.

Bram, A. D. (1997). Perceptions of psychotherapy and psychotherapists: Implications from a study of undergraduates. *Professional Psychology: Research and Practice, 28,* 170–178.

Brammer, L. M., & MacDonald, G. (2003). *The helping relationship: Process and skills* (8th ed.). Boston: Allyn & Bacon.

Brandell, J. R. (2004a). Introduction. In J. R. Brandell (Ed.), *Celluloid couches, cinematic clients: Psychoanalysis and psychotherapy in the movies* (pp. 1–17). New York: State University of New York Press.

Brandell, J. R. (2004b). Kids on the couch: Hollywood's vision of child and adolescent treatment. In J. R. Brandell (Ed.), *Celluloid couches, cinematic clients: Psychoanalysis and psychotherapy in the movies* (pp. 19–46). New York: State University of New York Press.

Brems, C. (2000). *Dealing with challenges in psychotherapy and counseling.* Pacific Grove, CA: Brooks/Cole.

Brunstetter, R. W. (1998). *Adolescents in psychiatric hospitals.* Springfield, IL: Charles C. Thomas.

Burnard, P. (1994). *Counselling skills for health professionals* (2nd ed). London: Chapman & Hall.

Callahan, J. (1998). Crisis theory and crisis intervention in emergencies. In P. M. Kleespies (Ed.), *Emergencies in mental health practice* (pp. 22–40). New York: Guilford.

Carkhuff, R. R., & Berenson, B. G. (1967). *Beyond counseling and therapy.* New York: Holt, Rinehart and Winston.

Cecchin, G. (1987). Hypothesizing, circularity, and neutrality revisited: An invitation to Curiosity. *Family Process, 26,* 405–413.

Chambliss, C. H. (2000). *Psychotherapy and managed care.* Boston: Allyn & Bacon.

Charles, M. (2004). Women in psychotherapy on film: Shades of scarlett conquering. In J. R. Brandell (Ed.), *Celluloid couches, cinematic clients: Psychoanalysis and psychotherapy in the movies* (pp. 67–94). New York: State University of New York Press.

Christensen, L. L. (1995). Therapists' perspectives on home-based family therapy. *American Journal of Family Therapy, 23,* 306–314.

Clark, D. C. (1998). The evaluation and management of the suicidal patient. In P. M. Kleespies (Ed.), *Emergencies in mental health practice* (pp. 75–94). New York: Guilford.

Clarkin, J. F., & Levy, K. N. (2004). The influence of client variables on psychotherapy. In M. J. Lambert (Ed.), *Handbook of psychotherapy and behavior change* (5th ed., pp. 194–226). New York: John Wiley & Sons.

Cochran, J. L., & Cochran, N. H. (2006). *The heart of counseling: A guide to developing therapeutic relationships.* Pacific Grove, CA: Thomson Brooks/Cole.

Collins, B. G., & Collins, T. M. (2005). *Crisis and trauma.* Boston: Houghton Mifflin.

Connors, G. J., Donovan, D. M., & DiClemente, C. C. (2001). *Substance abuse treatment and the stages of change.* New York: Guilford.

Conyne, R. K. (1999). *Failures in group work.* Thousand Oaks, CA: Sage.

Conyne, R. K., Wilson, F. R., & Ward, D. E. (1997). *Comprehensive group work.* Alexandria, VA: American Counseling Association.

Corey, G. (2004). *Theory & practice of group counseling* (6th ed.). Pacific Grove, CA: Brooks/Cole.

Corey, G. (2005). *Theory and practice of counseling and psychotherapy* (7th ed.). Pacific Grove, CA: Brooks/Cole.

Corey, G., & Corey, M. S. (2006). *I never knew I had a choice* (8th ed.). Pacific Grove, CA: Brooks/Cole.

Corey, G., Corey, M. S., & Callanan, P. (2003). *Issues and ethics in the helping professions* (6th ed). Pacific Grove, CA: Brooks/Cole.

Corey, G., Corey, M. S., & Callanan, P. (2007). *Issues and ethics in the helping professions* (7th ed.). Pacific Grove, CA: Brooks/Cole.

Cormack, P. H. (1988). Special and unusual events in residential treatment: Theoretical and clinical perspectives. In C. E. Schaefer & A. J. Swanson (Eds.), *Children in residential care* (pp. 89–103). New York: Van Nostrand Reinhold.

Cormier, W. H., & Cormier, L. S. (1991). *Interviewing strategies for helpers* (3rd ed.). Pacific Grove, CA: Brooks/Cole.

Cormier, S., & Hackney, H. (1999). *Counseling strategies and interventions.* (5th ed.). Boston: Allyn & Bacon.

Cortes, L. (2004). Home-based family therapy: A misunderstanding of the role and a new challenge for therapists. *The Family Journal, 12,* 184–188.

Crenshaw, D. A. (1988). Responding to sexual acting-out. In C. E. Schaefer & A. J. Swanson (Eds.), *Children in residential care* (pp. 50–76). New York: Van Nostrand Reinhold.

Cummins, L., Sevel, J., & Pedrick, L. (2006). *Social work skills demonstrated.* Boston: Allyn & Bacon.

Daniel, M. S., & Crider, C. J. (2003). Mental status examination. In M. Hersen & S. M. Turner (Eds.), *Diagnostic interviewing* (3rd ed.). New York: Kluwer Academic/Plenum Publishers.

Davis, S. R., & Meier, S. T. (2001). *The elements of managed care.* Pacific Grove, CA: Brooks/Cole.

de Shazer, S. (1984). The death of resistance. *Family Process, 23,* 79–93.

de Shazer, S. (1985). *Keys to solution in brief therapy.* New York: W. W. Norton.

de Shazer, S. (1988). *Clues: Investigating solutions in brief therapy.* New York: W. W. Norton.

de Shazer, S. (1991). *Putting difference to work.* New York: W. W. Norton.

de Shazer, S., Berg, I. K., Lipchik, E., Nunnally, E., Molnar, A., Gingerich, W., & Weiner-Davis, M. (1986). Brief therapy: Focused solution development. *Family Process, 25,* 207–222.

De Jong, P., & Berg, I. K. (1998). *Interviewing for solutions.* California: Brooks/Cole.

De Jong, P., & Miller, S. D. (1995). How to interview for client strengths. *Social Work, 40,* 729–736.

Derrig-Palumbo, K., & Zeine, F. (2005). *Online therapy*. New York: W. W. Norton.

DeSole, L. M. (2006). *Making contact*. Boston: Allyn & Bacon.

DiClemente, C. C. (1999). Motivation for change: Implications for substance abuse treatment. *Psychological Science, 10*, 209–213.

DiClemente, C. C., & Prochaska, J. O. (1982). Self-change and therapy change of smoking behavior: A comparison of processes of change in cessation and maintenance. *Addictive Behaviors, 7*, 133–142.

Diefenbach, D. L. (1997). The portrayal of mental illness on prime-time television. *Journal of Community Psychology, 25*, 289–302.

DiGiuseppe, R. A., & Muran, J. C. (1992). The use of metaphor in rational-emotive psychotherapy. In R. D. Weitz (Ed.), *Psychotherapy in independent practice* (pp. 151–165). New York: Haworth Press.

Dillon, C. (2003). *Learning from mistakes in clinical practice*. Pacific Grove, CA: Brooks/Cole.

Dlugos, R. F., & Friedlander, M. L. (2001). Passionately committed psychotherapists: A qualitative study of their experiences. *Professional psychology: Research and Practice, 32*, 298–304.

Donaghy, W. C. (1984). *The interview: Skills and applications*. Glenview, IL: Scott, Foresman.

Doyle, R. E. (1998). *Essential skills & strategies in the helping process* (2nd ed.). Pacific Grove, CA: Brooks/Cole.

Drisko, J. W. (2004). Common factors in psychotherapy outcome: Meta-analytic findings and their implications for practice and research. *Families in Society, 85*, 81–90.

Dubin, W. R., & Fink, P. J. (1992). Effects of stigma on psychiatric treatment. In P. J. Fink & A. Tasman (Eds.), *Stigma and mental illness* (pp. 1–7). Washington, DC: American Psychiatric Press.

Duncan, B. L., Miller, S. D., & Sparks, J. A. (2004). *The heroic client* (Revised ed.). San Francisco: Jossey-Bass.

Durrant, M. (1993). *Residential treatment*. New York: W. W. Norton.

Durrant, M., & Kowalski, K. (1993). Enhancing views of competence. In S. Friedman (Ed.), *The new language of change* (pp. 107–137). New York: Guilford Press.

Earley, J. (2000). *Interactive group therapy*. Philadelphia, PA: Brunner/Mazel.

Edwards, J. K. (1994). Children in residential treatment: How many, what kind? Do we really know? In G. Northrup (Ed.), *Applied research in residential treatment* (pp. 85–99). New York: Haworth Press.

Egan, G. (1994). *The skilled helper* (5th ed.). Pacific Grove, CA: Brooks/Cole.

Egan, G. (2002). *The skilled helper* (7th ed.). Pacific Grove, CA: Brooks/Cole.

Egan, G. (2006a). *Essentials of skilled helping*. Pacific Grove, CA: Thomson Wadsworth.

Egan, G. (2006b) *Skilled helping around the world: Addressing diversity and multiculturalism*. Pacific Grove, CA: Thomson/Brooks Cole.

Eichelman, B. S. (1995). Strategies for clinician safety. In B. S. Eichelman & A. C. Hartwig (Eds.). *Patient violence and the clinician* (pp. 139–154). Washington, DC: American Psychiatric Press.

Elleven, R. K., & Allen, J. (2004). Applying technology to online counseling: Suggestions for the beginning e-therapist. *Journal of Instructional Psychology, 31*, 223–227.

Ellis, A. (1971). *Growth through reason*. Beverly Hills, CA: Wilshire.

Ellis, A. (1977). Fun as psychotherapy. Audiorecording. Institute for Rational-Emotive Therapy.

Epstein, W. M. (1999). The ineffectiveness of psychotherapy. In C. Feltham (Ed.), *Controversies in psychotherapy and counselling* (pp. 64–73). Thousand Oaks, CA: Sage.

Epston, D., & White, M. (1995). Termination as a rite of passage: Questioning strategies for a therapy of inclusion. In R. A. Neimeyer & M. J. Mahoney (Eds.), *Constructivism in psychotherapy* (pp. 339–354). Washington, DC: American Psychological Association.

Fabian, E. (2002). On the differentiated use of humor and joke in psychotherapy. *Psychoanalytic Review, 89*, 399–414.

Falk, B. (1998). Social history. In M. Hersen & V. B. Van Hasselt (Eds.), *Basic interviewing* (pp. 73–85). Mahwah, NJ: Lawrence Erlbaum.

Faust, J. (1998). General issues. In M. Hersen & V. B. Van Hasselt (Eds.), *Basic interviewing* (pp. 1–22). Mahwah, NJ: Lawrence Erlbaum.

Fehr, S. S. (2003). *Introduction to group therapy* (2nd ed.). New York: Haworth Press.

Feltham, C. (1999). Contextualizing the therapeutic relationship. In C. Feltham (Ed.), *Understanding the counselling relationship* (pp. 4–32). Thousand Oaks, CA: Sage.

Finn, J. (2002). MSW student perceptions of the efficacy and ethics of Internet-based therapy. *Journal of Social Work Education, 38*, 403–419.

Fisch, R., Weakland, J. H., & Segal, L. (1982). *The tactics of change*. San Francisco: Jossey-Bass.

Flemons, D. (2003). *Of one mind*. New York: W. W. Norton.

Forman, B. D., & Silverman, W. H. (1998). *Answers to the 50 most important questions about private mental health practice*. Springfield, IL: Charles C. Thomas.

Foucault, M. (1965). *Madness and civilization: A history of insanity in the age of reason*. New York: Vintage Books.

Fox, R. (2001). *Elements of the helping process* (2nd ed.). New York: Haworth Social Work Practice Press.

Franzini, L. R. (2001). Humor in therapy: The case for training therapists in its uses and risks. *The Journal of General Psychology, 128*, 170–194.

Fry, W. F. (2001). Does Jay Haley have a sense of humor?. In J. K. Zeig (Ed.), *Changing directives: The strategic therapy of Jay Haley* (pp. 222–236). Phoenix, AZ: The Milton H. Erickson Press.

Fuertes, J. N., Bartolomeo, M., & Nichols, C. M. (2001). Future research directions in the study of counselor multicultural competency. *Journal of Multicultural Counseling and Development, 29*, 3–12.

Fuller, D. S. (1982). AMSIT: A description of the patient's current mental status. In R. L. Leon (Ed.), *Psychiatric interviewing: A primer* (pp. 74–85). New York: Elsevier.

Gabbard, G. O., & Gabbard, K. (1999). *Psychiatry and the cinema* (2nd ed.). Washington, DC: American Psychiatric Press.

Geller, J. D., Norcross, J. C., & Orlinsky, D. E. (2005). The question of personal therapy: Introduction and prospectus. In J. D. Geller, J. C. Norcross, & D. E. Orlinsky (Eds.), *The psychotherapist's own psychotherapy* (pp. 3–11). New York: Oxford University Press.

Gilroy, P. J., Carroll, L., & Murra, J. (2004). A preliminary survey of counseling psychologists' personal experiences with depression and treatment. *Professional Psychology: Research and Practice, 33*, 402–407.

Ginsburg, H. P. (1997). *Entering the child's mind: The clinical interview in psychological research and practice*. Cambridge: Cambridge University Press.

Goffman, E. (1965). *Stigma*. Upper Saddle River, NJ: Prentice Hall.

Golden, C. J., & Hutchings, P. S. (1998). Mental status examination. In M. Hersen & V. B. Van Hasselt (Eds.), *Basic interviewing* (pp. 107–128). Mahwah, NJ: Lawrence Erlbaum.

Goldstein, J. H. (1987). Therapeutic effects of laughter. In W. F. Fry, Jr., & W. A. Salameh (Eds.), *Handbook of humor and psychotherapy* (pp. 1–19). Sarasota, FL: Professional Resource Exchange.

Gordon, D., & Meyers-Anderson, M. (1981). *Phoenix: Therapeutic patterns of Milton H. Erickson.* Cupertino, CA: Meta Publications.

Gordon, T. (2001). *Leader effectiveness training L.E.T.* New York: Perigee.

Greenwald, H. (1987). The humor decision. In W. F. Fry, Jr., & W. A. Salameh (Eds.), *Handbook of humor and psychotherapy* (pp. 41–54). Sarasota, FL: Professional Resource Exchange.

Grodzki, L. (2000). *Building your ideal private practice.* New York: W. W. Norton.

Grodzki, L. (2003). *Twelve months to your ideal private practice.* New York: W. W. Norton.

Grohol, J. M. (2004). Online counseling: A historical perspective. In R. Kraus, J. Zack, & G. Stricker (Eds.), *Online counseling.* Boston: Elsevier Academic Press.

Gwynn, C., Meyer, R., & Schaefer, C. (1988). The influence of the peer culture in residential treatment. In C. E. Schaefer & A. J. Swanson (Eds.), *Children in residential care* (pp. 104–133). New York: Van Nostrand Reinhold.

Haber, S., Rodino, E., & Lipner, I. (2001). *Saying good-bye to managed care.* New York: Springer.

Haley, J. (1987). *Problem-solving therapy.* San Francisco: Jossey-Bass.

Haley, J. (1996). *Learning & teaching therapy.* New York: Guilford Press.

Hall, E. T. (1966). *The hidden dimension.* New York: Doubleday.

Halstead, R. W., Wagner, L. D., Vivero, M., & Ferkol, W. (2002). Counselors' conceptualizations of caring in the counseling relationship. *Counseling and Values, 47,* 34–48.

Hays, P. A. (2001). *Addressing cultural complexities in practice: A framework for clinicians and counselors.* Washington, DC: American Psychological Association.

Hillman, J. L. (2002). *Crisis intervention and trauma: New approach to evidence-based practice.* New York: Kluwer Academic/Plenum Publishers.

House, A. E. (2002). *The first session with children and adolescents.* New York: Guilford Press.

Howard-Hamilton, M., Ferguson, A., & Puleo, S. (1998). Multicultural counseling trends and issues: Implications and imperatives for the next millennium. In W. M. Parker, *Consciousness-raising: A primer for multicultural counseling* (2nd ed.) (pp. 257–275). Springfield, IL: Charles C. Thomas.

Hoyt, M. F. (2000). *Some stories are better than others.* Philadelphia: Brunner/Mazel.

Hughes, J. N., & Baker, D. B. (1990). *The clinical child interview.* New York: Guilford Press.

Hutchins, D. E., & Vaught, C. C. (1997). *Helping relationships and strategies* (3rd ed.). Pacific Grove, CA: Brooks/Cole.

Ivey, A. E., & Ivey, M. B. (2003). *Intentional interviewing and counseling* (5th ed.). Pacific Grove, CA: Brooks/Cole.

Jacobs, E. E., Masson, R. L., & Harvill, R. L. (1998). *Group counseling: Strategies and skills* (3rd ed.). Pacific Grove, CA: Brooks/Cole.

Johnson, L. N., Wright, D. W., & Ketring, S. A. (2002). The therapeutic alliance in home-based family therapy: Is it predictive of outcome? *Journal of Marital and Family Therapy, 28,* 93–102.

Johnston, F. E., Van Hasselt, V. B., & Hersen, M. (1998). Rapport, Empathy, and Reflection. In M. Hersen & V. B. Van Hasselt (Eds.), *Basic Interviewing* (pp. 41–56). Mahwah, NJ: Lawrence Ehrlbaum.

Kanani, K., & Regehr, C. (2003). Clinical, ethical, and legal issues in e-therapy. *Families in Society, 84,* 155–162.

Kanel, K. (2003). *A guide to crisis intervention* (2nd ed.). Pacific Grove, CA: Brooks/Cole.

Katsavadkis, K. A., Gabbard, G. O., & Athey, G. (2004). Profiles of impaired health professionals. *Bulletin of the Menninger Clinic, 68,* 60–73.

Katz, M. (1988). Crisis intervention in residential care. In C. E. Schaefer & A. J. Swanson (Eds.), *Children in residential care* (pp. 30–49). New York: Van Nostrand Reinhold.

Keats, D. M. (2000). *Interviewing: A practical guide for students and professionals.* Philadelphia: Open University Press.

Keeney, B. P. (1990). *Improvisational therapy.* New York: Guilford Press.

Kelley, L. (2006). How to motivate clients to show up for appointments. *Family Therapy Magazine, 5,* 35–37.

Kenny, M. (1998). Beginning the interview and confidentiality. In M. Hersen & V. B. Van Hasselt (Eds.), *Basic interviewing* (pp. 23–40). Mahwah, NJ: Lawrence Erlbaum.

Kinney, J., Haapala, D., & Booth, C. (1991). *Keeping families together.* New York: Aldine de Gruyter.

Kisthardt, W. E. (2002). The strengths perspective in interpersonal helping: Purpose, principles, and functions. In D. Saleebey (Ed.), *The strengths perspective in social work practice* (3rd ed., pp. 163–185). Boston: Allyn & Bacon.

Kleespies, P. M. (1998). The domain of psychological emergencies: An overview. In P. M. Kleespies (Ed.), *Emergencies in mental health practice* (pp. 9–21). New York: Guilford Press.

Kleespies, P. M., Deleppo, J. D., Mori, D. L., & Niles, B. L. (1998). The emergency interview. In P. M. Kleespies (Ed.), *Emergencies in mental health practice* (pp. 41–72). New York: Guilford Press.

Kleespies, P. M., Niles, B. L., Mori, D. L., & Deleppo, J. D. (1998). Emergencies with suicidal patients: The impact on the clinician. In P. M. Kleespies (Ed.), Emergencies in mental health practice (pp. 379–397). New York: Guilford Press.

Kleinke, C. L. (1994). *Common principles of psychotherapy.* Pacific Grove, CA: Brooks/Cole.

Kline, W. B. (2003). *Interactive group counseling and therapy.* Upper Saddle River, NJ: Prentice Hall.

Knapp, S., & Slattery, J. M. (2004). Professional boundaries in nontraditional settings. *Professional Psychology: Research and Practice, 35,* 553–558.

Kottler, J. A. (1994). *Advanced group leadership.* Pacific Grove, CA: Brooks/Cole.

Kottler, J. A. (1997). *Succeeding with difficult students.* Thousand Oaks, CA: Corwin Press.

Kottler, J. A. (2000). *Nuts & bolts of helping.* Boston: Allyn & Bacon.

Kottler, J. A. (2003). *On being a therapist* (3rd ed). San Francisco: Jossey-Bass.

Kottler, J. A., & Blau, D. S. (1989). *The imperfect therapist: Learning from failure in therapeutic practice.* San Francisco: Jossey-Bass.

Kottler, J. A., & Carlson, J. (2002). *Bad therapy: Master therapists share their worst failures.* New York: Brunner/Routledge.

Kottler, J. A., & Carlson, J. (2003). *The mummy at the dining room table: Eminent therapists share their most unusual cases and what they teach us about human behavior.* San Francisco: Jossey-Bass.

Kraus, R. (2004). Ethical and legal considerations for providers of mental health services online. In R. Kraus, J. Zack, & G. Stricker (Eds.), *Online counseling* (pp. 123–144). Boston: Elsevier Academic Press.

Lago, C., & Thompson, J. (2002). Counselling and race. In S. Palmer (Ed.), *Multicultural counselling* (pp. 3–20). Thousand Oaks, CA: Sage.

Lambert, M. J. (1992). Implications of outcome research for psychotherapy integration. In J. C. Norcross & M. R. Goldfried (Eds.), *Handbook of psychotherapy integration* (pp. 94–129). New York: Basic.

Lambert, M. J., Shapiro, D. A., & Bergin, A. E. (1986). The effectiveness of psychotherapy. In S. L. Garfield & A. E. Bergin (Eds.), *Handbook of psychotherapy and behavior change* (3rd ed., pp. 157–211). New York: John Wiley & Sons.

Lazarus, A. A., & Zur, O. (2003). Introduction. In A. A. Lazarus & O. Zur (Eds.), *Dual relationships and psychotherapy* (pp. xxvii–xxxiii). New York: Springer.

Lefley, H. P. (1992). The stigmatized family. In P. J. Fink & A. Tasman (Eds.), *Stigma and mental illness* (pp. 127–138). Washington, DC: American Psychiatric Press.

Leibert, T., Archer, J., Munson, J., & York, G. (2006). An exploratory study of client perceptions of internet counseling and the therapeutic alliance. *Journal of Mental Health Counseling, 28*, 69–84.

Leitner, L. M. (1995). Optimal therapeutic distance: A therapist's experience of personal construct psychotherapy. In R. A. Neimeyer & M. J. Mahoney (Eds.), *Constructivism in psychotherapy* (pp. 357–370). Washington, DC: American Psychological Association.

Leon, R. L. (1982). *Psychiatric interviewing: A primer.* New York: Elsevier.

Leong, F. T. L., & Lau, A. S. L. (2001). Barriers to providing effective mental health services to Asian Americans. *Mental Health Services Research, 3*, 201–214.

Leong, F. T. L., & Zachar, P. (1999). Gender and opinions about mental illness as predictors of attitudes toward seeking professional psychological help. *British Journal of Guidance & Counselling, 27*, 123–133.

Lindblad-Goldberg, M., Dore, M. M., & Stern, L. (1998). *Creating competence from chaos.* New York: W. W. Norton.

Lipchik, E. (1988). Purposeful sequences for beginning the solution-focused interview. In E. Lipchik (Ed.), *Interviewing* (pp. 105–118). Rockville, MD: Aspen.

Lipchik, E., & de Shazer, S. (1986). The purposeful interview. *Journal of Strategic and Systemic Therapies, 5*, 88–99.

Long, V. O. (1996). *Communication skills in helping relationships.* Pacific Grove, CA: Brooks/Cole.

Lukas, S. (1993). *Where to start and what to ask: An assessment handbook.* New York: W. W. Norton.

Lyman, R. D., & Campbell, N. R. (1996). *Treating children and adolescents in residential and inpatient settings.* Thousand Oaks, CA: Sage.

Lynch, O. H. (2002). Humorous communication: Finding a place for humor in communication research. *Communication Theory, 12*, 423–446.

Macaskill, A. (1999). Personal therapy as a training requirement: The lack of supporting evidence. In C. Feltham (Ed.), *Controversies in psychotherapy and counselling* (pp. 142–154). Thousand Oaks, CA: Sage.

Maples, M. F., Dupey, P., Torres-Rivera, E., Phan, L. T. et al. (2001). Ethnic diversity and the use of humor in counseling: Appropriate or inappropriate? *Journal of Counseling and Development, 79*, 53–61.

Martin, D. G. (2000). *Counseling and therapy skills* (2nd ed.). Prospect Heights, IL: Waveland Press.

Matsumoto, D. (2000). *Culture and psychology* (2nd ed.). Belmont, CA: Wadsworth.

McCain, V. M., & Day, H. D. (1999). Values held by office-based and home-based therapists in Northern New England. *Counseling and Values, 43*, 116–128.

McHenry, B., & McHenry, J. (2007). *What therapists say and why they say it.* Boston: Allyn & Bacon.

Meier, S. T., & Davis, S. R. (2001). *The elements of counseling* (4th ed.). Pacific Grove, CA: Brooks/Cole.

Miller, L. D. (2002). Overview of family systems counseling in a school setting. In L. D. Miller (Ed.), *Integrating school and family counseling: Practical solutions* (pp. 3–30). Alexandria, VA: American Counseling Association.

Miller, S. D., Duncan, B. L., & Hubble, M. A. (1997). *Escape from babel: Toward a unifying language for psychotherapy practice.* New York: W. W. Norton.

Millman, J., Strike, D. M., Van Soest, M., Rosen, N., & Schmidt, E. (1998). *Talking with the caller: Guidelines for crisisline and other volunteer counselors.* Thousand Oaks, CA: Sage.

Mindness, H. (2001). The use of humor in psychotherapy. In W. A. Salameh & W. F. Fry, Jr. (Eds.), *Humor and wellness in clinical intervention* (pp. 1–14). Westport, CT: Praeger.

Minuchin, S. (1974). *Families & family therapy*. Cambridge, MA: Harvard University Press.

Minuchin, S., & Fishman, H. C. (1981). *Family therapy techniques*. Cambridge, MA: Harvard University Press.

Minuchin, S., Nichols, M. P., & Lee, W-Y. (2007). *Assessing families and couples*. Boston: Allyn & Bacon.

Montgomery, M. J. (1999). *Building bridges with parents*. Thousand Oaks, CA: Corwin Press.

Mora, G. (1992). Stigma during the medieval and renaissance periods. In P. J. Fink & A. Tasman (Eds.), *Stigma and mental illness* (pp. 41–57). Washington, DC: American Psychiatric Press.

Morrison, J. (1993). *The first interview: A guide for clinicians*. New York: Guilford Press.

Murphy, B. C., & Dillon, C. (2003). *Interviewing in action: Relationship, process, and change* (2nd ed). Pacific Grove, CA: Brooks/Cole.

Nau, D. S., & Shilts, L. (2000). When to use the miracle question: Clues from a qualitative study of four SFBT practitioners. *Journal of Systemic Therapies, 19*, 129–136.

Nelson, T. S., Fleuridas, C., & Rosenthal, D. M. (1986). The evolution of circular questions: Training family therapists. *Journal of Marital and Family Therapy, 12*, 113–127.

Neukrug, E. S., & Schwitzer, A. M. (2006). *Skills and tools for today's counselors and psychotherapists*. Pacific Grove, CA: Thomson Brooks/Cole.

Nichols, M. P., & Schwartz, R. (2007). *The essentials of family therapy* (3rd ed.). Boston: Allyn & Bacon.

Norcross, J. C., & Connor, K. A. (2005). Psychotherapists entering personal therapy: Their primary reasons and presenting problems. In J. D. Geller, J. C. Norcross, & D. E. Orlinsky (Eds.), *The psychotherapist's own psychotherapy* (pp. 192–200). New York: Oxford University Press.

Norcross, J. C., & Guy, J. D. (2005). The prevalence and parameters of personal therapy in the United States. In J. D. Geller, J. C. Norcross, & D. E. Orlinsky (Eds.), *The psychotherapist's own psychotherapy* (pp. 165–176). New York: Oxford University Press.

Norman, E. (2000). Introduction: The strengths perspective and resiliency enhancement—A natural partnership. In E. Norman (Ed.), *Resiliency enhancement* (pp. 1–16). New York: Columbia University Press.

O'Hanlon, W. H. (1987). *Taproots: Underlying principles of Milton Erickson's therapy and hypnosis*. New York: W. W. Norton.

O'Hanlon, W. H., & Weiner-Davis, M. (1989). *In search of solutions*. New York: W. W. Norton.

O'Hanlon, B., & Wilk, J. (1987). *Shifting contexts: The generation of effective psychotherapy*. New York: Guilford Press.

Okun, B. F. (1997). *Effective helping: Interviewing and counseling techniques* (5th ed.). Pacific Grove, CA: Brooks/Cole.

Orlinsky, D. E., Norcross, J. C., Ronnestad, M. H., & Wiseman, H. (2005). Outcomes and impacts of the psychotherapist's own psychotherapy. In J. D. Geller, J. C. Norcross, & D. E. Orlinsky (Eds.), *The psychotherapist's own psychotherapy* (pp. 214–230). New York: Oxford University Press.

Orlinsky, D. E., Ronnestad, M. H., Willutzki, U., Wiseman, H., & Botermans, J. (2005). The prevalence and parameters of personal therapy in Europe and elsewhere. In J. D. Geller, J. C. Norcross, & D. E. Orlinsky (Eds.), *The psychotherapist's own psychotherapy* (pp. 177–191). New York: Oxford University Press.

Paris, E., Linville, D., & Rosen, K. (2006). Marriage and family therapist interns' experiences of growth, *Journal of Marital and Family Therapy, 32*, 45–57.

Parker, W. M. (1998). *Consciousness-raising: A primer for multicultural counseling* (2nd ed.). Springfield, IL: Charles C. Thomas.

Patterson, J., Williams, L., Grauf-Grounds, C., & Chamow, L. (1998). *Essential skills in family therapy*. New York: Guilford Press.

Patton, M. Q. (2002). *Qualitative research & evaluation methods* (3rd ed.). Thousand Oaks, CA: Sage.

Pedersen, P. (1999). Culture-centered interventions as a fourth dimension of psychology. In P. Pedersen (Ed.), *Multiculturalism as a fourth force* (pp. 3–18). Philadelphia, PA: Brunner/Mazel.

Pedersen, P. (2000). *A handbook for developing multicultural awareness* (3rd ed.). Alexandria, VA: American Counseling Association.

Pedersen, P. B., & Ivey, A. (1993). *Culture-centered counseling and interviewing skills: A practical guide*. Westport, CT: Praeger.

Petrocelli, J. V. (2002). Processes and stages of change: Counseling with the transtheoretical model of change. *Journal of Counseling and Development, 80*, 22–30.

Pitcher, G. D., & Poland, S. (1992). *Crisis intervention in the schools*. New York: Guilford Press.

Polanski, P. J., & Hinkle, J. S. (2000). The mental status examination: Its use by professional counselors, *Journal of Counseling and Development: JCD, 78*, 357–364.

Poorman, P. B. (2003). *Microskills and theoretical foundations for professional helpers*. Boston: Allyn & Bacon.

Pope-Davis, D. B., & Constantine, M. G. (1996). MCT theory and implications for practice. In D. W. Sue, A. E. Ivey, & P. B. Pedersen (Eds.), *A theory of multicultural counseling and therapy* (pp. 112–122). Pacific Grove, CA: Brooks/Cole.

Posthuma, B. W. (2003). *Small groups in counseling and therapy* (4th ed.). Boston: Allyn & Bacon.

Presbury, J. H., Echterling, L. G., & McKee, J. E. (2002). *Ideas and tools for brief counseling*. Upper Saddle River, NJ: Prentice Hall.

Pridmore, S. (2000). *The psychiatric interview: A guide to history taking and the mental state examination*. Amsterdam: Harwood Academic Publishers.

Prochaska, J. O., & DiClemente, C. C. (1992). Stages of change in the modification of problem behaviors. In M. Hersen, R. M. Eisler, & P. M. Miller (Eds.), *Progress in Behavior Modification, v 28* (pp. 183–218). Sycamore, IL: Sycamore.

Prochaska, J. O., DiClemente, C. C., & Norcross, J. C. (1992). In search of how people change: Applications to addictive behaviors. *American Psychologist, 47*, 1102–1114.

Prochaska, J. O., & Norcross, J. C. (2007). *Systems of psychotherapy* (6th ed). Pacific Grove, CA: Brooks/Cole.

Rastogi, M., & Wieling, E. (2005). *Voices of color*. Thousand Oaks, CA: Sage.

Rea, A. (2004). Now you're talking my language. *Psychologist, 17*, 580–582.

Reid, S. E. (2001). The psychology of play and games. In C. E. Schaefer & S. E. Reid (Eds.), *Game play: Therapeutic use of childhood games* (2nd ed., pp. 1–36). New York: John Wiley & Sons.

Reik, T. (1968). *Listening with the third ear*. New York: Pyramid Books.

Reiter, M. D. (1999). *Exploring the structure of home-based therapy: A qualitative inquiry of family therapists' perceptions*. Unpublished doctoral dissertation, Nova Southeastern University, Fort Lauderdale-Davie.

Reiter, M. D. (2000a). Utilizing the home environment in home-based family therapy. *Journal of Family Psychotherapy, 11*, 27–39.

Reiter, M. D. (2000b). Structuring home-based therapy: Four phases to effective treatment. *Journal of Family Social Work, 4*, 21–35.

Reiter, M. D. (in press). The use of expectation in solution-focused formula tasks. *Journal of Family Psychotherapy*.

Reiter, M. D., & Shilts, L. (1998). Using circular scaling questions to deconstruct depression: A case study. *Crisis Intervention and Time Limited Treatment, 4*, 227–237.

Riemer-Reiss, M. L. (2000). Utilizing distance technology for mental health counseling. *Journal of Mental Health Counseling, 22*, 189–203.

Rogers, C. R. (1951). *Client-centered therapy*. Boston: Houghton Mifflin.

Rogers, C. R. (1961). *On becoming a person*. Boston: Houghton Mifflin.

Rogers, C. R. (1989a). The characteristics of a helping relationship. In H. Kirschenbaum & V. L. Henderson (Eds), *The Carl Rogers reader* (pp. 108–126) Boston: Houghton Mifflin.

Rogers, C. R. (1989b). Reflection of feelings and transference. In H. Kirschenbaum & V. L. Henderson (Eds.), *The Carl Rogers reader* (pp. 127–134). Boston: Houghton Mifflin.

Rogers, C. R. (1989c). The necessary and sufficient conditions of therapeutic personality change. In H. Kirschenbaum & V. L. Henderson (Eds.), *The Carl Rogers reader* (pp. 219–235). Boston: Houghton Mifflin.

Rogers, C. R., & Stevens, B. (1967). *Person to person: The problem of being human*. Walnut Creek, CA: Real People Press.

Roller, B., & Nelson, V. (1991). *The art of co-therapy*. New York: Guilford Press.

Ronnestad, M. H., & Skovholt, T. M. (2003). The journey of the counselor and therapist: Research findings and perspectives on professional development. *Journal of Career Development, 30*, 5–44.

Rosenberg, T., & Pace, M. (2006). Burnout among mental health professionals: Special considerations for the marriage and family therapist. *Journal of Marital and Family Therapy, 32*, 87–99.

Rosenthal, R. H., & Akiskal, H. S. (1985). Mental status examination. In M. Hersen & S. M. Turner (Eds.), *Diagnostic interviewing* (pp. 25–52). New York: Plenum Press.

Roysircar, G. (2003). Counselor awareness of own assumptions, values, and biases. In G. Roysircar, P. Arredondo, J. B. Fuertes, J. G. Ponterotto, & R. L. Toporek. *Multicultural counseling competencies 2003: Association for multicultural counseling and development* (pp. 17–38). Alexandria, VA: American Counseling Association.

Roysircar, G., Webster, D. R., Germer, J., Palensky, J. J., Lynne, E., Campbell, G. R., Yang, Y., Liu, J., & Bodgett-McDeavitt, J. (2003). Experiential training in multicultural counseling: Implementation and evaluation of counselor process. In G. Roysircar, D. S. Sandhu, & V. E. Bibbins (Eds.), *Multicultural competencies: A guidebook of practices* (pp. 3–16). Alexandria, VA: Association of Multicultural Counseling and Development.

Rupert, P. A., & Morgan, D. J. (2005). Work setting and burnout among professional psychologists. *Professional Psychology: Research and Practice, 36*, 544–550.

Rutan, J. S., & Alsonso, A. (1999). Reprise: Some guidelines for group therapists. In J. R. Price, D. R. Hescheles, & A. R. Price (Eds.), *A guide to starting psychotherapy groups* (pp. 71–79). San Diego: Academic Press.

Saleebey, D. (2002). Introduction: Power in the people. In D. Saleebey (Ed.), *The strengths perspective in social work practice* (3rd ed., pp. 1–22). Boston: Allyn & Bacon.

Satcher, D. (1999). Mental health: A report of the surgeon general. Retrieved February 3, 2006, from http://www. surgeongeneral. gov/library/mentalhealth/.

Satir, V. (1967). *Conjoint family therapy*. Palo Alto, CA: Science and Behavior Books.

Satir, V., & Baldwin, M. (1983). *Satir step by step*. Palo Alto, CA: Science and Behavior Books.

Saunders, M. S. (2002). The clinical effectiveness of psychotherapy. In C. Feltham (Ed.), *What's the good of counselling & psychotherapy?* (pp. 240–255). Thousand Oaks, CA: Sage.

Saunders, S. (1999). It has been amply demonstrated that psychotherapy is effective. In C. Feltham (Ed.), *Controversies in psychotherapy and counselling* (pp. 74–85). Thousand Oaks, CA: Sage.

Sayyedi, M., & O'Byrne, K. (2003). Therapist: Heal thyself! In J. A. Kottler & W. Paul Jones (Eds.), *Doing better* (pp. 233–246). New York: Brunner-Routledge.

Schmidt, J. J. (1991). *Survival guide for the elementary/middle school counselor*. New York: Center for Applied Research in Education.

Schmidt, J. J. (1999). *Counseling in schools* (3rd ed.). Boston: Allyn & Bacon.

Sciarra, D. T. (1999). *Multiculturalism in counseling*. Itasca, IL: F. E. Peacock.

Selvini Palazzoli, M., Boscolo, L., Cecchin, G., & Prata, G. (1980). Hypothesizing—circularity—neutrality: Three guidelines for the conductor of the session. *Family Process, 19,* 3–12.

Semrud-Clikeman, M. (1995). *Child and adolescent therapy*. Boston: Allyn & Bacon.

Shapiro, E. (1999). Cotherapy. In J. R. Price, D. R. Hescheles, & A. R. Price (Eds.), *A guide to starting psychotherapy groups* (pp. 53–61). San Diego: Academic Press.

Shea, S. C. (1998). *Psychiatric interviewing: The art of understanding* (2nd ed.). Philadelphia: W. B. Saunders.

Sheffield, J. K., Fiorenza, E., & Sofronoff, K. (2004). Adolescents' willingness to seek psychological help: Promoting and preventing factors. *Journal of Youth and Adolescence, 33,* 495–507.

Shilts, L., & Gordon, A. (1992/1993). Simplifying the miracle. *Family Therapy Case Studies, 7,* 53–59.

Shilts, L., & Gordon, A. B. (1996). What to do after the miracle occurs. *Journal of Family Psychotherapy, 7,* 15–22.

Shilts, L., Rambo, A., & Huntley, E. (2003). The collaborative miracle: When to slow down the pace of brief therapy. *Journal of Systemic Therapies, 22,* 65–73.

Signorielli, N. (1989). The stigma of mental illness on television. *Journal of Broadcasting & Electronic Media, 33,* 325–331.

Simon, B. (1992). Shame, stigma, and mental illness in ancient Greece. In P. J. Fink & A. Tasman (Eds.), *Stigma and mental illness* (pp. 29–39). Washington, DC: American Psychiatric Press.

Skinner, A. E. G., & Latchford, G. (2004). International and multicultural issues. In R. Kraus, J. Zack, & G. Stricker (Eds.), *Online counseling* (pp. 241–254). Boston: Elsevier Academic Press.

Smith, T. B., Richards, P. S., MacGranley, H., & Obiakor, F. (2004). Practicing multiculturalism: An introduction. In T. B. Smith (Ed.), *Practicing multiculturalism: Affirming diversity in counseling and psychology* (pp. 3–16). Boston: Allyn & Bacon.

Snowden, L. R., (2001). Barriers to effective mental health services for African Americans. *Mental Health Services Research, 3,* 181–187.

Snyder, W., & McCollum, E. E. (1999). Their home is their castle: Learning to do in-home family therapy. *Family Process, 38,* 229–242.

Sodowsky, G. R., Kuo-Jackson, P. Y., & Loya, G. J. (1997). Outcome of training in the philosophy of assessment: Multicultural counseling competencies. In D. B. Pope-Davis & H. L. K. Coleman (Eds.), *Multicultural counseling competencies: Assessment, education and training, and supervision* (pp. 3–42). Thousand Oaks, CA: Sage.

Sommers-Flanagan, R., & Sommers-Flanagan, J. (1999). *Clinical interviewing* (2nd ed.). New York: John Wiley & Sons.

Sommers-Flanagan, R., & Sommers-Flanagan, J. (2003). *Clinical interviewing* (3rd ed.). New York: John Wiley & Sons.

Sparks, J. A. (2002). *Media madness: The construction of mental illness in popular culture.* Unpublished doctoral dissertation, Nova Southeastern University, Fort Lauderdale-Davie, Florida.

Spears, S. S. (2004). The impact of a cultural competency course on the racial identity of MSWs. *Smith College Studies in Social Work, 74,* 271–288.

Sperry, L., Carlson, J., & Kjos, D. (2003). *Becoming an effective therapist.* Boston: Allyn & Bacon.

Spiegel, D. (1999). Introduction. In D. Spiegel (Ed.), *Efficacy and cost-effectiveness of psychotherapy* (pp. xi–xv). Washington, DC: American Psychiatric Press.

Spitz, H. I., & Spitz, S. T. (1999). *A pragmatic approach to group psychotherapy.* Philadelphia, PA: Brunner/Mazel.

Sprengle, K. (2000). Sources of failure in home-based therapy. In N. A. Newton & K. Sprengle (Eds.), *Psychosocial interventions in the home* (pp. 67–80). New York: Springer.

Stein, J. A. (1995). *Residential treatment of adolescents and children.* Chicago: Nelson-Hall.

Stevanovic, P., & Rupert, P.A. (2004). Career-sustaining behaviors, satisfactions, and stresses of professional psychologists. *Psychotherapy: Theory, Research, Practice, and Training, 41,* 301–309.

Stewart, C. J., & Cash, W. B. Jr. (2003). *Interviewing: Principles and practices* (10th ed.). Boston: McGraw Hill.

Stine, J. J. (2005). The use of metaphors in the service of the therapeutic alliance and therapeutic communication. *Journal of the American Academy of Psychoanalysis and Dynamic Psychiatry, 33,* 531–546.

Stofle, G. S., & Chechele, P. J. (2004). Online counseling skills, part II: In-session skills. In R. Kraus, J. Zack, & G. Stricker (Eds.), *Online counseling* (pp. 181–196). Boston: Elsevier Academic Press.

Sue, D. W., Arredondo, P., & McDavis, R. J. (1992a). Multicultural counseling competencies and standards: A call to the profession. *Journal of Multicultural Counseling and Development, 20,* 64–88.

Sue, D. W., Arredondo, P., & McDavis, R. J. (1992b). Multicultural counseling competencies and standards: A call to the profession. *Journal of Counseling and Development, 70,* 477–486.

Sue, D. W. et al. (1998). *Multicultural counseling competencies: Individual and organizational development.* Thousand Oaks, CA: Sage.

Sue, D. W., & Sue, D. (2003). *Counseling the culturally diverse: Theory and practice* (4th ed.). New York: John Wiley & Sons.

Sue, D. W., Ivey, A. E., & Pedersen, P. B. (1996). *A theory of multicultural counseling and therapy.* Pacific Grove, CA: Brooks/Cole.

Summers, R. F., & Barber, J. P. (2003). Therapeutic alliance as a measurable psychotherapy skill. *Academic Psychiatry, 27,* 160–165.

Swanson, A. J., & Schaefer, C. E. (1988). Helping children deal with separation and loss in residential placement. In C. E. Schaefer & A. J. Swanson (Eds.), *Children in residential care* (pp. 19–29). New York: Van Nostrand Reinhold.

Taibbi, R. (1996). *Doing family therapy: Craft and creativity in clinical practice.* New York: Guilford Press.

Talmon, M. (1990). *Single-session therapy.* San Francisco: Jossey-Bass.

Tardiff, K. (1995). The risk of being attacked by patients: Who, how often, and where? In B. S. Eichelman & A. C. Hartwig (Eds.), *Patient violence and the clinician* (pp. 13–20). Washington, DC: American Psychiatric Press.

Teyber, E. (2006). *Interpersonal process in therapy.* Pacific Grove, CA: Thomson Brooks/Cole.

Thomas, V., McCollum, E. E., & Snyder, W. (1999). Beyond the clinic: In-home therapy with head start families. *Journal of Marital and Family Therapy, 25*, 177–189.

Thompson, C. L., & Rudolph, L. B. (1992). *Counseling children* (3rd ed.). Pacific Grove, CA: Brooks/Cole.

Thompson, R. A. (2002). *School counseling* (2nd ed.). New York: Brunner-Routledge.

Tolan, J. (2003). *Skills in person-centered counselling & psychotherapy*. Thousand Oaks, CA: Sage.

Tracy, E. M., & McDonell, J. R. (1991). Home-based work with families: The environmental context of family intervention. In K. G. Lewis (Ed.), *Family systems application to social work: Training and clinical practice* (pp. 93–108). New York: Haworth Press.

Trieschman, A. E., Whittaker, J. K., & Brendtro, L. K. (1969). *The other 23 hours*. New York: Aldine De Gruyter.

Turner, S. M., & Hersen, M. (1987). The interviewing process. In M. Hersen & S. M. Turner (Eds.), *Diagnostic interviewing* (pp. 3–24). New York: Plenum Press.

Turns, D. M., & Blumenreich, P. E. (1993). Epidemiology. In P. E. Blumenreich & S. Lewis (Eds.). *Managing the violent patient* (pp. 5–20). New York: Brunner/Mazel.

Van Hagen, J. (1988). Family work in residential treatment. In C. E. Schaefer & A. J. Swanson (Eds.), *Children in residential care* (pp. 134–144). New York: Van Nostrand Reinhold.

Ventura, M. (2005). The 8-minute cure, Psychotherapy. *Networker, 29*, 25–31; 60.

Wahl, O. F. (1995). *Media madness: Public images of mental illness*. New Brunswick, NJ: Rutgers University Press.

Wahl, O. F. (1999). Mental health consumers' experience of stigma, *Schizophrenia Bulletin, 25*, 467–479.

Wahl, O. F., & Roth, R. (1982). Television images of mental illness: Results of a metropolitan Washington media watch. *Journal of Broadcasting, 26*, 599–605.

Wainrib, B. R., & Bloch, E. L. (1998). *Crisis intervention and trauma response*. New York: Springer.

Walker, J. (2004). Psychotherapy as oppression? The institutional edifice. In J. R. Brandell (Ed.), *Celluloid couches, cinematic clients: Psychoanalysis and psychotherapy in the movies* (pp. 95–126). New York: State University of New York Press.

Walter, J. L., & Peller, J. E. (1992). *Becoming solution-focused in brief therapy*. New York: Brunner/Mazel.

Ward, P., & Banks, N. (2002). An analysis of the facilitative effects of gender and race in counselling practice. In S. Palmer (Ed.), *Multicultural counselling* (pp. 181–190). Thousand Oaks, CA: Sage.

Wasik, B. H., & Bryant, D. M. (2001). *Home visiting* (2nd ed.). Thousand Oaks, CA: Sage.

Watson, G. S., & Gross, A. M. (1998). History of the presenting complaint. In M. Hersen & V. B. Van Hasselt (Eds.), *Basic interviewing* (pp. 57–71). Mahwah, NJ: Lawrence Erlbaum.

Watzlawick, P. (1978). *The language of change: Elements of therapeutic communication*. New York: Basic Books.

Watzlawick, P., Bavelas, J. B., & Jackson, D. D. (1967). *Pragmatics of human communication*. New York: W. W. Norton.

Weick, A., & Chamberlain, R. (2002). Putting problems in their place: Further explorations in the strengths perspective. In D. Saleebey (Ed.), *The strengths perspective in social work practice* (3rd ed., pp. 95–105). Boston: Allyn & Bacon.

Welch, I. D. (2003). *The therapeutic relationship*. Westport, CT: Praeger.

Wetherell, J. L., Kaplan, R. M., Kallenberg, G., Dresselhaus, T. R., Sieber, W. J., & Lang, A. J. (2004). Mental health treatment preferences of older and younger primary care patients. *International Journal of Psychiatry in Medicine, 34*, 219–233.

Whitaker, C. (1976). The family is a four-dimensional relationship. In P. J. Guerin (Ed.), *Family therapy: Theory and practice* (pp. 182–192). New York: Gardner Press.

Whitaker, C. A., & Bumberry, W. M. (1988). *Dancing with the family: A symbolic-experiential approach*. New York: Brunner/Mazel.

White, M. (1999). *Re-authoring lives: Interviews & Essays*. Adelaide: Dulwich Centre.

White, M., & Epston, D. (1990). *Narrative means to therapeutic ends*. New York: W. W. Norton.

Wickman, S. A., Daniels, H. H., White, L. J., & Fesmire, S. A. (1999). A "primer" in conceptual metaphor for counselors. *Journal of Counseling & Development, 77*, 389–394.

Wiger, D. E., & Huntley, D. K. (2002). *Essential of interviewing*. New York: John Wiley & Sons.

Williams, E. N., Polster, D., Grizzard, M. B., Rockenbaugh, J., & Judge, A. B. (2003). What happens when therapists feel bored or anxious? A qualitative study of distracting self-awareness and therapists' management strategies. *Journal of Contemporary Psychotherapy, 33*, 5–22.

Wilson, C., & Powell, M. (2001). *A guide to interviewing children*. New York: Routledge.

Winters, A. M., & Duck. S. (2001). You ****!: Swearing as an aversive and a relational activity. In R. M. Kowalski (Ed.), *Behaving badly: Aversive behaviors in interpersonal relationships* (pp. 59–79). Washington, DC: American Psychological Association.

Wohl, J. (2000). Psychotherapy and cultural diversity. In J. F. Aponte & J. Wohl (Eds.), *Psychological intervention and cultural diversity* (2nd ed., pp. 75–91). Boston: Allyn & Bacon.

Wolin, S. J., & Wolin, S. (1993). *The resilient self*. New York: Villard Books.

Woodford, M. S. (1999). Home-based family therapy: Theory and process from "friendly visitors" to multisystemic therapy. *Family Journal: Counseling and Therapy for Couples and Families, 7*, 265–269.

Yalom, I. D. (2005). *The theory and practice of group psychotherapy* (5th ed.). New York: Basic Books.

Yalom, I. D. (1985). *The theory and practice of group psychotherapy* (3rd ed.). New York: Basic Books.

Yan, M. C., & Wong, Y-L, R. (2005). Rethinking self-awareness in cultural competence: Toward a dialogic self in cross-cultural social work. *Families in Society, 86*, 181–188.

Yorgason, J. B., McWey, L. M., & Felts, L. (2005). In-home family therapy: Indicators of success. *Journal of Marital and Family Therapy, 31*, 301–312.

Young, M. (2005). *Learning the art of helping* (3rd ed.). Upper Saddle River, NJ: Prentice Hall.

Zack. J. S. (2004). Technology of online counseling. In R. Kraus, J. Zack, & G. Stricker (Eds.), *Online counseling* (pp. 93–121). Boston: Elsevier Academic Press.

Zeig, J. K., & Munion, W. M. (1990). What is psychotherapy? In J. K. Zeig & W. M. Munion (Eds.), *What is psychotherapy* (pp. 1–14). San Francisco: Jossey-Bass.

Zelvin, E., & Speyer, C. M. (2004). Online counseling skills, part I: Treatment strategies and skills for conducting counseling online. In R. Kraus, J. Zack, & G. Stricker (Eds.), *Online counseling* (pp. 163–180). Boston: Elsevier Academic Press.

Zur, O. (2002). Out-of-office experience: When crossing office boundaries and engaging in dual relationships are clinically beneficial and ethically sound. In A. A. Lazarus & O. Zur (Eds.), *Dual relationships and psychotherapy* (pp. 88–97). New York: Springer.

Zwiers, M. L., & Morrissette, P. J. (1999). *Effective interviewing of children*. Philadelphia: Taylor & Francis Group.

Index